Lecture Notes in Computer Science   1765

Edited by G. Goos, J. Hartmanis and J. van Leeuwen

Springer
Berlin
Heidelberg
New York
Barcelona
Hong Kong
London
Milan
Paris
Singapore
Tokyo

Toru Ishida   Katherine Isbister (Eds.)

Digital Cities

Technologies, Experiences,
and Future Perspectives

 Springer

Series Editors

Gerhard Goos, Karlsruhe University, Germany
Juris Hartmanis, Cornell University, NY, USA
Jan van Leeuwen, Utrecht University, The Netherlands

Volume Editors

Toru Ishida
Kyoto University, Department of Social Informatics
Yoshida-honmachi, Sakyo-ku, 606-8501 Kyoto, Japan
E-mail: ishida@i.kyoto-u.ac.jp

Katherine Isbister
Netsage Corporation
3001 19th Street, 2nd Floor, San Francisco, CA 94110 USA
E-mail: isbister@netsage.com

Cataloging-in-Publication Data applied for

Die Deutsche Bibliothek - CIP-Einheitsaufnahme

Digital cities : technologies, experiences, and future perspectives /
Toru Ishida ; Katherine Isbister (ed.). - Berlin ; Heidelberg ; New
York ; Barcelona ; Hong Kong ; London ; Milan ; Paris ; Singapore ;
Tokyo : Springer, 2000
 (Lecture notes in computer science ; 1765)
 ISBN 3-540-67265-6

CR Subject Classification (1998): K.4, C.2, H.4, K.8, I.2

ISSN 0302-9743
ISBN 3-540-67265-6 Springer-Verlag Berlin Heidelberg New York

Springer-Verlag is a company in the BertelsmannSpringer publishing group.
© Springer-Verlag Berlin Heidelberg 2000
Printed in Germany

Typesetting: Camera-ready by author, data conversion by Boller Mediendesign
Printed on acid-free paper   SPIN: 10719693   06/3142   5 4 3 2 1 0

Preface

Digital city projects – building platforms to support community networking – are currently going on world-wide. European and American cities, as well as Asian cities, are creating digital meeting places and information resources for local residents and remote visitors. The Kyoto Meeting on Digital Cities covered successes and design challenges of currently implemented digital cities. In this volume, we have gathered and grouped papers from the workshop into seven sections, which reflect different perspectives and approaches to this large (and growing) research area.

We begin with papers that present a broad theoretic and analytical perspective on digital city creation. Here you will find wide-reaching analysis of first-generation digital city and community networking efforts (Aurigi, Serra, van den Besselaar), as well as analysis of what is desirable and feasible in next-generation digital cities (Ishida, Mitchell).

In the next two sections, we include reports on current digital city and community network efforts from around the world, including Belgium, Canada, China, England, Finland, Italy, Japan, The Netherlands, Sweden, and the United States. These papers discuss planning, design, evaluation, and iteration. We hope they will provide useful insights and lessons to others who are currently creating digital cities. Following these papers is a section, which explores specific applications of the digital city – from education to job hunting to disaster management.

The remaining three sections present technological innovations to support and sustain digital cities. We have divided these technologies into three broad areas: those that aid in visualization of the digital city, those that support mobile exploration of digital city resources, and those that seek to build social interaction and encourage community formation in digital cities.

The Kyoto Meeting on Digital Cities brought together researchers and practitioners from around the world, and sparked exciting dialogue and debate about digital cities and their future. We sincerely hope this volume will serve the same purpose for our readers. We would like to express our great appreciation of the co-organizers and the local arrangement people of the meeting: they are Yoh'ichi Tohkura, Jun-ichi Akahani, Kaoru Hiramatsu, Stefan Lisowski, Kenji Kobayashi, Kenji Ishikawa, Hideyuki Nakanishi, Masayuki Okamoto, Satoshi Oyama, Yang Yeon-Soo, Saeko Nomura, Hirofumi Yamaki, Takushi Sogo, Shoko Toda, and Yoko Kubota. Special thanks to Makoto Takema, who did tremendous work in editing this volume.

January 2000

Toru Ishida
Katherine Isbister

Table of Contents

DESIGN AND ANALYSIS PERSPECTIVES

DIGITAL CITY EXPERIMENTS

COMMUNITY NETWORK EXPERIMENTS

APPLICATIONS OF DIGITAL CITIES

VISUALIZATION TECHNOLOGIES

MOBILE TECHNOLOGIES

SOCIAL INTERACTION AND COMMUNITYWARE

Designing the Digital City

William J. Mitchell

School of Architecture and Planning, MIT

Abstract. The forms that cities take, the ways they function, and the mixes and distributions of activities within them have always been influenced very strongly by the capabilities of their underlying network infrastructures. Furthermore, cities have often been transformed by the introduction of new infrastructures. It is impossible to imagine Rotterdam without its canals and connection to the North Sea, Chicago without its railroads, Los Angeles without its freeways, or any large modern city without water supply, sewage, electrical, and telephone networks. Today, a new type of network infrastructure — high speed digital telecommunications — is being overlaid on cities everywhere. Its effects will be at least as revolutionary as those of the new network infrastructures of the past. It is already causing traditional building types and neighborhood patterns to fragment, recombine, and form startling new arrangements. This process will continue and accelerate. In this paper I describe the new digital infrastructure, analyze its major spatial effects, consider some illustrative examples of the resulting fragmentation and recombination, and discuss possible design responses with particular attention to social equity and long-term sustainability.

Digital cities are being developed all over the world. Digital cities integrate urban Let us ask some fundamental, practical questions about the role of digital telecommunications and ubiquitous computation in shaping our future cities. What new opportunities do these technologies provide to produce cities that are attractive, equitable, and sustainable? What unwanted side-effects must we contend with? And what strategies should architects, urban designers, and urban planners pursue to take maximum positive advantage of the potential benefits while avoiding the possible downsides?[1]

Network Infrastructures

We can best approach these questions, I believe, by reflecting upon the roles of earlier network infrastructures — water supply and sewer systems, streets and roads, canals, railroads, electrical grids, telegraph, telephone, and broadcast systems — in forming urban structures and patterns. Most obviously, these networks augment the

---

[1] These strategies are discussed in more detail, with extensive supporting documentation, in William J. Mitchell, *City of Bits: Space, Place, and the Infobahn* (MIT Press, 1994), and William J. Mitchell, *E-topia: Urban Life, Jim — But Not As We Know It* (MIT Press, 1999).

T. Ishida, K. Isbister (Eds.): Digital Cities, LNCS 1765, pp. 1-6, 2000.
© Springer-Verlag Berlin Heidelberg 2000

affordances of the places they serve, and so support activities that would not otherwise be possible there. Furthermore, they allow greater concentration of human activities by connecting urban locations to distant hinterlands.

Thus, for example, a piped water supply system allows habitation of sites that would otherwise be too barren to support life. And, by drawing upon a far-flung catchment area, it can support a much greater population than local water resources would otherwise allow. Similarly, sewer systems disperse waste that would otherwise accumulate locally, road systems allow trade with the food-producing countryside and other cities, electrical supply systems mitigate the effects of darkness and climatic extremes, and so on.

We have to consider not only the immediate effects of particular networks, but also the ways in which multiple networks interact to produce joint effects. An irrigation network might allow a desert location to produce crops, for instance, but it is also necessary to have road or rail access to get those crops to market. Water supply and transportation networks may allow population to concentrate at a location, but this population will not be sustainable unless there is also effective waste removal.

As geographers and planners have long-since discovered, the interactions of these networks with patterns of land use are complex. On the one hand, construction of networks creates the possibility of new land uses at the locations served. On the other, existing land uses generate demands for network service. Urban spatial development is best understood, then, as a recursive process, unfolding over lengthy periods of time, in which network infrastructures and land-use patterns evolve by continually responding to one another.

When a new type of network infrastructure emerges, it is not deployed across homogeneous terrain; it is overlaid on a spatial pattern that has developed in response to its predecessors. Typically, by creating new relationships among existing activities and introducing new activities, new network infrastructures produce significant transformations of such existing patterns. Since the industrial revolution, in particular, we have seen the effects of overlaying modern transportation, electrical supply, and telephone systems on older urban fabrics. Conversely, we have also seen the effects of removing network infrastructure or getting bypassed by it; there are numerous sad examples of towns and cities that have declined when railway or riverboat service ceased, or when interstate highways passed them by.

What, then, are the effects of overlaying digital telecommunications on existing urban patterns? How will this new type of network interact with existing ones? And what sorts of transformations can we expect to result?

Fragmentation and Recombination

The basic function of digital telecommunications, of course, is to allow human interaction at a distance. To the extent that remote interaction successfully substitutes for face-to-face, traditional requirements for adjacency among activities — the bonds that have always held buildings, neighborhoods, and cities together — are eliminated. However, only some — by no means all — such bonds are loosened or removed. You may now do your banking remotely, for example, thus eliminating the need for face-to-face interaction with a teller at a local branch bank. But, if you want to get your hair cut, you still need to go to the hairdresser's for a face-to-face interaction. The net effect is neither decentralization of everything nor rampant centralization (as some early commentators had suggested), but a complex process of fragmentation and recombination of familiar building types and urban patterns. It is much like a chemical reaction in which some bonds are broken, others remain, new ones form, and a new compound — with interesting new properties — results.

Consider, for example, the now-familiar effects of online bookselling. By making use of Web sites instead of traditional sales floors, online book retailers such as Amazon.com radically decentralize the activities of browsing and purchasing; instead of taking place in a few retail establishments at central locations, these activities are distributed to Internet-serviced desktops in huge numbers of homes and offices. The space to accommodate these activities, which had once been grouped with other retail space, now fragments and recombines with domestic space and work space. At the same time, book storage and distribution functions equally dramatically centralize. They no longer need to be clustered with browsing and purchasing, as in a traditional bookstore, but are now performed at a few national centers located at convenient air transportation hubs; this allows both economies of scale and maintenance of much larger stocks than are possible in scarce and expensive urban retail space. And back-office functions such as billing and stock control, which reduce to manipulation of digital data, no longer need to near either the books or the customers, and can float free to wherever teleworkers are available at a price the management is willing to pay.

There are implications not only for location of activities, but also for transportation demand. With old-fashioned bookstores, books were delivered in bulk to the stores (that is, to intermediate storage points), then carried away by purchasers. With online bookstores, the emphasis shifts to express package delivery from the national distribution center to widely scattered homes and workplaces.

You can carry out this sort of analysis for just about any of the emerging online retailing or service industries, and the results vary according to the natures of the particular products or services offered. Books are small, high value, imperishable, and a delivery time of a day or two is generally acceptable, so national distribution centers make sense. The same goes for music CDs, videos, consumer electronics, and many drugstore items. But groceries are bulkier, less valuable, and more perishable, so they demand regional distribution centers rather than national ones, and fleets of specialized local delivery vans rather than national package express systems. Hot pizzas are even more perishable, and require nearby local production and distribution centers. On the other hand, computer software, digital music recordings, and digital videos can be delivered online (provided that the bandwidth is sufficient), so the distribution centers can be located just about anywhere there's good network service, and telecommunication does not just restructure transportation requirements but completely substitutes for transportation.

Finally, we should not forget that delivery points for products and services — homes and workplaces in particular — are likely to change in response to their new roles within these systems. At the very least, they need network connections for placing orders; today, these typically take the form of PCs running Web browsers, but we are likely to see increasing use of smart appliances and closets that electronically order their own supplies, and sensor-equipped spaces that can summon medical and security services. The humble mailbox is likely to evolve into a larger and more sophisticated repository that can keep perishable goods from deteriorating and keep high-value goods secure. And home TVs, VCRs, CD players, radios, and videogame consoles will evolve into much more intelligent systems for finding, ordering, retrieving, organizing, displaying, and paying for digitally distributed entertainment, news, and educational materials.

The Redistribution of Office Work

What happens to office work space under these conditions? Once again, we can begin to discover the answer by disaggregating the functions of a traditional office and considering the differing implications of telecommunications for each one.

Traditional office buildings provide individual workspaces such as private offices and cubicles, convenient access to files and other work materials stored on-site, access also to machines such as copiers and printers, and group work and meeting spaces such as conference rooms and foyers. Access to people and facilities is controlled by receptionists. Layout and circulation are organized for maximum convenience and efficiency of internal interactions. Locations, typically, are in downtowns serviced by transportation networks or in suburban office parks with convenient automobile access. Each of these characteristic features is affected differently by digital telecommunications, so that office space also fragments, redistributes itself, and recombines with other activities rather than simply relocating.

First, in the era of the networked laptop computer, email, and sophisticated telephone services, private work spaces do not need to be grouped together in office wings and cubicle farms; employees can effectively take their private work home, on the road, or to customer or supplier sites. When files are converted to digital form and put online, it is no longer necessary to be physically adjacent to them. Copiers, printers and the like are becoming smaller and less expensive, so it is possible to distribute many of them to scattered locations instead of maintaining a few large ones at central locations. The most obvious results are the home telework space (recombination of office space with domestic space), the hotel room increasingly functioning as work space (and equipped to do so), and the airport lounge and airplane seat as workplaces. Furthermore, the centralized private offices and cubicles that remain may no longer be semi-permanently assigned to individuals, but may be part of a pool for temporary assignment as required.

On the other hand, face-to-face meetings remain crucial for many purposes. Thus office workplaces in central locations are likely to emphasize provision of meeting space, together with meeting support facilities such as food service and short-term accommodation. And there is likely to be continued growth of short-term meeting facilities at central locations, such as hotel meeting rooms, airport business centers, and convention centers.

Within this new spatial pattern, receptionists can no longer control access to people, facilities, and information in the traditional way, and supervisors cannot perform their functions by means of direct visual surveillance. These functions are largely taken over by software. Instead of having to walk past a receptionist to get to a confidential file, for example, an employee now has to log in to a secure area of cyberspace. When software functions in this way, much of the need to group activities in secure, supervised areas disappears.

Thus, for all these reasons, the adjacency bonds that have held the components of traditional office space together are weakened or broken, and these components can respond to other spatial imperatives. There is much more flexibility in the location of private work, and this allows more of it to take place at home (reducing commuting), on the road (reducing employee down-time), and at customer sites. Simultaneously, central locations and transportation nodes attract face-to-face meeting spaces and associated services, and can achieve economies of scale in provision of these.

Similar analyses can be made of the school, the university campus, and the hospital. Remote access to information resources means that there can be much more flexibility in the location of private study space, and remote monitoring and telemedicine capabilities provide comparable flexibility in sites for many types of medical care. But those aspects of education and medical care that continue to require face-to-face interaction will still tend to gravitate to central locations conducive to economies of scale and efficient provision of related services.

New Homes and Neighborhoods

In the case of residential space, a variety of scenarios — responding to needs of different cultures and subcultures, different segments of the population, and different values and priorities — are likely to unfold. For some of the affluent elite, the loosening of traditional locational constraints will open the way to a footloose existence as electronically connected nomads pursuing business and recreation across the globe. For those entranced by the old dream of rural retreat, it will provide the means to create isolated electronic cottages.

Most interestingly, though, the processes of fragmentation and recombination that I have sketched here will provide opportunities to recreate highly desirable neighborhood patterns that were torn apart in the cities of the industrial era. In these cities, a coarse-grained urban fabric typically developed; workplaces grouped in industrial areas and central business districts, housing grouped in bedroom suburbs, and lengthy daily commutes resulted. Today, when an increasing amount of work is information work that can be electronically supported and flexibly located, it is possible to recombine the home and the workplace — in many ways, to recreate a pre-industrial land-use pattern in the post-industrial era.

This electronically mediated live/work pattern yields a higher daytime population in residential areas than the commuter suburb, which then has the potential to support neighborhood services such as cafes, health clubs, hairdressers, business centers, child care and elderly care, and so on. These, in turn, provide the opportunity to create lively streets and public spaces. The result — if it's done well — can be an urban fabric of vigorous, pedestrian-scale neighborhoods that take advantage of the affordances of remote electronic connection to produce a high density of face-to-face interactions at the local level.

Kyoto's traditional *machiya*, in fact, demonstrate how this can work. In the *machiya* districts, townhouses accommodate both living space and work space, and there are numerous restaurants, bars and other local service facilities scattered throughout the fabric. The workspace has mostly been devoted to light industrial use, such as textile work. The live/work mix has been reasonably acceptable as long as these uses have not generated too much traffic, noise, and pollution, but it begins to show strain when the typical side-effects of light industry become prominent. This fine-grained mix would function even more effectively if information work, which does not produce the undesirable side-effects of light industry, could be substituted.

This strategy has much in common with strategies advocated, in the United States, by the New Urbanists. But whereas New Urbanist projects frequently rely too much on nostalgic recollection of days gone by — the image of a traditional Main Street rather than a convincing effort to generate the social and economic conditions that could make a Main Street work today — this sort of re-weaving of the urban fabric focuses on creating a robust underlying spatial structure that responds positively to today's emerging realities, and it does not commit designers to styles and images drawn from the past.

Summary: Re-weaving the Urban Fabric

In summary, I suggest that the deployment of digital telecommunications infrastructure creates a radically new logic governing the mix and distribution of living space, work space, and service locations within the urban fabric. The responsibility of urban designers and planners is neither to embrace this new logic uncritically, nor to hunker down in dogged resistance to it. It is, instead, to understand the opportunities that this new logic presents for re-weaving the urban fabric, and thus to find new ways to pursue the ancient goals of equity, sustainability, and delight.

Understanding Digital Cities

Toru Ishida

Department of Social Informatics, Kyoto University

Abstract. As a platform for community networks, information spaces using the city metaphor are being developed in worldwide. This paper compares the trials of digital cities. Four digital cities, those of America Online, Amsterdam, Helsinki and Kyoto, are introduced. It is interesting to note that each digital city has a different goal: to explore a vertical market, a public communication space, a next generation metropolitan network, and a social information infrastructure for the 21st century, respectively. Their different services, system architectures, and organizations result from the different goals. Digital cities will change together with the advance of computer and network technologies. No digital city can remain at its current status. This paper reviews those digital cities to have a better understanding of their current status and future.

1. Introduction

Digital cities are being developed all over the world. Digital cities integrate urban information (both achievable and real-time) and create public spaces for people living in the cities. From 1994, more than 100 European local organizations started to discuss digital cities. The topics include telematic applications, car-free cities and so on. In the US, on the other hand, AOL started a regional information service called "digital city" for several tens of major US cities. In Japan, the Digital City Kyoto Project was launched to create a social information infrastructure towards the 21st century.

Why do regional information spaces attract people given that we are in the era of globalization? We understand that the Internet has triggered global businesses, but at the same time, it enables us to create rich information spaces for everyday life. In the US, 80% of incomes are spent within 20 miles from home. Even though the economy has become more global, everyday life remains local. Business requires homogeneity to allow global competition, while life is inherently heterogeneous reflecting the different cultural backgrounds. If you visit various digital cities in the world, you will find differences in the functions provided.

People now start to incorporate the Internet technology into their life. For people with problems with their health, the worldwide network cannot have much impact. Local networks of people with the same problem are more valuable. Digital cities will provide the infrastructure for networking local communities.

T. Ishida, K. Isbister (Eds.): Digital Cities, LNCS 1765, pp. 7-17, 2000.
© Springer-Verlag Berlin Heidelberg 2000

According to the statistics available in 1999, the US has a largest number of Internet users. UK, Canada, Japan and Germany follow in this order. With regard to Internet applications, however, the ratio of Internet users to the entire population is more important. This ratio exceeds 40% in northern Europe and northern America, and is about 15% in Japan and other European countries.

The difference in the Internet user ratio significantly affects the use of networks in society. In Japan, the typical Internet user is male, in his twenties or thirties, and is a businessman. In northern Europe, networking people with high blood pressure is being tried, but this would be hard to promote in Japan. The social use of the Internet depends on the people who actually use the Internet. Therefore, it might take a few more years for digital cities to take an important role in Japanese society.

The rapid advance of Internet technologies makes any prediction rather suspect. Given this qualification, this paper visits several digital cities and then reviews the goals, architectures, technologies and organizations of digital cities in the world to have a better understanding of their current status and future.

2. Visiting Existing Digital Cities

2.1 AOL Digital Cities

We first visit digital cities in the US. When we search "digital cities" in the US, many instances are seen to have been created by America Online (AOL). AOL was founded in 1985 and their Internet service has more than 17 million members. AOL provides locally focused online network services for 65 cities and the number is growing.

Each AOL digital city collects tourist and shopping information of the corresponding city. Besides those information services, AOL provides local advertising opportunities for vertical markets including auto, real estate, employment, and health. The AOL digital city is the largest and most popular local information service in the US. It receives more than 4.5 million visitors every month. Though similar services are available like Yahoo.local, which collects local information for twelve cities, AOL seems to be a leader in this field. The success of AOL digital cities shows that people need regional information services for their everyday life.

Figure 1 shows an example of the AOL digital city for New York. The city delivers locally relevant news, community resources, entertainment, and commerce. Unlike general search engines, such as Yahoo, which aims at retrieving information from the world, digital cities focus on local information. To collect academic research results from the world, general search engines are convenient. However, for people living in or visiting New York, since they are interested only information related to New York, a digital city is easier to use.

 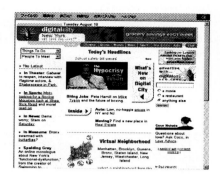

Figure 1. AOL Digital Cities
http://www.digitalcity.com/

2.2 Digital City Amsterdam

The European Digital Cities Conference has been held annually from 1994 to discuss a wide variety of topics. An example of the experiments performed is Digital City Amsterdam, which started four year ago[1]. This city was built as a platform for various community networks and thus particularly focuses on social interaction among citizens.

Figure 2. Digital City Amsterdam
http://www.dds.nl/

The digital city Amsterdam was first created for communication between the municipal council and citizens. All communication was presented via text and modems. Terminals were placed at public spaces such as libraries. The success of this experiment increased the interest of the citizens in the Internet. In the first ten weeks, 10,000 people registered with the digital city and 100,000 accesses were recorded. The system continued to grow, and in 1996, an average of 48,000 users visited the digital city every week.

2.3 Virtual Helsinki

Helsinki Arena 2000 Project started in 1996, under the initiative of the Helsinki telephone company (HPY) [8]. The goal of the project was building the next generation metropolitan network. This network enables citizens to communicate with each other using live video in both directions: members of a classic car community can cooperate on repairs by using live video transfer.

Figure 3. Virtual Helsinki
http://www.hel.fi/infocities/

In parallel to the development of high speed networks, a trial of building a 3D virtual city is underway. The virtual Helsinki is the face of this project, and the entire city of Helsinki is currently under construction in a virtual space. As the 3D models become more accurate, more computational power and communication bandwidth will be required to view digital cities at home. This virtual city will be a human interface for new broadband network services. Though there is a big discussion on whether or not 3D virtual reality is useful, the 3D Helsinki is accepted by the Finnish people who prefer new technology. Finnish activities are very strong in communication networks. Finland is now a leading country in Internet use, home banking, and mobile phones. It is very impressive to find that this revolution is on going in a northern country with only 5 million people.

2.4 Digital City Kyoto

In October 1998, a project started to develop a digital city prototype as a social information infrastructure for Kyoto[7]. Unlike other digital cities, the project is research oriented, and is being pursued by universities and basic research laboratories.

Within the first year of the project, various experiments were conducted. Digital City Kyoto makes available different city metaphors: a 2D map and a 3D virtual space, both of which are easy for non-technical people to understand. A large number of WEB pages (2600 in September 1999) are being collected and linked to the 2D/3D city. Real-time sensory data from the physical city is also mapped to the digital city. As the human interface, a whole Shijo street (2Km long) has been implemented in a 3D virtual space with the cooperation of the shopping street community. People can get information related to the physical city such as traffic, weather, parking, shopping, and sightseeing. Digital City Kyoto also encourages social interaction among residents and tourists. For oversea visitors via the Internet, a digital bus tour with a guide agent that supports cross-cultural communication is currently under development.

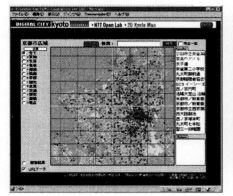

Figure 4. Digital City Kyoto
http://www.digitalcity.gr.jp/

Exciting ideas from researchers start triggering local communities and governments, but more time is required for the prototype to become a really useful digital city.

3. Comparative Analysis of Digital Cities

This section provides comparative analysis of the four digital cities presented in Section 2 from several different aspects.

3.1 Goals of Digital Cities

Each digital city has its own goal. The goal depends on the organization that took the when forming the project.

America Online's digital cities aim at growing their business in so called vertical markets. On the other hand, Digital City Amsterdam is intended to provide a public communication space to people living in the city. In Helsinki, the next generation metropolitan network is being planned. In Kyoto, a social information infrastructure for urban life (including shopping, business, transportation, education, welfare and so on) is the goal of the project.

Digital cities commonly provide both profit and non-profit services and have a dilemma in balancing the two different types of services. Without profit services, digital cities become unattractive and fail to become a portal to the city. Without non-profit services, the city may become too homogeneous like AOL digital cities as a result of pursuing economic efficiency. In any case, digital cities are forced to face competition with private companies, which provide only profit services. Can digital cities compete with those companies? In the US, it seems the answer is no, but in Europe, it may be yes since there is a tradition of public organizations providing high quality information[1]. As proof, the largest TV broadcasting stations are often run by non-profit organizations. The answer in Asia including Japan is not known and left to future.

Technology may move the border between profit and non-profit services. Digital cities often provide free e-mail and free desk space services. Digital cities try to guarantee an equal opportunity to any one who wants to access the Internet. Since free e-mail services can become commercial like hotmail.com, it is no longer clear whether this service is profit or non-profit.

Urban planning is another motivation of digital cities[9]. The Virtual Los Angeles is designed to allow community members to directly participate in the urban planning process, and is a good example of a high quality 3D virtual city[3].

3.2 Architecture of Digital Cities

Figure 5 shows the three layer model used for designing digital cities. The first layer is called the *information layer* where WWW archives and realtime sensory data are integrated and reorganized using the city metaphor. The geographical database is used to integrate those types of information. The second layer is called the *interface layer* where 2D maps and 3D virtual spaces provide an intuitive view of digital cities. The animation of moving objects such as avatars, cars, busses, trains, and helicopters demonstrate dynamic activities in the cities. The third layer is called the *interaction layer* where residents and tourists interact with each other. Social interaction is an important goal in digital cities. Even if we build a beautiful 3D space, if no one lives in the city, the city cannot be very attractive. Similarly, even if we have a virtual town where people often visit to chat, if there is no connection to the corresponding physical city, this town cannot be an information infrastructure for the city.

---

[1] Personal communication with Peter van den Besselaar.

Community computing experiments [5,6] especially agent/multiagent technologies, have been conducted to encourage interactions in digital cities.

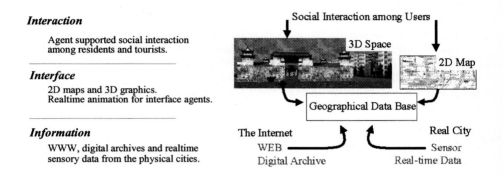

Interaction

    Agent supported social interaction among residents and tourists.

Interface

    2D maps and 3D graphics.
    Realtime animation for interface agents.

Information

    WWW, digital archives and realtime sensory data from the physical cities.

Figure 5. System Architecture of Digital Cities

How are digital cities directly connected to physical cities? In Helsinki, HPY (a metropolitan telephone company) is planning to build a high-speed network. The amount of budget is 20 million USD in 1998, and 600 million USD over five years starting in 1999. Under this plan, to fully utilize the new network, the digital city must be tightly connected to the physical Helsinki. This is why the 3D virtual city is the core of the project.

Amsterdam seems quite different. This digital city is not just a local network for the city of Amsterdam. Generally, people in small cities tend to prefer local topics. But the inhabitants of large metropolitan areas, like Amsterdam, mostly come from other cities. Their interests are not necessarily local to Amsterdam.

Though Digital City Amsterdam succeeded to introduce a city metaphor into regional information services, since there is no direct mapping between digital and physical Amsterdam, the ratio of Amsterdam-based digital citizens decreased from 45% in 1994 to 22% in 1998. This fact highlights the design issue of how much reality we should put into digital cities. If we make digital cities without strong connections to the corresponding physical cities, the connection may gradually disappear. However, Amsterdam organizers think of this as a good sign. Do the organizers really want the digital city to become an imaginary city? This is probably because of the size of the country and a role of the city in the country. In Netherlands, there are 14 million people living in a small area. Amsterdam is the capital and 1.5 million people are living in the greater Amsterdam area. The political power of Amsterdam makes it possible for the digital city to keep centripetal force beyond the physical boarder of the city. In another view, the boarder of the country (the boarder of the language) contributes to the effectiveness of the centripetal force of the digital city. There is a reason why the project welcomed the growth of the digital city beyond its corresponding physical boarder.

In Kyoto, though the project does not run on high speed networks, since the goal is to create a social information infrastructure of Kyoto city, the link between digital and physical cities is strong. As the level of real-time sensory data is increased, the link will be naturally strengthened. There is no reason to restrict communication within the city. However, only 10% or so of the population in Japan are Internet users, and most of these are "office workers familiar with technology." Accordingly, the Internet has had a very limited influence on daily life. Due on this fact, the goal of the digital city project (to create a social information infrastructure of Kyoto) may become vague without the strong connection created between the digital and physical cities. While Netherlands can be the border of Digital City Amsterdam, Japan is too large to act as the border of Digital City Kyoto. Amsterdam is the capital of Netherlands, but Kyoto is not.[2] The strong connection between digital and physical Kyoto was designed by learning from Amsterdam experiences.

3.3 Technologies for Digital Cities

The following technologies are unique to digital cities.

Technology for information integration is essential to accumulate and reorganize urban information in a comprehensive manner. Digital cities typically handle WEB pages and realtime sensory data from physical cities. A large amount of high quality digital archives can also be accessed from digital cities.[3] The idea of "using a map" is commonly observed in digital cities. Amsterdam uses an abstract information map, while Kyoto uses a city map. In the latter case, technologies are needed to integrate different kinds of urban information by using geographical information systems (GIS). GIS may become a key technology for digital cities.

Technology for public participation is unique to digital cities. To allow various individuals and organizations to participate in designing and building digital cities, the entire system should be flexible and adaptive. For designing such systems, multi agent systems are promising. For designing a human interface that supports both content creation and social interaction, a new technology is required to encourage people with different backgrounds to join digital cities. In Amsterdam, a city metaphor is used to create a new form of public participation. Recent activities on digital cities also include 3D technologies. The question is, however, what level of 3D reality is technologically and psychologically appropriate for implementing digital cities. Another question is who should/can develop and maintain the 3D digital cities. Again, public participation is a key to solving these problems.

---

[2] Kyoto was a capital of Japan from 8th century to 19th century
[3] Digital archives are extensively being developed under the leadership of Kyoto city.

Technology for social agents is being tested. So far, most digital cities adopt the direct manipulation approach to realize friendly human interfaces. The direct manipulation approach allows users to explicitly operate information objects. An agent (human-like dog-like, bird-like and whatever) is a relatively new approach in this field. Since agents often have the ability to communicate with users in natural language, users can access information without explicit operation. This allows a digital city to keep its human interface simple and independent of the increase of stored information.

Technology for information security becomes important as more people join digital cities. For example, it is not always appropriate to make links from digital cities to individual homepages. We found that most kindergartens declined our request to link them to the digital city. As we have social laws in physical cities such as peeping-tom laws, digital cities should introduce such laws in their information spaces. These issues are being discussed, but not yet introduced in any of digital cities.

3.4 Organizations of Digital Cities

Organizations of digital city projects result from their goals. AOL digital cities are operated by a for-profit company. In other digital cities, public sectors are more or less running the projects. Digital City Amsterdam is operated by a non-profit organization called DDS (De Digitale Stad), which consists of 30 members including system managers, programmers, html managers and WEB designers. DDS pays salaries to those members, and uses any monies collected for the organizational goal.

In Helsinki, the Arena 2000 consortium was formed under the initiative of the Helsinki Telephone Corporation (HPY). The city government and various companies including IBM and Nokia are involved in the project. It seems the rapid expansion of wireless telephone network triggered this project. If there is no advance to fixed networks, the market will shift to wireless networks. The 3D virtual city is being developed by ARCUS Inc. This company is trying to sell their technology to other cities in Europe, and has created a virtual Bremen at the request of the city of Bremen.

The digital city Kyoto project is a three-year initiative sponsored by NTT Open Laboratory. Established in October of 1998, the project consists primarily of researchers from NTT and Kyoto University, but also includes a wide variety of people from other organizations. In August 1999, the digital city Kyoto forum was launched. The forum includes several universities, companies, local communities and governments in/near Kyoto. Various activities are expected in the next two years.

4. Conclusion

We reviewed digital cities in the world. Table 1 summarizes the comparison results. Digital cities started with quite different motivations including a vertical market, a public communication place, a next generation metropolitan network, and a social information infrastructure. Digital cities have changed and will continue to change with new technologies.

Table 1. Comparison of Digital Cities

	AOL	AMSTERDAM	HELSINKI	KYOTO
Goal	Vertical market	Public communication space	Next generation metropolitan network	Social Information infrastructure for everyday life
Architecture	Accumulating urban information	Loosely coupled with the physical city Platform for community networks	High speed network Tightly coupled with the physical city	Tightly coupled with the physical city Multi layer architecture: information layer, interface layer, and interaction layer
Technology	WEB Chat	City metaphor for public participation	3D virtual city Network technology	3D virtual city Information integration Social agent
Organization	Profit organization	Non profit organization	Digital city consortium initiated by Helsinki telephone company	Digital city forum (Universities, companies and local governments)

Digital cities have a variety of directions: tourism, commerce, transportation, urban planning, social welfare, health control, education, disaster protection, politics and so on. People can easily imagine possible applications suitable for digital cities. Digital cities can incorporate real-time sensory data from the corresponding physical cities. More sensors are being embedded into cities in recent years. Many of them can be shared by citizens to increase welfare and to guard against disasters. Once people experience the usefulness of real-time sensory information in digital cities, they will start to announce various live data including vacancies in restaurants, parking lots and so on.

Digital cities attract people because different expertise can contribute to building a new city. Digital cities will provide an opportunity to people to create a public information space for their everyday life.

Reference

1. P. van den Besselaar and D. Beckers, "Demographics and Sociographics of the Digital City," *Community Computing and Support Systems*, Lecture Notes in Computer Science 1519, Springer-Verlag, pp. 109-125, 1998.
2. DingPeng, MaoWeiLiang, RaoRuoNan, ShengHuanYe, MaFanYuan and T. Ishida, "A Pilot Project of Digital City Shanghai - Shanghai Tourist Information System," *Digital Cities: Experiences, Technologies and Future Perspectives*, Lecture Notes in Computer Science, Springer-Verlag, 2000 (in this volume).
3. W. Jepson and S. Friedman, "The Virtual World Data Server & The Virtual Los Angeles Project," http://www.aud.ucla.edu/~bill/ACM97.html.
4. K. Kuutti, "Design for Motivation," In Terms of Design Workshop, Helsinki, May 1999.
5. T. Ishida Ed., *Community Computing: Collaboration over Global Information Networks*, John Wiley and Sons, 1998.
6. T. Ishida Ed., *Community Computing and Support Systems*, Lecture Notes in Computer Science 1519, Springer-Verlag, 1998.
7. T. Ishida, J. Akahani, K. Hiramatsu, K. Isbister, S. Lisowski, H. Nakanishi, M. Okamoto, Y. Miyazaki, K. Tsutsuguchi, "Digital City Kyoto: Towards A Social Information Infrastructure," *Cooperative Information Agents III*, Lecture Notes in Artificial Intelligence 1652, pp. 23-35, Springer-Verlag, 1999.
8. R. Linturi, M. Koivunen and J. Sulkanen, "Helsinki Arena 2000 – Augmenting a Real City to a Virtual One," *Digital Cities: Experiences, Technologies and Future Perspectives*, Lecture Notes in Computer Science, Springer-Verlag, 2000 (in this volume).
9. W. J. Mitchell, *City of Bits: Space, Place, and the Infobahn*, MIT Press, 1996.

Digital Cities: Organization, Content, and Use[1]

Peter van den Besselaar*, Isabel Melis[#], and Dennis Beckers*

*Social Informatics, University of Amsterdam
Roetersstraat 15, 1018 WB Amsterdam, The Netherlands
[#]Independent journalist, Amstel 49, 1011PW Amsterdam, The Netherlands
{peter,beckers}@swi.psy.uva.nl - imelis@direct.a2000.nl

Abstract. Digital cities are developing on many places, and settings, aims, design, organization, and functionality differ among the various systems. Do differences in content influence use and users? In this paper we compare two relatively successful but dramatically different digital cities. The study is based on quantitative and qualitative research, using various data. Although digital cities are generally conceived as local information infrastructures, and as a means for enhancing democratic participation, users primarily appreciate it as a tool for communication. We also observed, among others, how cyberspace reproduces the dynamics of 'established and outsiders', which inclines us to think that 'virtual public space' is not as open as is often claimed.

1. Introduction

Sociologists have been studying since long the complex relationship between the city and technology, and more recently between urban society and information and communication technologies (ICT) [1, 2, 3, 4]. Modern ICT is reshaping the global economy and its geographical dimension, and this results in what Castells [5] has called *the network society*, which functions as a *space of flows* between those cities and regions that participate in the generation of profits. Depending on the local opportunities for making profits, parts of the world are connected to or disconnected from this space of flows. The network society differs from the earlier industrial society, in that the centers of the international system are not fixed anymore, but are flexible determined from the perspective of the global system. Local societies have to compete more than ever for their position in the global network, and it is generally accepted that the availability and quality of the ICT infrastructure is a necessary condition for 'being connected'. Many initiatives have been undertaken to create this infrastructure, using headings like 'telecities' and 'digital cities' [6, 7]. Although the creation of this electronic overlay is in the first place based on the needs of modern *globalized economy*, the new media also have effects on *local urban life*.

---

[1] This paper summarizes some of the findings of two research projects [17, 22, 23], on which we will publish more extensively elsewhere. The authors gratefully acknowledge the digital cities in Amsterdam and Parthenay for their cooperation in the research underlying this paper.

T. Ishida, K. Isbister (Eds.): Digital Cities, LNCS 1765, pp. 18-32, 2000.
© Springer-Verlag Berlin Heidelberg 2000

In this paper, we are interested in the local dimensions of ICT networks, that is the digital city as an infrastructure for enhancing local social life. Related to the idea of community networking [8], the general aim of local computer networks is to provide an information and communication infrastructure to improve local participation and local (economic) development, and to create an electronic public space [9]. Castells claims that the new communication technology extends already existing networks, without substituting any other way of communication [5, p363]. Although these new tools correspond to our new way of living based on individuality and on the home, they are supposed not to question traditional values [5, p369-70]. Whether this is true is still to be seen, since digital cities are an emerging phenomenon and constantly in flux. Users are building and rebuilding them in specific local situations, and technological tools for local computing are constantly developing [10, 11, 12, 13].

Digital cities are interpreted in different ways. They can be seen as a *local social information infrastructure*, providing information over the 'real' city to locals and of course to visitors of the real city [14]. The digital city can also be approached as a *communication medium*, influencing the personal networks of inhabitants of a digital neighborhood [15]. Another view is the digital city as a tool to improve *local democracy* and participation [9, 16], in fact the basic idea behind the digital city in Amsterdam [17]. Fourth, we can characterize the digital city as a free space to *experience and experiment* with cyberspace [18]. Finally, the digital city can be seen as a practical resource for the organization of every day life. One can think of local electronic commerce, and the provision of online public services as a support of local economic activities. However, the digital city may also become an experiment with new forms of solving problems and coordinating social life. Where currently most activities are coordinated by the market or by the state, the digital city may become a tool that enables people to do things by *mobilizing the available local resources*, using existing and emerging social networks.[2] Think of 'local trade exchange networks', and other examples [19, 20, 21]. Using the term 'digital city', one expects a local computer network that, like a 'real city', offers all of these functions. In practice, this is of course not yet the case.

Studies on digital cities generally focus on only one of these functions. We have chosen a different approach, and evaluate it from the user's point of view. In this paper we present some results from a comparative study of two European digital cities, that differ considerably in terms of their setting, their aims and organization, and their design: *De Digitale Stad*[3] (DDS) in Amsterdam, the Netherlands, and the *In-Town-Net* (ITN) in Parthenay, France. We will try to answer the following questions: What functionality is offered by digital cities, in terms of information, communication, political debate, 'experience', and practical resource. To what extent are the offered possibilities used? Who is using the digital city, and what are the motivations of the users?

---

[2] Theoretically, this last point relates to the question to what extent ICT changes the relative costs of the various modes of coordination, production and transaction [17, 20].

[3] Dutch for *The Digital City*.

2.   Data and Method

The comparison of the *content* of the two digital cities is based on a content analysis during the summer of 1998. Web pages are classified in terms of the informational content (is the information general or for practical purposes; is it local information or not), and the communicational possibilities (the availability of email, chat, discussion lists, forms) [22].

Who is using the digital city? For the DDS we have surveys from May 1994, May 1996, and May 1998 [23]. For the ITN we have a similar survey from February 1999, and information about users from the administrators of the system. The surveys are not representative, and are more informative about the active users than about all users.

What do people do in the digital city? The questionnaires give information about this, although again, respondents cannot be considered as 'representative'. The DDS surveys are more informative, as we have three of them, with large numbers of respondents, enabling more a detailed analysis than in the case of the ITN. We also had access to log files of a two weeks period, which give a rich picture of what users do [22]. In the ITN log file, only the web page through which the user enters the digital city is registered, and consequently this log file is less informative. The two information sources cover different populations. The log files cover every visit, including occasional visitors, while the questionnaires reflect mainly opinions of the more frequent users who consider themselves as inhabitants of the digital city.

Why do people use the digital city? Open interviews of approximately one hour were held with a stratified sample of *local* users, male and female, at various ages, and of different social status. In the case of the ITN, the interviewed people were selected from the email-directory. The DDS users were selected from the 1998 questionnaire. The interviewees were between 12 and 57 years old, but the youngest DDS user was 24. We analyzed the protocols of the interviews to clarify the use profile, the communicational aspect of the digital city, the opinion on the ITN or DDS, and the opinion on the 'digital city' concept. The answers have been sorted out by sex and age to find possible differences answers for men versus women and for users below 30 years old versus users above 30 years old (the median age).

3. Two Digital Cities: DDS Amsterdam and ITN Parthenay

As far as we know, the term *digital city* originates from an experiment in Amsterdam, early 1994, when a political-cultural center and a group of computer activists[4] launched the DDS. The history of the DDS has been described on various occasions [17, 24, 25], thus we only summarize here a couple of main points, relevant for our analysis in this paper. The DDS started as an experiment to provide an electronic

---

[4] Hacktic, the computer activists group, became later in 1994 the first Dutch Internet access provider XS4ALL. In 1998, it was taken over by Dutch Telecom.

democratic forum to the citizens of Amsterdam, to bridge the gap between the inhabitants and local politicians. For ten weeks, before municipal elections, the visitors of the DDS were able to look online into municipal documents, request specific local information, ask for a free email address and have free access to the Internet. The DDS was the first open access to the Internet in the Netherlands, and consequently the DDS experiment benefited from extensive media coverage. The number of users grew fast: 10.000 users in ten weeks time. Such a successful start asked for continuation, but public funding would end. The next step was to become a foundation and a year after its launch the project was financially self-supporting. Since then, the number of citizens in the DDS has increased steadily and reached 120.000 citizens by the summer of 1999. It has developed into an infrastructure that is by far the largest digital city in Europe. Although it started as a grassroots initiative, there is no formal representation of the users in the board of the DDS.

Inspired by the FreeNets in the USA and in Canada, the founders invented the concept of the digital city as an electronic public domain in cyberspace, to foster social and political debate, free expression and social experimentation in cyberspace.[5] Other goals are innovation in the field of new media, support local (economic) development, and providing advice and services to small businesses in the field of Internet and the WWW. More recently, the DDS went through a re-orientation toward providing content, especially related to political and social issues.

The DDS is a non-for-profit organization, which raises income out of other activities, to maintain the digital city. It seems to be a sustainable solution, independent from subsidies, but competition with other systems that provide similar services becomes important. The digital city system is the 'unique selling point', that positions the organization on the market for consulting, website design, and WWW projects. Also some money is generated through renting space for companies and organizations in the digital city, and from advertisements. Finally, it has various sponsors. The DDS has an annual turnover (in 1999) of about $1.000.000, and employs some 30 people, of which five have a management role, five are in systems design, and another five are programmers.

Maintenance of the DDS is costly, and users complain about technical problems and declining free service. DDS is relatively often 'down', and also the links to the personal homepages (the houses) are problematic. The awareness tool (pressing the 'who is here' button) indicates already for three years that it does not work properly. Consequently, one knows only very partially who else is in the DDS.

The other digital city we studied is the one of the French municipality of Parthenay, a little town of 18.000 inhabitants, three hours southwest of Paris. Parthenay launched the ITN in November 1996, after successfully experimenting with a bulletin board system (BBS) for several months. The implementation of new technologies in Parthenay can be seen as another step in the municipal policy to involve citizens in the city's life and to promote the development of the local economy of this isolated

---

[5] As the DDS wants to be a virtual community, and not Internet provider, Internet access became quite soon restricted, to avoid membership only because of a full free access to the Internet.

rural region of Poitou-Charentes. This has been achieved thanks to a policy aiming at a deep transformation of the local society. The mayor's credo in the benefit of ICT is an essential part of the results. In his words: "The challenge of the digital city is to reinvent the city. It is a fantastic opportunity to propose new public services, to promote a new and creative partnership among local actors and reinvent the governance of the city for a better democratic public sphere in the city." [26]

Four main elements have contributed to the success of the experiment. First of all, Parthenay was selected to participate in a series of experiments at European level [27, p42] for the local implementation of new technologies, financed by the European Commission. Second, the population was already used to active participation through a consistent policy conducted by the socialist mayor in the last 20 years, promoting active citizenship[6] in the town. E.g., Parthenay holds the record for the number of associations per inhabitants (10 per 1.000 inhabitants, three times the European average). Third, the local authorities have chosen a social-pull approach to involve the citizens from the very beginning in all stages of the different projects. The aim was to adapt the technology to the need of the people. Fourth, this has been organized in a democratic way: by ensuring free access to the electronic tools from different public places. These learning centers were opened in strategic public places to reach different segments of the population. In addition to this, the municipality negotiated 1.000 computers ('1.000 micros' campaign) at low price (4.000 FFR.) to help the people who wished to have a computer at home but could not afford market price. Since October 1997, the municipality offers free access to Internet to all citizens of Parthenay, be it from their home or from a public terminal. The town has its own server to connect its employees, citizens, firms and five bigger companies that already have their own Intranet. In September 1998, the population of registered users rose above 2.500 persons and was considered to be the most successful digital city in France [25, p164].

In contrast with the DDS, the ITN is maintained by the city hall, and therefore not depended on the income generating capabilities of the digital city itself. On the other hand, the viability of the digital city becomes completely dependent on political priorities.

4. Morphology of Digital Urban Spaces

Both the DDS (http://www.dds.nl) and ITN (http://www.district-parthenay.fr) started with BBS technology, and developed quite fast into a WWW based system. This transition implies that the systems became more information-oriented, while communication facilities are less developed. Both have their own modem bank to enter the digital city, although DDS users generally enter through an Internet provider. Both digital cities are collections of websites, grouped into various topics (municipality, culture, sports, education, etc). The interfaces are very different: the

---

[6] Active citizenship refers to the very literal sense of being active in the local social life. This requires from each citizen autonomy, responsibility, co-operation, innovation and creativity.

ITN has a classic hierarchical structure, where the DDS implemented the city metaphor in a quite literal way [14, 17].

The homepage of the ITN shows directly the main menu of topics with their icons. One also finds a left column with basic services like checking your (free) email, access to newsgroups and discussion lists, what's new in the digital city, information for visitors, and a personalized entrance where you can get a regular up-date of your favorite topics. The In-Town-Net provides information, announcements, agenda of activities, and web pages of citizens, associations, businesses, shopping malls, etc. The digital city homepage is divided in 20 topics that correspond to the departments of the town hall, and each head of department is responsible for the development of his/her corresponding topic.

The basic structure of the DDS is one of topical squares, e.g., the music square on which various organizations in the music field have their 'office' (a homepage or link to a homepage). On every square, we find on the left various navigation tools, including the 'who are here?' button, and the access to email. On the right side, one finds the communication tools: the DDS magazine, one of the Web-cafe's, the discussion lists related to the topic of the square, and more recently, the access to the DDS broadcasting system. Around the squares we find the neighborhoods, where digital citizens have ca a homepage. The squares form a *city map,* which provides an overview of the DDS. Figure 1 shows the homepage of ITN (right), and the 'music square' of the DDS.[7]

Fig. 1 Two interfaces

When the DDS started with its WWW interface, it was quite advanced. After three years, the interface is still satisfactory in terms of the organization of the information. However, there is a clear need for much more sophisticated communication and awareness tools. Recently, several new communication possibilities were introduced, like the digital living room, and the DDS broadcasting. The new interface to be introduced shortly, will particularly improve these aspects.

---

[7] The *city map* of the DDS, and a *neighborhood* with *houses* are shown in [14] (in this volume).

We compared the DDS and the ITN first in terms of the distribution of sites over categories, second in terms of the percentage of sites with general, practical, and local information, and third in terms of the communicative possibilities:[8]

- The DDS is divided in 35 topics for a total of about 260 sites and the ITN in 20 topics for a total of about 680 sites (summer 1998). The large number of sites in ITN is due to the fact that the ITN does not charge local companies for hosting their website. Apart from this, the distribution of sites over the various categories is fairly similar, as the following classification shows. Business (13% DDS vs. 26% ITN), education (7 vs.11%), health (7 vs. 3%), computers (6 vs. 3%), media (12 vs. 10%), leisure (33 vs. 28%), and politics (22 vs. 20%)
- Another way of comparing is in terms of the nature of information supplied per site. General information is in 95% of the DDS sites, and in 66% of the ITN sites, and for practical information the figures are 83% and 90% respectively. General *local* information can be found in 33% of the DDS sites, and in 24% of the ITN sites. Finally practical *local* information is in 45% of the DDS, and in 49% of the ITN sites.
- The communication possibilities for are much more developed in the DDS than in ITN: in the DDS, 81% of the sites have email, 12% chat, 19% newsgroups, 35% have forms to reply, and only 15% do not have communication facilities. For ITN the figures are respectively 53%, 0.6%, 9%, 12% and 43%. Finally, the DDS sites have more often information in foreign languages (mostly English) than ITN sites: 47% vs. 22%.

Summarizing, DDS offers more general information than practical information, while for ITN this is the other way around. The DDS offers much more communication facilities, and more international exposure. On the other hand, the amount of *local* general and practical information is highly similar. In the DDS it is much higher than one would expect, as the DDS does not see itself as a local computer network for Amsterdam, while in the ITN case it is unexpectedly low, as ITN defines itself explicitly as local. Finally, except for business, the thematic categories have similar shares in both digital cities, despite the fact that both have been build by different people, in different institutions, and in different social, cultural and economic contexts.

5. Profiles of the Online Dwellers

DDS users may be occasional visitors (tourists) or registered users. Registered users are given a free email address, can make use of the chat rooms, participate in the Multi User Dungeon facility located in the underground of the DDS (the metro), are allowed to vote in online referenda, and can build their own *house* (web page). In October 1998, the counter of the DDS acknowledges 95.000 citizens. Visitors travel anonymously through the DDS, but without these possibilities. In the ITN, registered users can use a free email address, a free Internet connection (only for users living in Parthenay), have the option to appear in the directory of users and can create their own web pages. In October 1998, ITN had 2,400 registered users.

---

[8] We have not included personal sites in this comparison: approx. 2500 (DDS) and 50 (ITN).

The respondents of the questionnaires were mainly registered users, so we do not know much about visitors who walk through the digital city, or simply visit one site. On the other hand, the respondents can expected to be the most enthusiastic and frequent users, the data may enable us to answer the following questions we are interested in here: 1. Do digital cities attract the local population, or do they also serve users from a wider geographical area? 2. Does the population of digital cities users reflect the population of the 'real city', or is it more like the Internet population: male, young, and highly educated? 3. Do user populations of the DDS and ITN differ from each other? To answer these questions we have focused on three main variables: gender and age distribution, and the percentage of local users.

Table 1. Profile of the users of DDS and ITN

	DDS*			ITN**
	1994	1996	1998	1998
Inhabitants 'real' city	724000	718000	726000	18000
Users digital city	10000	48000	80000	2400
Female users	9%	16%	21%	33%
Local users	45%	23%	22%	42%
Age distribution:				
Users aged under 19	6%	8%	20%	2%
Aged 19 – 25	29%	48%	38%	20%
Aged 26 – 30	23%	15%	15%	11%
Aged 31 – 40	27%	16%	15%	29%
Aged 41 – 50	12%	9%	8%	27%
Aged above 50	3%	3%	4%	11%
* Surveys, May 1994, 1996, 1998				
** Sample of ITN administrators, October 1998				

Gender distribution is more balanced in the ITN than in the DDS. The surveys show that in the DDS the share of women rose from 9% in 1994 to 21% in 1998. For the ITN, figures from the administrators (Oct. 1998) indicate that of the registered users 67% are men and 33% are women. This is unusually high since most research in this field concludes that, at least until recently, the Internet is a male dominated environment.[9] This high number of female users could be the result of the seven computer centers in public places, with the objective to train the population in the use of new ICT. This didactic approach may attract a more diverse population and has indeed proved to be very successful in the case of Parthenay in helping people to learn how to use a computer in general, and the In-Tow-Net in particular. The number of public Internet terminals in Amsterdam to access the DDS is very low, and no human assistance is available to help the beginner. For an organization like the DDS it is financially not possible to create public access in a way the ITN does. On the other hand, in the Netherlands (and especially in Amsterdam), the percentage of people with a computer is comparable to the US [23, p67], and many people have Internet access through school, university, or their workplace.

---

[9] Lohr, "Who uses Internet?", 1995. McLeod, "Internet users abandoning TV". 1996. Quoted in [5, p. 359].

The *age distribution* tends to confirm that the ITN users are more representative for the population of their 'real' city: 70% of the users are over 30 years old, while for the DDS nearly 75% are under 30 years old. The surveys show a growing number of very young people in the DDS. The share of children under 18 has more than tripled between 1994 and 1998. The data on the ITN suggest that only 2% of the registered users are younger than eighteen. This percentage certainly is underestimated, since we observed that in practice children are not systematically reported when they ask for an email account.

Despite a nearly similar percentage of local content in the two digital cities (see section 4), the share of *local users* does differ greatly. In the DDS, the percentage of local users has dropped from 45% in 1994 to 22% in 1998. The DDS is thus loosing its close connection with Amsterdam and attracts a majority of users from all over the country and even some from abroad. As the DDS is three years older than the ITN, it has had more time to be better known both nationally and internationally. However, results from the 1996 survey reveal that two years after its creation, the percentage of local users had already decreased from 45% to 23%. While in the ITN, after two years the percentage of local users is still 42% (survey January 1999).

We emphasize here that non-local DDS users refers to users living anywhere but Amsterdam. While for the ITN, non-local users are living in Parthenay's environment since residence in Parthenay and surroundings is compulsory for registration, and our data concerns registered users only. In addition to that, Amsterdam, as cultural capital of a small country, has more potential to attract a wider number of online non-local visitors than a very small town like Parthenay in a large country. There is also a different attitude on the side of the administrators: the DDS foundation aims at a wider public, and the services are available for everybody who wants to register. Parthenay's authorities, in contrast, have no intention to go beyond local needs.

In conclusion, despite the similarities in information supply, the DDS is more a virtual city, with a fairly homogeneous population, and does not reflect the heterogeneous *urban* population. The DDS is, as we called it elsewhere, more like a digital suburb, or a digital campus [17]. The ITN, on the other hand, is appears to be more heterogeneous and more a computer network for a local community. However, in both cases various categories of the population are strongly underrepresented, like minorities, the lower educated, the elderly, the unemployed, and housewives.

6. Patterns of Use

How are digital cities used? During the period covered by the log files, the DDS counted about 325000 'hits', of which 13% personal pages. The ITN counted almost 9000 'hits'. The personal pages took 45% of these 9000, and one single personal page devoted to the TV soap opera *Star Trek* accounted for half of these.

Analyzing the two log files, we found that that there is a large difference between the supply of sites per categories, and the use of those sites. Second, a few sites attract a lot of the visits, while 78% of the sites in both digital cities were not visited at all during the period covered by the log files. In both digital cities, the 10 most visited sites (out of 250) are good for about 85% of all hits. The distribution of visits over the subject categories is as follows: Business: DDS 9% (DDS) vs. 21% (ITN); Computer: 19 vs. 3%; Education: 3 vs. 22%; Health: 7 vs. 4%: Leisure: 12 vs. 21%; Media: 34 vs. 6%; Politics: 16 vs. 23%. The differences are considerable, and reflect the large number of web sites of local firms and the active role of the schools in Parthenay. In the DDS, the high score for the 'media' category is due to the popularity of three sites, of which Kidon (a site with links to many media around the world) should be mentioned. This site attracts international attention, and counted 42.000 hits. The 'computer' category is also popular in the DDS, reflecting its young male population. In both digital cities, the 'politics' category is popular, but looking more detailed we see differences. In the DDS the attention goes to decision making issues, and to one political party, while in the ITN it is more practically oriented: town hall, cadastral map, etc.

The DDS questionnaires partly lead to a different picture, especially in terms of the popularity of subject categories. However, this may reflect the different use by the more frequent users, who seem to be focused more on the DDS itself, on computers, and on leisure and lifestyle, and less on media and politics. Use of the DDS related to work and professional activities indeed is low, and decreasing, as the results of the questionnaire shows.

Comparing the visits in terms of the type of information supplied by the visited sites, we see that in the DDS non-local (general and practical) information is popular, and is visited three times more than the sites with local information. The ITN users, on the contrary, go to sites with practical local information 1.5 times more than to the sites with non-local information.

Finally, in both digital cities, sites with communication facilities are more popular than sites without those facilities. The questionnaires support this, and show that *communication* is increasingly important for users. This requires changes in the design of digital cities, as WWW based systems are strong in information but weak in communication facilities.

7. Users' Motivations

In order to get a better picture of motivations for using the digital city, we conducted 27 interviews among a sample of users. The interviewees are early users, and 90% of French and Dutch interviewees started to use their digital city in the first 2 years of operation. They are still heavy users, as at least 75% claim to use the digital city daily for a short visit (half of the interviewees spend not more than 15 minutes in their digital city). ITN interviewees mention culture, computer, and education as preferred topics, while the DDS interviewees mention the digital city square, books and politics. The interviews suggest that users value the *communicational aspect* of their digital city more than informative or practical content. Most interviewees communicate with others in their digital city, meet other people, have the feeling that they communicate more or better thanks to their digital city, they like computer mediated communication

(CMC) and visit personal pages from others. Nevertheless, we have noticed some restrictions in this field. ITN interviewees declared that they usually read the newsgroups but hardly ever participate to the discussions. One reason is that it is always the same little group of persons who participate and they do not want to join them since they have not proven to be constructive and open to opinions of others. Another reason is because of the size of Parthenay: as a little town, everybody knows each other and they do not wish to share their opinion with everybody. For the DDS, some interviewees told that they do not participate in chat conversations because they do not feel welcome. As an interviewee said: "I got in there and it did not feel right, as a newcomer". Another interviewee: "I wanted to go in the metro by myself and I got lost and people were making fun out of me saying: look at the beginner! It's also like that a little bit in the chat rooms, when you don't feel welcome, you're a new being and you stay there, like the DDS belongs to *them* and not to anybody else." Such comments suggest that parts of the digital city are 'taken over' by active users - the established - who behave as a closed community and are perceived accordingly by the outsiders. These processes of norm building and tension among users are precisely what may indicate the rise of a virtual community[10]. Surprisingly, we have noticed that interviewees from Parthenay meet more people in person thanks to the digital city than the Dutch ones, despite the fact that the DDS organizes meetings for its users. This is an unexpected result as one may think that in a big town, where loneliness and anonymity is higher than in a small town, people may use their digital city to have the opportunity to meet other people.

Concerning the *local/non-local dimension* of the digital city and its use, there is a clear difference between French and Dutch interviewees. French interviewees are quite divided concerning the local/non-local dimension of their digital city while for the Dutch interviewees the DDS is clearly an opening to the outside (namely the Internet) although some of them wish that it had a stronger commitment in the local dimension. Consequently, in Parthenay half of the interviewees agree that the ITN is preferably for locals, while quite a few of the Dutch interviewees believe that the DDS is preferably for people from outside Amsterdam, despite the fact that all our Dutch interviewees are living in that city.
Interviewees are quite elusive about what they *like about their digital city*. For some of them it's a practical tool, others see it is an initiation to Internet, a few like it because it's free and the rest refers to the contact with people. However, interviewees are also critical about their digital city since half of them have complaints. But in general, interviewees remain quite positive about their digital city. For all of Dutch interviewees and 80% of the French, the digital city is useful and 70% of interviewees from both towns feel more or better informed thanks to their digital city and 70% of the total interviewees agree that their digital city is a good example to follow.

What should be the *role of a digital city*? From the answers, we could distinguish 3 opinions, related to respectively the geographical dimension (the local/global link), the social dimension (a communicational tool), and the technical dimension (the electronic age). Even if interviewees have different opinions and definitions about the concept, most of them believe that there will be more digital cities in the future. Younger interviewees are more confident about the future of the concept than older

---

[10] See [28] for an analysis and examples of virtual culture and virtual community building.

ones. Most of the French interviewees would even find it useful or necessary to have a digital city in every town while the Dutch were less enthusiast about the idea. Part of the Dutch interviewees would support the creation of a digital city only in big cities. They could not see the interest of implementing an electronic network in a small town where nothing happens… While on the French side, their experience and evaluation show that even small cities can benefit from it. The great majority believes that more people will communicate electronically in the future because it is cheaper, flexible, fast, reliable and efficient. They think that computer mediated communication is already part of the society and will penetrate even more all sectors of human life. Two interviewees mention that this new communicational tool may help isolated people. Another comments that "we were the phone generation" and one Dutch interviewee warns us: "the future generation of illiterates will only watch television"!

The analysis of the interviews demonstrates that interviewees are rather positive about their digital city from which they value above all the communicational dimension. The primary role of a digital city should be to help communication among people, second to be a local network and third to provide a free access to new technologies, in other words, to be an electronic local network.

8. Conclusions and Discussion

Interesting conclusions emerge from the comparison of the two digital cities. Digital cities can be seen as information infrastructure, as communication facility, as tool for local democracy and participation, as space for virtual expression and experience, and as resource for everyday life and for problem solving. In this paper we compared two relatively successful, but radically different European digital cities in terms of the design, organization, functionality, users and use. In a continuum from virtual topical communities to local community networks, we can put the ITN close to community networks, and the DDS close to the virtual community side, if we base our classification on aims and organization of the systems. Now what does this imply for users and use? And what does this teach us for the further improvement of local computer networks?

Similarities
Personalised and individualised interaction – We can say with Castells [5, p. 369] that what users of the digital cities are primarily seeking through the use of the computer, is personal interaction with other people. Questionnaires as well as the interviews tend to illustrate a strong interest emphasis on the communicational aspect of the digital city. In contrast, the use of the DDS and the ITN as access to local resources, and as a democratic tool is low. Users claim to communicate more thanks to their digital city, even in a small town like Parthenay. This possibility to communicate and meet people gives "a more human vision of the Internet", as an interviewee mentioned. This goes against arguments predicting that computer mediated communication will lead to less interaction among people "incapable of action, frozen in front of their computer" [29, p118] and that "our postmodern era

appears to be decadent and devoid of social responsibility" [29, p11]. Interviewees opposed this vision, that often appears in the media, as in the following comment of an interviewee: "They say that new technology kills human communication but I work in the social sector and I am strongly in favor of human bonds and still totally disagree with this statement. On the contrary, after a certain point, one feels the need to meet in person your electronic interlocutors. It's an opening on the outside world". Castells [5] also refers to an individualization of communication and information versus mass media communication. The interviews support this: "Everybody has its own style and its own little subculture and it is getting increasingly difficult to find people with the same interests and the same lifestyle, so Internet makes it easier to find these people... The whole moral of this technique is that it is very individualistic."

Positive evaluation – Interviewees share a positive approach to electronic networks. They agree in the useful dimension of their digital city, believe that there will be more digital cities in the future, and say that their digital city is a good example to follow. They welcome the idea to see more digital cities and believe that more people will communicate electronically in the future.

The "established/outsiders" patterns – Both digital cities clearly reveal the existence of a virtual community through processes of norm building, resulting in similar patterns of established users versus outsiders, as in the 'real' society. This suggests that new bonds are created, and users experience an appropriation of this newly created virtual public space. Even if electronic networks foster citizens interaction, this does not imply that the result of these interactions will lead to a more democratic, participative and inclusive society.

A learning tool for the electronic age – Digital cities are already organized in topics and expressed in the local language, which helps the new user to understand how to use CMC, and provides a familiar and protected environment that guides the user and avoids that he/she feels lost in cyberspace. Thus one clear objective and a direct effect of the use of a digital city is to accelerate this learning process and help the people to use new communicational and informational tools in their daily life.

Differences
Users profile – While the DDS still presents a rather homogeneous population of users, the findings about the ITN suggest a better representation of the population of the 'real' town as far as sex and age are concerned. The main reason for this seems to be the constant effort in Parthenay to involve the local population into the development of use of new technology through free public multimedia centers, strategically located to serve different social classes and age profiles. This didactic approach shows its results today and will most probably have a deeper impact in the long run. This in contrast to the DDS, where users are involved only as builders of their personal homepage.
Local/global dimension – Both digital cities are developing in opposite directions. The DDS is more global in terms of users profile and use, despite a significant proportion of local content. The ITN remains strongly local in use and content. We

can only stress here both the influence of users and the administrators determination on the local/global perspective.

Organization of the digital city – The two digital cities represent completely different models of organizing and maintenance. The DDS is a self-supporting non-for-profit organization, and therefore independent from changing political priorities. On the other hand, to maintain the digital city in Amsterdam, the DDS needs to be able to generate money on the market for Internet services and projects. At the same time, the DDS needs to compete with other systems that may supply similar functions to the users. To remain attractive for its current population of users, the DDS needs to remain innovative and to experiment with new technical possibilities. The current design is getting a little 'old fashioned', and this explains the declining level of activities in the DDS, as one can notice recently.

The ITN on the other hand, as it is maintained and funded by public funds, has a monopoly as local computer network for the community of Parthenay. This has obvious advantages, but at the same time, makes the digital city vulnerable for changes in political priorities, locally, as well as on the national and European level. What model will be the more sustainable, is still an open question.

Bibliography

[1] S. Graham & S. Marvin, *Telecommunications and the city*, London, Routledge, 1996.
[2] O. Jonas, *La cite interactive*, L'Harmattan, Paris, 1997.
[3] W.J. Mitchell, *The city of Bits*, Cambridge, MIT, 1995.
[4] S. Sassen, *Global cities, the impact of transnationalism and telematics*, Tokyo: United Nations University Press, 1999.
[5] M. Castells, *The rise of the network society*, Oxford: Blackwell, 1996.
[6] E. Mino, "Experiences of European Digital Cities", Lecture Notes in Computer Science (in this volume), Springer-Verlag, 2000.
[7] B. Peeters, "The information society in the city of Antwerp", Lecture Notes in Computer Science (in this volume), Springer-Verlag, 2000.
[8] D. Schuler, *New community networks, wired for change*, New York: ACM Press, 1996.
[9] A.Aurigi, "Digital city or urban simulator?" Lecture Notes in Computer Science (in this volume), Springer-Verlag, 2000.
[10] T. Ishida (ed.), *Community Computing and Support Systems*, Lecture Notes in Computer Science, vol. 1519, Springer-Verlag, 1998.
[11] T. Ishida (ed.), *Community computing*, John Wiley & Sons, 1998
[12] W.J.Mitchell, *E-topia; It's urban life Jim, but not as we know it.* Cambridge, MIT Press, 1999.
[13] W.J.Mitchell, "Designing the digital city", Lecture Notes in Computer Science (in this volume), Springer-Verlag, 2000.
[14] T.Ishida, "Understanding the digital city" Lecture Notes in Computer Science (in this volume), Springer-Verlag, 2000.
[15] K. Hampton & B. Wellman, "Examining community in the digital neighborhood". Lecture Notes in Computer Science (in this volume), Springer-Verlag, 2000.
[16] A. Ranerup, "On-Line Forums as an Arena for Political Discussions", Lecture Notes in Computer Science (in this volume), Springer Verlag, 2000.

[17] P. van den Besselaar & D. Beckers, "Demographics and sociographics of the Digital City", T. Ishida (ed.), *Community Computing and Support Systems*, Lecture Notes in Computer Science, vol. 1519, pp. 109-125, Springer-Verlag, 1998.

[18] H. Rheingold, *The virtual community*. Harper, 1993.

[19] N. Constructor & A. Bishop, "Reconfiguring Community Networks, the case of Prairie-KNOW", Lecture Notes in Computer Science (in this volume), Springer-Verlag, 2000.

[20] S. Miyagawa & I. Kaneko, "Design and Development of Community Oriented Tools. Lecture Notes in Computer Science (in this volume), Springer-Verlag. 2000,

[21] R. Loewenberg, "Davis Community Network", Lecture Notes in Computer Science (in this volume), Springer Verlag, 2000.

[22] I. Melis, *The local electronic network society*. MA thesis, University of Amsterdam, 1998.

[23] D. Beckers, *Use and users of the Amsterdam digital city*. MA thesis, University of Amsterdam, 1998. (Dutch)

[24] L. Francissen & K. Brants, "Virtual Going Places, Square Hopping in Amsterdam's Digital City". Tsagarousianon, Tambini, Bryan (eds.), *Cyberdemocracy, Technology, Cities, and Civic Networks*. London, Routledge, 1998.

[25] P. Wade & D. Falcand, *Cyberplanete, notre vie en temps virtuel*, Autrement, Paris, 1998

[26] M. Hervé, *Telematics strategy and partnership in a town*, 2nd European Digital cities Conference, Strasbourg, December, 1996

[27] E. Eveno, *Les pouvoirs urbains face aux technologies d'information et communication*, PUF, Paris, 1997.

[28] S.G. Jones, *Virtual Culture*, London, SAGE, 1997.

[29] C. Boyer, *Cybercities*, New York, Princeton Architectural Press, 1996.

Digital City or Urban Simulator?

Alessandro Aurigi

Centre for Advanced Spatial Analysis, University College London
1-19 Torrington Place, Gower Street, London WC1E 6BT, UK
Tel. +44-(0)171-3911808
Fax +44-(0)171-8132843
a.aurigi@ucl.ac.uk

Abstract. Much has been said in Europe about the 'digital city' phenomenon. However, we should question about the actual progress that these sites have made in these five years, as well as about the direction and trend of this progress.

New powerful functionality is available to the digital city that could facilitate the establishment of collaborative, communicative and inclusive virtual environments. But can we really recognise a trend towards increased public participation in European cities, as a direct consequence of digital city development?

This paper argues that this is not the case at the moment. To build more effective urban information systems we need to involve a plurality of actors in the design of virtual cities, and link digital developments to more traditional activities and initiatives that aim at enhancing public participation.

1. Introduction

About five years ago, a series of experiments aimed at exploiting the potential of computer networks for the establishment of electronic public spaces in European cities was born. Following the example of some well-established American 'free-nets' and drawing from the pre-existing culture of 'Bulletin Board Systems' that had been present in the European scene for years, these early experiences were going to establish a 'movement' of civic websites that would spread all over Europe. There were some notable differences between these new initiatives and BBS. First, they aimed at embedding themselves, more or less strictly, within real urban spaces. Second, the audience they were supposed to address was much wider, as several of them were trying to experiment with teledemocracy at the urban and regional level. Third, governments – local and central – as well as other community organisations got involved to a certain extent. Fourth, the Internet and the World Wide Web soon became the channel through which these 'digital' or 'virtual' cities – as many of them started being called – worked. These factors seemed to indicate that one of the major roles that these Internet sites were going to play was regenerating the public sphere of our cities, by providing a public electronic platform where citizens and communities could really exploit the communicative and inclusive potential of the new technologies.

T. Ishida, K. Isbister (Eds.): Digital Cities, LNCS 1765, pp. 33-44, 2000.

After five years, however, it is important to make an effort to go beyond the massive hype that is too often dominant in debates about the emergence of the Information Society.

It has to be noted that, as complex and multi-faceted civic problems are, digital city initiatives have tended to differentiate. Many orientations have emerged, that put more emphasis on addressing certain issues rather than others:

"First, there are attempts to use virtual cities to stimulate local economic development, through the provision of incentives to high tech innovation and 'friction free' arenas within which linkages can be created between local firms, service providers and consumers. Second, virtual cities can be 'electronic democracy' initiatives, aiming both to widen social access to the Internet and improve relations between citizens, elected representatives, and public and private service providers. Third, they can be attempts to engineer a new 'electronic public realm' for cities, supporting the development of on-line debates, discourses and 'communities' which feed back positively on the social dynamics of the 'host' metropolis. And, finally, they can be purveyors of new practices of urban management, supporting the electronic delivery of public services and 'intelligent' ways of managing urban services such as education, transport, waste, social services and planning" [1]

This paper however sticks to focusing on the relationship between the several digital cities and the public realm of their 'real' counterparts, as most initiatives being developed worldwide still claim to be geared to enhancing community life and participation in the real city. It is legitimate then for this paper to raise a series of questions about the actual progress that city and community-related web initiatives have made in these five years in addressing public participation and involvement objectives, as well as in being truly inclusive. In the second part of the paper attention is drawn on a few important design and policy issues that seem to have been overlooked so far in shaping the 'virtual city'.

2. Beyond the Urban Brochure?

If we think about the numerous changes that the emergence of the Information Society is already catalysing within cities, it is quite clear that the construction of civic websites is, in this context, just the tip of the iceberg. However, the function of the virtual city has been seen as a potentially important one just for this reason. Like the tip of the iceberg lets us know that there is something huge down there, the virtual town can give visibility and readability to the several bits – electronic and physical – of the real urban space. Therefore the shaping of these sites has been seen as a crucial exercise by scholars like Steve Graham, when he argues that:

"The challenge to planners and local policy makers is to try and construct the meaningful, accessible and local virtual cities which support the positive publicly-supported urban vision of trying to re-connect the often fragmented elements of cities together" [2, 201].

Taking this concept further, we can argue about the social relevance of initiatives such as public virtual cities, that could provide the environment where members of the public, and particularly those belonging to disadvantaged communities, can assert

their rights of citizenship, access, and interaction within those information highways of the 'space of flows' that otherwise would bypass them [3, 31].
However, research carried out during 1997 on city-related Web sites in the European Union [4] showed that, despite an impressive number of major European cities and towns being extremely active in constructing their digital urban analogies, the overall level of sophistication, complexity and above all participation-oriented features, was very low.

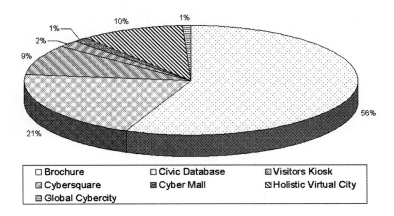

Fig. 1. Typological distribution of city-related Web sites in the EU in 1997

The majority of cities had opted for using the Internet to build sorts of 'electronic brochures' (see Fig.1) dominated by the ethos of city marketing whilst ignoring the participative and inclusive potential of highly interactive electronic environments. Only about 10% of the over 200 sites visited and analysed had something to offer on this side, while "many decision makers [were] sticking to old, reassuring media paradigms based on the ideas behind TV broadcasting and paper-based publishing" [1].
It seems though that levels of complexity, sophistication, and above all interaction of the virtual city are going to increase dramatically, thanks to the recent wave of research and development of innovative software aimed at enriching the experience of those who browse the Internet. Three dimensional environments that allow free movement and interaction – including dialogue – between multiple users can be created and put online as it is happening here at the Centre for Advanced Spatial analysis, UCL, with Andy Smith's "30 Days in ActiveWorlds" (http://www.casa.ucl.ac.uk/30days/) (see Fig.2) and "Virtual London" (http://www.casa.ucl.ac.uk/london/) projects. Proper 'digital cities' such as Virtual Helsinki (http://www.arenanet.fi/helsinki/) are taking advantage of similar techniques, and surely many others will follow. For instance, one of the first and most famous digital cities in Europe, Amsterdam DDS, has announced that it will soon implement

a 3D interface as well. All of this has in theory the potential to enhance many sites that in the 97 study were classified as brochures and urban databases.

Fig. 2. '30 Days in Activeworlds', a multi-user 3D community developed in CASA/UCL

Yet, it could be argued that more technologically sophisticated interfaces and increased functionality could still be 'invested' towards a more efficient place promotion, to attract tourists and foreign investors and customers, still remaining indifferent or even opposed to an active involvement of local communities and the support of public discourse. This tension between local interests and global, centrifugal, vocation of the digital city mirrors, rather than overcoming it, a crucial problem embedded in the post-modern real city. Enzo Mingione, for example, has noted that:
"The much expanded role of non-residents (e.g. businessmen, investors, tourists, shoppers, students, cultural visitors and commuters) complicates urban life and produces a new type of socio-economic environment, no longer dependent nearly exclusively on the number of permanent residents (Martinotti, 1993). It is on this ground that a fracture between tax-payers' interests (mostly residents and local businesses) and city marketing interests (mostly oriented towards capturing, at whatever the cost, increasing numbers of city users and regular business visitors) is widening fast and in some cases assuming greater importance than traditional class conflict" [5, 197]
Electronic urban design exercises could then end up mimicking some of the current trends in the design of physical urban spaces, limiting themselves to the production of exclusive 'spaces' that leave the needs and activities of traditional residents apart. Examples of urban design and regeneration exercises that tend to set these kind of priorities are easy to find. Elizabeth Wilson gives us a Parisian, pretty well known example:

"The Parc de la Villette is designed for tourists rather than for the hoarse-voiced, red-handed working men and women who in any case no longer work or live there. Thus it is in the great cities of the world at least, but also certainly in any smaller cities that can capitalize on an historic past, or an industrial peculiarity - not only is the tourist becoming perhaps the most important kind of inhabitant, but we all become tourists in our own cities…" [6, 157].

Other aspects of the technological progress that is going to make virtual cities more complex and interesting are the growing research efforts in information systems that can be used to provide civic services and sophisticated information over the Internet. Iperbole, one of the pioneering civic networks in Italy run by the municipality of Bologna, is working very hard to provide citizens with innovative services in a wide range of fields, like paying taxes and fees over the Net, checking planning applications, setting up e-commerce in a dedicated electronic district, and several others (http://www.comune.bologna.it/e_bologna_digitale.htm).

Also, Geographic Information Systems (GIS) that were previously available only on expensive and difficult to use Unix workstations are slowly migrating to desktop PCs and to the Net itself (see Fig.3). Although these systems have currently limited functionality once they are put on the Web, many projects, sometimes embedded in digital city sites, are being developed worldwide to publicly provide sophisticated information and, in some cases at least, stimulate public participation on the related themes.

Fig. 3. 'London Environment Online' (LEO), an Internet GIS developed at CASA/UCL

Enhanced services and information seem to have the potential of making the virtual city more useful, relevant to city life and participative. We should keep in mind, though, that there is not a unique way to configure these tools, and a logic of control and service provision could take over the public space vocation of the virtual city. Who decides what is useful and what is not in the digital city? And who sets the priorities, defining what needs are more urgent or important to address? And finally, what are the actual chances for the potential inhabitants of the virtual town to communicate, be visible and influence the decision-making processes in both the electronic and real urban space? Hoogvelt and Freeman (1996), for example, note that: "communities on-line grow from communication rather than information retrieval" [7], which means to us that a virtual city with high-tech facilities, rich information, service provision and an advanced interface, could still fail to let people communicate and participate. The next section will show how real this risk is.

3. All Geared Up and Not Much to Say

What does a virtual city need to really support public discourse and enhance the public sphere of our cities? How can the advanced interfaces and services be used to really boost public participation and exchange? Andrew Shapiro focuses on these problems speaking about two different possible designs of a virtual city. The first, that he calls 'Cyberbia', is a commodified space in which reality is highly idealised, and no disturbances can happen as "...you can shape your route so that you interact only with people of your choosing and with information tailored to your desires" [8, 10]. He therefore proposes an alternative type of virtual city, called 'Cyberkeley', conceived to guarantee freedom of speech and the presence of public spaces that he defines "virtual sidewalks":
"Consequently, it should be clear that Cyberbia - like suburbia - simply allows inhabitants to ignore the problems that surround them off-line. In Cyberkeley, by contrast, people may be inconvenienced by views they don't want to hear. But at least there are places where bothersome, in-your-face expression flourishes and is heard. These public forums are essential to an informed citizenry and to pluralistic, deliberative democracy itself" [8, 10].
Although this proposal has not been fully implemented by digital city initiatives, as far as inescapable 'virtual sidewalks' are concerned, many practitioners have understood the potential of public forums and their important role in a cybercity. The more sophisticated examples of digital city in Europe are based on the implementation of communicative features that complement a rich provision of information. However, enhanced services, rich information, and communicative facilities might still be not enough to have a real impact over citizens' involvement, thus making the virtual city really 'alive'. How can this be argued? A simple observation of what is going on in the discussion areas of some allegedly successful and advanced European digital cities gives us a reason to reflect. I will make three brief examples here, two from Italy, Rome and Bologna, and one from the Netherlands, Delft. These choices are not casual, as the Netherlands seem to be the most active Northern European country in setting up digital cities, capitalising on the example and paradigm of DDS Amsterdam. Italy is definitely the virtual city leader in Southern Europe [4], with some notable examples such as Bologna (see Fig.4) that are winners of numerous European awards like the so-called Bangemann Challenge in 1997, Euro-Med Net award in 1998 and the recent 'special jury award' at the 'Les Rubans des Villes Numeriques' meeting in France last March.

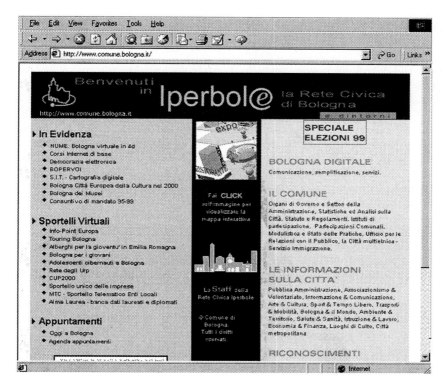

Fig. 4. The 'Iperbole' Web site

- Romacivica (http://www.romacivica.net) is the civic network of Rome. In March '99, a 'snapshot' of its discussion groups revealed that overall participation and communication was nearly non-existent. Over a week of normal activity, the most 'crowded' groups had been the 'cultural happenings' and the 'traffic calming' ones, with just 6 messages posted each. Some areas that were dealing with crucial themes such as 'immigration', 'environment' or 'drug addictions' got 1 or 2 messages, which in some cases were just non-relevant adverts. In all of the 18 newsgroups, the total number of people who had posted something was just 10, in a city that counts millions.

- Iperbole (http://www.comune.bologna.it) is the award-winning digital city of Bologna. In March '99, a similar observation to the one relating to Rome, resulted in an impressive number of active groups and a good traffic of messages within 12 days. This could be expected, as Iperbole is a pretty successful experience, running for over 5 years and supported by an interesting set of policies to increase usage of the virtual city. However, a close consideration of what was being written, showed that the type of participation that users were indulging in was very much on the leisure side, whilst social problems were discussed very little. The most successful areas were 'jokes' with 110 messages, '2nd hand' with 107 messages, and 'computers' with 75 messages.

On the other hand, 'multiethnic' had only 2 non-relevant messages, 'euro-citizens' had 3, and 'politics' had 8, just to mention a few.
- De Digitale Stad Delft (http://www.dsdelft.nl) in the Netherlands was observed in June '99. It had only 5 discussion groups in its space dedicated to citizens. A look at the 'politics' group was not very encouraging. Over the last 365 days, 17 different users had posted only 21 messages.

These examples show how negligible public participation of citizens in electronic debates within virtual cities is at the moment. This phenomenon tends also to be part of a vicious circle, in which the decision-makers and the public servants who would be supposed to be important actors in the discussion fail to grasp the real potential of the electronic environment, thus themselves failing to participate. The fact that few people frequent the public forums and that the number of messages is low, makes a very good case for 'calling yourself out' of the electronic town. Speaking with some policy-makers in Bologna, for instance, I was told:
"Once in a while we have a look at the discussion groups, but I have to admit that they have many defects. If I told you that we have learnt something from there that would allow us to change municipal organisation for the better, I would be just silly" [9].
Another prominent local politician of Bologna was referring directly to decision-making processes when he affirmed: "I believe that for the moment there is no influence whatsoever from Iperbole on decision-making processes" [10].

4. Towards Designing the Participative Virtual City

Generally, what has been noted so far suggests that the technologically deterministic vision that sees positive changes in society being inevitably generated by the implementation of a new technology, is a flawed approach to the problem of civic regeneration and the creation of effective electronic public spaces. We should not expect that urban problems can be fixed just by 'throwing in' a new piece of technology, as the crucial issue is not what this technology can do, but what kind of relationship and interaction will – or will not – be established between technology and society. Designers and managers of virtual city initiatives ought to avoid concentrating on just pure technical issues, and give some consideration to the ways the virtual city embeds within urban environment and society.
Partly, the failures of many digital city initiatives in establishing and keeping an active population of real citizens can be explained by referring to the ever-existing problem of social polarisation in the use of high technologies. It can be argued that there are not many participants because there are not many people able to surf the Internet, and that the social composition of this group of 'cybernauts' is still strongly unbalanced, making the digital city "more a place for a (new) elite and a number of 'techno-freaks' than for 'ordinary' citizens" [11, 242].
These problems are, of course, well known and being tackled with several measures. In Bologna, for instance, digital city promoters have been implementing policies that allowed more 'netizens' to join in, including senior citizens, women and the unemployed, like offering free Internet connectivity to residents for a long period of

time, public access points in libraries as well as computer literacy classes. So, something else seems to be missing from the picture, as local communities still tend not to be interested enough in what the virtual city has to offer in terms of communication and participation.

I would like to conclude this paper by suggesting three main issues that deserve particular consideration form the designers and those involved in shaping virtual cities. By these points I would like to argue that so far the virtual city has been too often looked at as a software product geared at some kind of end-users, whilst it should be seen as a process embedded in the city itself, and interacting with its communities from the very beginning of its life. In particular, the issues that I am suggesting to take on board are the following:

- First, we should reflect about the fact that digital cities are usually the result of a technology 'push'. This means that they are established and developed not to respond to some kind of demand from the general public and the urban communities. The attitude of virtual town shapers is 'proactive', tending to offer a series of facilities that are seen as due opportunities for the local community members who still do not even know about them. Therefore it seems normal and almost inevitable to create a digital environment and its services and then offer it to its potential users. This means that the vast majority of the initiatives is still designed according to a top-down process that sees communities as the − often unaware − 'clients' of the digital city (regardless of the fact that the service could be apparently offered for free, which after all usually means that it is paid by tax money or advertising). This attitude has so far put severe limits to the involvement of local community groups in the definition of aims, needs and design features of the digital city, making them just guests or at most information providers, but denying them influence in the governance and shaping of the virtual town. As a result of this, electronic citizens are supposed to interact in newsgroups, chatting areas and the like within an environment they are not in control of, and that they have not shaped at all. There are signs of this detachment between community and information system in developing virtual cities. It happens that multi-ethnic cities like for instance Bristol in the UK, that have a developing digital city (http://www.bristol.digitalcity.org), fail to represent − and therefore probably involve − the Asian communities that live there, as well as the social problems and potential that exist in the real town. What is offered instead is a pretty sanitised virtual environment that ends up being nearly desert, at least in terms of interaction and communication. I would like to argue that the involvement of local communities in cyberspace should start from the conception and design phase of the systems they will be supposed to use. Contributions from members of the public are simply necessary to develop the right ideas to bring the fragments of the real city together in the virtual one. If a virtual city project is concerned about dealing with the local citizens, its promoters should ask themselves whether it is more likely that members of the public would identify with an initiative that they have contributed to design, or whether they would prefer to use a product over which they had no say at all.

- Second, and closely connected to the previous point, I would argue that most digital cities − if not all − are being shaped according to paradigms familiar to computer scientists and bureaucrats, and end up prioritising what these professionals are most interested in. This depends on the fact that often virtual cities are seen as a computing exercise in the 'Human-Computer Interface' field, or at most as a tool for administrative efficiency and transparency. Gabriele Bollini, an environmental planner working for Bologna City Council and using Iperbole, when interviewed about the relationship that planning officers were establishing with the initiative said plainly that:

"Surely there are not interested people [in Iperbole] within the Planning department. In the Mobility department people seem more active, but my impression is that they end up uploading textual information into the system, without feeling very involved" [12].

This indicates that many of the categories traditionally involved in the management of the real city have a marginal role – or more often no role at all – in the running of the virtual city. It is hard to explain why this is happening. On the one hand it might be that the paradigm of the 'broadcasting' information system – when not of the 'classical' database – dominates the scene leaving little space for alternative conceptions and visions of the virtual city. In his interview, in fact, Bollini seemed to be extremely keen to get involved, as he had many ideas to use the digital city for planning and public participation purposes. But he seemed to be at the margins of the initiative, certainly not directly participating to its shaping. On the other hand, many planners did not want to be bothered by the potentiality of the new system. He had to admit that many of his colleagues deliberately avoided public consultation tools and procedures, as they considered them "a useless obstacle to their own knowledge" [12].

Whatever the reasons, this lack of pluralism of visions, if it can be defined as such, limits the scope, complexity and functionality of the electronic environment. In particular, the involvement of those people who are traditionally concerned with the organisation and development of the real city, such as planners, architects and urbanists, would be important to promote the virtual town as a thriving parallel public space. William Mitchell for instance states that there must be someone who knows how to deal with certain issues:

"A space is genuinely public, as Kevin Lynch once pointed out, only to the extent that it really is openly accessible and welcoming to members of the community that is serves. It must also allow users considerable freedom of assembly and action. And there must be some kind of public control of its use and its transformation over time. The same goes for public cyberspace, so creators and maintainers... must consider who gets in and who gets excluded, what can and cannot be done there, whose norms are enforced, and who exerts control" [13, 125].

However, many digital initiatives end up being developed as places highly specialised towards single uses (information broadcasting, tourism and place promotion, etc.) or aims (interface design, testing of IT techniques), and their social potential is lost.

Third, the development of virtual cities rarely involves the use of a combination of digital and traditional strategies and methods. This is in contradiction with the 'recombinant' [13] nature of the digital city, according to which physical and virtual bits of the same urban space exist and work together, rather than two separate levels of reality. As the electronic town is supposed to establish a relation – possibly beneficial – with the real town, policies and initiatives of a non-digital nature, such as computer literacy campaigns and public consultations and workshops, should be considered as an essential part of the development strategy, not just an option. Virtual cities need real communities, and need to think about them. As Julian Stallabrass argues:

"The virtual community demands a real one prior to it in order to function successfully. That communities can for the moment flourish is due to the still relatively closed and technophile nature of the Net, which is just what gives it its coherence" [14, 14].

The literature about Public Participation Geographic Information Systems (PPGIS) shows that initiatives aimed at empowering local people through the use of new pieces of technology – in the specific case GIS – always imply the implementation of a combined development strategy, where high technology goes together with more traditional participatory techniques. In Hawaii for example, the City of Honolulu developed together with members of the public a 'Traffic Safety GIS' that took advantage of "a participatory process where in residents come together to inventory and identify traffic problems" [15, 5]. Many other similar examples are available, all showing that if it can be true that the use of digital tools can generate new opportunities for communities, we always need to start from the real world in order to get these digital tools right, as well as involve people effectively.

5. Conclusions

We have seen that the digital city needs an all-round involvement of actors and experts, as well as a development process that addresses issues of inclusiveness, participation, and grounding into the real city and its real people and problems.

If these issues are not properly tackled, the virtual city simplifies itself to be either a civic database, a glossy brochure to promote bits of the real town, a nice exercise of 3D modelling, or a system that provides communicative facilities without really reaching the people who should use it. Either way, this kind of digital city risks to become an idealised icon of the more complex urban cyberspace that could inhabit it. Or, if we want to quote Mike Davis, it could be seen as an 'urban simulator' as some physical theme-park like experiments already are:

"Designed by master illusionist Jon Jerde, City Walk is an 'idealized reality', the best features of Olvera Street, Hollywood and the West Side sinthesized in 'easy, byte-sized pieces' (…) Indeed, some critics wonder if it isn't the moral equivalent of the neutron bomb: the city emptied of all lived human experience. With its fake fossil candy wrappers and other deceits, City Walk sneeringly mocks us as it erases any trace of our real joy, pain or labor" [16, 18].

If we want virtual cities to be "places of meaning, representation, politics, interaction and experience" [1] we should design them **with** communities, rather than **for** them. This would be a significant step forward to create and run forms of public cyberspace that support diversity and inclusion or, in other words, the participative virtual city.

References

1. Aurigi A. and Graham S. (forthcoming) "Cyberspace and the City: The 'Virtual City' in Europe" in Watson S. and Bridge G. (ed.) *The Blackwell Companion to Urban Studies*, Blackwell: Oxford
2. Graham S. (1995) "Cyberspace and the city", *Town and Country Planning*, August 95
3. Castells M. (1999) "The Informational City as a Dual City: Can It Be Reversed?" in Schon D., Sanyal B. and Mitchell W. *High Technology and Low Income Communities*, MIT Press: Cambridge, MA
4. Aurigi A. (1998) "Entering the Digital City: Surveying City-Related Web Sites in Europe" in *European Digital Cities – 3rd Conference: The Road to Deployment – Proceedings*, European Digital Cities EC DG XIII-C
5. Mingione E. (1995) "Social and Employment Change in the Urban Arena", in Healey et al. (ed.) *Managing Cities, The New Urban Context*, Wiley and Sons
6. Wilson E. (1995) "The Rhetoric of Urban Space", *NLR* 209
7. Hoogvelt A. and Freeman M. (1996) "Community Intranets", Mimeo
8. Shapiro A.L. (1995) "Street Corners in Cyberspace", *The Nation* 3-7-1995
9. Rovinetti A. (1997) Interview carried out by the author
10. Grandi R. (1997) Interview carried out by the author
11. Brants K., Huizenga M., van Meerten R. (1996) "The new canals of Amsterdam: an exercise in local electronic democracy", *Media, Culture & Society*, Vol.18
12. Bollini G. (1997) Interview carried out by the author
13. Mitchell W. (1995), *City of Bits: Place, Space and the Infobahn,* MIT Press: Cambridge, MA.
14. Stallabrass J. (1995) Empowering Technology: The Exploration of Cyberspace, *NLR* 211
15. Kim K. (1998) "Using GIS Technologies to Empower Community Based Organizations in Hawaii", paper presented at the Project Varenius Specialist Meeting on Empowerment, Marginalization, and Public Participation GIS, October 1998.
16. Davis M. (1992) "Beyond Blade Runner: Urban Control - The Ecology of Fear", *Open Magazine Pamphlet Series*, Westfield

Next Generation Community Networking: Futures for Digital Cities

Artur Serra

Center for Internet Applications (cANet).
Universitat Politecnica de Catalunya, Campus Nord. Modul D6-008
08034 Barcelona, Spain
artur@ac.upc.es
http://www.ac.upc.es/homes/artur

Abstract. Based in the results of the EPITELIO project (1996-98), an European founded research project on Telematics against Social Exclusion, this paper describes the possibilities of a new generation of community networking. The world is becoming digital and urban. For the first time, a global network society (M.Castells) is emerging. In parallel, an increasing gap between the connected populations and the unconnected ones are deepening. Next generation community networking is a possible solution for bridging such gap. As the Internet is now a convergent information infrastructure technology, community networking can works as a kind of convergent information society technology. Digital cities and community networks organizations can work together towards this new social platform of the digital era.

1   Introduction

The world is becoming digital and urban. Internet is the convergent digital technology allowing a convergence of the information and communications technologies. The next generation of Internet will accelerate such a convergence worldwide between text, audio and video in a common global information infrastructure. In September 1999, The Internet has approximately 201 million users worldwide. It embraces 44 million hosts or identified computers. The net of nets is in his 11th year of annual doubling since 1988. At the end of year 2000, the number of Internet users can be 300 millions, the 5% of world population. In 2006, the Internet is likely to exceed the size of the global telephone network by virtue of the IP telephony, or voice telecommunication over the Internet. It seems a lot but we notice that only half the population on Earth has ever made a telephone call.

The Internet2 generation is attracting already the attention of research groups, companies and governments all over the world. The US is developing two big programs: the "Internet2" program and the Next Generation Internet. At the moment, there is a web of Internet 2 projects what interchange traffic at the Science, Technology and Research Transit Access Point established in Chicago by the NSF. It is the new hub of interconnecting all the current projects on Internet2 in the planet. The

T. Ishida, K. Isbister (Eds.): Digital Cities, LNCS 1765, pp. 45-57, 2000.

Internet is becoming more and more a global information infrastructure for all the countries in the world. Next year 2000, for the first time since the beginning on the Internet, there will be more Internet users outside of the US, than in the country where the system began 30 years ago.

The Internet is a new global information infrastructure, with some particular characteristics like openness, interactivity and global dimension that make it very different from the rest of information and communication networks. Because of his beginning as a product of a public research, their protocols remain publics, open, and free. And because his enormous amount of useful information and knowledge the commercial world was interested in its fast commercialization globally. The result has been a new system, very different from the old telecom and television networks, a peculiar non-governmental system that keeps going only coordination of a non-for-profit and non-governmental institutions like IETF, ICANN, ISOC, Web Consortium, CERT...

The expansion of this new global information infrastructure although is setting now big economic, social and cultural opportunities and dangers to our societies. In the next years key research issues will deal with this transit from computer networking to community networking. New forms of organizations (new companies, new Universities, new policies...) are flourishing as genuine spin off of such new infrastructure. Old and new institutions are beginning to compete upon such new platform. At same time, in the global area, new countries like Finland or Ireland as emerging as pioneers in the digital era, meanwhile others are lagging behind. The same is happening in developing areas. Singapore, Taiwan or Mexico has set up Internet2 programs before most of the European countries. The key strategic research issues in the next years will focus on the problems and solutions this new technology creates in our societies.

A new phase of the Internet´s evolution is starting: the societal phase. In the last global conference of the Internet Society , INET99 in San Jose, California, the ISOC established the Internet Societal Task Force (ISTF), chaired by Vint Cerf. This is a new initiative complementary to the Internet Engineering Task Force (IETF). Its mission: dealing with the societal opportunities and problems that Internet is enabling in our societies. In the list of urgent topics you can find between others: e-commerce, security, privacy or community networking. The motto of this new task force is "Internet is for everyone".

May be we are in a critical moment in the evolution of the IT program. Our analysis indicates, (as work hypothesis) that we can be just in the middle of the Information and Communication Technologies wave, started 25 years ago. If we follow the Kondratieff-Schumpeter cycle theory, the next 25 years of this wave will be the years of the building of the new economic, social and cultural organizations and institutions appropriated to such infrastructure. It will be the phase of the InterCommunity issues. These new institutions, key actors of the new Internet-based society, will be developed as a result of new breakthroughs in new research areas still in the infancy.

In parallel with the deployment of the information infrastructure, the world is becoming urban also. Manuel Castells [1] and Jordi Borja [2] have analyzed this process of fast urbanization in the globalization race. Just the next decades, for the first

Table1. Map of possible evolution of IT research areas.

Information Society Technologies. (IST)	*Cultural engineering *Community networks engineering *Education engineering *Research collaboratories engineering *Electronic commerce engineering. *E-PUB, network communication.	*Inter-Community (Global Information Society based on Internet) (2nd order convergence technology) 1990s-2020s
Information and Communication Technologies. (ICT)	*WWW *Internetworking *AI *Software engineering *Hardware engineering. *Electronic engineering	*Inter-net (Global Information Infrastructure) (1st order convergence technology) 1960s-1990s

time in the history of mankind, the majority of the population will move to urban and suburban areas. The digital world in which we are beginning to live will be at the same time an urban world. The past United Nations Conference on Habitat II in 1996 forecasted a global population of 8.290 million people for the next 30 years (2025), a 43% increase. The 61% of this population will live in cities and 79% of such population will live in developing countries. Needless to say that although this process will continue, there will be still a 39% of the population that will live in rural areas, which, at least technologically, it could be served by satellite and cellular Internet.

The problem is the vast majority of such populations will not enjoy the access to the Internet and the benefits of the digital era at least some new solutions will be developed. A recent report from the UNDP, "Globalization with human face" [3] notices that the 93.3% of the Internet users belong to the 20% richest population. South Asia with the 23% of the global population has less than a 1% of Internet users. How the majority of this population could benefit of the Internet? What could be the social structures that could take advantage of such new infrastructure? Can we develop any kind of convergent social technology able to facilitate to the vast majority of mankind the access and the benefits of the new digital era? Can be community networking part of such solution? What can be a next generation community networking?

2   Community Networking Technology: Some European Experiences

2.1   The Epitelio Project (1996-1998)

The European Union lags behind the US and Japan in the information and communications technologies. With the exception of the Scandinavian countries, the number of Internet users in major European countries usually are half of the US or Canadian Internet populations. In the other side, there is a truly "European" sensibility for considering the societal issues of the digital era. Finally, the European Union is in a very interesting period. It is now the only continent in the world in a process of open social experimentation. Nobody knows how the process of "European construction" will end. Nobody knows if the creation of the unified common currency will have a happy end or not. Nobody can conclude how many countries will participate finally is such process of unification. Briefly, we are in a process of a big social experiment. In that moment, the continent has a very good chance: to combine this economic and social experiment with the new information and communication technologies. In other words, to take advantage of the new technologies for building the new Europe, and at the same time, to influence the social moment of this new technologies making innovative proposals from the economic and social areas, in which Europe usually has an special sensibility. In 1994, the Bangemann Report produced a first strategic document[1] underlying that the European way were based in the vision towards a truly Global Information Society, beyond the simple information infrastructure. During 1994 and 1998, the EU supported a European Digital City program, promoted by the big municipalities in the EU implementing a variety of telematic services for citizens. In the same framework program, the Epitelio Project took place.

Epitelio network configured a consortium of European universities, companies and NGOs dedicated to use the telematics in helping the European strategy towards social cohesion. Epitelio was a TURA (Telematics for Urban and Rural Areas) project looking for telematics applications to fight social exclusion. Its duration was 18 months. The Epitelio was an instrumental European project for coordinating this movement of community networks in Europe.

A full report [4] of such project was presented in the III EDC Conference in Berlin. The first steps in coordinating the European movement of community networks started in 1997-98 in two conferences in Milano and Barcelona, under the umbrella of such project. It was a real expression of the citizen movements in several countries, supported more or less from universities, some companies and city hall officials. This movement is more related to the citizen than to the city.

What we have learned in the EPITELIO project?

a) *Community network is a computer system and also a new social network. It creates new social identity.* If the origins of the community networking starts with group communication, the result is the creation of a new group structure, with a new legal status like some of the community networks in EPITELIO already have. (f.e.Ravalnet). In the design and development of such networks there is a participation of several actors: a knowledge innovator (usually the academic research team), a social innovator (the local activist) and some times even an economic entrepreneur (o young SME dedicated to sell computers or helping some technical assistance). Eventually, some people from the City Hall can also play this innovative role from the inside of the municipality. (f.e. CornellaNet).

b) *Participatory design methodologies haves to be adopted and adapted.* We used the classical participatory design approach to engage users in helping us to design the tools and systems. This is fine but not enough. It is necessary to adapt this methodology to help not users but citizens to define their own communities, not only systems.

---

[1] Bangemann Report, http://www.ispo.cec.be/infosoc/bckg/bangeman.html

We call it "participatory social design" technology, according with the social nature of community networks.

c) *Local and global can be linked.* We started several local community network in the city of Barcelona (with several neighborhood networks, like Ravalnet or Nou Barris Net), in Manchester (Manchester Civic Network). At the same time we fostering other projects already established like the Rete Civica de Milano in Lombardia. The collaboration of both networks has produced the first two European Conferences on Community Networking. In the first one, ECN97 in Milano we explored the European collaboration. Several European community networks participated like the Amsterdam DigiStaat (50,000 users), FreenetFinland (60.000), Iperbole-Bologna (10.000), Communities On Line (UK), VECAM (France, and Spain (BCNet, TINET (4.000 users), Mataro On Line). At the end of these conferences, a promoters group was established. Finally, in June 99, the EACN was born as an international association under the Belgian law. In the second ECN'98 conference in Barcelona we explored the global dimension of CNs. We invited a broad representation of Community Networking organizations from around the world: the AFCN from the States, Tele-communities Canada, the Victoria CN Association from Australia, the emerging movement of community networking from Russia and other similar initiatives from Argentina and Japan. The main lesson was to notice how similar were the problems of CNs had in their local activities and how *local and global* cooperation could be achieved through computer networks.

d) *More "normal" you are more bandwidth you need.* From the computer point of view, EPITELIO started using BCSCW and other cooperative tools. We explored the interoperability between the BBS First Class software and the Collabra conferencing system. Our team designed a service for an Internet citizen address (ICA)[5]. That evolved in an architecture called LocalNet [6][2]for integrating all local services in a common platform. But what really works is public access with a lot of bandwidth. Chat, games, radio on the net, web sites with a lot of graphics are the most popular applications in Ravalnet, the most successful experiment in the poorest neighborhood of Barcelona.

e) *A physical center helps a lot in rooting the CN in the community.* The best combination we found is the combination of a Community Technology Center (a local for civic uses) that at the same time plays the role of promoter of a Community Networking in his neighborhood.

f) *CN can be a new research field.* We identified Community Networks as a well international established field for creating cooperative systems to fight the social exclusion and to enhance a common sense of digital citizenship. We have analyzed particularly the Canadian experience and our national users organizations. Even we organized a first research workshop[3] in the ECSCW Conference in Lancaster. Doug Schuler, author of an important book on community networking and leader of Seattle Community Network [6] organized in Seattle 1998 [4]a second one and finally a third

---

[2] LocalNet, http://www.canet.upc.es/localnet-eng.html
[3] Worshop on CN as a new reseach field. ECSCW 1997 Conference.
   http://www.canet.upc.es/ws
[4] Doug Schuler, CN Workshop 1998
   (http://www.scn.org/tech/the_network/Proj/ws98/index.html)

one in Copehangen in 1999[5]. This research field can be one of the most promising new "information society technologies".

Briefly, the main lesson we learned from this project was that in the Internet era, *a new kind of civic associations are emerging where the citizens can speak and act by themselves through this kind of new platform, called community network, rete civiche, xarxes ciutadanes o redes ciudadanas.* Community networking seems a kind of "social technology" that could help to develop an open model of digital society. Community networks have usually the same kind of open, interactive and global environment established by the Internet. It is a brand new social technology, like the Internet. In the other side, we discovered the lack of attention of the local authorities (especially in big metropolis) in understanding the interactive and distributed nature of the new computer networks and the impact of such technology in a new model of politics based in the same principles of interactivity and distribution of powers. With the exception of a couple of Digital Cities projects, Bologna and Antwerp, the rest of Digital Cities initiatives are mainly web sites with more o less rich database of local information, maintained by local authorities. A big challenge in Europe in the Internet era seems the transit from the Welfare State to the Information Society: from Welfare to Information, from State to Society. Some key question seems more and more relevant in defining of this information society at the local level: Who is the digital city? Does a digital city need digital universities and schools? Does a digital city need a e-business community? Does a digital city have only virtual architecture or a mixed of virtual and physical spaces? Is the digital city only a communication tool or it is a new kind of institution? Briefly, what does an open digital city mean? A next generation community networking can be useful to define this model of open digital city.

3   Next Generation Community Networking

Computer networking have a relationship with the emergence of new social networking structures. Community networking is one of such phenomena. Before describing a next generation of community networking, let us explore a little bit the origin of such community networking field.

3.1 Community Networking Beginnings: The Computer Mediated Communication Model

At the beginning there was group communication. The "many to many" new model of communication was allowed by the electronic conferencing systems. It was a radical change in relation with the mass media, where few communicate one-way with many. The precursors of modern community networks are the first Conferencing systems created by Murray Turoff and Roseanne Hitz in the 70s [7]. Turoff introduced the

---

[5] Doug Schuler. CN Workshop 1999 .
   (http://www.scn.org/tech/the_network/Proj/ws99/index.html)

concept of Computerized Conferencing and was responsible for the implementation, utilization and early evaluation work on this unique combination of an information and communication system. He developed and implemented the first Computer Mediated Communications System (CMC) tailored to facilitate group communications (Delphi Conference in 1970) as well as four of these systems and have advised on the development and design choices for a number of others in both industrial and governmental organizations. Finally, he developed for the first time the idea of "Network Nation" in 1978.

At the beginning was a communication system, and the communication created community. The core application in all community network is the conferencing system, be a newsgroup system, be a distributed lists server, or whatever system for group communication. It seems there is a kind of test to evaluate if a CN works or not: if the group communication works, the community network works. The communication created communities. The old Computer Mediated Communication field (CMC) created the first computer conferencing systems, the basic element of the first Computer Communities, Networked Communities or Community Networks, as you prefer.

Still today the most successful community networks seem to be those whose group communications systems work fluently and with a high degree of participation. In the COMIC project we studied the case of I*EARN is an example (Serra, A. 1995), and by extension the APC. Electronic communication is basic for the health of community networks. Community networks develops with group communication. But Community Network is something more than a group communication system. It creates identity. Communications are one of the key functions of a community, but community has other goals: economic development, training, creation of identities, "Cyberspace", "e-address", "homepage", "netizen", are describing community spaces, functions, not only communications systems, not only media services. As Fiorella di Cindio has shown [8] community networks deal with citizenship. "Les maisons font la ville, mais les citoyens font la cite". (JJ. Rousseau) is a preferred quote of Fiorella de Cindio[8], founder of the Rete Civica de Milano. In that sense, in Europe, the term digital cities refers more to "la ville", community networking to "la cite".

3.2   The Freenet or Local Community Model. Tom Grudner

A second wave brought the freenet systems, and with them the idea of the local on line community and universal free access service. The freenet defined themselves from the beginning as computer services for the community, stressing the free access the local civic participation as common rights of everyone. The Cleveland Freenet, the first freenet in the world, saw itself as a set of services for the citizens, a local citizen network.

The big one, the National Capital Freenetin Ottawa, Canada, one of the most successful experiences, still defines itself in that way: "The National Capital FreeNet is a free, computer-based information sharing network. It links the people and organizations of this region, provides useful information, and enables an open exchange of ideas with the world. Community involvement makes FreeNet an important and accessible meeting place, and prepares people for full participation in a rapidly changing communication environment".

As the community network experiences matures, people begins to consider the CN as a community in itself, not only a service to a community. Their members begin to feel a sense of belonging, they are members of a network build in an electronic space. People increasingly doesn't feel themselves only as "users of a tool", but as members of a network, its network. For example, people in Tarragona freenet, TINET (Spain), call themselves "tinetaires", or members of TINET. There are not only internauts or citizens of Tarragona. They are both. The Rete Civica di Milano has as motto: "La Rete siete voi", "You are the network". The main contribution of the freenet experience was the demonstration that people not only communicated over the Net. They felt members of a community, a new kind of community. It was a change from CMC to community networks, an evolution from communication to community.

Also in the 80s Tonia Stone in Harlem started the movement of Community Technology Centers[6] with Playing to Win, proving that even excluded groups could benefit from the digital tools and services. A major contribution was how physical location is important to gather people in the community. Technology was rooted in the city, the neighborhoods, the real communities.

The explosion of Internet has made the success even global. Community networks once organized as local bbs systems now are connected to other networks through Internet, making the community network a global web of on line communities. We are entering maybe in a third phase of Community Networking, the Internet - Community Networks.

3.3   The InterCommunity Model

3.3.1   An Everybody's Community Networking?

Internet is not only a communication medium. It is facilitating the emergency of a new set of social networks and institutions, at the local, regional, national and global level. Community networking is one of them. Digital universities, e-publishing companies, community media centers, on line schools, collaboratories...a complete set of "on line communities" is emerging from the fabric of the old industrial society. ISOC proposes that "Internet is for everyone". Can we imagine a community network with everyone in the community. Suppose this trend of building on line communities upon the computer networks develops next years. Suppose the gap between a global computer infrastructure and a local citizens can be bridged. We could see in the next years an strong push towards a flexible alliance of on line communities of different nature and types (virtual universities, online civic networks, virtual companies, digital NGOs, etc.) in one country, in a set of countries, and in the global arena. We could imaging the coordination of all these online communities, by territories, by professions, by economic interests, A kind of federation or confederation of community networks could be of the possible outcomes of the trend towards connecting every citizen to the Net and the transformation of the Net in a set of online coordinated communities. The Intercommunity could be a theoretical hypothesis to envision this horizon. *By Inter-*

---

[6] CTCNet, http://www.ctcnet.org

Community we define this grid of new social networks built upon the Internet. As the Internet is the keystone of the new information infrastructure, the InterCommunity can be the social web of the new information era. It can be also a very dangerous model of social enforcement.

This model can be express in a very diverse way. From bottom up, we can conceived a variety of *intercommunities* as different local sets of on line communities. One of the experiments we started in Barcelona was inviting the other local digital communities to work together. The Internet Fiesta was a good opportunity last year. Promoted by the local chapter of ISOC, it gathers the support of the Group of Digital Journalists, the BCNet and other community networks, groups of schools, media companies, etc. An kind of local intercommunity was organized in such way. *This local intercommunity can be the Next Generation Community Networking.*

3.3.2   Localnets

Locality is one of the distinctive features of the community networks. By localnets we understand in the first place the local Internet community. It can be one of the first features of the next generation community networks. Usually we thing of Internet as a global network. But 50% of the normal communication of the Internauts in taking place locally. At the same time, currently we have a 10-30% of the population in a big metropolitan area connected to the Internet. Is it possible to organize a common set of agreements between the local Internet actors to facilitate this local communication, even to create some kind of common digital local identity? At the ECN'98 our research group presented the idea of localnet. A city needs the agreement of several local actors around the basic services that this community needs to share. The same can be true in a digital city. Localnet can be the basic architecture that can allow this agreement. Established inside the Internet system, localnet allows to the participants at the local level to define a "territory" designed to meet the requirements of their local community, being part at the same time of the global network. Localnet is a logical network, that can be evolve into a federation of similar networks in a region, nation or at the global level. Possible features.

a) Local integration of local services. Localnet is a logical integration of services in a common Internet domain. Usually, what you have now in a city is a collection of many local services developed by a heterogeneous set of actors (individuals, students, local administrations, small or big companies, NGOs...) without any common sharing of Internet domains. LocalNet allows at the first step the local integration of local services by offering a local common domain to all of these services as an snail mail architecture does. Technically, what you can do is to create a name server, or DNS (Domain Name Server). This service allows to you offering to every local service in the city be part of the localnet. F.e. All the services that want to be in the Barcelona localnet they only need to obtain a city sub-domain , f.e. upc.bcn.es, keeping at the same time your own domain. A localnet will allow integrating several systems and services already developed in Internet. You can develop inside the Local Net several common services like *a local search engine* (f.e. Altavista) that could search in all the sub-domains under the city domain; *a local directory* (like Yahoo) organized by topics or areas interested to the localnet; the coordination of several city sub-domains could allow you make searches by a set of cities or countries.

b) A virtual public network inside Internet. A localnet is not an Intranet. In a private Intranet, you cannot access from the Internet to his private services. But the localnet is at the same time Internet at the local level. What is possible is that some of the localnet services could be private. But the localnet is a virtual public network inside the Net. A community network can be seen already as a localnet service.

c) A framework for developing new local services.

-Any new local service can be part of a localnet. An open digital city must be as open as the current industrial city, even more. Any company, university, NGO, individual of the local community can organize his service as part of the localnet. They only need to give a sub-domain of the local domain, and it will appear in the local net. Independently, they can keep their current domain in the general Internet.

-Any citizen can have a localnet electronic address. We have developed the idea of an Internet Citizen Address, that in fact will be a localnet citizen address. The local authorities in combination with the local ISP can provide one the citizen address based in neighborhood, city, nation structure and the other the connectivity, as well as an alias system to have two addresses (the civic one and the professional one) with a single account.

-A localnet proxy can be developed. A local proxy can facilitate the access to the local information and the ISP can offer this value added service for their clients.

-A localnet news, agenda and newsgroups common service can be provided. It is difficult to have access to the several newsgroups, new media and agenda a big city is developing. The localnet can facilitate the creation of several services to group these disperse local resources.

-A local certification service for all the current network services is possible based in the localnet.

-The control of the quality of service is not yet solved in Internet. The local character of the services is not a warranty of their quality. We can expect an explosion of local information services with low quality. There is a increasing research on value filtering (f.e. Alexa) and other systems to reduce the amount of trash we received daily. Local Net will not solved this problem. What we can think is about establishing inside the LocalNet, specific local subnets, may be more selected, for specific purposes or projects. Edunets, communitynets, etc. can be sub-areas inside the Localnet that allow people to define the specific group of persons with a common set of goals and objectives for work. But at the same time, the small group produces a loss of openess and variety you can find in the global spaces. We need to be prepared to live an open world and at the same time defining innovative spaces inside this new ocean. But in any case, an Open Digital City can be a testbed of this new digital era and a new perspective for the Community Networking movement.

3.3.3   Globalnets

Some authors analyze a current dichotomy in digital era: in one side, the general process of globalization is considered in technological and economic terms. In the other side, they describe a logical reaction to that evolution from local cultures and identities. It seems to present the following dilemma: the technology is global, but the people are local. One of the main lessons we have learned from the EPITELIO project is that the real novelty of using the Internet is not local communication, but how local people are beginning to deal with global communication. A next generation community network is a kind of test bed for proving such local/global combination in communication and more important in identities. Local and national communication creates local and national identities. Remember that "natio" in the medieval universities was the way students organized themselves by languages, national languages. Now we have a new medium where people, normal people, are communicating and organizing themselves locally and globally. For the first time, global communication is in the hand of local people. Localnets can become globalnets. Local community networks are beginning to coordinate nationally and globally. A next generation of community networks can provide a better framework for such coordination.

In the era of Internet, community networks can exploit their possibility of acting globally. There is no reason why a local community cannot communicate and organize globally. Can the digital citizen can act globally? It is still not clear who will take advantage of such global process. Leading countries in the national era like France are experimenting difficulties to grasp the advantages of the digital era. In the contrary other countries, regions or cities like Finland, Singapore or Barcelona are playing fairly better in such new arena. More languages you will speak more possibilities you will have to communicate and act globally. In community networking a combination of local languages and international languages seems the most useful and normal combination.

3.3.4 Internet2, Platform for Next Generation Community Networking

Internet 2 is a new research program to establish a new generation of Internet able to solve the problems that has the current Internet. Mainly: the integration of text, voice and video in a common platform and the warranty of quality of services based in such integration. Besides it try to establish an unlimited structure of addresses IP, avoiding the shortcut of the current system. As the first Internet the research community took the lead in such program. But Internet 2 is not an infrastructure for the academic communities. In fact, working in EPITELIO, we discovered the bandwidth paradox: computer scientists do not need too much bandwidth. The less computer literate your are the more bandwidth you need. At the extreme, the complete illiterate cultures are the ones that only will communicate verbally and visually through the network. That means that Internet2 is for people at the end. Connecting local communities at the global level using multimedia network technology to organize common live activities like education, games, debates...by the citizens and for the citizens could be a big field of services and applications in the next generation community networks. In Barcelona, a couple of Cns, Ravalnet and CornellaNet, are experimenting now with LMDS, a "virtual fiber" technology allowing speeds until 2 megabits at the user. Videoconferencing is the testing application. A recent approved project on Internet2 in Catalonia, I2-CAT, is inspired in such approach.

3.3.5. Community Networks as Innovative Knowledge Networks

Community network started with group communication (M. Turoff's CMC) and free access (Tom Grundner's freenets). Other major contribution has been the creation of Community Technology Centers (Tonia Stone) and the community media centers. Can a next generation community networking become a set of community research centers? Can a normal community networker be a researcher?

The modern society extended the basic literacy (read, write, mathematics, and basic sciences) needed to work in an industrial environment to everybody. This was the basic role of the elementary school. Now our societies are entering in a global information society, in a knowledge society, and these basic skills are not enough. A new curricula in information technology and information society, jointly with the new technical skills, is needed for everybody. Community networking and community technology centers, centers for everybody, are beginning to play this basic role of training in the knowledge and skills need for living in the digital era. Are they only training centers? How about research centers? As Noshir Contractor [9] from University of Illinois suggest the mapping of knowledge networks in the community can be a crucial role of community networks. A next generation community networking can explore the possibility of "knowledge management" in his community. Can a community network become a collaboratory, a virtual research facility for his community? Internet was an invention of the research community. A major effect of his generalization could be the extension of his research culture, the innovation culture to every citizen in every community. Computer networking, community networking and knowledge networking could be a possible evolution to describe the process of the digital era.

4   Conclusions

In the evolution of the digital era, it seems that we are in a critical moment. As the Internet (I and II) seems to get recognition as the new global information infrastructure, next year the key research issues will focus on information society technologies to facilitate the building of a new set of digital communities upon such new infrastructure. Embryonic forms of such new digital societies can be discovered in the community networking movement. On the basis of the lessons we learned in a European project called EPITELIO, dedicated to develop community networks in several European countries, we have produced a new model for a next generation community networking. This model we call InterCommunity tries to take advantage of the unique features of the Internet infrastructure, openness, interactivity and global dimension, in order to facilitate the design and development of a similar and coherent grid of social networks upon such infrastructure, from the local level to the global one.

This new generation of community networks can be instrumental for understanding what an open digital city mean, a kind of city as much as divers, plural and open as our current lively cities. A broad perspective of mutual collaboration like the one established by the Digital Cities Workshops conducted by Professor Toru Ishida[10] from Kyoto University can be overseen.

References

1. Castells, M. The Information Age: Economy, Society and Culture. Vol 1-The Rise of the Network Society. Blackwell, Oxford. UK (1997ª). (Spanish. La Era de la Informacion. Vol 1. La Sociedad Red. Madrid. Alianza Editorial.1997)
2. Castells, M, Borja, J. Local y Global. La gestion de las ciudades en la era de la informacion. Taurus.Madrid. 1997.
3. HDR 99. Globalitzation with human face. UNDP. New York. 1999.
4. Serra,A. The Role of Community Networking in Deploying the Strategies for Digital Cities. Berlin. III EDC Confernce. Dec.1-2 1998
5. Ardaiz, O,Navarro, L.,Serra, A., Turro, J.,The Internet Civic Address Service. Bruxelles. Workshop on Trans- EuropeanGeneric Services 4 March 1998. http://www.ac.upc.es/homes/artur/ica.html
6. Schuler,Doug. New Community Networks, wired for change. New York. ACM Press. 1996
7. Starr Roxanne Hiltz, &Turoff, Murray. The Network Nation. Human Communication via Computer. The MIT Press. Cambridge MA. (1993,First Ed. 1978)
8. De Cindio, Fiorella. Community Networks, Citizenship and Democracy: Key Issues for the Millenium. EACN Workshop. Paris. 1999. http://www.eacn.org/fr_about.htm
9. Noshir S. Contractor, Daniel Zink and Michael Chan. IKNOW: A Tool to Assist and Study the Creation, Maintenance, and Dissolutiion of Knowledge Networks. In Toru Ishida Ed. Community Computing and Support Systems. LNCS 1519. Springer-Verlag. Berlin. 1998
10. Ishida, Toru, Community Computing and Support Systems. LNCS 1519. Springer-Verlag. Berlin. 1998

Experiences of European Digital Cities

Eric Mino

TeleCities c/o Eurocities – 18 square de Meeûs, B1050 Brussels – Belgium
Tel: +322 552 0868 – Fax +32 2 552 0889
eric.mino@enter.org
http://www.edc.eu.int/telecities/

Abstract: This paper presents the current developments of Digital Cities in the European Union. Starting from the point of view of local authorities and their specific role in the development of the Information Society, three applications clusters are proposed: i) Economic development or regeneration; ii) Social cohesion and quality of life; and iii) better management of the city administration and its infrastructures. The paper also reviews the limits of current pilot projects and gives an outline of the enabling technologies in use or planned in a near future. Finally, strategic success factors for the development of Digital Cities projects are presented on the basis of ten case studies carried-out in small and large cities.

1. Introduction

Cities and towns, by their very nature, represent- the 'chemistry' of all the social, economic and cultural changes of the Information Society at the local democratic level. Since 1993, TeleCities has been bringing together cities and towns sharing similar interests and goals for the development of telematics applications in an urban context.

This network of cooperation was launched by a small group of members of Eurocities (the association of European metropolitan areas grouping over 80 cities of more than 250 000 inhabitants over 20 European countries). Today TeleCities has its own elected Steering Committee and its own rules democratically defined by its members at the Annual General Meetings. The network has expanded its scope and now represents over 100 cities and towns (with populations ranging in size from a few tens of thousands of inhabitants to several million) from the European Union and Central and Eastern Europe as well as private observer members (e.g. Philips, Telecom Italia, ICL, BULL, SUN). As the democratic expression of user needs and demand for telematics applications in the urban context, TeleCities has the essential role of maintaining a high profile and understanding of the implications, risks and opportunities offered by the new Information and Communication Technologies (ICT) for local authorities/city governments. This level of political commitment from the most senior politicians representing local interests across Europe, is what differentiates TeleCities from other initiatives and networks, and is why TeleCities

T. Ishida, K. Isbister (Eds.): Digital Cities, LNCS 1765, pp. 58-72, 2000.
© Springer-Verlag Berlin Heidelberg 2000

stresses the importance of universal access to the information society and of support for cultural and linguistic diversity at all levels.

TeleCities provides an open cooperation network for the development of European Digital Cities. This framework allows the cities and towns to reach a consensus on the demand for telematics services, applications and infrastructures which support the regeneration of urban areas through socio-economic development. Thus it enables them to develop new strategies to fight unemployment and social exclusion and improvement of quality of life.

This support from TeleCities for the development of urban telematics projects and strategies is on a cohesive, trans-European basis so that cities can participate in the building of the Global Information Society, as outlined by the G7 conference of February '95, the Delors White Paper and the Bangemann report.

2. Major Role of Local Authorities

The globalisation of the economy puts more and more pressure on local developments: cities must achieve a world-class local economy. This goal implies the development of local partnerships that extend beyond local governments: involving citizens, business, media and community organisations. The role of these new partnerships is to develop new initiatives and raise the awareness of local actors.

At the same time our information needs are increasing but remain overwhelmingly local, as stated by Robin Gaster –President of North Atlantic Research- at the recent congress on World urban economic development "… the future of the web is not global, it is local".

In Europe local authorities are central to the development of an efficient, effective, equitable, open and accountable Global Information Society for a number of reasons.
- Local and regional governments control, directly or indirectly, between 25% and 40% of total public expenditure and they are central to stimulating a critical mass of users for a real uptake of the Information Society.
- Local governments handle the vast majority of day-to-day government interaction with citizens, firms and the voluntary sector and are therefore central to spreading the benefits of the Information Society as widely as possible.
- Local governments are key players in protecting the weaker members of society and are therefore central to the prevention of a two tier information society.
- They provide an invaluable core element for full scale validation and demonstration projects, due to their key co-ordinating role and multiple linkages to different social and economic actors and their wide range of responsibilities.
- Local governments play a key role in the development and support of empowering mechanisms for citizens.
- While the information society does permit the creation of geographically dispersed communities, the vast majority of everyday life takes place within the local or

regional domain and it is on this scale that most communities function. The construction of "community on line" will therefore need to begin at the local level.

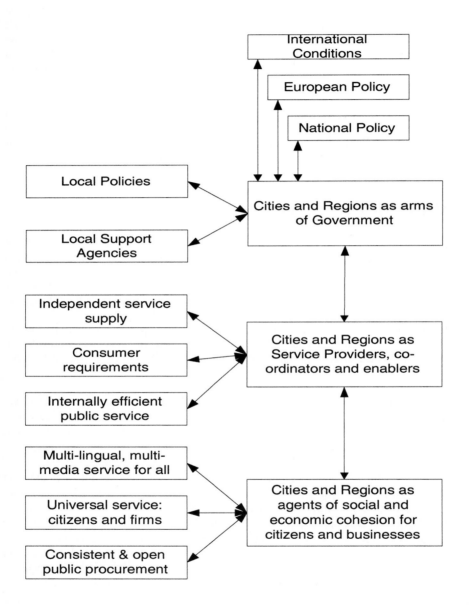

Fig. 1. Major roles of local authorities in the development of the Information Society

There are major variations between countries and between different types of areas (cities, towns, rural areas) which generate a range of advantages for developing, demonstrating and evaluating information society applications. However, local authorities must face a number of key challenges if they are to play a full role in the development of an information society in Europe:

- managing the technical complexity of integrating a wide range of telematics applications;
- managing the organisational complexity of bringing together a diverse group of actors;
- defining the appropriate policy and regulations to guarantee equitable services at an affordable price;
- promoting organisational change in the context of tight controls on public expenditure; and, clearly demonstrating the benefits of the new ICT applications to all local relevant actors.

3. Key Applications of Information Society Technologies in Cities

The application areas of telematics in urban are very numerous. But we can consider that these applications or services are contributing to tree main policy objectives: i) Economic development or regeneration; ii) Social cohesion and quality of life; and iii) better management of the city administration and its infrastructures. Of course all these policy objectives are inter-linked and a single application can contribute to more than one policy objective, but we tried to cluster the application areas around the policy objectives for which the foreseen impact is the most important.

The EDC survey carried out among European cities in 1998 shows that according the municipality decision makers the most pressing urban problems are related to social integration, economic development and transportation/environment issues. Although decision makers do not perceived yet the "problem solving capacity" of telematics for social and economic problems, they believe that it can help in providing better services to citizens, increasing administration efficiency, improving the education system and attracting new business.

3.1 Economic Development and Regeneration

A variety of strategies are currently being implemented by cities acting either independently or jointly:

- Developing advanced infrastructures with the objective of attracting company relocations;
- Promoting the development of new activities linked to the use of new technologies;
- Territory and local know-how promotion based on electronic catalogues (e.g. multimedia resource centre of Nice Cote d'Azur chamber of commerce: http://www.fr-rrc.com)

- Promoting the use of telematics by local economic players to strengthen their economic competitiveness. This area includes training programmes targeted to Small and Medium size Enterprises or provision of e-commerce facilities.

3.2 Social Cohesion and Quality of Life

The European model of the Society is oriented towards social cohesion. This concern is reinforced by a high level of unemployment (more than 10% in most of the European member states). For that reason, a large number of initiatives have been launched in this area and in the "more traditional" of the improvement of the quality of life.

- School networks. Schools on the net are largely promoted by cities in the framework the European Net Days or other national initiatives. The involvement of local authorities is usually limited to the provision of the infrastructure as the educational content is managed nationally. Innovative applications are foreseen in support to pupils with difficulties, in the "networking" of schools from various countries or in improving the dialogue between parents, schools and teachers.
- Services for the elderly and disabled people. Telematics can remove geographical and physical boundaries giving equal opportunities to less favoured citizens (e.g. in booking transportation, tele-shopping, video-conferencing, tele-alarm systems, social information services).
- Citizen participation (the so-called Tele-democracy). It concerns a constant dialogue between the citizens and government. The "well-informed citizen" is able to react on issues relevant to public authorities and to contribute to the planning for the future.
- Culture and tourism. Tourism and cultural activities represents an important part of the urban economy. Interactive electronic catalogues linked to booking and payment systems represent the typical telematics applications. The main advantage being that the same system can be used at both local and global levels.
- Health and social affairs. Telematics can impact on different communities: the citizens, the hospitals and healthcare providers. Although projects are usually launched in close collaboration with healthcare centres and providers, the main target audience of cities is the citizen :with services such as: online health education, screening, diagnosis and advice services, home surveillance.
- Adult education or "life long learning" became a necessity for almost everybody as the idea of a career for life does not anymore exist. The access to distance learning resources offer considerable opportunities. In cities the access to distance adult education resources is usually linked to labour or professional training agencies.
- Labour and employment. The applications are ranging from job-market information systems to training facilities to launch new activities, usually based on an extensive use of new media technologies.

3.3 Managing the City Administration and the Urban Infrastructures

Here telematics technologies are used to improve the functioning and the management of various public services.

- In the field of administrative procedures, there are a wide range of applications. With the aim of bringing municipal services closer to the citizen (e.g. through self-service kiosks, call-centers or satellite agencies), local authorities are moving from "mass produced" and unresponsive information services to integrated service delivery (including fully legal certification and payment). Cities are now planning to use telematics not only to provide information but also guidance or advice and to deliver formal documents (such as certificates, electronic receipts, driving licenses, passports) or to collect local taxes electronically.
- Urban planning is more and more supported by telematics tools such as Geographical Information Systems. These tools allow the consultation of a wide range of local players (including the citizens) and an effective collaboration for the urban spatial planning and related decisions.
- Telematics for urban transport is mainly used to address efficiency, safety as well as the impact on environment.
- Applications to the urban environment are mainly related to environmental management support systems, emergency management systems and information services.
- Security systems based on video-monitoring of risky location (e.g. metro stations) helps of prevent crime and vandalism.

3.4 Current Experiments at European Level

In the framework of the EC Telematics Application Programme, some 60 European cities and regions have already started up pilot projects following strategies which are either implicit (based on the opportunities) or more explicit (defined according to priorities set by the municipal authority). These projects range from a "simple" web server on the analogue telephone network which enables PC owners to access services via an Internet provider to more complex solutions based on intranet technologies which integrate the whole chain of the production and provision of services.

However these experiments are still restricted in a number of areas:
- a relatively low rate of penetration on both geographical and social levels;
- the exploitation of synergies between those involved in investment and in operations;
- impact analysis and the analysis of economic viability;
- stabilisation and standardisation of technological solutions;
- areas of application still very sector-specific;
- requirements in terms of regulation (or deregulation) and legislation.

This is quite understandable, as the Information Society is still at an early stage. These projects permit industry to fine-tune the technological solutions it needs while also enabling the public sector to familiarise itself with the organisational issues involved in their introduction.

But now we have to go further and attempt to expand these experimental services to a significant scale in order to analyse their usefulness and define the conditions required for them to be utilised in a realistic way. For this to be done, it is necessary that the complementarity of European, national, regional and local initiatives should be maintained and reinforced.

3.5 Today and Future Enabling Technologies

The EDC survey'98 shows that the Internet is almost the universally accepted medium for electronic services, it is used by 90% of all authorities surveyed. Videotext/ minitel (used by 23%) are declining in importance compared to 1996. There was also an increase in multimedia kiosk implementation (now at 38%) and telephone-based services (now 32%). Fax on demand is still not very widely used (12%).

The priority given to the Internet is an indication of local authorities' proactive approach to using this important new medium, as it allows fast prototyping and a kind of universal access. Considering the low availability of internet in most European households, local authorities are also providing access through multimedia kiosks (see PDWEB and INFOSOND projects), call centres (where the operators have access to the services via the Internet), self-service PCs available in so-called telematics centres and interactive TV (e.g. web TV).

The table 1 provide a list of advanced technologies used among the surveyed cities. Obviously, this list is in no way exhaustive and can only serve as an indication of readiness of European cities to adopt advanced technologies. A clear divide emerges:

- For technologies like Geographical Information Systems and intranet the benefits of every day use are already evident and they are becoming standard technology.
- A middle layer of technologies is "in the waiting room", as ATM, smart cards, etc., for which already some (mostly) prototypical applications exist.[1]
- There are other technologies whose usefulness is not at all evident to authorities (e.g. virtual reality).

In the future the technologies growth areas (e.g. implementation or extension planned) are smart-cards applications (for security in electronic transactions), intranets (know as community intranets or "in-town nets") and 'intelligent' call centres (merging voice and web technologies). It is quite clear the massive use of smart cards will have a considerable impact on telecommunications infrastructure both in term of real time applications (e.g. security, authentication) and of management features (e.g. billing).

---

[1] GPS which was expected in this category, is a technology that is more oriented to the transport sector

Most used (i.e. fully available or in trial use)	Percentage of users
Geographic Information Systems (GIS)	70 %
an own (internal) intranet	54 %
high speed multimedia networks (e.g. ATM)	28 %
JAVA-based applications (other than intranets)	24 %
smart cards	22 %
Intelligent software agents	18 %
Telephone call centre with automatic speech processing	14 %
Satellite-based positioning (GPS)	9 %
Virtual reality applications	9 %
Expert systems/ artificial intelligence applications	7 %

Table 1. Status of current technology use among cities surveyed

The end users terminals used in homes, office or community places are ranging from multimedia PCs, networked computers, digital TVs with set-top boxes to multimedia kiosks (with screen touch access or voice synthesis) and mobile personal assistants. Public kiosks are implemented in more and more cities as they provide a suitable access route for the citizens with limited resources, but usually they are located in public places where human support facilities are available.

In terms of telecommunication infrastructures, it appears clearly that the Internet is the preferred medium to provide the citizens with the necessary access to the new applications. The main reason is that the Internet provides a low cost and easy to access communication solution where performance, security and quality of service are secondary issues for the citizens. Most of the applications are based on basic-rate ISDN (i.e. 64 or 128kbps), but within 5 years the demand for downstream line rates between 2Mbps and 25Mbps will be evident in the access side (with several 100kbps upstream). Finally there is an emerging demand for higher bandwidth services over radio links for real information delivery independently of the location of the end-user.

4. Digital Cities Strategic Success Factors

As described above, telematics can have positive effects on a wide range of public services (economic development, urban planning, transport, etc.). But the deployment of these applications is very complex due to the large number of players involved as well as re-organisation process required. More and more cities are introducing a telematics section in their overall city strategy.

The development of urban telematics policies in Europe, having roots in earlier IT strategies, dates mainly from the early 1990s. It has been included in European agendas (e.g. the Bangemann Report) and in a number of strands of the EC Telematics Applications Programme (1994-1998), above all the Telematics for Urban and Rural Areas (TURA) and the Integrated Applications for Digital Sites (IADS) action lines.

Key success factors have been identified on the basis of a survey among ten cities carried out in 1996 in the framework of the European Digital Cities project: (Antwerp (BE); Barcelona (ES); Cologne (GE); The Hague (NL); Lewisham/South East London (UK); Marseille (FR); Rome (IT); Ronneby (SE); Southampton/Hampshire (UK); Vienna (AT)). These success factors have been grouped in three categories: telematics policy, development of telematics applications/services and the deployment at a larger scale of pilot services.

4.1 Telematics Policy Structures and Processes

The key features include the following:
- Successful cities and regions have tended to develop explicit telematics strategies, often contained in public documents, although these have been developed in an iterative way, building on experiences gained in development projects.
- Successful cities and regions have moved towards seeing telematics technologies within the wider context of their general strategies in fields such internal organisation, economic development and service delivery.
- Successful cities and regions have sought to develop telematics strategies that are more than just the sum of current projects.
- Successful cities and regions have built telematics strategies around clear overarching goals – generally including greater efficiency, better quality services, a closer relationship with citizens.
- The strategies of successful cities have the explicit backing of the leading political actors, often the mayor but also other leading politicians.
- Successful cities have clear "product/service champions" within the administration for the development and deployment of telematics technologies.
- Telematics strategies have been developed in the context of a specialist telematics institute, unit or committee that can provide an institutional driver for telematics within the administration.
- These new institutions are often semi-autonomous from the municipal administration, enabling them to bring in new skills and attitudes, to break with the bureaucratic traditions of public administrations and thus to form effective partnerships with the private sector.

These key features have been validated at a larger scale by the EDC survey in 1998 (among over 190 European cities) which indicates that cities are establishing structures coordinated strategic planning of technology policy (specific department, chief executive office or joint working group).

4.2 Developing Telematics Applications and Services

All of the ten case studies had significant activities in the development or at least the implementation and validation of advanced telematics applications – technical research and development and the testing and evaluation of pilot implementations. The key features include:

- Successful development was associated with having a critical mass of research projects, including those funded under the EC Telematics Applications Programme, but also projects funded from other European funds (research activities, trans-European networks of telecommunications, or European Regional Development Funds) and from national initiatives.
- European funding, in particular, played a central role in the development of telematics applications, in particular helping cities in three key ways:
  - first, EU projects have enabled the cities to experiment in the field of telematics, testing the best ways forward and developing solutions that are fitting to their specific requirements;
  - second, EU projects have enabled the cities to move more quickly towards their stated goals by binding in industrial partners and creating a "leading edge" within the administration; and
  - third, EU projects have helped cities to learn from each other, reducing duplication and also helping to speed development.
- A central focus for telematics technological and project management expertise has been established, either as a separate unit within the administration or as a semi-autonomous institute or centre closely linked to the administration.
- Strong partnerships with industry based on clearly understood mutual benefits and a shared vision of the central aims of the project.
- Successful cities have maximised the benefits of European networks of cooperation between cities, such as TeleCities, by seeking out partners for projects and establishing a genuine division of labour between partners.
- Successful cities and regions have been able and willing to *learn* from other cities, rather than ignoring other's experience or, alternatively, slavishly copying them. Within the Telematics Applications Programme, in particular, a new "division of labour" is emerging as cities have discovered their own particular specialist expertise and that of others through the increasing exchange of information.
- There is an increasing focus in the ten case study cities on the integration of applications from different areas to provide an integrated informational environment for citizens, local business communities (in particular Small and Medium size Enterprises) and functionaries within the administration.

- The key technological issue in successful cities is the insistence on "open systems" that avoid getting administrations tied into a single supplier and facilitate further development and integration of applications.

4.3 Deploying Telematics Services

The development of successful telematics applications relies on the eventual transfer of technologies and their associated processes from the experimental stage into full scale everyday use within cities and regions. For many of the case study areas, it is this issue in particular that they are tackling and, although there are a number of success stories, there is, perhaps, less experience to draw on at this stage that in the policy development and telematics development processes. Nevertheless, we can point to some of the features:

- The transfer of applications from the experimental stage to the "full scale" deployment stage needs to be based on a sound business case.
- Successful cities have sought to deploy telematics technologies in conjunction with wider organisational and cultural changes in the public administration.
- In particular, successful deployment of telematics has been associated with the re-engineering of service delivery functions and, in some cases, with the establishment of new structures such as neighbourhood offices or one stop shops.
- The successful transfer of telematics research and development work requires close relationships between telematics developers and key "change agents" in mainstream service departments.
- Industrial partners have a key role in the transfer of telematics developments, in particular in their commercialisation and wider dissemination of telematics applications to other cities and regions.
- European and national city networks are important conduits for the dissemination of experiences, methodologies and technologies.

4.4 Main Phases of Development

To conclude this chapter, let us list the key factors bearing on the success of a Digital Cities project:

1. The definition of a strategy based on a strong political will, the identification of priority areas of application and the possibilities offered by the technology. This strategy will be fine-tuned on the basis of the lessons learned from the pilot projects. But it is obvious that there can be no universally applicable model. After all, there are major differences between countries and between the different types of districts (big cities, small towns, rural districts), between their specific situations and between their existing infrastructures.
2. Consultation with representative local groups involved (potential users, providers, university and research centres etc.).
3. The definition of an organisational strategy, including specifically public-private or public-public partnerships and whatever reorganisation is necessary.
4. The setting up of pilot projects involving end users and publicity campaigns.

5. Assessment of the results and fine-tuning of the expansion strategy.
6. Campaigns to raise public awareness and training courses for users.

5. Conclusions

Most of the experiences presented in this paper have been collected and analysed in the framework of the European Digital Cities (EDC) project, a four years project (1996-1999) supported by the European Commission under the Telematics Applications Programme (Research and Technological Developments). Although this project will finish at the end of 1999, the TeleCities organisation, which has been created in 1994 and has coordinated the EDC project, will continue to bring together European cities and towns to collect, analyse and disseminate the results of Digital Cities pilot or deployment projects.

These exchanges at both policy and practical levels will be extended to major players outside Europe through the Global Cities Dialogue (to be launched in November 1999) in order to capitalise the results of experiences carried out throughout the World.

6. References

1. Graham Stephen and AURIGI Alessandro (1997), *'Virtual Cities, Social Polarization, and the Crisis in Urban Public Space'*, in *Journal of Urban Technology*, vol. 4, Nr. 1, April 1997, pp. 19-52.
2. Graham Stephen and MARVIN Simon (1996), *Telecommunications and the City - Electronic spaces, urban places*, Routledge, London/New York.
3. Aurigi, Alessandro (1997): *Entering the Digital City: Surveying City-Related Web Sites in Europe*, paper presented in the 3rd European Digital Cities Conference; Berlin, December 1997.
4. Castells, Manuel (1997): *The Network Society*, Cambridge, Massachusetts; Oxford: Blackwell.
5. Kluzer, Stefano and Farinelli, Marco (1997): *A Survey of European cities' Presence on the Internet*, Working paper No 31, Databank Consulting: ACTS; FAIR: Milan.
6. Nunn, Samuel and Rubleske, B. Hoseph (1997): *Webbed Cities and Development of the National Information Highway: The Creation of World Wide Web Sites by U.S. City Governments*, Journal of Urban Technology, Vol. 4, No 1, April 1997, pp: 53 – 80.
7. Cornford James and Naylor, Robert –CURDS- (1998) : *Good practice case studies in European Digital Cities*
8. Centre d'étude sur les réseaux, les transports, l'urbanisme et les constructions publics – CERTU- (1998) : *Collectivités locales et télécommunications*
9. Rete Urbana delle Rappresentanze (RUR) : *Le città digitali in Italia*, 1998
10. League of California Cities. *League of California Cities Telecommunications Policy of Universal Access*. Abstracted from the League's World Wide Website, 1998.
11. Organisation for Economic Cooperation & Development. *Governing metropolitan areas: reinforcing local democracy*, Conference Proceedings Athens, Greece, 1998.
12. Rupprecht Siegfried, *Results of the European Digital Cities –EDC- survey 1998*, 1999

13. European Digital Cities project: http://www.edc.eu.int (the site includes a library section with the full reports on the EDC survey'98, the EDC good practice case studies, EDC conference proceedings)
14. European Commission Telematics Applications Programme : http://www2.echo.lu (EC Research, Technological Development and Demonstration programme launched in 1994, ended in 1998, but with some project still running till 2000)
15. INFOSOND project: http://www.infosond.org (Information On Demand)
16 PDWEB project: http://www.pdweb.com (Public Data web: development of multimedia kioks)

Appendix: TELECITIES: The European Digital City Partnership

TeleCities is an open network for concerted urban development through Telematics.

It was initiated by the Eurocities Technological Cooperation Committee in 1993 as a working group of cities wishing to cooperate in developing the potential of telematic applications in the order to support the economic regeneration and social and cultural development of cities throughout Europe. Finally in April 1994 at the first Annual General Meeting where a Steering Committee was elected, TeleCities was launched as a democratic network of cooperation.

One reason for the success of the TeleCities cooperation network is the opportunity offered to local and regional decision makers to meet, to exchange experiences and to articulate the urban demand with regard to common issues concerning the deployment of the Information Society.

With 103 members, including 93 from 13 member states of the European Union, TeleCities brings together a rich diversity of skills expertise and experience and represents the whole spectrum of the European urban telematics demand. It aims to build a consensus on the development of a harmonised information infrastructure including the widest possible range of practical applications and services.

OBJECTIVES

The objective is to provide an open cooperation network for European Digital Cities, through which they will achieve a common definition regarding the urban demand for telematics services, applications and infrastructures which support the regeneration of urban areas through:

• Economic development and strategies to tackle unemployment, including teleworking.
• Social development and improved quality of life.
• New solutions to fight social exclusion.
• Maximising the benefits of the Information Society in the urban environment.

In identifying appropriate telematics services and applications responding to user needs and clearly defined by the cities themselves, TeleCities also promotes the development of technological solutions lending themselves to interoperability, interconnectivity and moving towards standardisation. For these reasons together with the willingness to develop innovative public-private partnerships, the network is not only open to cities, towns and to regional institutions, but also to technology and service providers who can participate as observer members.

PRIORITIES

The TeleCities priorities are to:

Support the development of telematics projects and strategies on a cohesive, trans-European basis.
- Identify projects of common interest where European financial support would give a clear added value element to telematics applications.
- Develop an effective dialogue with relevant European Institutions working in the field of new Information and Communications Technologies (ICT).
- Participate in the building of the Global Information Society, as outlined by the G7 conference of February '95, the Delors White Paper, the Bangemann Report.

ACTIVITIES

- organisation of conferences, workshops and seminars to develop consensus on key telematics issues (next conference: Bari, 4-5 October '99)
- publication of materials (newsletter, brochures, electronic bulletin boards, WWW) providing information on relevant telematics activities;
- the running of a co-ordination office to disseminate state-of-the-art shared knowledge of the telematics issues in urban areas;
- Develop an effective dialogue with relevant European Institutions working in the field of new Information and Communications Technologies (ICT).
- Participate in the building of the Global Information Society, as outlined by the G7 conference of February '95, the Delors White Paper, the Bangemann Report.
- operation of inter-city electronic communications facilities to exchange information and data files;
- preparation of the uptake by the local urban and regional planners of the results emerging from the Telematics Applications Programme and the joint preparation of operational plans on topics identified as strategic, by and for, the cities;
- setting up of working groups to address major urban issues identified by policy and decision makers. The subjects to be covered by working groups are:
    - Public Administration and City Information Highway
    - Standards and legislation
    - Economic Development (with an emphasis on SMEs)
    - Teledemocracy
    - Environment
    - Quality of Life
    - Healthcare
    - Employment and Teleworking
    - Education and Training
- setting up of joint pilot projects under the TeleCities umbrella co-funded by the European Commission.

Network Membership

President: Rome , Vice-President: Stockholm.

Other Steering Committee members: Amaroussion, Antwerp, Barcelona, Cologne, London-Lewisham, Vienna, Nice, The Hague, Bologna (observer), Manchester (Observer)

Other Members from the European Union: Aalborg, Aarhus, Amsterdam, Bari, Berlin, Belfast, Besançon, Bilbao, Birmingham, Bonn, Bradford, Brighton & Hove, Bristol, Cardiff, Copenhagen, Edinburgh, Eindhoven, Espoo, Frankfurt, Gent, Göteborg, Grenoble, Groningen, Hamburg, Hammersmith & Fulham, Helsinki, Heraklion, Hull, Islington, Kirklees, Knowsley (Liverpool borough), Köln, Las Palmas, Leeds, Leeuwarden, Leipzig, Lille, Linköping, Linz, Lisboa, Liverpool, Livorno, Lyon, Maastricht, Madrid, Marseille, Milano, Modena, Montpellier, München, Næstved, Nantes, Napoli, Newcastle, Norwich, Nottingham, Nürnberg, District of Parthenay, Porto, Orebro, Ronneby, Rotterdam, Salerno, Sheffield, Siena, Southampton, Strasbourg, Sunderland, Tameside, Tampere, Torino, Toulouse, Utrecht, Valencia, Venezia, Wageningen, Zarautz.

Members from the rest of Europe: Gdansk, Geneva, Iasi, Katowice, Korça, Lodz, Ostrava, Riga, Swarzedz, Vilnius.

Associate members: CIPAL (provinces Limburg and Antwerpen), Technopol Brussel-Bruxelles, Province de Liège, Oxfordshire County Council (observer).

Business representatives: Bull, ICL, Helsinki Telephone Company, Ericsson, SUN Microsystems, Urba 2000, KT-Datacenter, 3Com Europe, Philips, Olivetti Telemedia, Novell, Telecom Italia.

The Information Society in the City of Antwerp

Bruno Peeters

Vice Mayor of the city of Antwerp, responsible for communication,
governmental organisation and decentralisation
President of Telepolis Antwerp
President of DI@ (Digital Infoport Antwerp)

Bruno.Peeters@Antwerpen.be

Abstract. In Antwerp the dream of an information highway became reality a
long time ago. Antwerp has its electronic highway and every day it grows new
side-roads and exits. The main aim is to bring the inhabitants, authorities,
companies and services of Antwerp closer together. Naturally the city
government plays an important part in providing the best ways to serve its
community. The project "Antwerp an Intelligent City?" anticipates on the
information society by inventing, creating and implementing telematics
solutions for citizens and civil servants. And thus it supports a constant
dialogue between the local government, the business community and the
population.

1. The Metropolitan Area Network for Antwerp

In 1994 Antwerp completed a 70 kilometre fibre optic network called "Metropolitan
Area Network AntwerP" or MANAP. This modern telecommunications network
connects the main buildings – 46 in total – of the city departments in Antwerp: district
houses, police stations, hospitals, universities, libraries, museums and so on. The
network is based on the ATM protocol (Asynchronous Transfer Mode) and was the
first of its kind in the world when it was established. MANAP creates great
possibilities for data transfer, electronic mail, Lan-to-Lan connections, multimedia
applications, transfer of medical images and video conferencing.
One of the main advantages of this network is its great accessibility, both in time and
place. Anyone, anywhere in the world, can get information at any time day or night.
MANAP creates a platform for a variety of applications. The most important will be
presented in this article.

1.1. The Digital Metropolis of Antwerp (http://www.antwerpen.be)

On June 14th 1995 the Digital Metropolis Antwerp (DMA for short) was launched.
Antwerp was then the first city in Belgium to have a web site of its own on the
internet. At that time the Digital Metropolis Antwerp presented mainly governmental
and cultural information. Only 6 months later an extra dimension was added: the

T. Ishida, K. Isbister (Eds.): Digital Cities, LNCS 1765, pp. 73-82, 2000.
© Springer-Verlag Berlin Heidelberg 2000

virtual community. Since the creation of this virtual community everybody can become a virtual inhabitant and can participate in a completely new world. By becoming a virtual inhabitant you get a free e-mail address and free web space (750 k). This community is a "freenet" in the sense that users do not have to pay any subscription fee.

In June 1998 the fourth and current version of the virtual community was born. Almost all the information of the Antwerp governmental departments is present and updated on a regular base. Today the virtual community has over 30.000 active inhabitants. Together they send and receive over 500.000 e-mails per month.

Thanks to DMA, Antwerp has a virtual desk and can provide a round-the-clock service, 7 days a week. Citizens can now, for instance, book a city guide via the Digital Metropolis Antwerp or fill in an electronic report card, a quick way to report minor problems in their environment or infrastructure in need of repair.

Fig. 1.

1.2. Telemedicine

Before MANAP was established, hospital patients often had to be transported from one public hospital to another for an examination. Today all 8 public welfare hospitals are connected to the optic fibre network, which means they can send scanned images digitally to the place of diagnosis. This method not only saves a lot of money, but it also means a considerable increase of the patients' comfort.

1.3. Integration of Telephone Exchanges

The 30 digital telephone exchanges of the administrative departments, with their 5.000 telephones, are an integral part of the network. This means that the internal telephone anf fax traffic of the civil servants is free of charge. For the citizens a city contact phone number (22 11 333) was started. They can call this number with all their problems and questions. From there the caller is then directly reconnected to the right city department, wherever it is located in the city.

1.4. Distant Learning

Video conferencing has become common in Antwerp because it is easy to transmit moving images through the fibre optic cable. Video conferencing is often used for the education and training of civil servants. Today 5 locations are fully equipped for video conferencing.

The distant learning project also includes the creation and use of interactive courseware. Digital training programmes are put on a central server within reach of every employee. In 1998 4.000 courses (28.000 training hours) using PC based training packages were organised. In the same period 450 trainees were supported by a remote coach via video conferencing.

1.5. Culture on the Internet

The 12 municipal museums of Antwerp are on the internet to ensure world-wide publicity. They are setting up a digital collection, which will make the artistic wealth of the museums fully and interactively accessible by the internet. So thanks to this system the public can access art collections which have been hidden in the archives for decades because of lack of exhibition space or because these objects are too fragile to be exposed.

Next to the virtual museum Antwerp also has a virtual library. This virtual library links the public libraries, the university libraries and city libraries to each other. As a user, you can search for titles in all the participating libraries.

1.6. Remote Building Management System

As a first step towards a complete remote building management system an application has been installed which permanently and automatically controls the quality and the temperature of the water in all 8 municipal swimming pools.

This system can and will be elaborated in the future into a city management system, including alarm systems against theft or fire, access control for municipal buildings, pollution detection, electricity and heating measurement in public buildings and service flats.

1.7. Reservation and Booking System for Cultural Events

Thanks to a centralised ticketing system, event organisers and ticket agencies always have the most up-to-the-minute information on available seats. So with this system a seat can be booked directly for different cultural events in different locations.

1.8. Notulus: Decisions from Local Government

The complete official decision life cycle of the city and district council is managed by Notulus, a workflow system. The system is used by those who make a first draft suggestion for a decision and by the people who safeguard the information in the municipal archives. Notulus is available on the intranet of the city of Antwerp. This means that you can work in a deconcentrated way and that the users are scattered all over the city. All civil servants with intranet access can consult the decisions of the mayor and the aldermen, of the council and the district councils at all times. Furthermore via a full text information retrieval system you can search in the document database in an easy and effective way.

2. Strategy

All the above examples are part of an all embracing strategy of the city of Antwerp with respect to information technology and the information society.

In 1992 the Antwerp city council took an important decision. The aim was to "Reduce telecommunication costs within the city of Antwerp and offer high quality services to the citizens by building a high performance network for the city administration." The municipal government agreement for the period 1995-2000 added two additional important goals, i.e. the inner municipal decentralisation and the refinement of local democracy.

What does this mean?
- Decentralisation and expansion of the municipal structure.
- Accessibility and openness.
- Providing comprehensible information.
- Providing optimal and adequate participation opportunities.
- Providing the best possible service.
- Revaluation of the municipal council.
- Maintaining an open and fraternal atmosphere in the municipal council.
- A substructure of competent, well educated and motivated personnel.

In a world where information and knowledge are becoming more and more important, local government has to provide its citizens, visitors, companies and workers with the necessary information in an efficient and cost-effective way. All the information and the services must become more accessible and easy to use. Citizens must have one single contact point, even if they want to perform transactions with several different city departments. Contacting the local public administration must be an efficient and pleasant experience. That is the reason why the city of Antwerp started with the central number 22 11 333.

The Digital Metropolis Antwerp (the official web site of the city of Antwerp) was started in 1995 to realise these goals. With this site the city wants to use all the newest communication technologies and wants to set up interactive communication links with the population. It also helps to run a smoothly operating decentralised government and a deconcentrated administrative organisation.

A decentralised government implies the application of the subsidiarity principle. This means giving decision making power to (more) local politicians. By doing this the city can more effectively respond to the local needs. At the same time the city of Antwerp wants to bridge the legendary gap between the citizens and the local government in order to bring the government closer to the community.

The advantage of a deconcentrated administrative organisation with multiple district houses that provide all the necessary services, is that you can directly respond to the citizen's needs. Furthermore you can provide quality service without delay. In order to realise this deconcentration, a complete reengineering of the administrative organisation was needed. This meant that 60% of the 8.000 civil servants had to be moved to the different districts where they are closer to the population. At the same time the overall structure of the administrative services was simplified drastically. The 70 city departments were organised into 9 business units.

The existence of the Metropolitan Area Network for Antwerp (MANAP), the concept of the Digital Metropolis Antwerp and the availability of new telematics applications were indispensable tools to bring these enormous reorganisations to a good end.

3. Creating Access

Providing services is not the only task of a city. It also has to create access to this information. Several projects have been realised to provide complete access to all the information.

- Cybercafes were opened where everybody can surf free of charge. Today Antwerp has three public cybercafes, all located in public libraries. The first cybercafe with 10 computers was opened in the central public library in the city centre. The other two with each 5 computers are located in public libraries in the districts (i.e. the district of Deurne and Ekeren). Before the end of 1999 a fourth cybercafe will be opened, again in a district (i.e. Hoboken). These cybercafes are very popular. Each cybercafe has more or less 1.000 visitors per week. Internet freaks as well as people that have never surfed before visit the cybercafes. A survey that was conducted in 1998 showed that almost 60% of the visitors was introduced to the internet in one of the cybercafes.
- The cyberbus is a similar initiative. It is a mobile cybercafe with 10 computers, a scanner and 3 printers installed in a bus. This cyberbus visits schools and public events to promote the opportunities of the internet and the Antwerp virtual community. Up to now 30.000 people have been introduced to the internet via the cyberbus.

Fig. 2.

- Free internet introduction classes are organised on a regular base. These classes are open for everyone; clubs, individuals, groups, companies, etcetera. These internet introduction classes are very popular. That is why they are already organised for the third time. This year and next year 2.000 people will be introduced to the information highway.
- Forty information booths have been installed in strategic places, such as the city hall, the district houses, museums, the Chamber of Commerce, etcetera. Via these information booths you can access the internet.

Fig. 3.

- The media kiosk is the newest initiative to bring information closer to the people. The media kiosk is a combined booth with a traditional telephone booth on the one side and an information pillar with a touch screen on the other. Today 6 media kiosks are already operational. They can be found in the streets of Antwerp. Via the media kiosk you can get and print information on events, hotels, catering, public transport, etcetera.

Fig. 4.

4. Partnerships

A number of initiatives, like the media kiosk and the virtual library, are embedded within the context of broader formal co-operation agreements with partners of the private or academic sector. These agreements are mutual engagements towards co-operation in a number of concrete projects, aiming at a win-win situation for both partners.

Co-operation agreements have been established with a number of importants companies: the former national telecom provider Belgacom, the Antwerp university and polytechnics, the Antwerp Chamber of Commerce, the Flemish employment office and Telenet, a consortium of cable television networks providing telecommunication services in Flanders.

In February 1999 the Digital Infoport Antwerp (DI@) wasd founded. DI@ is a co-operative association, oriented to the formation of public-private consortiums which realise innovative projects for the information society. The public partners, like for instance the city of Antwerp, get an added value by acquiring the input from the private partners. For the partners of the private sector on the other hand, the city of Antwerp is a well equipped and well organised test case. They get the opportunity to develop new products for their commercial market.

The participation in European projects is also an example of active partnership. These projects are attractive because of the funding of the European Commission, but also because of the added value that is created by co-operating with other important European cities. Through these European projects there is an important exchange of experience and know-how. And often they become an effective catalyst for new ideas and new services. The Pan-European knowledge exchange has become so important that during the second half of 1999, the first steps will be set to establish a specific "know-how and technology transfer centre". The purpose of this centre will be to trigger and support bilateral exchange projects between European cities. The European Commission has already expressed its interest to support such a centre, at least in the first phase. Later on the centre should become self-sustainable and commercial.

5. Shaping the Future

We are evolving at top speed towards an information society in which the borders between telecommunications, computer networks and audiovisual technology are becoming blurred. Since Antwerp started early, lots of technical, organisational and psychological barriers had to be overcome. But starting early has its benefits because you reach the stadium of maturity earlier. This is especially true for the creation of the information society, because it involves a lot of organisational and psychological issues.

Thanks to this experience Antwerp has the opportunity to launch a lot of new initiatives to bring the information society closer to the people. At the end of last year a series of innovative project outlines were launched:

- Traffic guidance: an all-embracing management system for smooth intermodal passenger transport.
- VILA: sophisticated training facilities supported by networking and artificial intelligence.
- TOMMI: a compact guide which receives its information on the spot using wireless communication.
- Digital patrimony: unlocking the secrets of the past from the city's archives, with advanced search facilities.
- Multimedia kiosk: a media kiosk with new multimedia functionalities such as image, sound, speech, smartcard, etcetera.
- Electronic office counter: electronic processing of administrative transactions and procedures.
- Forum: support for communications between the general public and the process of democratic decision making.
- Distributed call centre: an all-knowing city administration, accessible via various communication media.
- MANAP^2: unrestricted access tot the urban network combined with watertight security.

If you would like a CD-rom with an attractive multimedia presentation of these projects, contact Paul Van der Cruyssen (+32-3-216.77.44) or send an e-mail to paul.vandercruyssen@telepolis.antwerpen.be.

These project descriptions are now the basis for an intense search for partners who are willing to join a consortium for the development. This can either be in the context of a project funded by the European Commission or in the context of the Digital Infoport Antwerp.

6. Telematics Service Publisher

In the meantime Antwerp has learnt from experience. Providing integrated telematics services in a city with the participation of diverse entities from the public and the private sector is a complex business. Providing telematics services has become a key operational activity.

Most people think that overcoming the technical problems is the most difficult part. But in fact this is not true. Next to the obvious technical work, lots of other more complicated and often unexpected obstacles must be dealt with. Examples of these obstacles are the users' needs and behaviour, the economic viability, the need for reengineering organisations, the psychological and legal barriers, etcetera.

In this context a specific "Telematics Service Publisher" in a city is a possible solution. This should be a dedicated organisation with the mission to bring telematics services from various providers together in a consistent, integrated and easily accessible way. Next step then is to offer all these telematics services to the community. A Telematics Service Publisher has to act as a mediator between the individual telematics service providers and the users of these services. The city government, as a democratic representative of the population, should take the initiative to establish a Telematics Service Publisher. Depending on the local context, the city may delegate the activity to a business (outsourced or self owned) or it may be organised as a cross-department committee within a city. However the consequence of outsourcing the activity completely is a lack of control and a loss of expertise within the local authority. Keeping everything within the administration is not a good solution either since a public administration is not flexible enough and needs too much time to take a decision. This is of course impossible in the fast changing world of telematics. The best solution is to combine the two models and to establish the Telematics Service Publisher as a private-public body, combining the best of both worlds.

7. Conclusion

The city of Antwerp knows since quite some time that telematics has a strategic value for the government of today's cities. It has become as important as the management of the city's budget and finances.

Antwerp has gone a long way already with relatively positive results. Confirmation of the fact that the city of Antwerp is on the right track came in June 1999. Then

Antwerp won one of the awards in the prestigious "Global Bangemann Challenge", a world-wide telematics competition.

But the most challenging period is still to come. The opportunities of the information age will not cease to grow. So Antwerp will continue its efforts and will keep on using the newest possibilities for the benefit of its citizens.

Helsinki Arena 2000 - Augmenting a Real City to a Virtual One

Risto Linturi, Marja-Riitta Koivunen, Jari Sulkanen

Helsinki Telephone Corporation, Finland

Abstract. Helsinki Arena 2000 is a large consortium project headed by Helsinki Telephone Corporation. It has been running since early 1996. The main goal of the project is to provide the citizens of Helsinki an enabling platform through an affordable high bandwidth multimedia network in the year 2000. The project consists of three simultaneous development processes. The first process develops and tests services and user interfaces to them integrating the results of many national and international multimedia research projects. The second process creates an easy user interface to the services through a real 3D model of the city of Helsinki. This gives us many possibilities in augmenting the real city and provides a totally new viewpoint to the large web information systems. Finally, the multimedia network which already works in some areas of the city is being extended to other areas. Unlike other networks that provide high bandwidth from the service provider into the homes, this multimedia network is the first commercial network which is capable of transmitting guaranteed good quality video between any two homes. This gives the citizens many new possibilities for communicating with each other as well as with the local communities and businesses. Furthermore, homes connected to multimedia network are able to transmit video up to thousands of other homes.

1. Introduction

Helsinki Arena 2000 is a large consortium project headed by Helsinki Telephone Corporation. The administrators of the City of Helsinki are in major role in the consortium. Other participants represent the local businesses and universities, but also global information and telecommunication companies like IBM, ICL and Nokia. Many companies

T. Ishida, K. Isbister (Eds.): Digital Cities, LNCS 1765, pp. 83-96, 2000.

view Finland as an information society laboratory because of the high mobile phone and internet penetration. This and very technology friendly user base makes Finland a promising place to experiment with new models of network behaviour.

Helsinki Arena 2000 project aims to provide the citizens of Helsinki advanced web platform and services through an affordable high bandwidth multimedia network. These services as well as the multimedia network are planned to be widely available by the end of year 2000. This year is important because it is the year when Helsinki celebrates its 450th anniversary and is one of the cultural capitals in Europe. So at year 2000, plenty of cultural activities will be available through the network. In addition to providing ready-made services to the citizens, the aim is that the citizens themselves can exploit the possibilities of the network in their personal communities adding more value to their life. The support of high quality two-way video connections and multicasting gives a lot of possibilities for this.

The project has been running since late 1995. It consists of three simultaneous development processes. The first process develops and tests services and their user interfaces mainly in various pilot projects. The second process is developing an easy user interface to the services through a real 3D model of the city of Helsinki. Finally, the multimedia network which covers some areas of the city has been extended to cover all of Helsinki in late 1999.

The starting-point of Helsinki Arena 2000 are the needs of the citizens in their daily life. This includes considering their roles and activities within a family, in their free-time, as employees or students in an organisation and as inhabitants of the city. This goal is somewhat similar to the goals in electronic villages that start from citizens grass-root needs aiming to give everybody a possibility to participate. Blacksburg Electronic Village [1, 2] is a good example of that. The goals of Helsinki Arena 2000 project differ somewhat from the interactive TV based networks, such as Time Warner Full Service Network or GTE mainStreet. These TV based networks are typically more closed and they provide their customers rather completed and polished sets of services [3]. In Helsinki Arena 2000 project our aim is that the citizens of Helsinki have an important role in developing new uses of the network. In this and in the sense of the 3D user interface perhaps the closest ideological counterpart of the project can be found in Digital City Kyoto [4] even though that project does not concentrate on the physical network issues.

In order to get most of the citizens into the network, a lot of education is needed. First, it is important to awake the interest of the citizens to the Helsinki Arena 2000. This is already happening as the 3D model of the actual city makes many people very enthusiastic and curious. Also the video-phone is interesting when people see its possibilities in their daily life. The second step is to eliminate their fears to technology. The 3D model works also here as it creates a conception that using computers is as easy as walking down the streets of Helsinki. As we anticipate that the web browsers will develop into more usable direction [5], we also believe that this will be true in near future. Naturally, technical help solving problems with the computers needs to be easily available. Finally, we need to provide the citizens interesting and easy-to-use services that help them in their daily life. Even though the concept basically relies on citizens and businesses creating their own services for each other there are many platform type services that need to be created centrally. In addition we see that a fundamental change in behaviour patterns can be speeded up by creating services as examples and as basic attention grabbers in order to get a large enough user base to start growing its own services.

In Finland many people have a positive attitude towards new technology that adds value to their daily life. There are over 60 cellular phones per 100 Finns. Furthermore, according to Statistics Finland in spring 1999 there were about 110 Internet host-connections per 1000 Finns. By the end of 1999 the Finnish government starts issuing electronic identities to the citizens. These enable people to sign official documents and contracts over the net. Finland is also world leader in electronic banking with over 20% of the population using home banking systems. These are leading figures in the world. This is a good starting-point for getting users interested in Helsinki Arena 2000.

Many viewpoints can be taken to the Helsinki Arena 2000 project. Here we will mainly concentrate on discussing the development of the services, the 3D-model and the network, their basic concepts and how these can be easily provided to the citizens. The usage of the 3D model of the city as a user interface to the services is in key role here. This city model gives us many possibilities in augmenting the real city and provides a totally new viewpoint to the large web information systems.

2. Development and Piloting of Services

Our goal in developing the virtual city is that it will be profitable both to the end-users and to the businesses. By profitable we mean not only that the businesses can maintain their services without subsidiaries but also that the taxpayers or community members find the public services or community provided services worthwhile to use their tax or membership money on. The multimedia network is nothing but the technology to enable communication and make services available. The video-phone is one of the very basic services. In addition, we need to have a wide selection of other services that the users want and a user interface through which these services are easily accessible. To get the companies interested in investing and developing services we need users, and to get above a critical mass of users we need to offer them interesting services.

In Helsinki Arena 2000 we have solved this typical booting problem by starting several pilot and research projects which develop and test services with the users and act as catalysts. Services developed with the city of Helsinki are in a central role in this development. These are developed in EU supported projects, such as Infocities and Equality. In addition, we have also other EU projects as well as several projects with Finnish National Multimedia Program (KAMU) and Eurescom, which is a research consortium of the European public network operators. In addition, we are hoping to encourage various hobbyist and special interest groups to use the network for their own interests. To get a sample view of the service development the Infocities services developed in Helsinki are discussed in more detail in chapter 2.1.

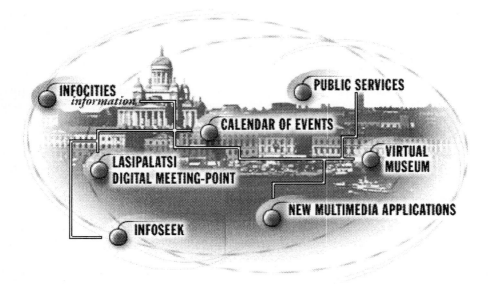

Figure 1: Web Interface to Infocities Services.

2.1 Infocities Project as an Example of Service Development

Infocities is a European Commission funded project in TEN Telecom program. Digital services for the citizens are developed in seven European cities Helsinki being one of them. In Helsinki the services are developed in co-operation with Helsinki Telephone Corporation and the city of Helsinki. These services include public and civic services, Helsinki City Museum services and cultural services. In addition, the Virtual Language School developed in the National Multimedia Program is being tested by users.

Many public and civic services are traditionally provided to the citizens by the different bureau's of a city. The development of the integrated public and civic services started from thinking about these services from the citizens' point-of-view. The services were organised according to the different roles of the citizens, such as a tourist, a house builder, an organiser to a happening. Furthermore, we also wanted to find out any new needs in citizens every-day life. Our hope was that Helsinki could provide better services with less burden to the employees of the city. Finally, we considered how the multimedia network and the possibilities it offered could enhance these services. For instance, ip-phone and video based techniques are being experimented on.

The services of Helsinki City Museum are developed to the ordinary citizens interested in the history of the city and also to the school children. Our aim is to make history so interesting by using multimedia and visualisation that many new citizens would be interested. For instance, the 3D modelling offers the museum people tools to show already non-existing buildings, such as a model of the centre of Helsinki at 1700 before the current empire style centre was built. By making the historical information available to the web will also help its use. It may hopefully even attract new people to visit the real museums.

Figure 2: The Lasipalatsi building in the past.

The Lasipalatsi project connects the citizens both in the real as well as in the virtual world and offers citizens advanced web based services. In the real city, Lasipalatsi is a building located in the middle of Helsinki. It has a digital library and freely available computers connected to Internet. It also offers citizens a digital meeting point which connects the real meeting point in Lasipalatsi building to the meeting points in some other cities. In addition there is a virtual version of Lasipalatsi.

Virtual Lasipalatsi has been an experiment with several services. An user survey has already been conducted on the users of the 3D-meeting place in Virtual Lasipalatsi. Less than half of the users were able to function without any technical troubles with their viewers. Visual 3D layout was considered very good and the 3D-meeting point was considered very good service by 73% of the surveyed users. 79% of those that had visited several times intended to come again. 30% had used user to user communication, 29% had used 3D- product presentations and 25% had followed live radio broadcasts or live disc jockey performances. Only 2% had used electronic shopping in the Telco store and 4% had user other Telco services provided in Virtual Lasipalatsi. When we studied frequent visitors the picture was slightly different. Communication with other visitors amounted to 75% and live radio broadcasts to 54% and getting aquinted to other people to 54%. People generally wished for more cultural content. Overall the results were considered encouraging in this early phase.

3. The Helsinki Arena 2000 -Network

The multimedia network offers citizens different access and bandwidth levels. At the moment, we test most service-concepts for web with ISDN based lines. There are currently 50 thousand ISDN lines, from a total of 700 thousand telephone lines, provided to Helsinki Telephone customers and they get a discounted telephone rate from normal calling price when they connect to the multimedia network. XDSL connections have been available in some areas from 1997 and in 1999 they will be available throughout all Helsinki including suburbs. In 2000 the whole operating area of Helsinki Telephone will be covered. Even so the user base of xDSL connections starts to grow slowly and is not expected to rise over ISDN volumes until 2003.

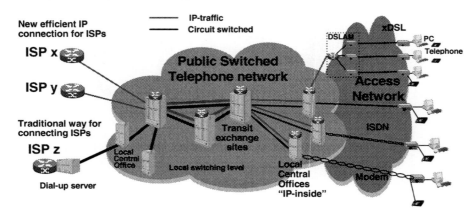

Figure 3: Helsinki Telephone new multimedia network

Through the multimedia network access and core services the network is available for all ISP:s who wish to provide their services through a common access point. Efficient usage of network resources allow for a lower price for connections than regular telephone network local call prices which are already among the cheapest non substituted prices in the world according to various studies.

There are several areas of development which have required extensive study and where equipment and software suppliers have only recently been able to provide satisfactory standards based solutions. These include open multicasting, quality of service concepts, multipoint internet based video conferencing platforms and QoS-usage based billing infrastructures. Also efficient customer connection and maintenance systems have been developed only lately for xDSL accesses. These are all crucial issues for the community oriented business model that has been selected.

4. User Interface to the City and Its Services

Many different spatial 2D and 3D metaphors for hypertext information have been built and studied [6] to improve the user interface. Also the city metaphor has been used to visualize general hypertext information [7]. The aim in using the spatial metaphors is to visualize larger information spaces with landmarks instead of just showing a single information node at a time. This helps the searching, comparing, analyzing and combining the information. The spatial environments can be extremely useful if natural mappings to the information are found from the point-of-view of the user tasks [8]. So the understanding of the user's task should be the moderating variable when the spatial coding is evaluated.

Information of the services that closely relate to the city seems to be a perfect case for applying the city metaphor. First of all, this virtual city exists also in the real world. So it is at least partly known to many of its inhabitants, which makes the city itself meaningful. This helps in navigation and in creating a cognitive map that structures the services of the city. The city itself is also static, which helps the users to orient themselves and navigate within it. Furthermore, the virtual city will familiarize its users with the places and services of the real city. This is extremely useful for people who have moved in recently and even for those long time residents who want to learn more about the suburbs of their city. Finally, the 3D model interests people and hopefully motivates them to learn to use computers.

The city metaphor nicely visualizes data that can be given an intuitive location within the city. In some cases, it might even work nicely with other kinds of data, such as the use of a non-existing city model for ordinary hypertext data [7]. It could be even possible to use the city as a memory aid resembling the memory techniques where things are associated with objects along a familiar walking route. A sample view to the city with different types of links are shown in Figure 4.

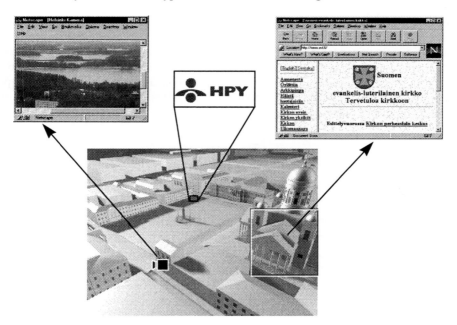

Figure 4: A view to the city with a video -, a phone -, and a web-page link.

The 3D city concept enables location based search, which is naturally used in parallel with text based search robots and agents. However, we do not want to be constrained by the 3D model when other presentations seem to be more suitable. Therefore, we also offer ordinary graphical 2D web-pages and panorama views. All these views can be mixed with each other so that a user can select to mainly work on her 2D pages and follow links to the 3D city when needed. Alternatively, she can use the 3D city as an interface to the services in other formats.

The different user interfaces are probably going to attract different users and also different communities. In addition, they will attract the same users at different times. The 3D model may be very useful for visualizing some data. In addition, it is more entertaining than the ordinary web-pages. For instance, it might be just fun to walk the streets of the virtual Helsinki when you are not in a hurry. You might look what kind of restaurants exist near your apartment, maybe even look inside from a video window or see what kind of sports or exercise services are located within a walking distance from your home. Also you might wander around hoping to meet someone with whom to discuss about this virtual city.

4.1 Technical View to the City

From the technical point-of-view the virtual city itself is a large web information system which will be connected to an information database of the actual services offered to the users. The information system can be divided into five layers as shown in Figure 5. The bottom layer consists of databases, such as the structured 3D city model, web-link information and advertisements that can be shown in the virtual city. These should be easily updated by the businesses and communities through web. Various geographic information system databases are important also in the business sense. As the model will be commercially financed and will cover all of Helsinki there needs to be easy ways to support various GIS-applications and advertisement-type usage in order to get as many potential interest groups as possible to take part in paying for usage of the model or inclusion in it.

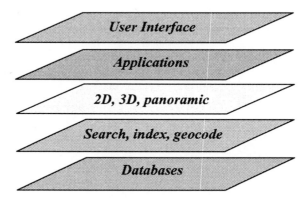

Figure 5: The Layers of the Virtual City Information System Model

The next layer is a system software layer that contains search robots, indexing and geocoding engines. These engines make searches and filter the databases. They are accessed through the positioning layer, which shows the results as 2D maps, part of the 3D city model or as different kinds of pictures (panoramic, still and video-images). Different applications are built on top of these bottom layers. They include multi-user applications, city-camera applications and games. The top layer of this model is a user interface layer. It consists of a general user interface and specific application interfaces which form a user interface to the virtual city.

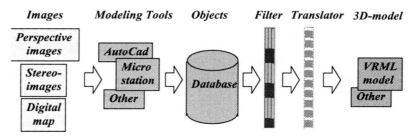

Figure 6: Phases of 3D Modeling.

The structuring of the 3D-world is very flexible as can be seen in Figure 6. The source material is modeled into hierarchical objects which are stored into the database. Different models can be created from the database according to the goals of the modelers. For instance, if the file size is important, as in Internet, some details can be filtered away from the model making it considerably smaller. Various static GIS data and links can be automatically incorporated in the model and also dynamic positioning data can be incorporated. Currently, VRML translator is used to form the visible 3D world but enhancements are being made in order to distribute workloads and throughputs of the system. The next generation viewers and database servers will only transmit and use those objects and detail levels that are necessary for each user. A garbage collection system is also in development to support users who move through various areas in the city model without closing the model in between.

4.2 Arcus City Modeling Process

The modeling and the tools for the model have been developed by Arcus Software. The Arcus modeling process consists of creating a base model and a model with facades and object handles with various attributes attached to them. Base model starts with aerial photos. They are taken from an airplane with flying altitude of 900 - 1200 meters. Photos are then used for stereo mapping. A 3D-stereographic line map is made from stereo pair photos and a 3d sulface model is made from this line map. Parallel with this work diagonal aerial photos are taken from a helicopter. This starts the second phase of modelling the facades. Flying altitude is 200-250 meters. Photos of building basements are taken from street level. Building facades are modeled using Arcus software tools and photos. Facades are modeled using doors, windows and other real world objects instead of mapping digital bitmaps on walls. These have been pre-designed to various building style libraries to create efficient modelling environment. Model includes very little dumb geometry. Most things are stored as intelligent objects. Street is a street, window is a window, tree is a tree etc.

As the final model consists of relatively optimized objects with bitmaps only as optional decorations the model size is very small. This is extremely important as the model will be distributed on line and design goal has been that it should be usable over ISDN-lines. Different parts of town are modeled with different amount of details. City center, main streets and sub urban centers are modeled with high amount of details. Side streets and sub urban areas are modeled with less details. Landmark buildings are most important because they are used for recognizing places.

The following estimates give a fairly good approximation of model sizes and required effort converted to commercial modelling prices of professional modellers. Helsinki center model will be finished in the year 2000. The model will cover 30 km2 and the required storage or file size of the complete model without application dependant data is 300-400 MB. Cost estimate is $ 1 million. Helsinki metropolitan model will be finished in 2002 covering 450 km2 and a population of 1 million people. Size of this model is approximately 700-900 MB and estimated modelling cost will be $ 5 million. A completely different set of values is reached in Kainuu which is also being modelled and finalized in 2002. Kainuu is a province of 24 000 km2 and population of 100 000 people. The whole province of 24 000 km2 will be modelled and it will include besides provincial model also models of rural villages and surroundings 600 km2 and urban center models 10 km2. Estimated modelling cost is $ 0.5-0.75 million. This efficiency is largely based on converting automatically digital maps from the rural areas to Arcus modelling objects.

Average modeling cost is: city center areas, $ 30-40 000/km2, sub urban areas, $ 10-20 000/km2

5. Applications of the 3D City Model

The 3D city model integrated with the 2D metaphors inspires many exciting new uses. Location based search adds interesting new possibilities for interaction. All kinds of data can be looked through the city model user interface. The data can be related to video commerce, multi-point video telephony, entertainment, virtual meetings, community meeting points, or real-time video from public places of the city. It will be exciting to see how far it is possible to go with this kind of a user interface. This will be examined as the Helsinki Arena 2000 project evolves.

Sample applications are discussed in the following chapters. Some of the discussed functions are already implemented, at least as pilot versions, and others are just being brainstormed.

5.1 3D Phone Catalog

One already implemented experiment is the use of the city model as a phone catalog with names and phone numbers connected to the corresponding building (Figure 7).

Furthermore, as the multimedia network is connected to the normal telephone network, these numbers can be called by just clicking on them. This gives new possibilities to situations when a user remembers a building by its look but names or numbers are missing. For instance, you might want to contact a nice shoe store you visited lately, but can only remember its location. Also your little daughter might want to call her friends in the neighborhood, but she only knows how to get to their houses. In the city model this can be done by clicking the phone icon attached to the door of the building. The experiment showed that it is practical to create the telephone links automatically from telco databases and the telephone line co-ordinates and addresses.

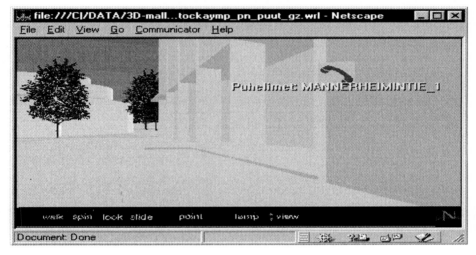

Figure 7: Telephone numbers attached to an address in the virtual city model.

5.2 Search for Local and Mobile Services in the Real City

There is an ongoing research activity between Hewlett-Packard Bristol Labs, Helsinki Telephone and Arcus where integration of mobile data is studied. Intention is to create a distributed messaging environment where all moving vehicles such as buses and, taxis could be shown as corresponding avatars with their links in the model. This system needs to be distributed in two ways. It needs to be open so that anyone can start sending their own message streams in the virtual city. In addition, any user should be able to freely select which part of the information flow he wishes to receive through his communication link. Furthermore to support extendibility there should be no central server. Currently the intention is to study whether we could move from HP's preliminary platform to their forthcoming commercial but freely distributed E-Speak-technology. Helsinki Telephone has already announced a service for voluntary publication of the positioning data of mobile phones. This information will be linked to the respective mobile services in the virtual model.

In addition, to providing users information from moving objects in he form of avatars in the virtual city there are plans to integrate the yellow pages information to the virtual model. In these plans the yellow pages and other telephone catalogue search facilities become essential part of the city model so that the user of the model can get pinpointed to all barbers or all restaurants and possibly even see immediately if they can make reservations. There is also a study going on about getting tourist guidance type information on objects of interest near by.

5.3 Meeting Places in Real and Virtual Surroundings

Helsinki Arena 2000 project aims to support rich communication among the ordinary citizens. This means that also different network communities should be supported. Some of these communities will be formed totally virtually while others have very strong connections to the physical world. Different design dimensions for these communities are discussed in [9].

In the virtual Helsinki you can meet your friends as avatars just as you meet them in the real Helsinki. In the virtual world you just do not have to leave home when it is raining or snowing heavily. You can use the same popular meeting points, such as in front of Stockman's warehouse or at the Lasipalatsi Clock tower. You may even experience the same crowds together and possibly get to know some other people in these crowds.

In addition, to the real and virtual Helsinki, there exists an underground 3D meeting point which gives the designers and the users more freedom to explore the imaginary worlds, participate and create something of your own. We felt that there is a need for imaginary virtual meeting places besides the reality based ones also.

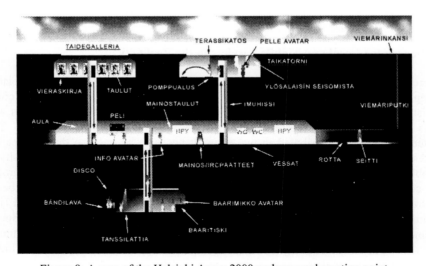

Figure 8: A map of the Helsinki Arena 2000 underground meeting point.

5.4 Possibilities for Route Guidance

Helsinki Telephone Corporation has a number and address service number, which is usually called 118 service. In addition to providing people with right numbers or addresses when name is given, it also provides more advanced services. For instance, it may find a person a restaurant according to her wishes or a repair shop when something has happened to a car. This service is also available through the web.

It has been studied how the 3D model of Helsinki would help the 118 service people when they are guiding the customer to a certain place. They could look the landmarks, such as big or easily identified buildings and give their directions by using these landmarks. There has also been a study on how the web based phone numbering service and search engine service for yellow pages could be combined with 3D-model.

A further version of these could be able to send fasted information of the notable landmarks and the destination even to the travelers mobile phones. Already it is possible for a user to show another user across the network how first to reach the correct destination in Virtual Helsinki. Currently this can be achieved with H.323 conferencing applications but more efficient methods are studied.

6. Conclusion

Helsinki Arena 2000 is an ongoing project whose near term goal is in year 2000. At the moment, isolated parts of the multimedia network are already available and larger scale availability is very near. Also the central parts of the virtual city model as well as some services are available for experimenting purposes and large scale production of the citywide model has started in early 1999 when the tools were ripe enough. As we gain more experience with the virtual city we will see more and more possibilities for its use. Already many citizens are giving us enthusiastic feedback about it after seeing some possibilities of the virtual city being demonstrated to them. However, there is still a lot of exciting work to be done to develop more ideas, experiment the services and the user interface, and test our virtual city with the users.

Acknowledgments

Many people contribute to Helsinki Arena 2000 in Helsinki Telephone Corporation, in City of Helsinki in Arcus Software and in other participating institutions. We want to give our special thanks to Aimo Maanavilja, Kari Lehtinen, Pertti Hölttä, Tauno Hovatta, Harri Palviainen, Timo Simula, Immo Teperi and Kyosti Laamanen who provided us many valuable comments. We are also grateful to Jukka Lehikoinen who was very helpful in finding us articles and books.

References

[1] Carroll, J. M. and Rosson, M. B. (1996) Developing the Blacksburg Electronic Village. *Communications of the ACM*, Dec 1996, Vol 39, Number 12, pages 69-74.

[2] Cohill, A. M., Kavanaugh, A. L. (ed.) (1997) *Community Networks: Lessons from Blacksburg, Virginia.* Artech House.

[3] Schwartz, E. (1995) People are Supposed to Pay for this Stuff? *Wired,* July 1995, pages 149-191.

[4] Ishida, J. Akahani, K. Hiramatsu, K. Isbister, S. Lisowski, H. Nakanishi, M. Okamoto, Y. Miyazaki, K. Tsutsuguchi, ``Digital City Kyoto: Towards A Social Information Infrastructure," M. Klusch, O. Shehory, G. Weiss (Eds.), Cooperative Information Agents III, *Lecture Notes in Artificial Intelligence*, Vol. 1652, Springer-Verlag, 1999, pages 23-35.

[5] Mohageg, M. et al (1996) A User Interface for Accessing 3D Content on the World Wide Web. *CHI'96*, pages 466-472.

[6] Card, S. K. (1996) Visualizing Retrieved Information: A Survey. *Computer Graphics & Applications*, Vol 16, No. 2, March 1996.

[7] Dieberger, A. (1993) The Information City: A Step towards Merging of Hypertext and Virtual Reality. *ACM Conference on Hypertext*, Seattle, November 1993.

[8] Shum, S. (1990) Real and Virtual Spaces: Mapping from Spatial Cognition to Hypertext. *Hypermedia*, 2(2), pages 133-158.

[9] Mynatt, E. (1997) Design For Network Communities, *CHI'97*

The Geographic Information System (GIS) of Turin Municipality

Guido Bolatto[1], Adriano Sozza[2], Ivano Gauna[3], and Maddalena Rusconi[4]

[1]Comune di Torino
via Pietro Micca, 21 - 10100 Torino (ITALY) Tel. 011/ 4421442 - Fax 011/ 4422950
guido.bolatto@comune.torino.it
[2]CSI - Consorzio Sistema Informativo
c.so Unione Sovietica, 216 - 10134 Torino (ITALY) Tel. 011/3168691 - Fax 011/ 3168498
adriano.sozza@csi.it
[3]CSI – Consorzio Sistema Informativo
ivano.gauna@csi.it
[4]CSP – Centro di Eccellenza
c.so Unione Sovietica, 216 – 10134 Torino (ITALY) Tel. 011/3168906 – Fax 011/3168322
rusconi@csp.it

Abstract. The essay bids a framing of the remarkable telematic services of the City of Torino. Core of the document is the description of the local Geographic Information System (GIS): the aim of the GIS on the Internet is to allow a shared use of data concerning land use and management, cartography, building rules, environment conditions. The system puts together information coming from different Departments of the Municipality. Access to the system is made possible through a series of subsystems, some already operative and some still under construction, all briefly described in the paper. Finally, an empiric example of the work procedures of the GIS structure is given with the description of the Digital Town Planning Scheme.

1   Introduction

Torino has always been in the lead with regard to innovative technologies. The municipality has been one of the firsts in Italy to develop on large scale the idea of "telematic citizens". (AM/FM Italy, 1992). Key aim is to improve citizens' quality of life through ICTs by:

- Providing wider access to city services.
- Developing the city's cultural heritage and tourism.
- Improving the educational and professional fields.

The City has set up an Internet-based common information system architecture that ensures flexibility in administrative performances and integration of the services offered. Internet thereby becomes a tool to convert local government into a democratic "open system", that makes the public services network accessible to all.
In this framework was born the first concept of a geographic web site, to provide access to the spatial information on the city to a large number of citizens and professionals (ASITA, 1997).

T. Ishida, K. Isbister (Eds.): Digital Cities, LNCS 1765, pp. 97-109, 2000.
© Springer-Verlag Berlin Heidelberg 2000

To carry out its telecommunication related initiatives the City avails itself of the expertise of the public consortium CSI-Piemonte (Information System Consortium). CSI is the largest software company in the Piedmont region and ranks among the top 20 Italian information service companies. The consortium is in charge of the management, development and updating of the whole municipal information system. Supporting structure of CSI is CSP (Centre of Excellence for Research, Development and Experimentation of Advanced Computer Science and Telecommunication Technologies), which deals with innovative projects of applied research in Telecommunication and Computer Science fields.

2   The Geographic Information System

2.1   GIS: Structure and Aims

The aim of the GIS on the web is to allow a shared use of data concerning land use and management, cartography, building rules, environment conditions, putting together different information coming from the many Municipal Departments (AM/FM Italy, 1993).
The complete loading and updating of the different geographic information should be able to satisfy different needs through a simple and fast way of accessing data of common use.
In designing the system three main user typologies were foreseen:

- Professionals: Engineers, architects, associations, companies, university, researchers
- Public offices (data users only)
- Common citizens

Professional users would have therefore the opportunity to search for laws, town planning schemes, urban regulations, and maps related to their work. Technical public offices, inside or outside the Municipality, with the need of consulting frequently the database, would maintain a constant contact and be always up-to-dated to the latest changes. The common users inquiring on their houses, their district, municipal services, public documents would obtain information easily and for free.
Today specific agreements with professional associations of Engineers and Architects are being signed to set up new telematic services based on the GIS on the web.
The GIS is organised on a series of digital maps (managed with the package "Geographic Resource Analysis Support System") and a series of spatial data (managed with a relational database) linked to the map. The different kinds of geographic information are stored in different sub systems where each map with its graphic elements represents a class of objects described through a series of attributes managed by the database.

Concerning the software development environment we should underline that it is a completely free environment, based on packages and software tools usually available on the Internet.

In particular the GIS web system was founded on the following tools:

Server component:

- GIS: GRASS 4.1 (Geographic Resource Analysis Support System)
- Web server: Apache 1.2.4
- Application server : Java 1.1.1
- Data base: My SQL 5.3 by TCX

Client component

- Browser supporting Java applet: Netscape 4.5, Hotjava

2.2   The Sub Systems Application

In order to offer a simple system, easy to consult, the access to the different kind of geographic information stored in the subsystems is organised through hierarchical menus that permit to choose and select the information required.

Access to the system is made through one of the subsystems. During the research it is possible to shift from one to another. Some of the subsystems are already completed and operative, while some other are still under construction:

- BASIC CARTOGRAPHY:
- Topographic map 1:1000
- 52 kinds of graphic objects

- TOPONYMY:
- Streets and squares codification
- Street numbers (addresses) codification
- Census sections
- Statistical zones
- Districts

- MASTER PLAN:
- Urban zoning
- Land use
- Environmental and Historical constraints
- Building rules

- ENVIRONMENT:
- Parks and green areas
- Air quality on the survey points
- Avenue trees

- MOBILITY:
- Traffic Master Plan
- Road classification
- Parking system

- PUBLIC PROPERTIES:
- Schools
- Public services
- Market areas

- CADASTRE:
- Parcel boundary
- Properties characteristics

- UNDERGROUND NETWORKS:
- Water
- Electricity
- Gas
- Sewers

The following page offers a short description of the origin and the contents of each subsystem:

- Basic Cartography: The basic cartography of the GIS is the topographic map of the city on a 1:1000 scale, that delineates the urban territory as it is, with all its physical objects: buildings, streets, railways, parks and so on. The map was created in 1985 through an aerophotogrammetric flight and successively updated through recurrent ground surveys. Today, every three months an updated version of the topographic map is made available. Any other geographic information of the system has been "leant" on the topographic map to guarantee geometric congruence among the graphic objects.

- Toponymy: It contains all streets and public space names and the geographic reference (instreet number) of each building too. To set up the GIS an important outcome was achieved: the localization of every town civic number and its positioning on the map. This means that it is possible to approach the map simply by starting from the address. The operation is significant too because it allows the linking to a geographic position of much of the information managed by the administration or coming from different sources (population register, census, cadastre, etc.). This permits then to carry out statistical processing on a geographic basis.

- City Master Plan: It manages all data linked to the land use and management: urban prescriptions, restrictions, documents, laws. The Master Plan can be described as a sort of draft of the future city development and of the urban projects to be implemented. The Plan contains also the Color Plan that sets rules for walls color restoration in the historical part of the city. A more detailed information on the Master Plan is given in the second part of the paper.

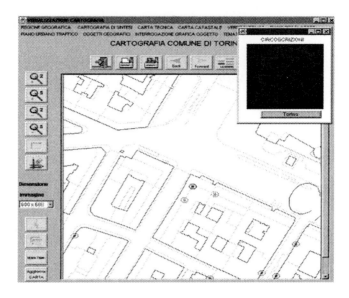

Fig. 1. Toponymy System

- Environment: This subsystem manages all the so-called environment quality indicators: air pollution dynamic, noise reduction zoning, parks and natural areas, cycling tracks, avenues trees plantation. As a matter of fact, Turin has a very important green heritage represented by its many planted avenues; therefore the GIS contains the geographic position and general information on about 60.000 trees of the town. Currently a complete register of all trees is under construction, in order to build a support tool for public offices for the routine green maintenance. Moreover the Municipality and in particular its Environment Department is setting up a Local Agenda 21Program: all geographic information related to this program will be available soon on the web.

- Mobility: It is mainly a information service on the Traffic Master Plan, that defines road use and classification, traffic restricted areas, parking use rules (on payment, free, etc.), road condition modifications due to public works or other events.

- Public properties: The subsystem, still under construction, will provide information on the location and characteristics of the different kind of public buildings like markets and connected parking lots, sport equipment, schools and children utilities, healthcare system, cultural services (libraries, museums, art galleries, theatres.

- Housing services: the sub-system, still under construction, will provide information on the location and characteristics of the public residential buildings (E.R.P.).

- Cadastre: This subsystem, under construction, will provide information on the real estate municipal taxes in the different urban zones, on their payment deadlines and other related documents.

Fig. 2. Avenue Plantation

Fig. 3. Traffic Master Plan

- Technical underground networks: This subsystem contains an experimental model to manage all tracks and links of the urban networks like electricity, gas, water supply, sewers, in cooperation with the utility companies that should provide directly maps and information about their own networks.

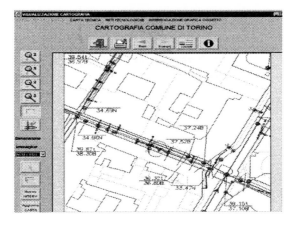

Fig. 4. The Works on Underground Networks

2.3   An Empiric Example: The Digital Town Planning Scheme

The aim of the Town Planning Scheme (*PRG - Piano Regolatore Generale*) is to set the general guidelines of the urban development, to specify the areas of complete transformation and of historical preservation, to fix all urban index, quantities and values that must be respected in all future intervention in the City.

The structure of the PRG is therefore formed by maps and by a series of rules that specify the prescriptions for all map areas.

The general users of the PRG are public offices that deal with land management and registration and professionals (architects, surveyors, and engineers) that need to know the actual situation of the areas they are working on.

The digital version of the PRG allows these users to consult the prescriptions of the PRG in an easier way and also to have links to general laws (local and national) which regulate the urban interventions.

The structure of the digital PRG is made of tables (managed with ACCESS and MYSQL) related to the numeric data of every single object of the system.

The tables are linked to the cartographic database on one side and to the prescriptions of the PRG itself on the other. The link is made through a code that characterizes each element.

The objects of the system have been identified comparing the map and the rules and have been organized on different levels. It was possible to create classes of objects, where elements of each class share the same general attributes.

The scheme of the structure can be represented as following:

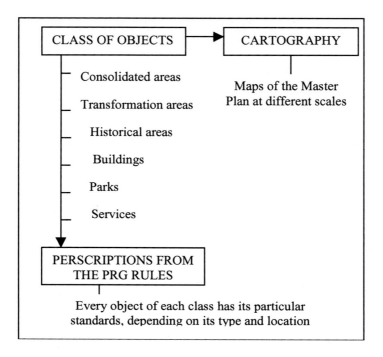

Fig. 5. Database structure

The query of the Plan begins from the map: the selection of an area starts a process that affects different levels corresponding to the classes. The key that allows this process is the code of each element. The output is visualised in a final report that summarizes all data on all single objects selected through the query.

2.4 The Query Process of the Master Plan on the Internet

The main web page of the GIS lists all available subsystems.

By selecting the sub-system *cartography* the related page is opened.
In this new page it will be possible to choose between the topographic map and the Master Plan cartography. By choosing the Plan option the access to this subsystem is made and the consulting alternatives are proposed to the users.

Fig. 6. The main page of the GIS

Fig. 7 The map choosing menu.

The query starts from one of the tables that form the general map. By selecting a particular area it is possible to obtain the information on all the objects that are touched in the query.

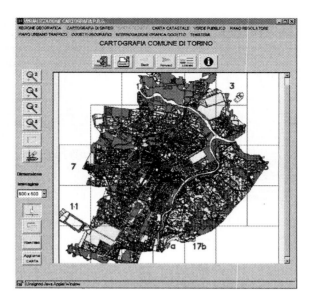

Fig. 8. Master Plan Consulting Options

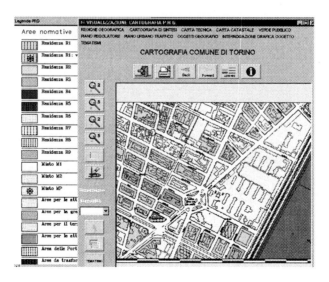

Fig. 9. City Master Plan: a Map Legend

The result of the query is visualized in a report (Figure 12) where every one of the seven folders corresponds to a class of objects and summarizes the data of the single object touched with the query and belonging to that class.

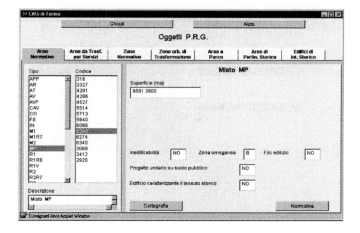

Fig. 10. Final output of the query

2.5   Next Implementations

Today new functions on the Internet GIS are being developed and will be added to the services available:

- map files download,
- services payment through smart cards,
- document authentication

Fig. 11. Example of Map Download

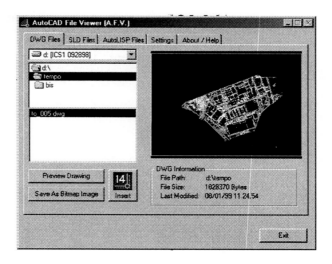

Fig. 12. Checking downloaded files

To pursue these goals as well as to enforce European cohesion, the Municipality has taken part in a European project named DISTINCT, which aims at developing and integrating smart card services (microchip card). Drawing together a number of tools, such as electronic signature, secure data transmission, and an open payment system, access to on-line services available at the Website is gradually made possible.

One of the first uses of the DISTINCT card known at local level as TorinoFacile (Turin-Easy), is the experiment of Internet use for the handling of housing permit applications and for accessing the City's IS urban planning information; the service is mainly addressed to Professional Associations.

The smart card will provide access to authorized users to specific sites within the municipal Website to consult procedures for the submission of building permit applications. Users can follow the whole procedure, inquiry on the status of specific requests, inquiry on any hypothetical procedural delay or stop. Such information exchange may naturally also involve bodies outside the municipal administration.

One of the pilot studies put into place is the access to City maps and geographical information via the smart card, using the network to enter the City's mapping archives (urban-planning maps and current regulations). It is conceivable an access extension to other departments (land-survey maps, surveying certificates, or zoning reports). Professional bodies will thereby be able to work with certified up-to-the-minute documents and, in turn, provide the City with surveys, plans and information, in electronic format, pertaining to new projects.

3. Conclusion

Some local administrations in Italy are actually following the example of Turin creating their own cartographic site on the Internet environment.

In the last two years about 15,000 users have visited the Turin GIS site. Certainly this is not a very big figure for a city of about 1 million inhabitants, but the number is progressively increasing. Moreover, many of the users contact the system administrator to ask for new functions and services and to offer useful suggestions.

Currently this experience remains an experimental system, but its approach is shaping a sort of standard inside the administration for presenting and making available geographic data to a wide set of users. Almost every month new sets of information are proposed by the different Municipal Departments to be added to the system.

In conclusion it can be stated that the network services for the exchange of geographic information that will find implementation in Italy in the next future in some way will bear a connection to the Torino example.

References

AM/FM Italy (1992). IV Conference, "GIS for Italy and Europe"

AM/FM Italy (1993). V Conference, "The public information heritage: Integration and valorization"

ASITA (1997). I Conference, "Images and geographic information"

Digital City Bristol: A Case Study

Annelies de Bruine

Hewlett-Packard Research Laboratories
Filton Road, Stoke Gifford, Bristol, BS 34 8 QZ, England, UK
annde@hplb.hpl.hp.com
http://www.bristol.digitalcity.org

Abstract. Digital City Bristol (DCB) aims to stimulate the provision of a sustainable and visually appealing Internet resource. Users of DCB can access public information about the city of Bristol, its organisations and its inhabitants. The web site is based around a graphical interface of piers in a harbour, each of which represents a different theme such as leisure, business, education or community groups. Initiated by Hewlett-Packard Laboratories, the project was developed with help of Bristol City Council, the University of the West of England (UWE), Bristol Evening Post and City NetGates Ltd. The pilot site was launched in March 1997.

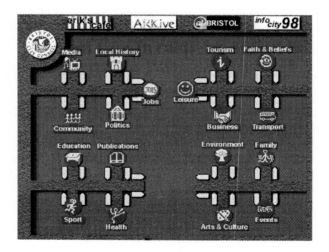

1 Introduction

Digital City Bristol started as collaboration between Bristol City Council, Hewlett-Packard Research Laboratories and the University of the West of England and was launched in March 1997. Nowadays there are five partners since City NetGates Ltd. and Western Media Publishing Ltd. joined the team in 1998.

T. Ishida, K. Isbister (Eds.): Digital Cities, LNCS 1765, pp. 110-124, 2000.

Digital City Bristol provides a way of grouping and indexing electronic information concerning the City in an attractive, readily understandable manner, which combines visual impact with valuable content. Information is grouped in themes and is then accessed as a series of pages using the Internet.

The visual metaphor for Digital City Bristol is that of a harbour. Information is grouped into 'piers' with 'houseboats' each represents a particular information theme. Themes for 'piers' of information include business, education, health, art & culture, sports, tourism, community, news & publications and information related to Bristol City Council services.

The harbor also has the capacity to provide a base for electronic information (home pages) relating to individuals and community organisations. It is anticipated Digital City Bristol will also have the potential to support electronic newsgroups and provide electronic mail in the future.

One of the major objectives of Digital City Bristol is to create a cohesive and holistic view of the City of Bristol. The aim is to project a well presented and visually interesting electronic image of Bristol as a thriving, dynamic and forward looking city and regional capital. As part of its wider IT in the Community initiative Bristol City Council is keen to explore opportunities to provide access to Digital City Bristol through 'public access' points located throughout the City.

2 Aims and Goals

The Aim of Digital City Bristol :
- To stimulate the provision of a sustainable and visually appealing Internet resource which represents the community that makes up the City of Bristol.
- To provide opportunities for community groups and individuals to gain new skills in digital content creation and to make new links within the local community and Internet community.
- To provide signposts to relevant and appropriate information about Bristol, its organisations and its inhabitants.

Objectives:
- To enable relevant digital resources to be accessed via a visually appealing framework.

The principles of Digital City Bristol:
- Responsible information provision.
- Local ownership.

The goals:
- The long-term goal of DCB is the ownership of a digital network and of digital resources by a public/private sector partnership concerned with achieving the economic regeneration of the City of Bristol and the participation of all Bristol citizens in digital media.
- For all: free information about the City of Bristol.
- For citizens and community groups in Bristol: Opportunities to establish a presence on the World Wide Web.
- For businesses: Sponsorship and marketing opportunities.

Free web space for community organisations

Targets:

- For all: Access to public information about the City of Bristol, its organisations and its inhabitants
- For citizens and community groups in Bristol: Links to other relevant and appropriate web sites and digital resources. Home pages signposting the activities and resources of citizens and community groups. A virtual meeting place and an electronic communication network for the City of Bristol.
- For business in Bristol: Links to appropriate web sites and resources.

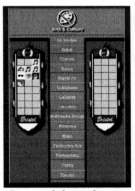

Pier with houseboats

On a pier

Digital City Bristol is more than a portal site for Bristol. Although the web site is the most important feature, there is lot of attention for (IT-) awareness raising activities, public access, training, research and co-operation with community groups in the city.

3 History

Digital City Bristol was launched in March 1997 as a pilot project. During this phase of development the management committee was made up of representatives from Bristol City Council, the University of the West of England and by Hewlett-Packard Laboratories (HPLabs). The management committee has now expanded to include City NetGates Ltd. and Western Media Publishing Ltd. These organisations are commercial organisations with a different perspective, which had a positive influence on DCB. A co-ordinator got appointed to chair the management meetings and the digital city grew because of the amalgamation with the Bristol Directory of City NetGates.

Getting decisions from a diverse range of organisations can be tricky. There are small, medium and large organisations in the key partnerships all of whom have wider agendas and their own business to sustain. This can lead to differences.

Communication within the management committee has not always been easy, because of the different cultures of the organisations. It took some time to get to know each other. After a few years there is an excellent and close relationship of trust between the partners and they share common aims, even though the motivation for these common aims vary with each of the participating organisations. The committee is able to further develop DCB in what seems to be a loose organizational structure. The representatives of the participating organisations have been the same throughout the development and this continuity of people has been key to the success of DCB.

An advisory committee, which represents a range of citywide community, business and training organisations, exists to gain valuable grassroots feedback and advice. The advisory committee is group of around 16 organisations from all sectors with focus on voluntary sector involvement. The advisory committee meets in theory quarterly and is chaired by a Councilor from Bristol City Council. In fact this group meets very infrequently and has not met for some time.

Extension of the ownership and changes to management arrangements are by agreement of the management committee. Based on the experiences of the pilot project phase, DCB, with the newly formed management committee, started a two-phase program of development.

Phase 1:
Re-launch of the World Wide Web site with a new graphical interface and a dynamic, database led infrastructure. Launched September 1998.
Phase 2:
The introduction of more interactive elements to the World Wide Web site, to include virtual meeting and communication areas, multi-media and interactive spaces and dynamic news feeds. Development began January 1999.

In July 1999 726 home pages are linked to DCB, the hitrate on the site is approximately 7,600 a day with a peak of almost 12,000 on one day. Only 22 individuals have their web pages on the houseboats.

All the numbers are going up, DCB is growing. Now the time has come to focus on communication in the digital city and to investigate the commercial potential for DCB to make it self sustainable.

Statistics DCB 03-Aug-1999	Monthly Report
	Each unit (▬) represents 15,000 requests, or part thereof.

General Summary

(Figures in parentheses refer to the last 7 days).
Successful requests: 1,899,046 (53,254)
Average successful requests per day: 5,022 (7,607)
Successful requests for pages: 483,822 (14,496)
Average successful requests for pages per day: 1,279 (2,070)
Failed requests: 24,025 (890)
Redirected requests: 86,538 (2,405)
Distinct files requested: 3,279 (1,836)
Distinct hosts served: 34,938 (1,842)
Corrupt logfile lines: 4
Data transferred: 6,070 Mbytes (190,057 kbytes)
Average data transferred per day: 16,439 kbytes (27,151 kbytes)

month:	#reqs:	%reqs:	kbytes:	%bytes:	
Jul 1998:	1919:	0.10%:	6174:	0.10%:	▬
Aug 1998:	4109:	0.22%:	14746:	0.24%:	▬
Sep 1998:	82585:	4.35%:	266711:	4.29%:	▬▬▬▬
Oct 1998:	169952:	8.95%:	520549:	8.37%:	▬▬▬▬▬▬
Nov 1998:	136918:	7.21%:	428013:	6.89%:	▬▬▬▬▬
Dec 1998:	104784:	5.52%:	345357:	5.56%:	▬▬▬▬
Jan 1999:	149823:	7.89%:	478224:	7.69%:	▬▬▬▬▬
Feb 1999:	168552:	8.88%:	538986:	8.67%:	▬▬▬▬▬▬
Mar 1999:	194029:	10.22%:	623850:	10.04%:	▬▬▬▬▬▬▬
Apr 1999:	191836:	10.10%:	607004:	9.77%:	▬▬▬▬▬▬▬
May 1999:	199546:	10.51%:	651955:	10.49%:	▬▬▬▬▬▬▬
Jun 1999:	212344:	11.18%:	711261:	11.44%:	▬▬▬▬▬▬▬
Jul 1999:	262152:	13.80%:	950800:	15.30%:	▬▬▬▬▬▬▬▬
Aug 1999:	20497:	1.08%:	72219:	1.16%:	▬

Busiest month: Jul 1999 (262,152 requests).

4 Organization

The management committee is not formally organized. All five partners in Digital City Bristol have a representative in the management committee. The management committee meets every 3 months. Items discussed are key day to day running decisions, design, project management, new ideas for the site and progress monitoring. Also discussed in the last few meetings is how to generate income and how to get sponsorship for DCB.

The partners put time, personnel and equipment in DCB. The resources are scarce. Up until now no money has been exchanged within the organization of DCB. Every partner has its own input in DCB. This input is described in the next chapter. The following members of Digital City Bristol Management Committee provide sponsorship of the project and general management:

Stewart Long (Bristol City Council)
Linda Skinner, Marc Day (University of the West of England)
Erik Geelhoed, Phil Stenton, Annelies de Bruine (Hewlett-Packard Research Laboratories)
Johanna Nicholls, Peter MacLellan (City NetGates Ltd.)
Eric Rayner (Western Media Publishing Ltd.)

Digital City Bristol would like to see more partners actively involved in the digital city. A research project with Bristol University started recently. Also Venue Publishing has been contacted with the aim to add up to date content to the web site with information about what is happening in Bristol on a weekly or daily base.

Software Development:
Patrick Versteeg, Erik Geelhoed, Hewlett-Packard Laboratories (HPLabs)
Marc Day, Ian Rees, University of the West of England
Graham Willmott, City NetGates Ltd.
Graphic Design and HTML
Sierd Westerfield, Jon Bently, Aukje Thomassen, HPLabs
Marc Day, Ian Rees, University of West of England
Music Section and Erik's Café
Annelies de Bruine, HPLabs
Co-ordination:
Johanna Nicholls, City NetGates Ltd.
Public Sector and Community Involvement:
Bristol City Council
Academic and Research Involvement:
University of the West of England, Bristol
HPLabs, Bristol
Private Sector Involvement:
City NetGates Ltd.
Western Media Publishing Ltd.

The advisory committee, a larger group of around 16 organisations from all sectors with focus on voluntary sector involvement, is supposed to meet quarterly and is chaired by a Councilor from Bristol City Council. The two-tier structure was felt to be necessary to give a focus for key decision but a wider accountability to the wider Bristol community through the advisory group.

5 Current Status & Services

There are currently five organisations involved in the management and running of Digital City Bristol (DCB). There is no legal framework. The contributors to DCB take responsibility for particular activities based on availability of funds and people within their organisations. City NetGates hosts and maintains the server, Western Media Publishing are investigating commercial potential for DCB, UWE took the responsibility for free training in the community, Bristol City Council attached their public access point program to the DCB structure and HPLabs have taken responsibility for designing the interface and developing Erik's Cafe.

City NetGates Ltd.
City NetGates Ltd. is an established Internet services company based in central Bristol. It provides dial-up Internet access, web design services, Internet training and a range of networking and business solutions. In addition to theses packaged services, NetGates runs a lively city centre cybercafe, providing a public point of Internet access for Bristol in a friendly and informal atmosphere.
City NetGates was invited to attend an inaugural meeting in 1996 at HPLabs, when the DCB concept was first introduced. Soon after, the company registered the Internet domain on behalf of the project. City NetGates has always been keen to support and

contribute to the DCB project. This commitment was clarified by its decision to become a leading partner and member of the core management committee in 1998, having spent some time as a member of the advisory group.

Since becoming a management partner, City NetGates has contributed the following services and resources to the project:

- Consultancy and advice during the review of the pilot web site
- Design and creation of a database led and expandable architecture for the new web site and contribution to the creation of a new graphical interface.
- Configuration and set up of a new DCB server
- Ongoing accommodation of the new DCB server and ongoing provision of bandwidth for all DCB traffic
- Development of policy and administration documentation
- Ongoing project development and co-ordination resource

City NetGates Ltd. is very much in support of the DCB initiative. At the heart of the NetGates company ethos is an interest and concern in people rather than technology. Through its training courses, public cybercafe and local strategic partnerships, NetGates seeks to raise the level of awareness and understanding among the people in Bristol in the powerful potential that new technology can hold for them.

Western Media Publishing/Bristol Evening Post

The Evening Post is Bristol's daily newspaper. The newspaper has had its own web site for over two years and was a natural partner for DCB. As part of its role as the primary source of news and information about the city, the newspaper's web site is updated daily with a selection of news, stories and advertisements. Classifieds ads are databased allowing users to search for jobs, cars or rented property.

Western Media Publishing is working in close relationship with the other partners to create a web site promoting the city of Bristol and encourage people in the city to use information technology.

Western Media Publishing generously proposed to take the responsibility for marketing for a few months to get sponsors and advertisements in DCB, which can be a start of the self-sustainability of the digital city.

University of the West of England

The Centre for Research, Innovation and Industry at UWE became involved with DCB in the early stages of development. The University helped the initial pilot project to be established and co-ordinated its administration. UWE has also been active in helping to get community groups involved offering free web site training and web authoring.

Funded by the Single Regeneration Budget the Centre for Research Innovation and Industry (CRII) of the University of the West of England (UWE) has initiated a project entitled "Connections". The aim is to enable inner city Bristol community organisations to have access to the WEB. They'll be given a presence in the digital city, the project will help them construct their homepage, provide software for browsing the WEB, have email and develop ways to communicate to other community groups. The outcome will specify information requirements for the new media technologies for this sector. A wide range of community groups is now represented on the DCB web site.

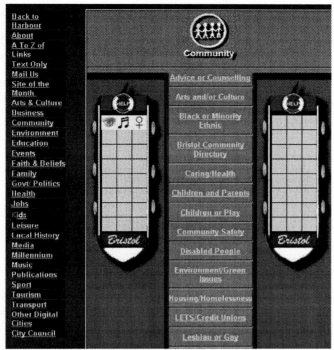

Community pier

The last design changes of the DCB web site have resulted in greatly enhanced, more attractive and faster graphics. The redesign was undertaken at UWE in collaboration with HPLabs.

Bristol City Council

A lot of digital cities are set up by the local government. Bristol City Council played an important role in DCB from the beginning. DCB is part of the wider IT in the Community initiative of the City Council, which aims to implement a number of projects which will raise awareness of the potential of IT and electronic information.

Information Technology has the potential to develop new types of relationships between the City Council and the public. There is an opportunity for the City Council (working with other partners) to make an impact locally, nationally and in a European context with a series of well-focused initiatives. These initiatives would make information of interest to the local and wider community available using electronic and digital methods as well as address the wider question of how Information Technology can be made more accessible to the local community

The fundamental contribution this initiative is making to regeneration is raising awareness and taking steps to assist in equipping a wide range of communities, individuals, voluntary sector groups and businesses with the IT skills required for the 21st century and beyond. Experience elsewhere in the UK, Europe and the USA indicates that this has the potential to build skills which create a wider range of employment opportunities for individuals and encourages the development of small private sector and community business activity related to IT.

DCB has done much to contribute to the image of the City as a leading edge, high technology city. The most frequently visited areas of DCB are the City Council pages and within those pages the tourist information and 'About Bristol' pages are the most popular. This in itself is opening up information about the city for tourism and inward investment in a way, which would not be possible using normal printed media/communication methods.

More than a third (35%) of the hits on DCB come from Public Access Points in the city. In April / May 1998, 21 Public Access Points were installed in libraries, community centres & the Hartcliffe Social Service / Housing Office as part of Bristol City Council's 'IT in the community' initiative. These touchscreen multi-media kiosks & multi-media PC's provide free public access to DCB, the Bristol City Council web site & other relevant Bristol Internet sites.

The City Council is keen to work with other agencies in enabling access to a wide range of additional electronic content. Developing local content for local people is an important part of the project and progress has already been made on this aspect of the project at several of the community based Public Access Points.

The City Council would like to see the network of Public Access Points extended throughout the City. As well as their plans to expand the network they are particularly keen to talk to organisations from any sector that might consider financing a kiosk or Public Access Point on their premises. In principle the City Council would be prepared to connect this to their internal network/Intranet and also provide a moderated 'live' feed to the Internet. This might be of particular interest to organisations who would wish to promote their own Web Site to Bristol people but lack the locally based expertise or resources to manage the security and administrative overheads associated with operating such an infrastructure. In addition Bristol City Council would also welcome enquiries from organisations interested in either advertising on our kiosk information pages or sponsoring individual kiosks.

A survey done in November 1998 pointed out that the Public Access Points are used most by people who already have access to a computer with an Internet connection at home and/or at work. 87% of the users had access elsewhere. People who didn't use the Public Access Points didn't know they existed and/or needed more training on how to use computers. People who are IT literate are more likely to use a Public Access Point than people who are IT non-literate. Together with the positive correlation between computer access and the willingness to use a Public Access Point, we can say that people who already have access to a computer are more likely to use a Public Access Point than people who don't have access to a computer are.

Bristol City Council placed the first Public Access Points in libraries and community centres. The public thinks these are the best places to put them, with supermarkets in third place. Location is an important issue; if the services are not convenient for use, it may discourage people from using them (Rigg et al, 1998). Respondents in the Rigg report mention post offices, libraries and banks because of the possibility of privacy, the convenience and neutrality of these locations. Post offices and banks are mentioned in both the Public Access user and in the non-users survey. However many of the non users surveyed don't know that Public Access Points exist though more than half of the non users surveyed want to use Public Access Points in the future.

The main reason people used a Public Access Point was out of curiosity. These findings are confirmed in Rigg et al (1998) where respondents said they would try something and 'give it a go', but that they would quickly be discouraged by negative experiences. Other reasons mentioned for using the Public Access Points were to get information about Bristol or to surf the Internet. In general, it was felt that the Public Access Points would improve communication with Bristol City Council.

Respondents wanted a connection to the Internet and E-mail facilities at the Public Access Points. This is also seen as a way of improving communications between Bristol City Council and the public. The introduction of such facilities should, however, be underpinned by sound policies on information access and security.

People who used the Public Access Points said they were easy to use though views regarding on-site staff availability and manuals were mixed.

There is a perceived need for more training. More than half of the respondents stated they require more training. The training requirement increases in the higher age groups.

Research Laboratories (HPLabs)
Hewlett-Packard Research Laboratories got involved in Digital City Bristol (DCB) in a time that there was a lot of interest in home computing and the Internet. DCB was set up partly as an experiment using it as a research platform. The digital city could be used for user studies, as a platform to test prototypes and to study interfaces.

Questions HPLabs would like to have answered are how people and organisations interact via the Internet, what are the personal uses of the Internet, what are the needs for interaction and where are the gaps in the technology with a view to identify opportunities for HP in this area.

However the project offered the scope for a much wider range of research. Part of the activities meant liasing with various entities in HPLabs, academia, cultural organisations and Bristol City Council to set a variety of research projects in motion as well as maintaining the HP tradition of good citizenship.

Interfaces
As input into the design of DCB (DCB) HPLabs compared a number of digital cities. All the digital cities in this study provided local mostly textual information about government, leisure, culture etc.

De Digitale Stad (DDS, Amsterdam) has been a major source of inspiration for the thinking of DCB. DCB judged three aspects particularly attractive: novel ways of representing the information space enhanced navigational cues and last but not least the social aspects of the city. Residents of the digital city can communicate with each other via the digital city computer interface as individuals or as groups thereby energizing the city.

The contents of the overview homepages for 16 digital cities were analysed for how the information space was represented, contents of information and the occurrence of residents. HPLabs scored whether or not the city had residents, whether there was a graphical information map rather than the use of blue hypertext lines or grouped icons, and whether there was information about the following headings: Government, Education, Health, Recreation/Tourism, Commerce and Art/Culture.

There were four cities that had residents. Only Amsterdam integrated information and residencies. Four cities featured a graphical map representing the information space. Most cities covered all the information categories.

Common to the digital cities in the 1996 study was the provision of local information about government, leisure, culture etc. For most of these, the information was textual with some images added. Only a few cities allowed residents. However judging from some of the sites more and more cities will feature residents in the future. Graphical user interfaces to capture the vast information space were not common practice.

The Amsterdam interface seemed to stand out in the way a large information space is represented in a single overview, whilst allowing growth and maintaining clarity. Also unique is the integration of living areas with the information space and the ability to allow some form of (currently maybe still primitive keyboard based) social interaction. (Geelhoed, 1996)

As a result of this study DCB decided to create a user interface with the metaphor a harbour. Bristol has been a major port in the past. The interface has a 3 tier structure which allows growth whilst maintaining clarity. Piers in the harbour have different themes and alongside each pier houseboats are moored for residents to 'live' on (e.g. put their home pages in). With this design the living areas for residents are integrated in the information space.

The left frame makes it possible to navigate in Digital City Bristol, even if the pages the user are looking at are on another server.

Erik's Cafe

After the design research and the redesign of DCB, another project HPLabs have been working on for the past months is Erik's Café. In Erik's users can find a dedicated virtual user studies lab. At the moment it is still under construction, but two questionnaires can be found for users to fill in. More questionnaires for user studies will follow.

The Music room in Erik's Café.

In July 1999 there were nine tunes from local producers in the jukebox in MP3 format for users to download.

Also in Erik's Cafe is the Music Room with a MP3 Jukebox. Music of local producers can be downloaded from the Music Room. Bristol is known all over the world for its music with bands like Massive Attack, Portishead and Roni Size & Reprazent. So a focus on music in DCB can attract more visitors from both in as outside the city.

Other features in Erik's Café are a reading room with a link to Bristol based eZines and pages with video clips (Real Video) from Bristol Events. Bristol events (carnivals, music festivals etc.) are filmed and a few small clips are converted to the Real Media format so people can watch clips of events, which have taken place in Bristol. DCB is talking to Future Radio, a local radio station, to broadcast Internet Radio from Erik's Café in the future.

In February 1999 a conference about 'Music on the Web' was held at HPLabs to create awareness about the Internet for the Bristol music industry. Speakers talked about different aspects of music on the web like audio files (MP3, Real Audio) and copyright. At the end of the conference people worked in workgroups to discuss music on the web and future plans for DCB. As a result a few meetings with people from the Bristol music industry were held and DCB organized a workshop 'Music on the Web' with live recording sessions. More workshops and maybe another conference about Music and the Internet will take place in the winter of 2000. A Music Pier is added to the harbour. The Music Pier is the first pier with a chat/forum; a place where users can post messages and discuss topics.

Research will continue at the Laboratory of Hewlett-Packard in Bristol, using DCB as a research platform. In the summer of 1999 HPLabs will focus the research on the usage of the DCB web site to support the marketing strategy for DCB.

6 Future Plans

After more than 2 years Digital City Bristol all partners involved are satisfied with the results. The amount of links to home pages and the amount of hits are both steadily growing and Digital City Bristol is well-anchored in Bristol's community sectors. There still more work to do though.

The DCB Music Conference; 'Music on the Web'
24 February 1999 at Hewlett-Packard Laboratories.

More Interaction

At the moment the web site is a good information source for Bristol. It is not very dynamic; more interaction can energize the digital city and make users come back to communicate with others. The chat/forum on the music pier and in Erik's Cafe is modest start, but more newsgroups are needed to make the web site a dynamic and more interesting place on the web. The management committee is also considering giving an E-mail address to all users, but security and administration is an issue.

More Involvement Bristol People

At the moment people see Digital City Bristol as a top down organisation, although that is not the intention of the partners involved in the project. More citizens should get involved in building and maintaining the digital city. The management committee should think about a policy how to involve the people of Bristol more. Raising awareness what Digital City Bristol is and how it works could be a start, so people have more understanding about the organisation and can then to decide to join in or not. Another solution can be working with volunteers and/or students. The problem is that none of the partners have the resources to supervise volunteers and/or students.

More Users Studies

Hewlett-Packard Research Laboratories and the University of the West of England want to use Digital City Bristol in general and Erik's Cafe in particular more for user studies. Questionnaires can be put in the user studies lab in Erik's Cafe and the partners can use Digital City Bristol more as an experimental platform for trying out new appliances and to gather information on the use of the Internet.

Community Groups
Digital City Bristol wants to continue the work with community groups in the area. By working in the community Digital City Bristol can create more content for the web site and at the same time raise awareness and train people in different areas in Bristol. Important is to increase the links with the grass roots by starting up the advisory committee again.

Marketing
Digital City Bristol and in particular Western Media Publishing are going to try to get local businesses to sponsor Digital City Bristol. With money from sponsoring Digital City Bristol can make some money and to put back in the project. Hewlett-Packard Research Laboratories will support the marketing strategy with data from user studies. Getting advertisement ion the web site and sponsoring for the project will generate money, which can go back into the organization. Money is needed for co-ordination, technical support, administration and marketing.

Grassroots Training
More training for people in Bristol is needed. Especially training in their own locality so it is easy for people to go to. The problem with training is again the resources; DCB needs money and people to set up and give the training.

More Public Access Points
Bristol City Council is working on more public access points in the city. In July 1999 38 multimedia computers and kiosks can be found in town and more will come in the next few years. If DCB wants more people to use the public access points, training needs to be provided. It is important to raise the awareness of the people that the public access points are in town for them to use and that they learn how to use them. Giving people full access to the Internet might attract more people to use the public access points.

All partners are committed to keep Digital City Bristol online and to make it grow to a lively and dynamic virtual city with a lot of information about the city of Bristol and with involvement of people who live, learn, work and play in the city. The management committee will work on long term planning about the maintenance and the self-sustainability of Digital City Bristol.

7 Conclusions

Digital City Bristol started as a pilot project more than 2 years. The web site is growing steadily and more people in Bristol know about the existence of the web site. In July 1999 more than 700 homepages are linked to Digital City Bristol and every week more requests for links come in every week.

Working with five organisations in the management committee has not always been easy because of the different cultures of the organisations, but now the relationship between the partners is excellent. The partners of DCB take responsibility for particular activities based on availability of funds and people within their organisations

For the future of Digital City Bristol it is important to start thinking more commercial. Resources are scarce because all partners are working on DCB in addition to the day job, which can be problematic. Digital City Bristol needs money to sustain itself and the management committee is investigating the commercial potential. Advertisement and sponsoring can help generating money for further development of the digital city.

The links with the local grassroots organisations has always been a strong point of Digital City Bristol. These links with the community organizations should be fortified and maintained. The training for community organisations has been successful and Digital City Bristol should look for a way to continue the training for organisations and individuals in Bristol. The people need more training so they can use one of the 38 public access points in the city and maybe become residents with a home page on one of the houseboats.

Projects like Erik's Café can help attracting more visitors to the digital city because it offers a dynamic content with Real Video, MP3s of local producers and links to events and conferences. During conferences and workshops people can learn about the Internet in general and about Digital City Bristol. It is important to focus on communication in the web site to make it more than an information database.

Research at HPLabs and the University of the West of England together with the commitment of Bristol City Council, the commercial input of Western Media Publishing and the co-ordination and technical support at City NetGates made Digital City Bristol what it is today. The five partners will continue working together to make Digital City Bristol grow and make it a virtual city of the future.

References

Geelhoed, E.N. (1996) Comparing Digital Cities. Internal Report HPLB.

Bruine, A. de (1998) IT in the Community, Analysis of Public Access Point User/Non User surveys. Report of Consultancy Services - Bristol City Council

Rigg et al (1998), The Electronic Government, Report for the Government

Digital City Shanghai: Towards Integrated Information & Service Environment

Ding Peng[1], Mao Wei Liang[1], Rao Ruo Nan[1],
Sheng Huan Ye[1], Ma Fan Yuan[1], Toru Ishida[2]

[1] Department of Computer Science, Shanghai JiaoTong University,
Shanghai, China
Dingpeng@ieee.org, Wlmao816@mail1.sjtu.edu.cn,
Rao-ruonan@cs.sjtu.edu.cn, Hysheng@mail.sjtu.edu.cn,
FyMa@shnet.edu.cn
[2] Department of Social Informatics, Kyoto University, Kyoto, Japan
Ishida@i.kyoto-u.ac.jp

Abstract. This paper aims to describe Digital City Shanghai (DCSH), which was designed to be an *integrated information & service environment* for everyday life. Section 1 provides a background of Shanghai. Section 2 discusses the motivation and guidelines of DCSH: *service-oriented, intelligent, participant-encouraged, and government-guided & commercialized*. Section 3 gives a rough skeleton of DCSH, which includes virtual government, virtual bank, virtual enterprises, virtual markets, digital library, digital hospital, digital community, and virtual school. The reality of DCSH is presented in section 4 based on the description of the current backbone of "InfoPort Shanghai." A comparison between DCSH and other digital cities is given in section 5. Section 6 is a detailed description of Shanghai Tourist Information & Services, which is a pilot project of DCSH.

1. Introduction

Shanghai is the biggest industrial city, the biggest economical center, and the biggest trade port in China at present. It was founded in the Tang dynasty, with more than 1500 years of development and progression, became the financial center of East Asia in the early 20 century. Now, the government, industry, academia and all residents are tightly linked and working hard to make Shanghai the economic center of Asia in the near future.

Shanghai is located on the East Coast of China at 31 14' north (latitude) and 121 29' east (longitude). It covers an area of 6340.5 km^2, which is 0.06% of all of Chinese. Most area of Shanghai is flat except for several small hills in the north, which makes Shanghai a pleasant place to live in. Shanghai consists of 15 districts and 5 counties with more than 13.0546 million residents by the end of 1997, representing 1.1% of the Chinese population. Table 1 summarizes the data.

Shanghai is famous for the richness of its water supply because the Changjiang River empties into the ocean to the east of Shanghai. There are many historic sites in

T. Ishida, K. Isbister (Eds.): Digital Cities, LNCS 1765, pp. 125-139, 2000.

Shanghai, for example, XuJiaHui church, TianShan park, People square, HuaiEnTang, and JingYiTang.

By the way, the fifth Fortune Forum Annual Meeting was held in Shanghai in September, because Shanghai was regarded as the most animated city in the world. Most of the presidents of the top 500 corporations in the world attended this forum and discussed the potential and development activities in Shanghai.

In section 2, we will introduce the motivation and guidelines of building Digital City Shanghai, which guarantee us not go to the wrong way at the very beginning. We give a rough skeleton of Digital City Shanghai in section 3 and so provide interesting and valuable information. We show in section 4 that Digital City Shanghai could be implemented step by step based on the current backbone of "InfoPort Shanghai." We compare Digital City Shanghai with other digital cities in section 5. In section 6, a detailed description of Shanghai Tourist Information & Services, which is a pilot project of Digital City Shanghai, is given. And some further developments are also discussed in this section. Section 7 is the conclusion.

Table 1. Statistics of Shanghai

Item	Value
Area	6340.5 km^2
Population	13.0546 million
Density of population	2059/ 1 km^2

Fig. 1. The map of Shanghai

2. Motivation and Guidelines of Building Digital City Shanghai

The design and implementation of DCSH is an urgent task because it is required by almost all groups in Shanghai, that is to say, individuals, government, industry, and cultural organizations. All groups will benefit much from DCSH in various ways. We predict some of the benefits in the following paragraphs of this section to demonstrate our motivation. It appears likely that the real contribution of DCSH to society will be even stronger than is described below.

For individuals (permanent residents and tourists), DCSH is the platform of *online living*. In other words, DCSH provides most of the information and services of everyday life, for example, news, business & economy, education, entertainment, health, recreation & sports, regional, science, society & culture, forum & chat room, shopping, stock, and a virtual community. All these information & services are real and dynamic because DCSH was modeled on the actual city, not an artificial construction.

In terms of government, DCSH provides the public with information and assistance on regulations. We find that some traditional government policies will be replaced by *online equivalents*, for instance, online policy distribution, online courts, and online tax offices. Government staffs can even use chat rooms to discuss tasks instead of face to face meetings. Higher level officials can get information and suggestions from common residents via the Internet far more easily than is possible in the traditional ways. That will bring more democracy to society. Moreover, there are also many services provided by DCSH, such as, social information collection, supported decision making, and resource distribution (population, roads, water supply, and energy supply). We can not predict the exact impact of DCSH on government, but we can foresee that DCSH will change the current method of governing in various ways.

For industry, DCSH is a perfect backbone for *online business*. Here we extend the definition of industry away from just factories and companies to all enterprises including markets, banks, insurers, and hospitals. We use just the one term for brevity. DCSH offers industry many opportunities that will greatly improve the efficiency and competitive power of industries. Some of them described here are works in progress. Finding partners is more easily achieved within DCSH than traditional ways because only mouse clicks are needed. Large-scale virtual corporations are feasible on the Internet regardless the real location of the companies. We can foresee that virtual enterprises with no real facilities will play an important economic role in the near future. DCSH not only provides new chances to industries but also creates economical potential in the real society.

Table 2. Benefits of DCSH to society

Groups	Benefits
Individuals	Distance education, distance health care, online shopping, online stocks, online entertainment
Government	Online policy dissemination, social information gathering, more democracy, resource distribution, online tax offices
Industries	Commercial information gathering, virtual corporations, online transaction, partnership searching
Cultural organizations	Cultural events PR, distance research corporation, cross-culture communication

For cultural organizations, DCSH is an excellent source of *online culture*. The term "cultural organization" here refers to all the entities that have relations with culture, and include schools, universities, institutes, libraries, museums, cinemas, tempers, and churches. Here are some new points: publicizing online cultural events greatly extends the scale of cultural events; online entertainment, which brings a new type of recreation to the people; distance education, whose goal is to offer more training opportunities to common citizens; distance research corporations, which enable different experts working together to create new solutions. Moreover, there are also many other interesting issues, for example, distance medicine, cross culture communication, virtual exhibitions, and virtual tours. We believe that more and more cultural events will be created within DCSH. We summarize the above points in table 2 in order to deepen the reader's understanding.

After describing the motivation of building DCSH, it is necessary to discuss the guidelines adopted. The guidelines are important concepts that we have to obey in the implementation of DCSH. We focus our attention on four main guidelines, they are, *services-oriented, intelligent, participation-encouraged, government-guided & commercialized.*

The first is *Services-oriented*. It means that DCSH is more than an information provider. In Shanghai, there are already many ISPs that offer information to the public, such as Shanghai Online (http://www.online.sh.cn), Kali (http://www.kali.com.cn), Shanghai Yellow Page (http://www.yp.online.sh.cn), Internet Shanghai (http://www.sh.com), Shanghai News (http://info-po.online.sh.cn). They provide various information on daily living from news, financial to education, health care and so on. DCSH will become a popular website if we provide the same things as these ISPs. Instead, DCSH aims to *integrate* all the websites and largely subsume them by doing far more than just providing information. From September 4 1999 to September 6 1999, the " 72 hour Online Survival " test was performed in Beijing, China. The goal of this test was to find out whether or not there were enough services for online living in the Internet in China. 12 participants were locked in a house with nothing but a PC connected to the outside world. They were required to find ways to survive using the PC and the Internet. The test showed that services for online living are not adequate. This interesting result is very important information for the design and implementation of Digital City Shanghai.

The second is *intelligent*. Artificial intelligence has been studied for more than 40 years and many results have been achieved. AI has been used commercially for more than 10 years. It is important to apply AI technology to DCSH, because almost all the services offered by ISPs in Shanghai are unintelligent at present. Intelligent services will dramatically decrease the time and energy expended by users, and significantly improves the quality of services. Intelligent agents are the most valuable technology that we intend to introduce to DCSH. For example, guide agents introduce DCSH to users; search agents find information, and retrieval agents organize the information gathered; planning agents help users in decision making; shop agents buy and sell on the user's behalf. We believe that AI is not just a toy for academic people but also a valuable technology that might impact the daily life of society. We are confident DCSH will become even more attractive with the use of more and more intelligence.

The third is *participation-encouraged*. DCSH is not just a single server, instead, it is a large-scale distributed system, and is intended to cover almost all activities in Shanghai. This goal is beyond the government and the more active people are, the bigger DSCH will become. We argue that it should be common resident-oriented instead of professional-oriented, in another words, DCSH should be built *by* common residents rather than *for* them. Common residents are encouraged to take part in the design, implementation, maintenance, and development of DSCH. DCSH is open to all the people in Shanghai, even worldwide, and we encourage the universities, research institutes, organizations, industries to join us. By contributing to the system they will benefit from it.

The last is *government-guided & commercialized*. DCSH is not going to be an academic project and so is unlike Digital City Kyoto (http://www.digitalcity.gr.jp). DCSH is also not going to be non-profit website for public communication such as Digital City Amsterdam (http://www.dds.nl). DCSH has to be profitable in order to stimulate the participation of more and more individuals, industries, organizations. Digital City Shanghai will require large investments at the beginning. All the companies, banks, and financial organizations, are encouraged to invest, and they will be rewarded in various ways: advertising, website operators, service providers, and so on. It is unimaginable that such a big system can be adequately implemented without macro-management being provided by the government. At the beginning, the government will establish the backbone of DCSH. Furthermore, the government can also provide support in many ways, such as (1) systematically organizing the information (2) making regulations for operation (3) broadcasting news and (4) making policies to support it. Another reason is that we do not want DCSH to be a system that exists only for profit just like Digital City of AOL (http://www.digitalcity.com). We also hope that there will be many innovative areas in DCSH that deserve study. It is up to the government to organize universities, institutes, and labs in cooperative efforts to find new ideas and new topics.

This finishes the description of our motivations and guidelines, and we'd like to roughly outline Digital City Shanghai in the next section.

3. Skeleton of Digital City Shanghai

William J. Mitchell argued that the net effect of city development is neither the decentralization of everything nor rampant centralization, but a complex process of fragmentation and recombination of familiar building types and urban patterns [3]. We agree with this and made it one of the important concepts in selecting the content of Digital City Shanghai. DCSH is big project and so it is not easy to give deterministic specifications of DSCH content; that is, what should be in, what should not? The following paragraphs roughly outline DCSH content and so provide interesting and valuable information.

Virtual government. Currently, most of the information exchanges between various government offices, for example, between city hall and counties, are handled via telephone, mail, or face-face meetings. Email is not widely used between government offices. We can foresee that virtual government will rapidly improve the speed of information exchange in the real government. Staffs can use email to send and receive information, use Webpages to release news, use chat rooms to discuss events, use video to hold online conferences and so on. We believe that virtual government will reduce the time, space, material, and labor needed to realize government, and will give more opportunities for common citizens to participate in policy discussions.

Virtual banking. E-commerce is very hot in Shanghai now. Whether or not it is feasible largely depends upon the banking system. We believe that most of the banks will be online in the future in Shanghai. By then people will be able to withdraw and deposit cash, and pay bills by credit card wherever they are. Currently, most of these processes must be done in a bank office, so many things must be changed to realize virtual banking.

Virtual enterprises. Some leading corporations, for example, IBM, Motorola, HP are becoming more and more virtual. They do not do everything by themselves, instead, they distribute some of their tasks to partners. This allows them to focus on market promotion, product development and so on. This style of operation makes enterprises more virtual, more global, and more competitive. Shanghai is standing on the starting line in this regard. Although there are already some companies using the Internet to locate partners, realize distant co-operation, and submit orders, they are still far from what we think of as " virtual enterprises". Most of the enterprises in Shanghai do their tasks in traditional ways, even worse, quite a large percentage is still not connected to the Internet. They represent a significant potential market both for enterprises and ISPs. We think that enterprises will become more competitive and energetic after they join DCSH.

Virtual markets. There are already some websites that provide online shopping services, such as Amazon (http://www.amazon.com), Ebay (http://www.ebay.com), BargainFinder: (http://bf.cstar.ac.com/bf), Jango (http://jango.excite.com), AuctionBot (http://auction.eecs.umich.edu), and Yahoo (http://www.yahoo.com). They provide a more efficient way to shop than the traditional method. In Shanghai, there are also some ISPs that provide this kind of service, for instance, Shanghai Online (http://www.online.sh.cn) and Kali (http://www.kali.com.cn). We suppose that most of the real markets in Shanghai will open their own websites in the near future. Furthermore, some new kinds of commerce will arise, for example, there will be online supermarkets that do not have a physical presence, they receive orders from the customers and pass them to the real markets, who deliver the goods to the customers. This can reduce transaction costs greatly. But this is just the beginning and there are many things to do if we are to build virtual markets in Digital City Shanghai.

Digital Library. There are now more than 100 libraries open to the public in Shanghai, including Shanghai Library, which is the largest, and about 30 university libraries. But only Shanghai Library and some of the university libraries are presently online. They provide some online services to users, for instance, online searching and online indexing. These are not enough. There are many new services that can be provided in DCSH, for example, online reading, which means that all the documents in libraries could be accessed and read online just like MSDN (http://msdn.microsoft.com). So there is a big gap between current online libraries and what we think of as digital library. Scott Robertson introduced a Digital City public library project and argued that willingness to share knowledge is one of the most basic changes in culture and technology that can lead to the effective use of an organization information resource [7]. This idea is valuable when implementing digital library in DCSH.

Digital Hospital. Distance medicine has been developed rapidly throughout the world as well as in Shanghai. A distance medicine system was established in ZhongShan hospital in 1998. Up to now, more than 3000 people have used this system for their health care. But this is just the beginning. There are more than 300 hospitals in Shanghai and most of them do not have a website, some are even not connected to the Internet. It is a big task to bring them into the digital hospital. Distance medicine is not the only function of the digital hospital, we can think more functions, for example, online consultation, online operation, and multi-hospital co-operation. DCSH surely will bring better health care to the whole society.

Digital community. Community networks were developed rapidly in Shanghai recently. The government invested much money in building the backbone of the community networks, which connect the subnetworks of nearly 1000 communities in Shanghai. But creating just the backbone is not enough. More important are the services offered to the citizens in the communities such as water supply, energy supply, food supply, emergency services, remote management, inter-community and communication. We can not describe what the digital community is exactly, but we believe the current community network in Shanghai is the first step towards the digital community.

Virtual school. There are almost 3 million students, from elementary schools to universities, and more than 5 million employees need post-school education in

Shanghai. But the 30 universities available are insufficient. A lot of high school students have no chance to enter university, and many employees do not receive post-school education. Virtual school is one feasible and efficient way for solving this problem. Courses can be opened to the public on the Internet and users (students and employees) can learn by themselves. This gives many chances to far more people than is possible with the traditional approach. A distance education system has already been built and has been serving the public in our university since 1998. The next step is to extend it to other universities, colleagues, high schools and elementary schools. We believe that the virtual school is one important part of Digital City Shanghai.

Some of the systems mentioned above are being built now, some are at the planning stage, and some remain just concepts. We encourage the submission of valuable ideas because DCSH is a totally open, distributed system.

4. Reality of Building Digital City Shanghai

The previous sections show that Digital City Shanghai is an ambitious project, and it can not be fully implemented instantaneously. Luckily we are not starting with our hands empty. DCSH does have a solid foundation, the project "InfoPort Shanghai", which was initiated by Municipal Bureau of Economics and Society Information in May 1996. The aim of this project was to build an information backbone for Shanghai. The first stage of "InfoPort Shanghai", which will finished by the end of 1999, already has many achievements. DCSH is to be built upon these achievements and could be regarded as the second stage of "InfoPort Shanghai".

By the end of 1998, there were 9 thousand kilometers of optical cable, 8 million telephones, and 2 million handy telephones in Shanghai. Some parts of Shanghai are already being served by SDH and ATM networks. The number of cable TV users exceeded 10 million and more than 2 thousand databases have been built to provide services to the public. The exact data of 1999 has not been collated yet, but we believe that all metrics will be largely increased. Table 3 shows the data as of the end of 1998.

Besides the infrastructures described above, many networks have also been built and opened to the public. Many companies, organizations, individuals are connecting

Table 3. Data on information infrastructure of Shanghai as of the end of 1998

Item	Value
Optical cables	9000 kilometers
Telephones	8 million
Handy telephones	2 million
Cable TV users	10 million
Databases	2000

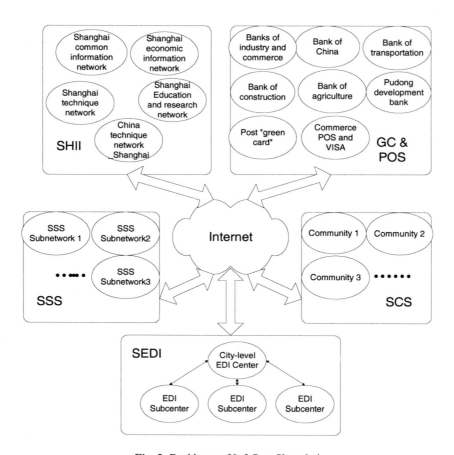

Fig. 2. Backbone of InfoPort Shanghai

to them and provide services to the public via these networks. This is the fundamental that Digital City Shanghai is based on.

The five main networks that construct the backbone of "InfoPort Shanghai" are Shanghai Information Interaction networks (SHII), Shanghai social security network (SSS), Shanghai electronic data exchange network (SEDI), Shanghai community services network (SCS), Shanghai golden card, and POS network (GC & POS).

Shanghai Information Interaction network connects all the information resources in Shanghai and provides an entrance towards the Internet. The first stage has been implemented and was opened to the public at the end of 1996. It now supports 5 systems with more than 1 million users. They are Shanghai Economic Information Network (http://www.sh.cei.gov.cn), Shanghai Common Information Network (http://www.online.sh.cn), Shanghai Technique Network (http://www.stc.sh.cn), China Technique Network_Shanghai (http://www.cnc.ac.cn), Shanghai Education and Research network (http://www.cernet.edu.cn).

Shanghai social security network (SSS) was initiated by the government to support various social insurance schemes. About 20 subnetworks have been implemented to provide services to the public such as endowment insurance, medicine insurance, confinement insurance, unemployment insurance, and injury insurance.

Shanghai electronic data exchange network (SEDI) is being built for the purpose of "trading without paper". It will fill the information gaps that exist among the main trading chains, such as CIQ, check, and shipping. Currently, the city-level EDI center and 3 subcenters have been implemented and it is now being extended to other fields.

Shanghai community services network (SCS) connects all the communities in Shanghai and provides information services to the public such as job searching, homemaking, community culture, and so forth. Currently, 50 percent of the communities in Shanghai are connected to SCS.

Shanghai golden card and POS network (GC & POS) mainly connects financial and commercial organizations and is the backbone of E-commerce in Shanghai. Eight main banks in China are connected to GC & POS. Those are Banks of Industry & Commerce, Bank of China, Bank of Construction, Bank of Transportation, Bank of Agriculture, Pudong Development Bank, Post "Green Card", Commerce POS & VISA. Figure2 shows the backbone of InfoPort Shanghai

DCSH will be implemented on this architecture and extend it step by step, section by section, function by function towards the goal: *integrated information & services environment*.

5. Comparison of Digital City Shanghai with Other Digital Cities

Although Digital City Shanghai is just at the stage of outlining and design conception, it is interesting and significant to compare it with other digital cities. It is better to give a detailed description on the status of current digital cites before we make the comparison. For brevity, we'd use the summarization made by Toru Ishida who divided digital cities into four kinds, which are *vertical market*, *public communication space*, *next generation metropolitan network*, and *social information infrastructure for everyday life*. An example of the first kind is AOL Digital Cites (http://www.digitalcity.com), which aims to collects tourist and shopping information of the corresponding city as well as local advertising opportunities for vertical markets including auto, real estate, employment, and health. The second is Digital City Amsterdam (http://www.dds.nl) which was built as a platform for various community networks and thus particularly focuses on social interaction among citizens. The third is Virtual Helsinki (http://www.hel.fi/infocities/), whose goal is to build the next generation metropolitan network to enable citizens to communicate with each other using live video in both directions: members of a classic car club can cooperate on repairs by using live video transfer. Digital City Kyoto (http://www.digitalcity.gr.jp) is trying to develop a social information infrastructure for urban life (including shopping, business, transportation, education, welfare and so on) [1].

Now we will compare these digital cities using five characteristics: goal, guideline, content, current achievement and organization. The many differences between DCSH and the other digital cities confirm that DCSH has a new style.

We think the outstanding point of DCSH is its goal, which is the integrated information & services environment. This makes DCSH a complicated, distributed system that involves almost all aspects of producing & consuming goods and services in Shanghai.

The other impressive difference is its organization. DCSH is a project that needs large scale cooperation among municipal governments, industries, and academia, while others are supported by specific organisations.

As for current achievements, we have to admit that AOL and Amsterdam are more advanced because they were founded earlier and have been open to the public for more than four years. We have just built a system named "Shanghai tourist information & services" as a pilot project. The experiences of other digital cities are valuable for us in implementing DCSH.

We can also see that Kyoto and Amsterdam are nonprofitable projects while DCSH is for profit just as AOL and Helsinki.

The other differences involve contents and guidelines. It would be counter productive to introduce too much detail and we'd like to move on to the pilot project of DCSH, Shanghai tourist information & services (STIS), which is described in the next section.

6. STIS - Pilot Project of DCSH

6.1 Reasons for Choosing STIS as a Pilot Project

DCSH cannot be implemented at once and must proceed step by step. The reasons for choosing STIS as the pilot project are (1) Geographic information is the basic information of STIS as is true for DCSH. It is offered by STIS now and can be used by DCSH in the future. (2) The information and services offered by STIS to tourists are also very important for the residents, for example, hotels, restaurants, shops, weather, landscapes, and etc. (3) DCSH is the first Digital City in China so we lack experience in both design and operation. We will gain valuable experience in building and operating STIS.

The website of STIS (http://www.tourinfo.sh.cn) was opened to the public on September 7th, 1999 and has been visited more than 20000 times.

STIS is the fruit of international cooperation among local governments, Shanghai Jiaoto University, and Kyoto University.

Tourist Bureau of Shanghai, who is responsible for all tourist events in Shanghai, initiated the project "Shanghai Tourist Information & Services " in March 1999 with a total investment of more than 3 million dollars. Moreover, it was the overall manager during STIS design and implementation. It provided all the tourist information using forms, tables, and pictures. After STIS completion, it became responsible for site maintenance.

CS Department of Shanghai Jiaotong University, which was established over 30 years ago, is responsible for providing STIS with technical support. Its duties includes conception design, detailed design, coding, integrating, testing and further development. More than 30 persons include 3 professors and 6 Ph.D. students contributed to this project. They are divided into three groups and deal with global design, E-commerce development and website building respectively.

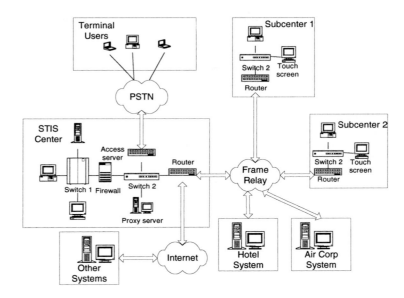

Fig. 3. Architecture of STIS

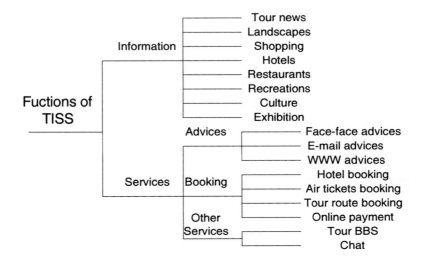

Fig. 4. Functions in STIS

Kyoto University is currently implementing the project Digital City Kyoto, which was initiated in October 1998 together with NTT Openlab. Collaboration started when T. Ishida visited the CS department of Shanghai Jiaotong University in April 1999 and contributed many ideas and suggestions to STIS.

6.2 Architecture of STIS

Figure 3 shows the architecture of STIS. The core of STIS is the STIS Center, which connects to 10 Subcenters (only 2 displayed in Figure 3), Hotel System, Airline System, and some other networks (Restaurant System, Train Corp. System, Shop System, which are not displayed in the Figure) via Frame Relay. Terminal users can access the STIS Center through their PCs or mobile notebooks via PSTN. The STIS Center is also connected to other systems (SCS, SSS, SHII, SEDI, GC&POS, which were described in section 4) via the Internet. Access servers, firewall, proxy, routers are all located in the center. Subcenters are composed of PCs and touchscreens that enable unskilled users to get information easily. Hotels and Airline companies have their own systems that were built to meet their special requirements.

6.3 Functions Description

The functions of STIS can be divided into two main parts, one is information supply and the other is service support. Figure 4 shows both. We mentioned in section 2 that one of the guidelines of DCSH is services-oriented. This was also one important rule we followed in building STIS. Accordingly, we focused our attention on both services and information in STIS.

The information in STIS includes tour news, landscapes, shopping, hotels, restaurants, recreations, cultural events, and exhibitions. Both tourists and residents need these kinds of information and they will be also useful in DCSH later.

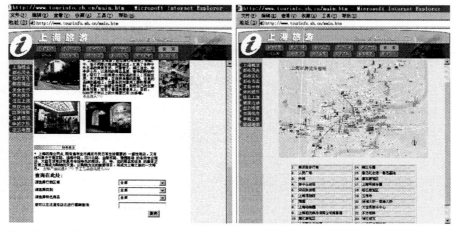

Fig. 5. Menu-based navigation in STIS   **Fig. 6.** Map-based navigation in STIS

STIS currently provides two main services, one is advice and the other is booking. More services will be provided in the future, and will be discussed next.

STIS now offers three kinds of advice services. Face-face advice requires the user to go to the advice center and talk to the staff, E-mail advice is done by the Q&A between users and staff, WWW advice is similar to an online forum. We provide booking services, as one application of E-commerce, because they are needed by almost all hotels, airlines, and restaurants. Moreover, we also provide tour BBS and Chat, which encourage the users to take part in the STIS.

Users can get the services in two ways. One is menu-based, and the other is map-based. In menu-based services, users can select items from menus or input keywords to make a query.

In map-based services, users can click on spots on the map and can navigate across all of Shanghai. Figure 5 and Figure 6 show the two styles of navigation, respectively.

6.4 Further Development

Intelligent is one of the building guidelines of both DCSH and STIS. Currently, all services are unintelligent, but we are planning to introduce intelligence to STIS. For example, advice services require the response of human staff (face-face, E-mail, WWW). We are going to build several advice agents that will mostly replace the staff. This will reduce the labor requirements dramatically and improve the quality of services in STIS. The others are intelligent queries. We are going to add fuzzy queries to help users in finding information more easily.

Table 4. Future services in STIS

Online journey planning	Online amusement park
Online tourist information live broadcast	Online highway tickets booking
Personal email	Online shopping
Online tourist group organization	Tour IC card
Online restaurant seats booking	Oversea tourists assistance
Online trade	Tour sales promotion
Tourist self-organization	Membership services

It is difficult to connect STIS to legacy systems such as hotel computer systems, airline computer systems, and cinema computer systems. Because all these computer systems were built before STIS and it is hard to make STIS totally compatible with them. We are now discussing with the appropriate bodies to find some solution.

The 3D environments in Digital City Kyoto and Virtual Helsinki is not only interesting but also useful. It would allow STIS to offer more services such as emergency control; visual traffic management; disaster simulation; and history recur. Accordingly, we are planning to build a 3D environment for two special spots, Waitan and Yuyuan, which are the most famous places in Shanghai as a start.

Table 4 shows the services we are planning to provide to the public through STIS in the near future. Some are personal services, including personal email, tourist self-organization, and membership services. Some are extensions of current hotel booking systems, online restaurant seat booking systems, and online highway ticket booking systems. Some are the beginning of the virtual market mentioned in section 3, and include online shopping, online trading, tour sales promotion, and tour IC card sales. They represent the early stage of a digital community, say, online amusement park, overseas tourist assistance, online tourist information live broadcasting and online journey planning, which is an excellent example of applying AI techniques.

7. Conclusion

In this paper, we describe Digital City Shanghai and its pilot project: Shanghai Tourist Information & Services. Digital City Shanghai is to be built as an *Integrated Information & Services Environment* for everyday life. It is a big distributed system that aims to bring together all the information systems in Shanghai and extend to provide more services to the public. Shanghai Tourist Information & Service provides two main functions to the public, they are information and services. The experience of building STIS is valuable for us when implement DCSH.

Recently Bureau for Social and Economic Information of Municipal Government initialed ITA 2000, which will be an integration of Exhibition, Workshop and Panel Discussion on Application of Information Technology for Cities Infrastructure. This is a continual event of promotion of digital cities. The information of ITA 2000 will be available soon.

Acknowledgement

Shanghai Jiaotong University and Kyoto University signed an agreement for long-term cooperation in September 1998. The dispatch of exchange students between them started in April 1999. This gives us the chance to take part in both the projects, STIS and Digital City Kyoto.

Many people have and are contributing to the STIS in the government, in Shanghai Jiaotong University, and other participating organizations. All these participants are creating new ideas, discussing, developing, and finally implementing STIS.

We'd like to give our special thanks to Ph.D. Wangzhaodong for his generosity in supplying documents on STIS. We also want to thank Ph.D. Zhaoyuyuan for his assistance in locating a lot of valuable material on the SHII.

Reference

1. T. Ishida, "Understanding Digital Cities,"Lecture Notes in Computer Science (in this volume), Springer-Verlag, 2000.
2. T. Ishida, J. Akahani, K. Hiramatsu, K. Isbister, S. Lisowski, H. Nakanishi, M. Okamoto, Y. Miyazaki, K. Tsutsuguchi, "Digital City Kyoto: Towards A Social Information Infrastructure,"M. Klusch, O. Shehory, G. Weiss (Eds.), *Cooperative Information Agents III*, Lecture Notes in Artificial Intelligence, Vol. 1652, pp. 23-35, Springer-Verlag, 1999.

3. W. J. Mitchell, "Designing the Digital City," Lecture Notes in Computer Science (in this volume), Springer-Verlag, 2000.
4. P. Van den Besselar and D. Beckers, "Demographics and Sociographics of the Digital City," Ishida (Eds.), *Community Computing and Support Systems*, Lecture Notes in Computer Science, Vol. 1519, pp. 109-125, Springer-Verlag, 1998.
5. Wangzhaodong, "Designing Report on Shanghai Tourist Information & Services," 1999.
6. K. Isbister, "A Warm Cyber-Welcome: Using an Agent-led Group Tour to Introduce Visitors to Kyoto," Lecture Notes in Computer Science (in this volume), Springer-Verlag, 2000.
7. S. Robertson,"The Digital City's Public Library: Support for Community Building and Knowledge Sharing," Lecture Notes in Computer Science (in this volume), Springer-Verlag, 2000.
8. T. Ishida Ed., *Community Computing: Collaboration over Global Information Networks*, John Wiley and Sons, 1998.
9. R. Linture, M. R. Koivunen and J. Sulkanen,"Helsinki Arena 2000: Augmenting a Real City to a Virtual One," Lecture Notes in Computer Science (in this volume), Springer-Verlag, 2000.

Experiments in the Digital 'Engineering City Oulu'

Lech Krzanik[1,2] and Minna Mäkäräinen[3]

[1]Universtity of Oulu, Department of Information Processing Science,
Linnanmaa, Box 3000, FIN-90401 Oulu, Finland,
Lech.Krzanik@oulu.fi
[2]CCC Software Professionals, Oulunsalo, Finland
[3]Nokia Mobile Phones, Oulu, Finland
Minna.Makarainen@nokia.com

Abstract. The paper outlines results of feasibility experiments with new functions for a local version of the digital city, performed under a collective name 'Engineering City Oulu' (ECO). We investigated design and implementation options supporting engineering services in the digital city. The options were oriented towards local needs and potentials of the Oulu economic area. Many technologies can be used to support user interaction in digital city systems, such as 3-d imaging, on-line sensory data, culture-sensitive instruction, etc. We focused on supporting engineering - a fundamental activity of real city users. In the experiments we emphasised conditions for active participation of users ('digital citizens') in the community decision making. A broad classification of engineering support in digital cities is introduced followed by motivation of the feasibility studies. Then the requirements for an innovative digital city are discussed. The main feasibility results are then presented including a selection of basic engineering models and an outline of the experiments new software, applicable in digital cities.

1 Introduction

The paper outlines results of feasibility experiments with new functions for a local version of the digital city, performed under a collective name 'Engineering City Oulu' (ECO). We investigated design and implementation options supporting engineering services in the digital city. The options were oriented towards local needs and potentials of the Oulu economic area. Many technologies can be used to support user interaction in digital city systems, such as 3-d imaging, on-line sensory data, culture-sensitive instruction, etc. We focused on supporting engineering - a fundamental activity of real city users. In the experiments we emphasised conditions for active participation of users ('digital citizens') in the community decision making.

Oulu is a growing high-tech city and a centre of industry in Finland with good flight connections. It has a large concentration of telecommunication software companies. Finland has an excellent telecommunication infrastructure and the highest density of mobile phones as well as Internet servers and connections in the world. Oulu is close to the Arctic Circle. The beautiful nature of the vast wilderness of Lapland is within an easy reach from Oulu. The Oulu economic area embraces the area of about 1000 square kilometres and has approximately 200 000 inhabitants. Lapland is known, among other reasons, as being the residence place of Santa Claus.

T. Ishida, K. Isbister (Eds.): Digital Cities, LNCS 1765, pp. 140-150, 2000.

In Section 2, following the ways of how the engineering services of digital cities are budgeted, we distinguish public sector engineering and industrial engineering. Public sector engineering refers to participation of citizens in such activities as designing road network, schools, bus lines and schedules, determining paths through a park, scheduling the service in a local church, setting priorities in subsidising cultural events, etc. The other type of engineering services is a representation of industrial engineering. While also having an important role in community integration and development, it will generally be associated with operation and development of local industry, and will refer to industrial projects which have major local impacts in terms of production quality, employment, creating new companies, building high-tech infrastructure, development of business co-operation, etc. In Section 3 we provide more details regarding the motivation of the feasibility investigations outlined in this paper. In ECO we'd like to extend the co-operation layer of the digital city with flexible planning and engineering functions. Our intention is to further increase the number of 'digital citizens' by making the digital city even more attractive and fulfilling users' expectations regarding co-operation, planning and engineering. In Section 4 we give a more detailed account of the requirements for an innovative digital city. Section 5 presents a selection of basic engineering models and Section 6 outlines the experiments with new software, potentially applicable in digital cities.

2   Ubiquitous Engineering

Engineering [8, 7, 4] consists in iterative development of solutions that satisfy a set of stated goals, under uncertainty, within constraints, with the application of heuristic selection rules and optimisations. It is a co-operative activity, usually involving many participants. It is based on experience and reusing previous solutions in related contexts. Engineering is performed as professional activity, as well as in everyday life. In a sense, everybody is an expert in some types of everyday engineering in some contexts. We engineer our work place, our holidays, etc. Engineering activities are applicable to diverse domains such as industrial engineering, education, medical services, entertainment (e.g., selecting a type of entertainment of interest), etc. All that motivates the introduction of engineering into the set of common digital city services. Engineering is an important part of every (real) city responsibilities. The citizen involvement and support has the potential of improving the quality of city decisions. The citizen-participative approach to the city's engineering decisions integrates the people with their local community.

The engineering method can be defined as 'the use of heuristics to cause the best change in a poorly understood situation within the available resources' [8]. Heuristics are hints or rules of thumb in seeking a solution to a problem. To control risks several heuristics may be proposed [8]: (a) Make only small change in what has worked in the past. (b) Arrange matters so that if they are wrong they can retreat. (c) Arrange matters so that they feed back past results in order to improve future performance. An important aspect of the engineering activity is the multidimensional nature of the performance criteria used for measuring the results and articulating fundamental values that can lead to the identification of decision opportunities and the creation of better alternatives [7].

Fig. 1. Samples of current Oulu city pages (by courtesy of City of Oulu, Computer Services Centre).

Two types of engineering can be considered in connection with a digital city: public sector engineering and industrial engineering. The distinction is important from the viewpoint of budgeting the development and operation of the engineering support.

For public sector engineering, the engineering activity is connected with basic functions of the real city and the respective resources may be controlled by the city itself. The access to this type of engineering support may be connected with common services such as local communication schedules. This type of engineering directly supports community integration and development. Public sector engineering refers to participation of citizens in such activities as designing the road network, schools, bus lines and schedules, determining paths through a park, scheduling the service in a local church, setting priorities in subsidising cultural events, etc. Public sector engineering is an on demand and interactive process. It offers communication with city decision makers and access to the current projects. User participation may be reduced to simple voting, but may also be associated with a deeper analysis of the design criteria, delivery priorities, and candidate solutions. Specialised agents may support consistency of the engineering contribution, and determine the segment of the citizen population from which the contribution came. A set of incentives should be considered in connection with public sector engineering. A sufficient incentive may be the ability to check and validate available options, to propose a new solution and receive follow-up information about the engineering project. A web page may offer a presentation of the criteria used and of the baseline currently in force, as well as an interactive summary reports of engineering results so far. User options can be interactively evaluated for impact, constraints, and consistency with other proposals. Interested users may participate in tuning the engineering process. Some users may wish to use a dedicated engineering language connected with more detailed specification of the solutions.

The other type of engineering applicable to digital cities is a public representation of industrial engineering. While also having a major role in community integration and development, it will generally be more associated with local industry. It may refer to industrial projects with local impacts in terms of production quality, employment, creating new companies, building high-tech infrastructure, development of business co-operation, etc. The engineering services available through a digital city will likely be an external representation of the industrial projects that may also participate in budgeting the respective digital city functions. The access can be encouraged through customer information services, new positions pages, etc.

3   Extending a Digital City to Cover for Engineering Services

To illustrate certain common issues with extending a digital city to cover for engineering services let's take a broader, virtual community view.

A virtual community is a community of individuals sharing interest in a similar topic, with common location in cyberspace – and not necessarily the common physical location [12]. The same concept is sometimes referred to as online community to emphasise the fact that the interacting individuals are real rather than virtual, and only the interaction occurs online. The online medium is expected to perform two groups of functions. One group of functions addresses capturing and presentation of exchanged information. It presents the engineering processes and artefacts from many perspectives. The multiple perspectives are tuned to the needs of various users. The other group of functions addresses the co-operation of the virtual community members on a wider scale. That group of functions also enables the resources of the community to be consistently viewed as a single logical entity by its users. There are design and implementation tradeoffs between these two groups of functions, for example in terms of the number of supported users versus the required user qualifications to co-operate within the technical framework provided by the media. Therefore solutions addressing wide user groups, such as a digital city, tend to focus on simple models of user co-operation. Solutions supporting refined co-operation models tend to restrict their membership. The membership and co-operation structures of virtual communities may vary from open forms as in the digital city to restricted forms as in a virtual organisation [12, 6, 11]. To demonstrate these tradeoffs let's compare two virtual community solutions: a digital city [5] and the Virtual Reengineering Community [17].

A digital city is a type of virtual community which supports the concept of 'an arena in which people in regional communities can interact and share knowledge, experience, and mutual interests' [5]. For example, the system architecture proposed for a digital city in [5] consists of three design layers. The first layer called the information layer integrates and reorganises WWW archives and real-time sensory data. Next, the interface layer provides an intuitive view of a digital city with 2D maps, 3D graphics and animations. Finally, the third layer called the interaction layer supports social interaction among residents and tourists. The co-operation functions involved in the third layer include, for example, newsgroups, email lists, bulletin boards, a digital bus tour for foreign visitors of the digital city, a helper character facilitating cross-cultural communication in digital cities.

The offered co-operation services are selected to support a large number of potential users. The size of the digital city population is a critical success factor. To illustrate possible effects of embedding more advanced engineering support in a digital city let's consider the Virtual Reengineering Community (VRC) introduced by the Software Engineering Institute [17]. VRC focuses on reengineering that offers an approach to 'migrating a legacy system towards an evolvable system in a disciplined manner. (...) At a high level, reengineering may be viewed as applying engineering principles to an existing system in order for it to meet new requirements' [17]. VRC distinguishes three categories of users and corresponding virtual community functions. The first category accessing the VRC web site are people who are interested in basic information about legacy system reengineering. The second category is made of practitioners who want to find out more about the tools and techniques available for their reengineering projects. The function geared to their needs is the "guide to the current practice". The third category of users are researchers active in legacy system reengineering. According to [17], 'It is this group of people that form the VRC. One might argue that anyone interested in reengineering may be legitimately considered part of the VRC, but we have chosen to form the VRC out of people doing active research in the field, keeping in mind the dual goal of facilitating technology transfer and fostering global research partnership.' Among the co-operative functions considered for the third category are the following: creation of a common intermediate data representation and tools for extraction of that representation, co-ordination of the respective work, providing an agreed-upon lexicon of terminology, providing independent evaluation of reengineering tools, classification of the research being carried out by the members of the VRC and fostering research partnerships between members of the VRC.

As can be seen from this example, the access to the co-operation layer of VRC is granted at the cost of restricting the number of users. Most likely if we added to the digital city services as advanced as in VRC, the membership would likewise decrease considerably. In ECO we'd like to extend the co-operation layer of the digital city with flexible planning and engineering functions without sacrificing the number of users. That is a foreground objective of our feasibility investigations. Our intention is to further increase the number of 'digital citizens' by making the digital city even more attractive and fulfilling users' expectations regarding co-operation and engineering.

There's a number of examples of digital cities with extended planning function. They are mostly oriented toward visual modelling. For example, the Virtual Los Angeles project [2] facilitated the city's rebuilding efforts by helping neighbourhoods envision redevelopment projects. The application gave individuals the potential to interact with each other in planning their own community. In our experiments we investigate opportunities for comparing many solutions not only visually, but also with a selection of multidimensional success factors.

4   Requirements for an Innovative Digital City

Oulu has a number of digital city services, some are demonstrated in Figure 1. We'd like to extend these services by providing more co-operative and dynamic view that would represent the changing nature of the real city and contribute to integrating the community. We intend to stress such issues as community networking, social interaction, and a user-participative approach to the digital city.

Apart from the foreground objective of extending the co-operation layer of the digital city with flexible planning and engineering functions without sacrificing the number of users, there are a number of other important goals that we considered. We were looking for a generic and tailorable engineering support suitable for a broad spectrum of various engineering problems in the digital city. In particular, we are looking for support for co-operative development of engineering specifications, evaluations and solutions. The generic model of the engineering process should be conceptually simple and accessible to most of the users.

The access to these features should be based on the use of common technical platforms and browsers. There should be an easy interface to existing tools that might support various aspects of engineering. The model should provide an integrated flexible view of the engineering method. We look for a generic engineering process that is consistent with current conventional digital citizen behaviour. We intend to give the user a dynamic view of the city, with the support for specifying, planning and evaluating changes to the city. The city decision-making should be a co-operative activity, with the subprocesses of the engineering process performed collectively, but at the same time suitably decomposed to be performed separately. The results should be reusable whenever possible.

There should be an option for small target devices such as communicators. The conceptual simplicity of the approach should support relatively easy implementation of respective versions for such devices. There should be an option for limited graphics. Numeric representation of engineering data should be widely available.

There are new challenges connected with implementing support for engineering activity in digital cities. Unlike in conventional digital city systems which are primarily a one-way medium for disseminating information, new approaches involve interaction among the stakeholders. The challenges include navigation structures designed to support specific work flow (the way in which the digital city is visited), a structured data model representing relationships among pieces of information, features that enable the users to process engineering data interactively, and support for distributed collaboration work style. We are also facing challenges and opportunities connected with global information exchange and design collaboration, and with personalised services.

5   Basic Models

The two models outlined in this section provided a basic reference for the examined implementations. The models are flexible and simple enough to fulfil the stated requirements.

Table 1. Subprocesses of the engineering process.

A	Need specification
B	Design specification, impact estimation, solution evaluation and selection
C	Media quality control
D	Evolutionary results delivery management
E	Engineering process tuning
F	Support of a specialised engineering language

The engineering process. Table 1 shows main subprocesses of the engineering process [3, 7]. The model that is general enough for various engineering applications. The subprocesses may proceed sequentially or in parallel. The digital city application should assure proper interaction with all of the subprocesses. Some application areas may skip or reformulate selected elements of the generic processA digital city application which includes engineering as one of its methods for community networking should take care about the correctness of the applied engineering process. . An engineering approach suitable in one context may not work in another context. It may be necessary to analyse all the subbprocesses to check whether the objectives are clearly stated, the solutions are consistent with the criteria, that the process is evolutionary, that reuse of components is supported by the necessary evidence of reusability, that a co-operative approach to engineering is supported involving an adequate representation of the stakeholders, etc. Often the interaction may result in a voting solution with system responses as in Figure 2. Media quality control can be implemented as a formal inspection process similar to one known from document quality control [4]. The process checks the quality of both the structure and the contents of media accessed by the user in the engineering process. The purpose of the evolutionary results delivery management is to offer an alternative way of working in projects where new or unsure results are expected. The engineering process tuning thread allows the user to customise the generic process model. Some processes may use a specialised engineering language that may have the capability of integrating all the subprocesses.

Generic requirements, personalised	Current baseline	Summary of all proposals (votes) since baseline	Impact of this proposal (vote): – individually – together with all proposals (votes) since baseline

Fig. 2. Frequent types of information provided by interactive city engineering support.

The digital citizen decision process. Not much is known about the particular behaviour of a digital city user - a 'digital citizen', especially with an innovative engineering services provided. Therefore for our purposes we exploited a, general

Table 2. Steps of the 'digital citizen' decision process.

Id	Step	User roles	Digital city roles
1	Need recognition	Users have to recognise a need to be satisfied through a digital city interaction.	Digital city provides advertising that supports generating the need. This include advertising on other web sites, URL publication, submitting to newsgroups, agents and event notification.
2	Reviewing information	Users search for criteria and solutions that satisfy the need.	Digital city provides a criteria and solution handbook. Digital city offers specialised directories and classifiers, search engines, information brokers, virtual catalogues, internal search and brokers on web site, links to external resources, discussion in newsgroups.
3	Analysis and evaluation	Users analyse, evaluate and compare solutions.	Digital city offers evaluation support, tuning the generic engineering models, provides help and explanation facilities. FAQs, summaries, references to related implementations.
4	Engineering transaction	Users commit a particular solution decision, and possibly agree on a particular way of being informed about the results.	Digital city provides facilities for solution specification, voting, etc. Specialised solution configuration managers (agents) facilitate decision statement.
5	Follow-up	Users get information about the state of the decision and engineering processes, evaluate delivered solutions.	Digital city supplies information about the state of the decision process, then about the final decision, and about the state of the engineering process. Provides citizen support and maintenance where applicable.

enough, user decision process demonstrated in [10] in connection with electronic commerce customer decision support systems. We included certain modifications. The outcome is presented in Table 2. We noticed that more active involvement of users in digital city activities introduces an element of transaction common to the electronic commerce domain. Apart from considerable similarities (for example, in the steps of Need recognition and Reviewing information), there is a number of important differences. For example, there is a more extensive and objective role of the digital city in Analysis and evaluation, Engineering transaction, and Follow-up. The Engineering transaction step consists in committing to certain selected solutions, rather than in purchasing. In Follow-up, extensive decision-making activity may take place before the actual implementation of the solutions starts. Perhaps the most important difference is that a digital city has more responsibility in providing the background information and models, preferably personalised, regarding the engineering process.

6   Examining Software Solutions

We conducted a number experiments using new software solutions. The main goal was to provide support for engineering in digital cities, and to assure accessibility, simplicity, and ease of use. The approaches presented below gradually move towards more complex solutions, however each time we try to capitalise on commonalties and provide a very flexible and usable generic solution. The solutions are, in turn: common data representation for the engineering process in a digital city, change management support, more advanced cases such as product line engineering. The experiments confirmed feasibility of the approach and the particular software solutions for engineering services in digital cities.

Common data representation for the engineering process. We looked for a feasible data representation for the engineering process. The feasibility was determined based on simplicity and flexibility of the representation that could be used to exchange information about the engineering activities and artefacts between different co-operating users. We required availability of suitable tools to generate data and to present results from the representation. Common accessibility of the tools was required. It was also required that the same representation could be relatively easy used with many third party tools possibly used in the engineering process.

The solution that we investigated [15] was an XML/XSL representation. The XSL specifications can be used with common browsers. A dedicated web site was established on which we provided XSL style sheets for various proposed standards to be used with a variety of engineering process types.

The experiments confirmed the usefulness of the XML/XSL approach. We had however to develop a non-conventional XML/XSL viewer, to work with a usual browser. The viewer displayed engineering data in a tabular form that constituted an easy and very flexible user interface. Ongoing developments investigate feasibility of the approach for portable devices. With this approach engineering data can be exchanged with any XML-sensitive tool thus providing the necessary data interoperability.

Change management. Change management is a fundamental type of engineering in usual digital city problems. It adds dynamics to digital city data through specification, designing and evaluation of changes. We looked for a generic change management process implementation that would provide the required flexibility, suitable for many practical instances of the engineering process.

Among the investigated solutions most promising was the approach that used separate specifications of the engineering process, change process, requirements traceability, and multidimensional numeric criteria to be used for evaluating changes and selecting change options [16].

The experiments proved the usefulness of the approach The numerical approach to change evaluation is suitable for web browsers of limited functionality. One problem that was solved only partially. It regarded complexity of possible change management models. While much of the results generated for test problems could be successfully presented with the XML/XSL viewer mentioned above, the processing of more complex engineering models had to be allocated to the advanced, dedicated SACHER change management tools [14] (the viewer handled the simple cases, e.g. worst-case impacts). It has been however confirmed that for simple cases, which are most important for the digital city applications, the XML/XSL viewer alone was an appropriate solution.

Other experiments. Other experiments have been started regarding product line engineering. The real city is a complex system with interrelated resource, activity, and artefact assets. To represent the real city problems in a digital city engineering environment one needs to share not only criteria and process/product *models* (e.g., as discussed above in the change management case), but also the available assets, including components and partial as well as final solutions. A product line is defined as a group of artefacts sharing a common, managed set of features that satisfy specific needs of a selected market or mission [1]. Product line practice is the systematic use of composable assets to modify, assemble, instantiate, or generate the multiple products that constitute a product line (a product line is built as a product family). Product line practice involves strategic, large-grained reuse as a way to generate engineering solutions. When dealing with large systems like real city, it is often most economical to engineer the solutions as a group of systems built from a common set of assets. We looked for a generic product line approach suitable for engineering services in digital cities, particularly for cases of industrial engineering.

The investigation included introductory tests with component-oriented versions of the change management approach discussed above. We avoided excessive complexity by careful decomposition of the models and introducing various types of quality control implemented as inspections of intermediate and final artefacts. The approach allowed the user to divide the engineering problem into two stages: asset engineering and solution engineering. Furthermore, the stages were decomposed into different architecture/construction phases: first the selection of architecture, which addressed the structure of solution and capitalised on commonalties, and then derivation of the solution by reusing from the available assets. By introducing a feature-based approach we managed to maintain end-user-orientation of the whole process. The approach was initially tested with an engineering problem regarding local GSM services [9].

The product line engineering case and other, more advanced cases have to be further investigated to obtain more substantial conclusions and implementation advice. The feature-based approach proved to be particularly useful.

7   Conclusion

Engineering is an important aspect of many domains of a real city life, with the potential of improving community networking and social interaction. If a digital city intends to map the fundamental services of a real city then engineering is a foreground activity to be supported. In ECO we started to investigate diverse aspects of introducing engineering to a digital city, with very promising initial results. Public sector engineering decisions, directly supported by the wider public, increase the citizen-participative style of the community and improve the community decisions. The support of selected types of industrial engineering, apart from other benefits, is expected to improve the operation of the community in terms of long term criteria such as employment or creation of new companies.

Acknowledgement

We wish to thank members of the related projects SACHER and MONICA for helpful discussions and for providing software used in the feasibility experiments. We also thank City of Oulu, Computer Services Centre, for providing digital city information.

References

[1] Bass, L., et al., *Second Product Line Practice Workshop Report*, CMU/SEI-98-TR-015. SEI, Pittsburgh, 1998.
[2] Chan, R., W. Jepson, and S. Friedman, Urban simulation: An innovative tool for interactive planning and consensus building. *Proc. 1998 APA National Conference, Boston, MA,* American Planning Association, 1998.
[3] Gilb, T., *Principles of Software Engineering Management.* Addison Wesley Publishing Company, 1988.
[4] Gilb, T., and D. Graham, *Software Inspection.* Addison Wesley Publishing Company, 1994.
[5] Ishida, T., et al., Digital city Kyoto: Towards a social information infrastructure. *Cooperative Information Agents III,* M. Klusch et al., Eds., LNAI 1652, Springer, Berlin, 1999.
[6] Ishida, T., Ed., *Community Computing and Support Systems.* LNCS 1519, Springer, Berlin, 1998.
[7] Keeney, R.L., *Value-Focused Thinking*, Harvard University Press, Cambridge, Mass.,1992.
[8] Koen, B.V., Toward a definition of the engineering method. *Proc.14th Conf. Frontiers in Education, Philadelphia, PA,* IEEE Press, 1984.
[9] Feature-driven concurrent product line engineering, *MONICA Report.* 1999, to appear.
[10] O'Keefe, R.M., and T. McEachern, Web-based customer decision support systems. *Comm. ACM,* Vol.41, Nr 3, March 1998.
[11] Pallot, M., and V.Sandoval, *Concurrent Enterprising: Toward the Concurrent Enterprise in the Era of the Internet and Electronic Commerce.* Kluwer Academic Publishers, 1998.
[12] Rheingold, H., *The Virtual Community.* Addison-Wesley, Reading, MA, 1993.
[13] Rummler, G.A., and A.P. Brache, *Improving Performance: How to Manage the White Space on the Organisation Chart.* Jossey-Bass Publishers, San Francisco, 1995.
[14] SACHER: Sensitivity analysis and change management support for evolving requirements. Project Programme. SACHER Consortium, Milan, 1998.
[15] XML/XSL data representation for change management. *SACHER Application Note 11.* SACHER Consortium, Oulu, 1999.
[16] Representing change management as a generic engineering process. *SACHER Application Note 12.* SACHER Consortium, Oulu, 1999.
[17] Tilley, S.R., and D.B. Smith, Documenting virtual communities. *Proc. SIGDOC96,* IEEE Press, 1996.

Reconfiguring Community Networks:
The Case of PrairieKNOW[1]

Noshir Contractor & Ann Peterson Bishop

244 Lincoln Hall
702 South Wright Street
Department of Speech Communication
University of Illinois at Urbana Champaign
Urbana IL 61801
USA
nosh@uiuc.edu

203 LIS Building
501 East Daniel Street
Graduate School of Library & Information Science
University of Illinois at Urbana Champaign
Champaign IL 61820
USA
abishop@uiuc.edu

Abstract. The advent of the Web has renewed interest in the use of information and communication technologies to support not only virtual communities but also traditional communities. This paper observes that the majority of successful applications to date tend to use technologies to substitute for and/or enlarge existing community interactions and transactions. We argue that this trend, unfortunately, deepens the digital divide between those who have social and knowledge capital and those who don't. In order to improve the conditions of low-income residents, there is a need to deploy tools that help to reconfigure rather than simply substitute or enlarge existing community interactions. This paper describes the methodology of asset mapping and the development and deployment of a tool called PrairieKNOW (Prairie Knowledge Networks On the Web) in Champaign-Urbana, Illinois' Prairienet community network. While Champaign-Urbana was ranked by *Newsweek* magazine as one of the ten most wired cities in the world, it also has a substantial low-income population that has traditionally been under-represented in their use of Prairienet.

---

[1] The conceptual development of IKNOW (Inquiring Knowledge Networks On the Web), of which PrairieKNOW is a derivative, was conducted as part of a research project funded by the National Science Foundation (ECS-9422730). PrairieKNOW's development and integration with Prairienet is also supported through the Community Networking Initiative (CNI), funded by the Telecommunications and Information Infrastructure Assistance Program (TIIAP) in the U.S. Department of Commerce and by the W.K. Kellogg Foundation. CNI is a joint effort of Prairienet, the Graduate School of Library and Information Science at the University of Illinois, and the Urban League of Champaign County. Karen Fletcher and Pamela Salela were especially valuable in developing the asset mapping concept for Prairienet. Prairienet's pilot asset mapping database was implemented by Andrea Ingram, with assistance from Denise DeBrock The database was implemented in PrairieKNOW by Dan Zink, Dana Serb, and Peter Taylor.

T. Ishida, K. Isbister (Eds.): Digital Cities, LNCS 1765, pp. 151-164, 2000.
© Springer-Verlag Berlin Heidelberg 2000

Introduction

Communities are social systems that enable actors (individuals, groups, and organizations) to communicate, to share resources, and to participate in efforts to address their needs collectively. Moreover Cohen and Axelrod (1998) note, membership in a logical category is not a sufficient condition to describe a community. Actors must also share common commitments. These commitments may be based on shared interests (e.g., those interested in economic revitalization), diverse but complementary interests (e.g., health care, childcare, education), or constructively antagonistic interests (providers and consumers of goods and services). When such communities share a common environment (where they work or live) they are also referred to as communities of practice or local communities (Koch, Rancati, Grasso, & Snowdon, 1999).

There has been considerable discussion about the implications of terms used to describe these communities of practice and interest especially when they are mediated by computing and communications technologies. In their description of the De Digitale Stad (DDS) project in Amsterdam, Van den Besselaar and Beckers (1998) describe their network as a Digital City, which is simultaneously similar to and different from a local or topical community network. "The DDS does not see itself as a local community network, because the scope of the Digital City is much larger – the content is not restricted to the Amsterdam region, and the services available for everybody who wants to register. ... The DDS is also not a topical community network, as it covers a large number of different topics" (Besselaar & Beckers, 1998, p. 113). Using the metaphor of a "city" carries with it connotations from traditional cities. "As in a real city, the Digital City supports highly diverse activities and attracts people from many places outside" (Besselaar & Beckers, 1998, p. 113). However, the metaphor also carries the negative connotations associated with the economic plight of the "inner city" neighborhoods and the flight to the suburbs (Wolpert, 1999). Indeed, Shaw and Shaw (1999, p. 317) reinforce some of these concerns when they yearn for a more pastoral characterization of the community as a "village": "Of the place where everybody knows each other's name, and where people are often working with their neighbors on projects to improve their community. Many people are yearning for that kind of world to return. ... This is the notion of a village or at least is the ideal of the village." Of course, the village metaphor also has its dark side "where many neighbors have only time, information or small amounts of food to offer others – the informal flow of resources decreases when it comes to items such as skilled work, material resources, or cash" (Espinoza, 1999, p. 156).

In addition to these multiple connotations, terms such as cities and villages suggest a geographical area comprised of neighborhoods. Wellman (1999, p. xii) cautions that communities must not be equated with neighborhoods: "Communities are about social relationships, while neighborhoods are about boundaries." Hence, Wellman (1999) argues, communities are more usefully defined not in terms of space or neighborhoods, but in terms of social networks (see also Chaskin, 1997).

. Castells (1996) extends the argument in his vision of a network society. The actors in these networks may be individuals, groups, associations, and/or organizations. The relationships among these actors include the flow of symbolic resources (such as communication, advice, social support, expertise), material resources (products and goods), or monetary resources (Monge & Contractor, in press). The network metaphor also dovetails well with the underlying technological infrastructure of community computing networks, though Agre (1999) points to the inherent tension between the concepts of "community" and "network" in this context.

Technologies and Community Networks

Historically, the advent of new communication technologies – the telephone, radio, television, and the Internet being recent examples - have been accompanied by considerable prognostications about their social impacts as "the ultimate transformer" for better or for worse. Utopians have waxed eloquent about the technology serving as an unalloyed blessing for the enhancement of community, while dystopians have characterized the technology as an unmitigated curse that will destroy community (Rochlin, 1997). However, the benefits of hindsight have given us an opportunity to examine historically the transient and long-term impacts of communication technologies on the fabric of communities. Scholars (e.g., Fischer, 1992; Malone & Rockart, 1991; Sproull & Kiesler, 1991) have gleaned a consistent pattern from these historical analyses. Our use of communication technologies goes through three stages: *substitution, enlargement,* and *reconfiguration.* In the first stage, *substitution,* the communication technology is adopted to accomplish the very same communication tasks we had done previously – albeit faster, cheaper, and perhaps more accurately. The reasons for an initial substitution effect can be found in studies that have shown that there are five factors which determine our likelihood to adopt an innovation (Rogers, 1983): (i) relative advantage of the innovation over an older product (or service), (ii) compatibility of the innovation with previous products (or services), (iii) observability of the benefits of the innovation, (iv) trialibility of the new innovation, and (v) adaptability of the new innovation. All of these factors are closely tied to the relationship the innovation has with previous ways of accomplishing a certain task. Hence it follows that for a new technology to be successfully adopted, it is at first considered as substitute for existing tasks. However, the benefits of substitution are often not sufficient to offset the investments in the technology, the training, and other sunk costs. Hence the ability of the technology to serve as an effective substitute and the need to recover the initial investment, leads to an increase in use of the technology, thereby ushering in the second phase – *enlargement.* Enlargement typically manifests itself in an increased use of the technology to sustain ongoing interactions, rather than to create new links. For instance, Fischer's (1992) social history of the telephone until 1940 illustrates how Northern California communities adopted and adapted the telephone to enhance, rather than broaden, their existing social networks. Thus enlargement serves to deepen rather than broaden existing communication network patterns. While substitution and enlargement are important milestones in the adoption of a communication technology, their impacts on society are only transient. The more enduring impacts of the technology are evidenced when the technology is used to *reconfigure* social practices. The use of new computing and communication technologies to support communities appears to be tracking this three-stage evolution pattern.

The first landmark event in the wide-scale deployment of community computing networks in the US was the creation of FreeNets. Free-Nets are "loosely organized community-based, volunteer-managed electronic network servers." (Victoria Free-Net Association 1994). They provide free dial-up access to the Internet and information about the local community (Beamish, 1999). The major impetus of FreeNets was the recognition that in order to harness the benefits of community computing networks, as a first step, the public needed low-cost (or no-cost) access to the network. Free-Nets belong to the National Public Telecomputing Network (NPTN), a nonprofit corporation established in 1989 to disseminate software and methodology for establishing community networks. It filed for bankruptcy in the fall of 1996.

The access framework continues to be an influential design imperative for community networks (Mitchell, 1999). The early notion of access (in terms of free dial-up to the servers) has now been broadened to include public access centers where hardware, software, and technical support are offered to neighborhood residents (Beamish, 1999). Further, there has also been an attempt to provide content that would motivate the use of the technology, especially by low-income groups. In particular, computer-based community networks (CNs) are not-for-profit institutions that typically provide online community information, Internet services, and user support to local residents and organizations (Beamish, 1995; Schuler, 1996). At their most vibrant, community networks develop and distribute tools such as software and computers; identify and encourage participation from community groups; provide training about use of tools and provision of information; foster a rich information space that includes email, listservs, and newsgroups; link real and virtual communities through social and information-sharing gatherings; and establish public access terminals in comfortable, neutral settings (Martin, 1997).

However, Beamish (1999, p. 363) concludes that "in spite of their rhetoric, far too many projects have been unable to go beyond the broadcast model and still see their target group as consumers rather than as producers of information. Too many ignore the capacity of the technology to support communication. And even sites that emphasize information over communication are unable to maintain a high standard of updated information." Beamish's observations underscore the notion that the early use of community networks appears to be based on (i) a failed broadcast "publishing" model, as a *substitute* for traditional media like radio, TV or the newspapers and (ii) an untapped communication model as a *substitute* for the telephone, letters, or face to face conversations.

Notwithstanding the limited success of community networks to serve low-income residents, the advent of the Web has triggered several community applications in other segments of society. There have been several successful demonstrations using the Web to support community activities such as the following: (i) online interaction starting with the well-documented success of the WELL (Rheingold, 1993); (ii) access to public information repositories; (iii) access to real time information (such as highway traffic); (iv) public information kiosks (for instance, Geokiosks in a Paris suburb that citizens can use to find the local dentist); and (v) public participation and discussion in political events, such as the Internet Voices Project to support deliberative discussion for the 1999 mayoral elections in Philadelphia (see http://internetvoices.asc.upenn.edu/). In parallel, and often in competition with grassroots community initiatives, the past year has seen a dramatic increase in the number of city-oriented commercial web services such as City Search, Yahoo,

Microsoft's Sidewalk, and AOL's Digital Cities (Shapiro, 1999). Beamish (1999, p. 352) notes that "a fundamental difference exists between grassroots community computing initiatives that see their users as residents and neighbors and the commercial ventures that view their users as consumers and customers." The exponential use of grassroots community and commercial Web services as a substitute for traditional broadcast and communication media in these applications has demonstrated their viability in offering cheaper, faster and more accurate communication and information transfer. Further, some of these applications suggest that we are moving from the substitution to enlargement phases of community computing.

Studies of this advancing "enlargement" phase have two implications for low-income community networks. *First*, investments in these efforts have put low-income communities into an even greater disadvantage. As pointed out by James Katz in the Benton Foundation (1998, p. 5) report on low-income communities in the information age, "The information poor will become more impoverished because government bodies, community organizations, and corporations are displacing resources from their ordinary channels of communication on to the Internet." As such they have exacerbated the Digital Divide (Wolpert, 1999).

Second, studies of this enlargement of electronic communication in society indicate that these communications increasingly are used to augment rather than substitute for face to face communication. Consistent with the evolution of a technology's use from the substitution phase to the enlargement phase many online interactions continue to be with people who are seen in-person at work or at leisure. In fact, despite the dramatic press coverage portraying virtual worlds whose "netizens" only meet online, the overwhelming evidence from systematic studies demonstrate that most ties combine in-person with computer-mediated contact (Castells, 1996; Rheingold, 1993; Wellman & Gulia, 1999). Castells (1996, p. 363) notes that computer-mediated communication "does not substitute for other means of communicating, nor does it create new networks; it reinforces the preexisting social patterns." These findings imply that computer mediated communication "may be a powerful medium to reinforce the social cohesion of the cosmopolitan elite" (Castells, 1996, p. 364). In deed, elsewhere in this book, de Bruine (2000) notes that 87% of the people using public access kiosks in the city of Bristol were those who already had access to computer in their homes. Hence, these developments do not augur well for low-income communities, where the challenge is to also help individuals reconfigure (mobilize new network links) rather than to simply augment existing network ties. Thus the technology bonanza further isolates precisely those people and organizations who are at the heart of local development efforts: those without the resources, expertise, motivation and experience to access and make effective use of local information infrastructure (Novak & Hoffman, 1998; Schön, Sanyal, & Mitchell, 1999; U.S. Department of Commerce, 1999).

In summary, while community networks have made important strides in providing access to computer-based tools and resources for a larger proportion of low-income community members, the infrastructure has attempted with limited success to substitute for traditional means of publishing and communicating. Further, even as these networks evolve into an "enlargement" phase and experience an increase in use, the networks tend to reinforce the existing community structures rather than help low-income residents reconfigure their networks by creating new ties that will help them mobilize their resources more effectively.

Special Challenges for Low-Income Community Networks

The critical needs of low-income residents—who in the United States typically include African-Americans, single parents, and seniors--include affordable health care and housing, crime prevention, family support and youth development. As social systems, low-income communities face distinct problems. Problem-solving is hampered because information regarding beneficial social services is fragmented, and community organizations find it difficult to share resources and coordinate their work (Dewdney and Harris, 1992; Venkatesh, 1997). In addition, a sense of isolation burdens many of our disadvantaged neighborhoods. Indeed, Rheingold (1993, p. 13) notes that the social glue that helps bind communities together are social network capital ("Who knows who?" and "Who knows who knows who?"), and knowledge capital ("Who knows what?" and "Who knows who knows what?"). Low-income communities are in dire need of tools that help provide members with this social glue. Computing and communications technologies offer the potential to support community-wide social systems by facilitating more extensive communication and coordination related to problem-solving efforts and the delivery of social services.

Hence, the unique challenge for low-income community networks is to provide an infrastructure that helps the residents realize and mobilize both their social capital and their knowledge capital (Amsden & Clarke, 1999). In what is arguably a hyperbolic observation, Resnick and King (1990) note that "There is no such thing as a poor community. Even neighborhoods without much money have substantial human resources. Often however the human resources are not appreciated or utilized, partly because people do not have information about one another and about what their neighborhood has to offer. For example, a family whose oil heater is broken may go cold for lack of knowledge that someone just down the block knows how to fix it." Although discussion of mobilizing human resources in low-income neighborhoods must recognize that the resources community members bring to the table are circumscribed by the opportunities they have had to develop their education levels and skills training, it points to a way that, *ceteris paribus*, communication technologies can be implemented to leverage and foster relationships among community members.

In an attempt to address this issue, Kretzmann and McKnight (1993) report the use of asset mapping to help with community renewal projects. Asset mapping is a way to identify and involve all the capabilities or capacities of a community to create community transformation, or to build community self-reliance. Asset mapping begins with a survey of capabilities in a community at three levels: (i) individual assets, which include the skills, resources, and expertise of individuals in the community, (ii) association assets, which include a list of citizen associations and non-profits and what they can accomplish, and (iii) institutional assets, which include information provided by institutions including businesses, government agencies, and city services. In addition, at all three levels, the assets mapped include not just the knowledge capital possessed by actors (i.e., the individual, associations and institutions) within the community, but also their social capital -- that is, the relationships and partnerships among these actors.

Several projects demonstrate that the process of convening citizens for the purpose of identifying and mapping these assets have been extremely productive. Practitioners of asset mapping chronicle several "Eureka" moments where members of a community can discover assets that they did not realize existed within the community. An example posted on the web (http://www.assetmap.com/About/about.html) illustrates this sentiment: "One of our most memorable sessions was in Virginia. Fourteen community teams were working on some preliminary asset maps, when we heard this cheer from one corner of the hall. The cheer was followed by this ecstatic yell: "Wow! Yes!! We´ve got everything we need right here!!!" The surprise and joy was absolutely wondrous. That community will succeed because they found the treasures they need to solve their problems -- right in their community!"

But sustaining and scaling up the asset mapping process for a community entails very high coordination costs – in terms of the time and effort required by the various actors on an ongoing basis. Further, the coordination costs continue to escalate as the community begins to harvest the information gathered in the asset mapping process into the asset matching process (linking "who has what" to "who needs what" or "who knows what?" to "Who needs to know what?). Coordination theory (Malone & Crowston, 1990) suggests that there is a real and, as yet, largely untapped opportunity for information technologies to reduce coordination costs. In this case, technologies offer the opportunity to reduce the coordination costs for a community to dynamically map, update, and access its asset maps, thereby exploring and cultivating its social and knowledge capital more effectively. The remainder of this paper describes our experiences in developing and deploying such tools within Prairienet – a community network serving the Champaign-Urbana community in the midwestern USA.

Prairienet: Champaign-Urbana's Community Network

The city of Champaign-Urbana was ranked by *Newsweek* magazine (November 9, 1998, http://www.newsweek.com/nw-srv/19_98b/printed/us/bz/bz0419_1.htm) as one of the ten most wired communities in the world. It is served by a nationally recognized computer-based community network (CN) called Prairienet (http://www.prairienet.org), which develops and consolidates community information in digital formats, provides free or low-cost access to Internet services such as electronic mail and web browsing, and offers significant user outreach, training and support.

CNs like Prairienet have been heralded as promising partners in local efforts aimed at both community development and bridging the digital divide that splits use of computer resources along socioeconomic lines (Chapman and Rhodes, 1997; Lillie; Virnoche, 1998). Information on Prairienet is organized (as it is in most CNs) following a city metaphor with information and organizations grouped into general categories, such as Health or Recreation. While a great deal of valuable local information is provided on Prairienet, the online information areas created by individuals and organizations do not typically include the kind of information that would provide answers to the questions about local problems and resources posed above. This arrangement does not optimally support local problem-solving and resource-sharing across organizations.

PrairieKNOW: A Tool to Support Prairienet

As mentioned above, the pervasiveness of electronic communication media in communities makes it increasingly difficult for economically disadvantaged individuals and community organizations to discern their community's knowledge networks. Specifically, it is increasingly difficult for individuals and organizations to accurately determine: "Who knows who?" and "Who knows who knows who?" "Who has what?" and "Who knows who has what?" "Who is addressing which community problems?" and "Who knows who is addressing which problems?" This difficulty presents a serious barrier to coordination and collaboration in community development efforts across local organizations. As part of the Community Networking Initiative (http://www.prairienet.org/cni), we are piloting an approach that uses networked information services to enhance community-wide collaboration. Our approach is derived from the concept of asset mapping (Kretzmann & McKnight, 1993) described above. Our pilot project is intended to develop more effective ways of identifying and mobilizing sharable assets that are currently hidden within organizations, and missing from Prairienet itself. We have developed PrairieKNOW, Prairie Knowledge Networks On the Web, to help enhance an organization's ability http://iknow.spcomm.uiuc.edu/prairieknow), to access the community's knowledge network. PrairieKNOW, which represents a new generation of software, sometimes called "communityware," makes visible the community's tacit social and knowledge networks (Contractor, Zink, and Chan, 1997). For a multimedia overview of IKNOW, see http://www.spcomm.uiuc.edu:1000/contractor/iknowtour.ppt.

PrairieKNOW represents an innovative application that complements the existing tools and resources currently found on Prairienet and most other CNs. We have collected and loaded into PrairieKNOW asset records from about 30 community-based organizations in the local region. The asset records contain fields for the following categories of information: major programs and services offered; target audiences; community organizations worked with in the past; past community development projects; resources available to share; resources needed; and contact information. Within PrairieKNOW, users can examine the existing network relations among the various organizations in the community.   For instance, they can identify those organizations that are directly and indirectly connected to one another through various community partnerships and projects. They can also examine the network of organizations that can offer or share a need for similar resources. More significantly, PrairieKNOW allows organizations in the community to visually map the network of local groups and institutions in terms of their matching resources. A screen shot from PrairieKNOW displaying the matching of these resources is show in Figure 1.

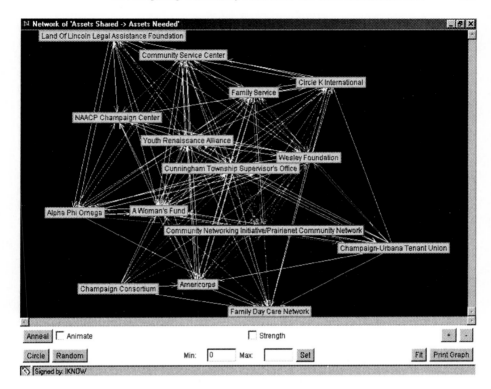

Fig. 1. Mapping and matching assets in the Prairienet community

These asset records have also been mounted directly on Prairienet in the form of simple web pages (http://www.prairienet.org/assets/). As part of our pilot project, we are exploring the strengths and weaknesses of these two technological platforms. One offers a high tech solution that allows sophisticated search, analysis, and display, but will require more advanced skills and equipment to use. The other offers a low-tech solution with minimal functionality but greater ease of use. Eventually we hope to develop an integrated solution that will make the power of PrairieKNOW readily available to all community members.

User Reactions to PrairieKNOW

In meetings attended by representatives of local community organizations, we have introduced the asset mapping concept, collected asset records, and obtained direct feedback from those who are both the creators and users of the local asset map we are developing. Organizations attending these ongoing meetings include the Urban League of Champaign County, Family Services, Senior Services, and A Woman's Place (which offers temporary shelter and social services to women and their children who are in need of emergency aid). Those attending the meetings were enthusiastic about the potential of asset mapping to facilitate collaborations across community institutions and felt that such an application would indeed address an important information and communication need. At one meeting, a representative from one organization noted they often have leftover food that goes to waste because they have no means to discover, quickly and easily, what other organizations might be able to use it. The representative of another organization quickly noted that they could use the leftovers, and the two people exchanged phone numbers so that, in the future, they could contact each other when food was available. This incident, with its ironic use of face to face communication to set up future contact via another traditional communication technology (the phone), demonstrates both the potential for cross-institutional resource sharing and the need for improved communication mechanisms to support it. Users also suggested enhancements that explicitly supported the asset matching process. For instance, one person suggested that the asset mapping should be augmented with an automatic alerting function to email people when a resource they needed was posted as an available resource in the asset record of another organization.

Meeting participants also identified important issues related to the adoption of online asset mapping. Concerns were raised about 1) the inability of community organizations who lacked computers and technical skills to participate in the system; 2) the demands associated with maintaining the online asset record repository; and 3) the need to keep private that information which organizations did not want to make publicly available.

Potential of PrairieKNOW to Support the Community

There are at least four ways in which PrairieKNOW can assist creating, sustaining, and growing knowledge networks within the community. First, it provides participating organizations with a set of visual tools to inspect, identify, and critically analyze the existing and potential collaborations and partnerships among the local government and non-profit, and health organizations in the community. Second, it offers participating organizations the ability to track over time the growth characteristics of the community network (in terms of its social and knowledge capital). Third, it provides participating organizations the ability to efficiently identify other organizations represented on Prairienet who offer specific complementary or similar services. This feature is especially beneficial for organizations assembling partnerships to address specific project concerns or funding opportunities. Fourth, it provides citizens in the community the ability to identify organizations on Prairienet which offer specific services.

Potential of PrairieKNOW to Support Research

The introduction of tools such as PrairieKNOW also raises several theoretically provocative and practically relevant questions about the emergence – creation, maintenance, and dissolution – of networks in communities. Fortunately, the tools also provide us the ability to unobtrusively gather comprehensive and accurate longitudinal data on the evolution of community knowledge networks. Specifically, it provides an opportunity to answer questions such as:

- How can tools like PrairieKNOW enhance Prairienet's ability to contribute to community-wide collaboration and problem solving? How can these old and new genres of community networking tools be most appropriately integrated, and in a manner that does not further widen the digital divide?
- What effect do tools like PrairieKNOW have on a community's power structures? Does it undermine the perceived centrality of those organizations which are currently viewed as important resources? What effect does it have on established means of cross-organizational communication and coordination?
- What configurations of community knowledge networks are more appropriate to specific types of tasks – such as planning an event versus mobilizing for a cause? To what extent are community knowledge networks reconfigurable to accommodate the community evolving needs?
- How does the use of tools such as PrairieKNOW alter the structures and growth of community knowledge networks?
- What theoretical mechanisms are most influential in "growing" a community knowledge network in terms of its size as well as the density of connections? To what extent does the initial configuration of the network influence the speed and characteristics of its growth patterns?
- How do exchange and trust mechanisms both explain the likelihood that organizations will remain members (or drop out) of a community knowledge network, and account for which information about organizational assets members are willing to make public?
- How can tools like PrairieKNOW achieve its goals while not violating the participating organizations' privacy?
- To what extent will cultural differences in community networks (Otani, 1999) impact the design and utilization of communityware tools?

Theoretical and methodological advances in the field of social network analysis promise to play an important role in helping us address these questions (Monge & Contractor, 1999).

Conclusion

This paper has attempted to make the argument that, like technologies in earlier times and other contexts, the initial use of technologies to support traditional communities has followed a substitution framework. Community computing networks were used as a substitute for traditional means of broadcast and interpersonal communication. For many sectors of contemporary society, the use of the technology as a substitute has transitioned to an enlargement phase stimulated by the increase in commercial services and the increased activity among certain sectors of the community – the so-called *digerati*. However, this enlargement has further exacerbated the digital divide between these sectors of society and the low-income community and has failed to yield direct benefits to low-income communities since it augments existing relationships rather than building new connections.

This paper has argued that in order for community computing networks to help bridge this divide, special attention must be given to tools that help to reconfigure, rather than simply substitute or enlarge the extant community networks. Reconfiguring the network serves to provide disadvantaged members of communities the opportunity to enhance and leverage their social and knowledge capital. Our initial experiences, using asset mapping as a methodology and PrairieKNOW as a tool, in the Prairienet community network indicate a high degree of demand and potential for this approach. While such tools will not compensate for other structural changes that seek to improve the condition of low-income communities, they can play a modest role in helping maximize the opportunities for the economically and socially disadvantaged within the existing structures.

References

Agre, Philip E. (1999, June 8). *Rethinking networks and communities in a wired society*. [Draft paper presented at the Midyear Meeting of the American Society for Information Science, Pasadena, May 1999]. Available: http://dlis.gseis.ucla.edu/people/pagre/asis.html

Amsden, A. H., & Clark, J. C. (1999). Software entrepreneurship among urban poor: Could Bill Gates have succeeded if he were black? ... or impoverished? In D. Schön, B. Sanyal, & W. J. Mitchell (Eds.). *High technology and low-income communities: Prospects for the positive use of advanced information technology* (pp. 213-234). Cambridge, MA: MIT Press.

Beamish, A. (1995). *Communities online: community-based computer networks*. Master's thesis, Massachusetts Institute of Technology, Cambridge, MA. [Online]. http://loohooloo.mit.edu/arch/4.207/anneb/thesis/toc.html

Beamish, A. (1999). Approaches to community computing: Bringing technology to low-income groups. In D. Schön, B. Sanyal, & W. J. Mitchell (Eds.). *High technology and low-income communities: Prospects for the positive use of advanced information technology* (pp. 349-368). Cambridge, MA: MIT Press.

Castells, M. (1996). *The rise of the network society*. Oxford, UK: Blackwell.

Chapman, G. & Rhodes, L. (1997, October). Nurturing neighborhood nets. *Technology Review*. [Online]. Available http://web.mit.edu/techreview/www/articles/oct97/chapman.html

Chaskin, R. J. (1997). Perspectives on neighborhood and community: A review of the literature. *Social Services Review, 71*, 522-547.

Cohen, M. & Axelrod, R. (1998). Complexity and adaptation in community information systems: Implications for design. In Toru Ishida (Ed.), *Community Computing and Support Systems, Lecture Notes in Computer Science 1519* (pp. 16-42). Berlin: Springer-Verlag.

Contractor N., Zink, D., & Chan, M. (1998). IKNOW: A tool to assist and study the creation, maintenance, and dissolution of knowledge networks. In Toru Ishida (Ed.), *Community Computing and Support Systems, Lecture Notes in Computer Science 1519* (pp. 201-217). Berlin: Springer-Verlag.

de Bruine (2000). Digital City Bristol: A Case Study. *Lecture Notes in Computer Science* (in this volume), Berlin: Springer-Verlag.

Dewdney, P., & Harris, R. M. (1992). Community information needs: The case of wife assault (in six Ontario communities). *Library & Information Science Research, 14*(1): 5-29.

Espinoza, V. (1999). Social networks among the urban poor: Inequality and integration in a Latin American city. In B. Wellman (Ed.), *Networks in the global village: Life in contemporary communities* (pp. 147-184) . Boulder, CO; Westview Press.

Fisher, C. (1992). *America calling: A social history of the telephone to 1940.* Berkeley, CA: University of California Press.

Koch, M., Rancati, A., Grasso, A., & Snowdon, D. (1999). Paper user-interfaces for local community support. In H-J. Bullinger & J. Ziegler (Eds.), *Human-computer interaction: Communication, cooperation and applications design. Proceedings of HCI International '99, Munich, Germany,* Volume II (pp. 417-421). Mahway NJ: Lawrence-Erlbaum.

Kretzmann, J. P., and McKnight, J. L. (1993). *Building communities from the inside out: A path toward finding and mobilizing a community's assets.* Chicago, IL: ACTA Publications.

Lillie, J. (1998). *Possible roles for electronic community networks and participatory development strategies in access programs for poor neighborhoods.* [Online]. Available: http://sunsit.unc.edu/jlillie/research/.

Malone, T. & Crowston, K. (1990). What is Coordination Theory and how can it help design cooperative work systems? *Groupware and Computer-Supported Cooperative Work.* E53-333: 375-384.

Malone, T. W., & Rockart, J. F. (1991). Computers, networks, and the corporation. *Scientific American*, 265, 128- 136.

Martin, C. V. (1997). Managing information in a community network. In A. M. Cohill & A. L. Kavanaugh (Eds.), *Community networks: Lessons from Blacksburg, Virginia.* Boston: Artech House.

McConnaughey, J. W., & Lader, W. (1998). *Falling through the net II: New data on the digital divide.* Washington, DC: National Telecommunications and Information Administration. http://www.ntia.doc.gov/ntiahome/net2/falling.html

Mitchell, W. J. (1999). Equitable access to the online world. In D. Schön, B. Sanyal, & W. J. Mitchell (Eds.). *High technology and low-income communities: Prospects for the positive use of advanced information technology* (pp. 151-163). Cambridge, MA: MIT Press.

Monge, P. R., & Contractor, N. S. (in press). Emergence of communication networks. In L. Putnam & F. Jablin (Eds.) *New Handbook of Organizational Communication.* Newbury Park, CA: Sage.

Novak, T. P., & Hoffman, D. L. (1998). *Bridging the digital divide: The impact of race on computer access and Internet use.* [Online]. Available: http://www2000.ogsm.vanderbilt.edu/papers/race/science.html

Otani, S. (1999). Personal community networks in contemporary Japan. In B. Wellman (Ed.), *Networks in the global village: Life in contemporary communities* (pp. 279-298) . Boulder, CO; Westview Press.

Resnick, P. & King, M. (1990). The Rainbow pages – building community with voice technology. In *Proceedings of Directions and Implications of Advanced Computing (DIAC-90) Symposium.* Boston, July 28.

Rheingold, H. (1993). *The virtual community: Homesteading on the electronic frontier.* New York: HarperCollins.

Rochlin, G. I. (1997). *Trapped in the Net: The unanticipated consequences of computerization.* Princeton, NJ: Princeton University Press.

Rogers, E. M. (1983). *Diffusion of innovations.* New York: Free Press.

Schön, D., Sanyal, B., & Mitchell, W. J. (Eds.). (1999). *High technology and low-income communities: Prospects for the positive use of advanced information technology.* Cambridge, MA: MIT Press.

Schuler, D. (1996). *New community networks: Wired for change.* New York: ACM Press.

Shapiro, A. L. (1999). *The control revolution: How the Internet is putting individuals in charge and changing the world we know.* New York: A Century Foundation.

Shaw, A. & Shaw, M. (1999). Social empowerment through community networks. In D. Schön, B. Sanyal, & W. J. Mitchell (Eds.). *High technology and low-income communities:*

Prospects for the positive use of advanced information technology (pp. 315-335). Cambridge, MA: MIT Press.

Sproull, L. & Kiesler, S. (1991). *Connections: New ways of working in the networked organization.* Cambridge, MA: MIT Press.

U.S. Dept. of Commerce. National Telecommunications and Information Administration. (1999). *Falling through the net: Defining the digital divide.* Washington, DC: NTIA. Available: http://www.ntia.doc.gov/ntiahome/fttn99

Van den Besselaar, P., & Beckers, D. (1998). Demographics and sociographics of the *Digital City.* In Toru Ishida (Ed.), *Community Computing and Support Systems, Lecture Notes in Computer Science 1519* (pp. 108-124). Berlin: Springer-Verlag.

Venkatesh, S. A. (1997). The three-tier model: How helping occurs in urban, poor communities. *Social Service Review,* 71(4), 574-606.

Virnoche, M. (1998). The seamless web and communications equity: The social shaping of a community network. *Science, Technology and Human Values,* 23(2), 199-220.

Wellman, B. (1999). *Networks in the global village: Life in contemporary communities.* Boulder, CO; Westview Press.

Wellman, B. (1999). The network community: An introduction. In B. Wellman (Ed.), *Networks in the global village: Life in contemporary communities* (pp. 1-48) . Boulder, CO; Westview Press.

Wellman, B. & Gulia, M. (1999). Net-surfers don't ride alone: Virtual communities as communities. In B. Wellman (Ed.), *Networks in the global village: Life in contemporary communities* (pp. 331-366) . Boulder, CO; Westview Press.

Wolpert, J. (1999). Center cities as havens and traps for low-income communities: The potential impact of advanced information technologies. In D. Schön, B. Sanyal, & W. J. Mitchell (Eds.). *High technology and low-income communities: Prospects for the positive use of advanced information technology* (pp. 69-104). Cambridge, MA: MIT Press.

The Mutual Development of Role, Rule, and Tool Through the VCOM Project

Shoko Miyagawa[1] and Ikuyo Kaneko[2]

[1]Steering committee of VCOM project
[2]The representative of VCOM project
[1,2]Graduate School of Media and Governance, Keio University,
5322 Endo, Fujisawa, Kanagawa, 252-8520 Japan
{miyagawa, kaneko}@vcom.or.jp

Abstract. Communities on the Internet have developed to the stage where they are no longer a mere "virtual existence". Though these network communities have little to do with "real society", they are nonetheless a very real existence as they have a substantial and firm effect on society. To enhance the activities of network communities, utilization of IT tools is indispensable. However, design and development of community-oriented tools is not an easy task because tools should reflect the characteristics shared in the communities, which never cease to change. In this paper, we propose three aspects to characterize network communities: role, rule and tool. We will also introduce the interpenetration of these three aspects through the activities of the VCOM project, which is driven by Keio University. Finally, we discuss the indispensable characteristics of IT tools for network communities, which are regarded as having an important role to play as a real existence in the future society.

1 Network Communities: The New Method of Problem Solving

As our society is becoming more complex and more diverse, there are more business chances due to the general trend of information sharing. The trend is accompanied by the emergence of a new class of problems, which cannot be solved by the conventional approach of either government or market. Environmental problems are a typical example of this class. It seems to us that such general movements in society are making voluntarily formed "communities" more important as units of trying to tackle problems. The recent emphasis on "communities" in the Internet seems to be a reflection of this phenomenon in society. The following are some achievement of these "communities."

Many people wish to quit habitual smoking. The going success rate in Japan for a regular hospital visit type treatment is estimated at roughly 10%. However, when a self-help group of people wishing to quit smoking was formed on the Internet, the result of the community was astonishing. More than half of the participants were reportedly successful in quitting smoking. The substance of the community is a mailing list on the Internet. This mailing list consists of hundreds of people who wish to quit smoking, some doctors, and people who tried to quit smoking in the past (and

T. Ishida, K. Isbister (Eds.): Digital Cities, LNCS 1765, pp. 165-178, 2000.

succeeded or failed). It is said that the key point of the success of the community is mutual communication among people trying to quit smoking and people who have experienced the same effort. It is note-worthy from the organizational point of view, that the organizational characteristic of the mailing list is neither hierarchical nor completely flat. The owner of the mailing list who is a medical specialist in quitting smoking, takes the lead along with many "supervisors" such as voluntarily participating doctors and experienced people. The "supervisors" are seen to be in a slightly "higher" position than the ordinary participants. Each party plays a role, which is dynamically and loosely defined according to the roles and actions of others. Here, a kind of mutuality and structure exist simultaneously.

In another case, a regional network community for helping elderly was established by more than 2,000 local residents in Machida city, Tokyo. It succeeded in founding a highly successful day care center in consort with the local government of Machida city. This grass-root effort enabled a very efficient use of monetary resources of the local and central governments.

Both of these cases employ a method of forming a "community of interest" as a substance of problem solving. This method is quite different from either "leviathan approach" or "privatization approach". The leviathan approach is to accumulate information in the hands of the government, thereby assigning the unique role of solution providing to the government. This was the solution for the famous "tragedy of commons" problem [8]. In the leviathan solution, the government centralizes control and becomes the sole power to decide who can use the meadow, when they can use it, and how many animals can be grazed. However, to maximize the utility of the meadow, the government must have complete information about the condition of the meadow and activities of the each herder, something which is hardly possible. With the government acting with incomplete information, herders must content themselves with less than maximum utility. Privatization is another way to solve the tragedy of commons. In the privatization solution, the common meadow is abolished and the meadow is parceled out to each herder as personal property. As a conclusion, new costs of investment in fences and their maintenance, monitoring and sanctioning intruders are needed [15].

Forming "Community of interest" is the third method for solving social problems. This method is a "brand new - age old" method because the community itself has a long history in our social institution. Originally, "community" meant a group of such that members shared or had common regional characteristics. Now, computer networks, which have surmounted regional boundaries, provide new virtual places where people get together and communicate with one another. We define such a new type of community without the restriction of regional boundaries as a "network community", discriminating it from the conventional definition of regional community. A network community is a community of interest based on voluntary participants. Members of a network community tend to have a high degree of interaction with one another, to share information and to make relationships dynamically [12]. Though many network communities utilize the Internet, the use of computer networks is not requisite in the definition of a network community. Rather it is a fact that computer networks have the potential to become a powerful tool for organizing network communities. In this paper, we focus on network communities that utilize the Internet as an essential tool for their activities. These network communities have recently begun to gain recognition as social entities. However, when we try to analyze the effect and the efficiency of such a network community, we are faced with two kinds of problems. The one is that very little study has been done on network communities as it is an extremely new form of organization, and therefore there exist almost no organizational theories on their behavior. The other is that the current Internet, in its present form, is not necessarily equipped with tools for promoting self-governance of a network community[2]. These two problems are tightly related with each other, that is, to develop community-oriented tools, it is necessary to examine and analyze the activity and management method of network communities carefully.

2 Rule, Role, and Tool: The Three Aspects

The characteristics of network communities can be described from the following three aspects. The first is "rule". This refers to the aspect of rule development. Rules of a network community tend to evolve voluntarily, and are not imposed from "above". What is important in the forming of a network community is the manner or method in which these rules are developed and achieved. It is an essential characteristics which makes a distinction between the voluntary network community and the hierarchical organization, in which rules should be established at the top of the organization and given from "the above."

The second is "role". This refers to the organizational aspect of a network community. Such a community is neither hierarchical nor completely 2 dimensional ("flat") but is instead managed in a fashion where in each member plays a role which is mutually agreed upon by the whole community. The relationship among the members is based on not a contract nor a compulsion but mutual agreement and respect. The relationship among the quit-smoking mailing list is an example of such characteristics.

The last one is "tools". Tools facilitate the realization of the first two, "rule" and "role", in virtual space by using information technology, which we will mainly discuss in this paper.

These aspects can be analyzed from the point of sociology. The concept of "social capital" describes the "richness" of human relationships such as mutual help and trust, which forms the basis of network communities and other ordinary communities. According to James Coleman, social capital is a kind of capital which is vested in the relationship among people, while goods, money or manpower is capital in themselves [4]. Coleman gave as examples of communities with rich social capital, (i) a group of people who belong to the same church, (ii) a relationship among a doctor and patients without lawsuit, etc. Putnam and Saxenian also explain the difference of political and economic performance between regions by the difference in the relationship of the members [16][17]. Coleman explains that the aim of forming a regional community is to accumulate and enrich the social capital of the community. Although these discussions of social capital are based on regional communities, the theory itself can be extended to more diverse types of communities of interests. In fact, social capital is much more important for network communities. The characteristics of "rule" and "role" are rather fragile when compared to that of traditional hierarchical organizations, and network communities are always exposed to the risk of free riding that this fragility involves. However, under the assumption of mutual help and trust, there is no need to prepare for such risks: no one need to be afraid of being taken advantage of by others' free riding, or there is no need to settle fences to protect one's private properties, as in the case of the "tragedy of commons." This analysis describes to us that social capital is a great incentive toward developing network communities. Discussions concerning social capital are also made by Contractor and Hampton/Wellman in this volume[5][7].

Another analysis that describes the incentive of forming network communities can be made from the point of organization theory. Transaction cost is the cost which emerges when participating in transactions of the marketplace [3][19]. The transaction cost model employs the assumptions of "bounded rationality", which is clarified by Simon [18] and "opportunism", instead of the classical assumptions of complete information and complete competition. Transaction cost is classified into two costs of "information search cost" and "monitoring cost", each of which corresponds to the assumptions of "bounded rationality" and "opportunism" respectively. When considering information search cost, it is said that the Internet decreases the cost for obtaining information but increases the amount and complexity of the information itself and therefore the cost for processing the information. It is inefficient for the traditional hierarchical organization to keep up with such complexity. On the other hand, network communities being loosely coupled organizations, can involve people of diverse roles, and therefore can keep up with the complexity more so than hierarchical organizations. When considering monitoring cost, which is closely related to the previous discussion of social capital, the voluntary manner in establishing rules of a network community realizes less or no sanctions for violation than that of hierarchical organizations, and therefore, less monitoring cost for violation. This analysis describes to us that a well-managed network community has advantages over the free marketplace or classical hierarchical organization.

Tools should be the implementation of these characteristics, however, current major technologies such as mailing lists, WWW, and databases have not achieved the realization of such implementation. Indeed, these tools per se are merely separate and incomplete parts of what we need. We need to integrate these tools. However, to make the integrated tool suit the objectives of each network community, the developers should know what is happening in and around the community. We will describe the efforts of the VCOM project as a legitimate peripheral participant of the network communities in the next section.

3 VCOM Project: History and Organization

VCOM (http://www.vcom.or.jp/) is an experimental research project to develop network communities using the Internet and other information networks since 1995(Fig.1).

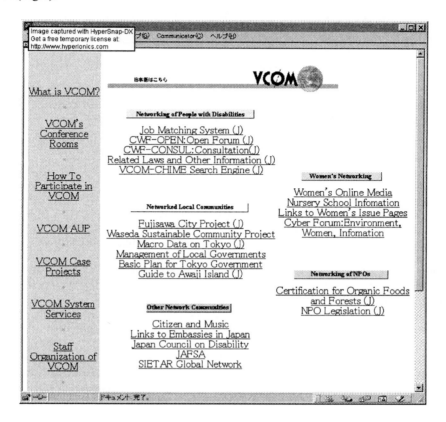

Fig. 1. The VCOM Homepage

The authors of this paper have been committed to VCOM as members of the steering committee for five years.

VCOM has its start at the Great Kobe Earthquake in 1995. After the Earthquake, a large number of Japanese people in general seemed willing to take part in activities to help out earthquake victims. A great many of them used PC networks and the Internet for daily communication and giving and receiving advice. In a way, the entire country of Japan acted as one big network community at that time. Users of PC networks and the Internet also tried to exchange and share information such as the whereabouts of people, items needed, and the conditions of the stricken areas. However, because PC

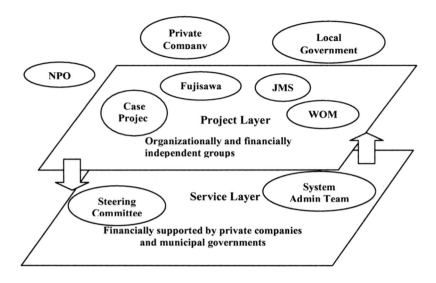

Fig. 2. VCOM Organization

networks including the Internet did not have transparent connectivity with one another to a satisfactory degree in those days, information of high social importance was confined to each network. InterVnet, founded right after the Great Kobe Earthquake was designed to be a device for sharing information across various PC networks and the Internet. The InterVnet offered transparent information exchange among the networks so that the same information could be read by any of the participating PC network subscribers. Millions of PC users were connected via the InterVnet [13].

The task of running the InterVnet was taken over, in May of 1995, by the VCOM project, which is carried out by a research group headed by Prof. Ikuyo Kaneko of Keio University SFC (Shonan-Fujisawa Campus). VCOM expands the activities of InterVnet to support more general network communities. There are three key concepts for VCOM: (i) voluntary networks, (ii) sharing socially valuable information, and (iii) new social systems with voluntary participation of citizens. The two main activities of VCOM are (i) to carry out various "case projects" to form and support network communities, and (ii) to develop community system tools and to provide internet services to case project participants.

Concerning the organizational structure, VCOM consists of two layers: the service layer and the project layer(Fig.2). The service layer provides various Internet resources to the case projects, such as WWW, mailing lists, user accounts, disk space, and Web-ML conference system that we developed to link mailing lists and archive browsing function via WWW. This layer is financially supported by private companies, which are the member of the consortium, and the municipal government. The service layer consists of the steering committee and the system administration team. On the other hand, the project layer consists of case projects, each of which is an effort to create or support a specific and real-world voluntary network community.

The case projects are financially and organizationally independent from the service layer. They set up their funds by membership fee, subsidies from the government, and/or donation etc. Each case project body is not an isolated and closed existence on the Internet, but rather is collaborating with other network communities or existing organizations such as local governments, private companies, or non-profit organizations to provide useful information and to solve socially important problems. Simultaneously, when developing new IT tools, each case project collaborates with system administration team.

The VCOM case projects are grouped into the following 5 groups.

GROUP 1 : Networking of People with Disabilities
- Job Matching Square
- CHIME's SQUARE

GROUP 2 : Women's Networking
- WOM(Women's Online Media)

GROUP 3 : Networked Local Communities
- Fujisawa City Project
- Project to Offer Financial and Other Macro Data of Tokyo
- RENET (Waseda Sustainable Community Development Executive Committee)
- Public Management Forum

GROUP 4 : Networking of Non-Profit Organizations
- C's(Information of NPO Legislation)
- AXIS(Organic Food and Forest Certification)

GROUP 5 : Other Network Communities
- Citizen and Music
- Macro Data of Tokyo

The following is an explanation of some of the case projects of VCOM and IT tools developed in each case project.

WOM

WOM(Women's Online Media) is made up of women from diverse backgrounds, including company employees, homemakers, and students. WOM aims at introducing women to the uses of electronic media, providing information about women, women's studies, and women's issues on the Net. In addition, WOM has several subgroups each of which discusses and studies specific topics such as working mothers, sexuality, nursing homes etc and presents the results of the study through the Internet. The WOM homepage is considered to contain some of the best women-related information in terms of volume and quality in Japan. WOM has developed a collaborative link management system based on a relational database system so that the members of WOM can easily collect and edit the set of links provided in its homepage.

Fujisawa City Project

In 1996, VCOM carried out a joint project with the Tokyo Metropolitan Government to promote citizen's participating in the process of formulating the "basic plan for the future of Tokyo" to be announced by the governor of Tokyo. Information was provided by the Tokyo Government through a homepage and an open discussion was held in an Internet-based conference room. Since 1997, a similar but more extended project has been executed jointly by the City of Fujisawa and VCOM. This project is similar to the ones in Davis or Amsterdam, but this is considered to be the first attempt in Japan to provide a citizens' participation platform on the Internet in a project of the local government[1][10]. An electronic conference system called "Community Maker" and its successor called "Community Editor" have employed to support communication, voting, and mutual reputation. The detail of this project will be introduced later.

Job Matching Square

Job Matching Square (JMS) is a packaged device that promotes the employment of people with disability in Japan. JMS provides a job matching database, a cases and law database, and a mailing list for individual consultation. The service of JMS started on July 1998, and has made significant achievement in the past year. The method and result of JMS are paid considerable attention from the administration office of the Japanese government[11].

AXIS

Credibility plays an important role in the activities of an NPO. For example, some NPOs certify organic products that are not grown in chemically fertilized soil and to which agricultural chemicals are not used. However, the criteria for "organic-ness" may vary, as does the manner in which the contamination is measured. In other words, the manner in which the certification is carried out, is equally important as, or more important than the fact that the product is certified. That is, credibility of the organization that certifies the product plays the important role. It is often the case that the government as a certifying agent may not receive sufficient trust by consumers as the government is perceived as often acting with a certain political intention. Thus, credible NPOs acting as certifying agent are important. AXIS provides various information concerning certification of organic food and well-managed forest. At the same time, a new challenge to distribute information concerning "trustworthiness" on the Internet will be performed in consort with researchers of Internet security.

Now, VCOM consists of 11 case projects and 85 people who have e-mail account at VCOM. Concerning mailing lists, the most popular communication device in VCOM, there are 150 mailing lists and about a total of 4200 subscribers. The VCOM WWW server contains 700Mbyte of contents and 10200 html files. The access count for the VCOM webserver is about 4000 a month to the toppage, and about 237000 a month as a total. VCOM is often introduced at government councils as a progressive challenge in forming network communities, and was also introduced in the white paper of telecommunication in 1998.

The characteristics of network communities in VCOM can be summarized as follows:

- Not limited to the Internet, but is simply the cyber face of a real world social entity.
- Forms self-governing communities of interest. These communities tend to be made up of parties which have different standpoints but are unified under one objective or interest.
- Not forming hierarchical type of organizations, but instead less strict and networked organizations in which each member has a role of one's own.
- Utilizes or develops information sharing tools to smoothen communication among members.

In other words, these characteristics are those of the open system and self-organizing process, which is called in the terminology of physics "dissipative structure" [19]. These patterns of self-organizing and autopoiesis are seen in many case projects which are "going well". In the dissipative structure system, elements are neither independent nor isolated: they interact and interpenetrate with each other by exchanging energy and materials. The same can be said for the structure of network communities: the three characteristics of rule, role and tool are not isolated but interact with each other. We will discuss more details of this interpenetration among rule, role and tool, focusing on two case projects concerning the digital city and the employment of people with disabilities.

4 Case Study: Fujisawa City Project

So far, there have been many discussions that the Internet is affecting the ways of society. Not only is the Internet employed as a new tool to promote the efficiency in business or research, metaphors of the Internet are also penetrating society in such a way that a new framework of business, organizational and social theory is being called for. However, another direction of influence is also emerging: the new framework of social entities is calling for new technologies and equipment for the Internet. The following is a case of how organizational characteristics, that is, rule and role, are affecting the implementation of tool in a network community.

The Aim and Key Body
Fujisawa is a city with 370 thousand people some 40 miles south west of Tokyo. The aim of the Fujisawa City Project is to establish a digital city of Fujisawa that promotes information publication and smooth communication between citizens and the local government, under the concept of "Open Governance" and "Development of Local Industry". This project started in September 1996 and became an official project of Fujisawa City in 1997. The key body of this project is a group consisting of 2 people from the VCOM project and 2 people from the Fujisawa City Government. An electronic conference room was employed to realize the communication place among citizens and the local government on the Internet. The results of the discussion held in the electronic conferences have been reflected to the policy making process of the local government, especially in the area of the re-development of the city center. The number of registrants of the electronic conference room at Mar. 1999 was 901 (529 in Mar. 1998), which is 170% increase from the previous year. The average of articles posted to electronic conference room in a month is 4,006 (1,199 in Mar.

1998). There are 121 conferences through the year and 61 of them were newly started between Apr. 1998 and Mar. 1999. This project was presented the Internet Award of 1998.

Before this project, VCOM performed an information publication project for the Tokyo Metropolis called the "Resident-friendly City Tokyo" plan, which started in January 1996. In this project, the process in which "Committee to Think" come up with the final set of recommendations, including all the discussions which took place at the committee sessions were made public through the "Committee to Think Homepage," and an open forum in which anybody could express opinions and request documents to the Tokyo Metropolitan Government on this issue and other related issues was set up as a conference room on the Internet. The Fujisawa City Project is the second challenge for VCOM concerning information publication of local government, and the first challenge of collaboration between Keio University SFC and Fujisawa City, where SFC is located.

With the beginning of this project in September 1996, the city government asked the citizens to participate the preparatory committee. The committee was made up of 20 citizens and 10 students from Keio University, members of the VCOM project, and city officers. The committee distributed a questionnaire to the citizens to inquire about the needs for the open governance. According to the results, 68% of citizens were interested in the local governance, but 82% of them felt difficulties to gain the information about the local governance and 92% of them wished to have a more convenient way of gaining such information. Also 91% of them felt difficulties in participating in the local governance and 96% of them thought it important that citizens participate in the local governance. Additionally, 94% of citizens expect information publication via the Internet[20]. Based on the findings of the inquiry, two mailing lists concerning governance information and life information were settled and made public to the citizens of Fujisawa city. These mailing lists were expanded to the electronic conference room, which will be described later.

Rule and Role: The Development of the Project
Size is not the only way in which the community of citizens developed. The method of the governance of the conference room was also revised so that it could provide a more convenient and helpful way of participation. At the beginning of the Project in 1996, the registrants were restricted to the residents or commuters of Fujisawa city. The moderators of each conference were also restricted to the graduate students of Keio University, who were entrusted by the city office. This restriction has its basis in the thought that as long as this service was held under the leadership of the city office, the responsibilities must be clarified and troubles must be avoided. However, as the conferences grew up to well-managed communities, it became clear that the registrants were well-motivated voluntary participants and these restrictions are abolished in 1997. The moderation of the whole conference room is entrusted to the steering committee, which consists of volunteers from registrants, and a new area of conferences called "citizens' area" was set up in addition to the traditional "city office area." Many discussions such as children who do not want to go to school, educational use of the Internet, cooking, and networking of housewives etc. are being held in the "citizens' area." The deregulation of the governance of the conference

rooms refers to the change of rules and roles based on mutual trust, which is accumulated in the repetition of interactions.

The Interpenetration among Role, Rule, and Tool: From Community Maker to Community Editor

Role and rule are not all that have been developed reflecting the accumulation of social capital. Tool has also been changed to implement the change of role and rule. The core system of this project is an electronic conference room called "Community Editor", which was developed in consort with the Editorial Engineering Laboratory and SoftFront, Inc. and was customized for this project in consort with the VCOM project and the Fujisawa City Government to support communication, voting, and mutual reputation. According to our experience and previous research during the early period of this project, most users, especially the beginners, often tend to hesitate in expressing one's casual opinion. In this system, users cannot only express their opinions and feelings by posting messages, but also by clicking one of the buttons corresponding to a sentiment such as "I agree", "I disagree", "I want more discussion" etc. This device provides a simple but significant way to reflect, at least in part, the sentimental of the "silent majority." In the process of the development of the Community Editor, interpenetration of role and tool were found. "Community Editor" is a new electric conference room system that was developed making use of the advantages of a former tool called "Community Maker". Some technological improvements were made, for example, the conferences and mailing lists became interlocking so that users can refer to all the information using the device of their preference. However, the truly remarkable improvement concerns the changes of role and rule. As described in the previous paragraph, the rule that restricted the moderators of each conference to people who were approved by the city office was abolished, so that any registrant could open new conferences. This deregulation, however, also brought about a new need of community care. Before the deregulation, the application process of opening a new conference was completely automatic, only by clicking buttons. The assumption was that this system would be used by authenticated and well-trained users. However, under a new assumption that not all the people who want to open a conference are trained well, a new support system had to be established. In the new system, instead of the automatic application, the set up of a new conference is done by a member of the steering committee. This change is seemingly retrogression, however, in the process of manual setup done by the steering committee, the chaperone can be support the new conference and the inexperienced moderators until the conference can function properly on its own. This change of the tool is reflecting the changes of role and rule, therefore this "retrogression" actually signifies the improvement of the community. The fact that these improvements are made through the discussion among citizens and are not forced on by the local government shows that voluntary participation and self-governance, which are the aims of the project, have achieved both the aspects of organization and the tool.

5 Conclusions and Discussions

We have discussed the three aspects of network communities through our experience of community forming and development of IT tools. All of these tools have been developed based on needs which emerged from the cross point of the activities of real society and virtual organization management. Through the analysis of the cases, it was clarified that "rule" and "role" of each community makes up quite a large part of the development process of these tools. Although all tools emerged to solve specific problems for each case project, none of them are merely an ad-hoc tool for a unique purpose. This suggests that analysis of rule and role will help to extract the general characteristics of network communities. Here, we describe two requisites in developing next IT tools for the network communities.

Involving the IT Developers
   The IT tools introduced in this paper are not actually new technology in the sense that they do not use particular newly developed computational or engineering methods. However, the design and the development of IT tools for supporting network communities is not easy work because the tool should also develop reflecting the development of role and rule. In this sense, design and development of the tools are a continuous process, much in the same way as the development of the community is. In the case of the Fujisawa City Project, Community Editor was designed and developed in consort with Editorial Engineering Laboratory and SoftFront, Inc. and customized for the Fujisawa City Project in consort with the Fujisawa City office, VCOM and volunteer citizens. However, generally speaking, because most of the network communities are non-profit organizations, to place an order for customized software with an outside developer is difficult for them, mainly in terms of budget. Therefore, another way of involving IT developers which takes advantage of the non-profit nature of network communities should be considered. One solution for this problem is to use the community as a testbed in developing IT tools for general communities. For instance, the Community Editor was actually developed with the idea in mind that it could be introduced into the market as a product after any revisions reflecting the results of the Fujisawa City Project. This means that the relationship between the Fujisawa City Project and IT developers is not simply a business transaction, but rather a collaboration. Other types of collaboration may be possible, however, the point is that continuous involvement and reciprocal relationship between the project body and IT developer should be realized for the development of sustainable IT tools for sustainable network communities.

Dealing with the "TRUST"
   We have mentioned the accumulation of social capital repeatedly in this paper. Actually, Fukuyama asserted by referring to James Coleman that social capital has great significance for almost all of the society including economy[6]. Therefore, IT tools for network communities will be greatly enhanced if the features of social capital may be incorporated. However, the trust, which is regarded as the substance of the social capital is difficult to handle as an element that controls the behavior of certain IT tools because it is still vague, invisible, does not have a certain format and does not have methods for computation. On the other hand, the demand for an

accreditation infrastructure for network community has gradually arisen. As we briefly introduced, a case project concerning organic food and forest certification called AXIS has just started. In this project, certification of organic food and forest performed by NPOs and how to establish the credibility of those NPO is discussed. It is being examined that the possibility to introduce a mutual accreditation infrastructure for network, which Yamasaki, Miyagawa et al have developed an experimental system of mutual accreditation based on digital identity certificate and digital attribute certificate mechanism, and have experimented using the pseudo job matching database of JMS [14]. In order to employ the prototype of the mutual crediting infrastructure as is, there remain several problems such as distribution of digital certificates, user interface, and privacy protection. Mutual accreditation infrastructure enables complex and flexible access control. There is also another kind of trust besides accreditation, which is based on the repetition. A person cannot be trustworthy simply by once acting in harmony with others, and it takes many repetitions to develop a trustworthy relationship. It means that the historical aspect is indispensable to deal with trust emerging from repetition. Applied social network analysis will be a help for this problem, however, we do not argue about this in this paper. The essential meaning of "trust" is too complex and context dependant to be described separately from the overall history of each network community. However, with the assumption of shared context in community, less complex types of credibility can be worth digitalizing because the shared context will complement the lack of history of interaction in the credibility information itself. The mutual accreditation infrastructure will be the first step to the coming post-capitalism and post marketalism society, which the Internet and other information technology can potentially enable.

In Japan, NPOs are paid considerable attention in expectation that they will act as a integral part of future society. Forming a community on the Internet is now becoming an indispensable method for those NPOs. The nature of mutuality which the Internet and network communities have will support the entry of more NPOs' to the Internet. The efforts for supporting network communities have just taken off and we still have much to do with it. The trend of the VCOM project has transited from provision of connectivity and homepage to the provision of original IT tools that satisfy the needs of the communities. Our next step is to realize an inter-community networking environment and a proposal of a new model of economy that involves network communities and NPOs.

Acknowledgements
    The authors would like to thank the members of the system administration team of VCOM for their help in developing the VCOM system and Shu Nakamae for his encouragement and discussion.

Reference

[1] P. van den Besselaar and D. Beckers, "Demographics and Sociographics of the Digital City," T. Ishida (Ed.), Community Computing and Support Systems, Lecture Notes in Computer Science, Vol. 1519, pp. 109-125, Springer-Verlag, 1998.
[2] M. Castells, "The Rise of the Network Society", Blackwell Publishers, 1996.

[3] R. H. Coase, "Industrial Organization A Proposal for Research", Policy Issues and Research Opportunities in Industrial Organization, New York, 1972.
[4] J. Coleman, "Foundation of Social Theory", Belknap Press, 1990.
[5] N. Contractor and A. Bishop, "Reconfiguring Community Networks: The Case of PrairieKNOW", in this volume.
[6] F. Fukuyama, "Trust", Free Press, 1995.
[7] K. N. Hampton and B. Wellman, "Examining Community in the Digital Neighborhood: Early Results from Canada's Wired Suburb", in this volume.
[8] G. Hardin, "The Tragedy of the Commons", Science, 162, 1968.
[9] E. Jantsch, "The Self-Organizing Universe", George Braziller Publishers, 1980.
[10] R. Lowenberg, "Davis Community Network (DCN): A Regional Community Networking Initiative in North-Central California", in this volume.
[11] S. Miyagawa, H. Ohashi, I. Kaneko, "Designing and Constructing Job Matching Service on the Internet for People with Disabilities", Proceedings of INET'99, 1999.
[12] S. Miyagawa, J. Murai, I. Kaneko, "Making Network Communities Work", Proceedings of INET'98, 1998.
[13] S. Miyagawa, I. Kaneko, G. Inaoka, K. Shimizu, "Constructing and Operating an Internet Site Supporting Network Communities", Proceedings of Internet Workshop '98, IEICE, Japan, 1998.
[14] S. Miyagawa, S. Yamasaki, "Trust and Reputation in the Internet --- Social Application of the Mutual Crediting System" (in Japanese) , Business Review Vol.46, No.2, Hititsubashi University Innovation Center, 1998.
[15] E. Ostrom, "Governing the Commons", Cambridge University Press, 1990.
[16] R. Putnam, "Making Democracy Work", Princeton University Press, 1993.
[17] A. Saxenian, "Regional Advantage", Harvard University Press, 1996.
[18] Simon, H., H : "Rationality as Process and as Product of Thought", American Economic Review, Vol.68, No.2, 1978.
[19] O. E. Williamson, "Markets and Hierarchies Analysis and Antitrust Implications", The Free Press, 1975.
[20] "The Annual Report of the VCOM Project '96" (in Japanese), 1997.

Davis Community Network (DCN):
A Regional Community Networking Initiative in
North-Central California

Richard Lowenberg

Executive Director, Davis Community Network
1623 5th St., Suite I, Davis, CA 95616, USA
Tel: 530-750-1170; Fax: 530-757-2938
http://www.dcn.davis.ca.us   rl@dcn.davis.ca.us

Abstract. Davis Community Network (DCN) is one of several hundred community networking initiatives now being spawned in the U. S. and throughout the world. Community networks are local responses to the needs of urban, rural and ever growing edge communities in a globally evolving information society. They are taking a variety of forms and fulfilling various functions in response to their social, economic and technical context. DCN is a notable example of the community networks that were jump-started with government or corporate funds in the early to mid-1990s. Broad based community partnerships, a sound economic foundation, an educated and participatory public, and clearly understood goals and benefits, are the still rare combination of factors that result in successful community networking ventures. Non-local factors, such as government policies and private sector telecommunication infrastructure deployment timeframes, also weigh heavily into the equation. The information society is in the early stages of an evolutionary development. Community networks must frequently reassess and reinvent themselves in response to greater local-global changes. Davis Community Network hopes to continue to learn lessons and to demonstrate possibilities, as all communities, homes and people eventually become nodes in a ubiquitously networked society.

1. Introduction

Davis Community Network (DCN) is this north-central California regional community's tele-portal to the Twenty-first century. When initiated, DCN was the first non-university campus Internet access provider in the local calling area. Today, as a 501(c)(3) non-profit research, education and community service organization, DCN is helping to make Davis and its neighbors smarter, more creative and healthier participants in the new Information Society.

DCN began in late 1993, with funding from the California Department of Transportation and University of California (UC Davis), to pragmatically demonstrate the benefits of tele-commuting and tele-work. At that time, a small group of concerned and active citizens formed DCN to serve the needs of an increasingly communications networked locality in ways that could not be properly met purely by the commercial marketplace.

T. Ishida, K. Isbister (Eds.): Digital Cities, LNCS 1765, pp. 179-193, 2000.
© Springer-Verlag Berlin Heidelberg 2000

Current efforts mark a maturing of DCN. As an organization, DCN now has a strong and representative Board of Directors, active working Committees, an Executive Director and staff. DCN also has a more robust financial base. A Civic Networking grant from the Corporation for Public Broadcasting is helping DCN and partners to develop an online Volunteer Management program, and assisting in the development of "WaterWorks", a public decision-support web site focussing on bioregional watershed issues. This pilot project is additionally supported by grants from the US Army Corps of Engineers, Hydrologic Engineering Center; the USGS National Spatial Data Infrastructure Program; and ESRI, Inc. Such efforts are augmented and made real by numerous on-the-ground regional data sharing partnerships. DCN is also a leading example and promoter of the California Smart Communities Project. The DCN network has over 1800 active online subscribers.

DCN is currently working through Memoranda of Understanding and local funding from University of California at Davis, Cities of Davis and West Sacramento, Davis Joint Unified School District, County of Yolo, and Davis Virtual Markets. DCN also has strong working relationships with the Yolo County and Woodland Libraries; as well as Davis Community Television (DCTV) and ISP partner Omsoft Technologies, with which we share facilities as a Network Operations Center (NOC). In addition, DCN is the founding partner of the Yolo Area Regional Network (YARN), and a newly initiated Regional Community Networking Partnership (RCNP), serving the multi-county Sacramento "Smart Growth" planning region.

DCN is a member of the Association for Community Networking (AFCN), and the Community Technology Centers Network (CTCNet).

Davis Community Network is working to build bridges between existing social organizations in this geographic area, with newly evolving networked processes and resources. It is helping to develop online applications that can add value and quality to peoples lives, and help localities thrive in this new tele-mediated society. DCN intends by example, to promote an Information Ecology.

2. DCN Organization

DCN has an active Board of Directors of up to 17 members, including 4 Officers. The Board is made up primarily of representatives from DCN's community networking partners, and chairpersons from its working Committees. DCN Committees are: Strategic Planning (SPC); Technical Operations (Tech Ops); Training; Public Education & Marketing; Finance; Information Providers (IPC); Web Team; Executive Committee; Public Access Working Group (PAWG) and Ad Hoc Committee on Content Policy (AHCCP).

DCN has a two person staff: Richard Lowenberg, Executive Director; and Annie Zeidman, Administrator & GIS Specialist. Jack Crowell, Network Administrator; and Marguerite Spencer, Bookkeeper/Accountant, are independent contractors; as are variously assigned project applications and content developers. DCN also has almost one hundred active volunteers serving on committees and working groups, fostering real 'community' within this network.

3. DCN Network Services

DCN contracts its dialup and network services through local Internet Services Provider (ISP) and computer support company, Omsoft Technologies. This arrangement keeps DCN, as a non-profit organization, from competing with private sector providers. In this new public-private sector relationship, Omsoft Technologies donates an agreed upon portion of its dialup and network accounts income to DCN, in support of value-added, community networking services such as public access, training, content brokering and hosting.

Omsoft Technologies currently provides DCN with 56Kb modem dial-up services, accounts maintenance and billing, new accounts registration, user and technical support, network services and partner institutions support. It also provides ISDN, spread spectrum wireless and newly available ADSL services in Davis and neighboring communities, and is contracted to maintain the DCN Network Operations Center (NOC).

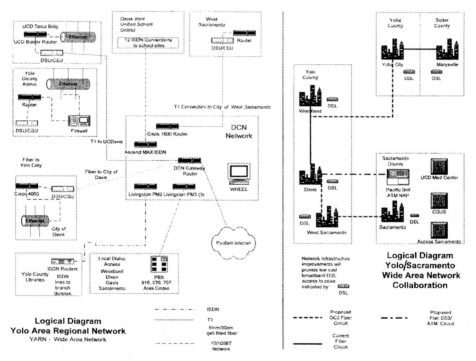

Figure 1. DCN Network Diagram

Additionally, Omsoft Technologies' founder, Robert Nickerson serves on the DCN Board of Directors and the Tech Ops Committee.

DCN is the registered owner of a number of area domain names (dcn.davis.ca.us; dcn.org; yarn.org); provides and administers domain name service (DNS), listserves, web hosting, telnet, email hosting and a few other related services.   Jack Crowell,

Network Administrator, maintains these and DCN's SUN and NT servers and other systems. The DCN Network Operations Center is the point of connection for over 300 phone lines; T-1 lines to City of West Sacramento and UC Davis; fiber to City of Davis; ISDN and soon to be upgraded to T1 connection to 12 Davis schools, networked connectivity for numerous apartment complexes and various commercial clients; and OC-3 to Pacific Bell; with all of the associated hardware (routers, hubs, switches, etc.) and software necessary to support these.

DCN's ISP partnered network services income and expenses constitute approximately one quarter of its total annual budget.

4. DCN Partnership Memoranda of Understanding (MOUs)

DCN is a partnership based organization. Certain key partnerships have been a mainstay of our existence and efforts for the past few years, helping to promote the development of additional such relationships. These community networking partnerships are maintained and annually renewed through MOUs which specify the nature of our mutual work, support and benefits, but are specifically not fee for services agreements. Current MOU partners are:

City of Davis:
DCN is to provide City staff, officials and the public with internetworking accounts and services; free public Internet classes at the City's computer lab; public access systems for the community; and host and develop community web content and online civic resources.

County of Yolo:
DCN is to provide administration and staff Internet accounts; support countywide communities' access and economic development opportunities; assist the County with online elections and voter information; and collaborate on development of countywide GIS mapping and web serving thereof.

University of California at Davis:
DCN is currently operating under an umbrella five year (1998-2002) MOU, which allows for development of project contracts and relationships with various schools and departments. Presently these include a long term interaction with the Information Technology and Computer Science Divisions on possible regional outreach of Internet 2 next year; Magic WAND (Wide Area Network Davis) wired and wireless networking of apartment and housing complexes around Davis; testbedding new technologies; and researching Internetworked economics and social processes. DCN is also working on projects with the Program on Nature and Culture; Community Development; Public Service Research Program; Environmental Sciences; Arts and Design; and Department of Agriculture and Natural Resources.

Davis Joint Unified School District (DJUSD):
DCN has been the schools' primary technology partner for many years, providing and maintaining network connectivity, planning and training for teachers and staff. Additionally, DCN has developed a secure web based Technology Inventory Database, and hosts school Internet accounts, web sites and email lists.

West Sacramento:
DCN provides the City of West Sacramento with T-1 connection to the Internet, and shares in a number of networked government and economic development projects.

Davis Virtual Markets (DVM) and Virtual Market Enterprises (VME):
These business sector ventures have been a dedicated partner for many years, providing assistance with development of the DCN Executive Director's web site; maintenance of DCN public access tele-computers; and brokering DCN/Omsoft dialup accounts.

These MOUs constitute approximately one third of DCN's annual budget.

5. DCN Projects: Grants and Contracts (1994-2000)

California Department of Transportation (CalTrans) Grant:
Funding of $500,000 to University of California at Davis, from 1994-96, initiated the California Smart Communities Program, and helped to realize and support DCN through its first three years. Vicki Suter, DCN's University liaison, managed the project and wrote primary sections of the Smart Communities Handbook.

California Smart Communities Project Contract:
DCN has been working under a renewed consulting contract from the California State University at San Diego, Smart Communities Institute, to promote Smart Communities projects and practices in northern California. DCN's Executive Director has worked with the City of Petaluma; other Marin and Sonoma County community initiatives; the Bay Area Council in San Francisco; various Sacramento area initiatives; consulted and presented on Smart Communities practices and experiences at conferences in the US, Europe and Japan; and authored a ten point Smart Communities Best Practices list.

Corporation for Public Broadcasting (CPB) "Civic Networking" Project Grant:
DCN was one of four CPB "CivicNet" Grant awardees in late 1996. The goal of this funding initiative was to promote and create examples for the civic applications of the Internet. DCN has undertaken two primary projects for this initiative. The Volunteer Management Project is designed to organize over one hundred volunteer groups and agencies in the region; to provide them with Internet access and training to improve organizational efficiency; and to develop a web-based Volunteer Management Database that will help to facilitate volunteer tasks, scheduling, and time valuation. The second project is a Bioregional Watershed Decision-Support System, with a web site titled "WaterWorks", described further in other parts of this report.

US Geological Survey's National Spatial Data Infrastructure (NSDI) Grant:
Inter-agency funding to the US Department of Agriculture's (USDA) Natural Resources Conservation Service (Yolo County NRCS office) and the Resource Conservation District (RCD), assigns DCN as project coordinator and subcontractor; with UC Davis, County of Yolo, and many other regional partners. Furthering the "WaterWorks" project, this grant has enabled DCN to set up an NT server for web accessible GIS maps, documents, metadata and database applications, including the newly orthorectified Yolo County Soil Survey. DCN is also coordinating the sharing of maps, data and technical standards among numerous public and private sector agencies and organizations, with the goal of freely providing these information resources for improved public decisionmaking.

US Army Corps of Engineers' Hydrologic Engineering Center (HEC) Contract:
The HEC office has contracted DCN to integrate WEAP (Water Evaluation and Planning), a hydrological analysis tool, initially developed as stand-alone software by the

Stockholm Institute and the Tellus Institute, with the "WaterWorks" Bioregional Watershed Decision-Support web site; and to provide WEAP training for project partners and end users.

ESRI's Conservation Technology Support Program (CTSP) Grant:
ESRI, Inc., the world's largest producer of GIS software and support services, through its Conservation Technology Program, has donated ArcView and ArcInfo based tools and training to DCN, in support of the "WaterWorks" project and our goals of becoming a regional public access GIS clearinghouse.

American Youth Soccer Organization (AYSO) Contract:
The Davis branch of the AYSO has contracted with DCN to develop and host an NT served web registration, scheduling and organizational database site, as a replicable toolset for other such community sports groups.

6. DCN Projects: Continuing and New Initiatives

Public Access, Outreach and Training:
DCN continues to build upon its capabilities to serve Davis and its mostly rural neighboring communities through a series of volunteer programs providing public access tele-computing sites and systems; free Internet use and applications classes; access and online content development sponsorship and donations; and computer re-furbishing and placement.

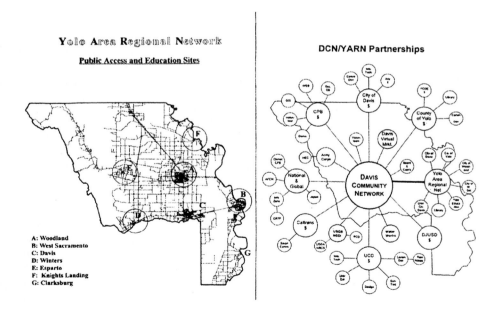

Figure 2. YARN Communities and Partnerships

DCN currently has provided systems and free connectivity at six sites in Davis: Senior Center, Teen Center, City Hall, Co-op Supermarket, Heron Technologies (computer store), Omsoft Technologies (ISP), and Davis Community Television (DCTV). Additionally planned countywide sites will be located in the communities of: Knights Landing (Grafton School), Winters, Esparto (new library), Capay Valley (Guinda Community Center), West Sacramento, Woodland (Latino Center, Schools, Library and Public Housing Center), Yolo County Office of Education, and Clarksburg. Some of these will also serve as Internet class sites.

Except for the hot Summer months, DCN provides free weekly Internet classes at the City Computer lab, and other sites as scheduled and available. These hands-on classes range from Drop-In (any questions answered), to HTML or Linux, to Train the Trainers. DCN also provides classes for schools' staff, teachers and parents, as requested.

DCN is also a partner in the UC Davis "Weavers" project, coordinated by the UCD Department of Agriculture and Natural Resources and Human and Community Development Program, to research and provide bi-lingual online access, information and education to regional migrant farm worker families and other underserved populations in the region.

The DCN Information Providers Committee's (IPC) Sponsored Projects are available to area organizations and groups wishing six month to one year donated Internet accounts, web hosting and disk space, technical assistance, or other possible services. To date, the IPC has sponsored over one hundred area organizations and projects.

DCN also coordinates an all volunteer Computer Refurbishing Project, in coordination with school districts, county and state agencies and other partners, to provide systems for public access sites and for needy high school students.

Environmental Decision-Support Program:
DCN is continuing to build upon its first phase work on the "WaterWorks" Bioregional Watershed Project. Further refinement will be needed for the web toolkit that integrates GIS, documents, databases, forums and analysis systems, to truly facilitate public decisionmaking, rather than overwhelm users with complex information resources. New and enhanced partnerships will continue to be developed to share data and agree on 'open standards' and metadata requirements. Additionally, Richard Lowenberg has been selected as a 1999-2000 Artist in Residence with the UC Davis Putah-Cache Bioregion Project.

DCN will continue to expand its capabilities as a regional GIS Clearinghouse, with DCN staff person, Annie Zeidman, serving as GIS Specialist. DCN's YARN project will organize a regional GIS Working Group, with active participation from UC Davis, county and city government staff, environmental groups, various government agencies and ESRI.

Voter Information and Election Reporting Project:
DCN & Davis Community Television (DCTV) are partnering with the Yolo County Elections Office (and California Voter Foundation), to provide web forums; issues and candidate information; position papers; precinct maps and census data; and other information that may promote greater participatory democracy. On election nights, over the past three years, DCN and DCTV have simulcast live web and cable television interviews and voter returns, with live public interaction and large viewership.

Numerous other small and large projects consume parts of DCN's schedule, as we continue to reinvent community networking on a daily basis. DCN provides both a pragmatic and conceptual framework upon which to build new technically, socially, economically and ecologically networked relationships for our evolving local-global society.

The following three initiatives: Yolo Area Regional Network; Regional Community Networking Partnership; and the Info/Eco Project, if realized as planned, will shape the next few years of DCN opportunity, direction and potential public benefit.

7. Yolo Area Regional Network (YARN)

Yolo Area Regional Network (YARN) is dedicated to the cooperative development of telecommunications systems and services for the benefit and enhancement of this regional community's social, cultural, economic, political and environmental future.

Incubating over the past two years as a project of the Davis Community Network (DCN), YARN has to date brought together a partnering of county and local governments, university and schools, public service organizations and business groups. It is now moving to incorporate as a non-profit public service and educational organization; inviting greater community sectors' involvement and participation; and developing strategically pragmatic and cooperative projects.

YARN, in this formative phase of its development, is composed of an Executive Committee with broad regional representation, and assigned working Committees. The Executive Committee currently includes Maynard Skinner, Chairman; Russ Hobby, UC Davis/DCAS; Tom Stallard, Yolo County Supervisor, and Kevin Yarris, Planner; Phillip Marler, Assistant Manager, City of Woodland; Carol Richardson, Manager, City of West Sacramento; Carlene Naylor, Yolo County Superintendent of Schools; Nanci Mills, Administrator, City of Winters; Jim Mullen, Davis Chamber of Commerce; Rick Guidara, MIS, City of Davis; and Richard Lowenberg, DCN and YARN staff person. Additional members representing county communities, institutions and businesses are now being added.

YARN's projects and staffing have been initially supported by DCN; County of Yolo; Cities of Davis, Woodland and West Sacramento; University of California at Davis; specific program sponsors, such as Pacific Bell; and the 1997-99 "Civic Networking" grant from the Corporation for Public Broadcasting. Additional sources of support are being developed.

Public conferences and workshops are a cornerstone of YARN's educational outreach efforts. YARN co-hosted three free public workshops in 1996; produced the 1997 Telecommunications Policy Summit, in Davis, which resulted in the formation of the County Telecommunications Policy and Planning Group; the April 22, 1998 COO/CIO Technology Summit and Policy Workshop, in West Sacramento; the May 15, 1998, Agriculture, Environment & Telecommunications Summit, held at the Heidrick Agriculture History Center, in Woodland; and the Schools, Libraries and Telecommunications Summit, held October 23, 1998, at the Yolo County Superintendent of Schools' conference facilities, in Woodland. Upcoming 1999-2000 programs include a series of public Y2K workshops, and a yet to be scheduled Summit on Economic Development and Telecommunications.

Yolo Area Regional Network is working to assess and GIS map existing and planned Internetworked systems and services in the region, with the goal of improving planning, innovative deployment and cost sharing of that infrastructure, while minimizing unwanted impacts on the environment, economy and society.   YARN is promoting and facilitating shared countywide telecommunications policy and planning initiatives, helping to formulate new ordinances and codes, as applied to cell tower placement; street cuts and rights of way; and agreements with telecommunications providers. YARN is also working to provide public Internet access systems at appropriate, mostly rural sites throughout the County, and will offer scheduled public training classes and seminars for schools, government, institutions, businesses, and various other regional communities of interest.

8. Regional Community Networking Partnership (RCNP)

Network of Networks and Community of Communities: A Geographical Spheres of Influence Approach to Integrating "Smart Growth" and "Smart Communities" in the Sacramento Valley Region.

Davis Community Network (DCN) and its Yolo Area Regional Network (YARN) project are working in this mostly rural, north-central California region, to promote and set practical examples for smart and vital community development in the emerging information society.

Recognizing that the forces and issues affecting Yolo County, its rural neighbors, and the largely urban and rapidly sprawling, neighboring Sacramento communities are not isolated, but are in fact complexly interrelated, DCN intends to nurture the creation of a larger initiative: the Regional Community Networking Partnership (RCNP). This urban-rural region includes many diverse agricultural, low income, multi-ethnic and racial, university, industrial, high tech, and sprawling suburban communities.   The proposed RCNP rural-urban, public-private venture intends to more appropriately and effectively plan and deploy new tele-technologies, applications and learning processes for the benefit of the regional environment and its people.

Project goals include:

a. Building upon ongoing, practical work of providing the community networking services of affordable local access, education, content, tools and applications development, and partnering.

b. Demonstrating diverse, next phase, socially / technically integrated, sustainable examples of regional community networking; with specific projects that are both practical and replicable.

c. Implementing an evaluative system to determine the economic, ecological and social value and effects of tele-networked systems and services deployment in the region, as a replicable model.

Taking an 'appropriate technology' approach, this project will utilize a range of Internet-worked systems, from low-bandwidth dialup access, ISDN and DSL services, to emerging fiber optic Internet 2 and National Telecommunications Optical Network (NTON) opportunities; providing email and web access, shared GIS and convergent multimedia applications.

The RCNP Project will undertake a detailed GIS mapping of regional telecommunications infrastructure, and relate it to newly collected social, economic and ecological data, for improved decision-support, analysis and evaluation, and as a model for replication by other regional communities and investors.

Initial partners include: (3) county and (9) city governments, federal and state agencies, community non-profits, libraries and school districts, computer and tele-communications companies, (2) universities, regional and national organizations.

Together, our work will hopefully lead to the phased creation of a regional 'information society' that promotes improved quality of life for all.

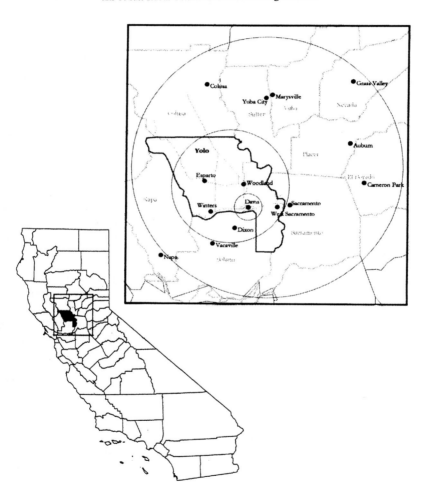

Regional Community Networking Partnership

An Urban-Rural Communities Networking Initiative

Figure 3. Regional Networking Spheres of Influence

9. Information Economics and Ecology (Info/Eco)

Smart Growth and Smart Communities: Smart About What?

With recent advocacy from the White House and state governments, "Smart Growth" initiatives are now being promoted in most US metropolitan areas, with particular emphasis focussed upon mitigating the impacts of rapid population growth; the automobile; land, water, air quality and other natural resources uses; and our desires for economic development. These largely reactive and often vested interest motivated planning processes have barely begun to consider the impacts and implications of evolving technological development, local-global internetworking of society, and the 'information economy'.

Government bodies, private sector groups and non-profit environmental, education and healthcare organizations are becoming involved in "Smart Growth" planning in the multi-county Sacramento 'capital region', where traffic impacts are increasingly untenable; state agencies intend to mandate transfers of northern mountain and valley waters to southern California; air quality looms evermore densely visible above the horizon; Central Valley agricultural fields are being replaced by sprawling subdivisions; and education is not keeping pace with new job requirements. Can application of Internetworked decision-support systems and processes help make a difference? What is the role of "Smart Community" initiatives in this context?

Networked Urban-Rural Communities: Stewarding Changing Relationships in the Information Society.

Consideration of communities in an increasingly information based society, and of our ability to act intelligently for their benefit, cannot be done without taking into account the evermore complex, socially dynamic, and economically critical relationships between cities, their rural surrounds, and all that is disturbingly filling in between. To separately address the problems, solutions and changing state of cities or rural communities, is to deny an ecological, whole systems approach to planning and living.

Few have studied or applied urban-rural relationships to the new information society. Digital thinking has further fostered an 'either-or' consideration of cities, rural areas and 'edge'. The need to better understand, to plan, and to make more intelligent, constituency-supported decisions about the impacts and implications of societal change is urgent. This task, though critically necessary, is a daunting journey into the heart of complexity. Internetworked tools and facilitated public processes may, however, offer the opportunity to do things a bit better.

Mapping Telecommunication, Education, Economics, and Community Development

Over the last few years, a select number of government agencies, corporate groups, and private foundations have funded and subsidized the development of local/regional telecommunications infrastructure and networked user applications, with the goals of promoting 'universal access', enhanced educational opportunities and 'smart' economic development. Measuring the success or failures of these initiatives is a difficult task. Anecdotal information and achievement milestones are only beginning to be documented. To date there has been no appropriate means for accurate determination of the relationship between telecommunications systems and services, and geographically specific and dynamic educational, economic or other demo-social trends. Without the ability to begin substantiating the impacts of these funding and subsidization programs, their effectiveness and continuing existence is in jeopardy, and many pioneering public networking initiatives will be left with a precariously uncertain future.

Improved methods are increasingly required for private sector investors; information technology companies; state and federal funding agencies; local government, schools, libraries, medical facilities, community groups and local businesses to determine the areas and amounts for their investment in and deployment of telecommunications systems and services; for understanding direct and indirect effects thereof; and for determining specific social needs and appropriate ways to fulfill these in an economically phased and sustained process.

Will Newly Structured Public-Private Investments in Building a Networked 'Information Society' Prove Their Economic and Social Worth, by Fostering Improved Quality of Life for All?

The Info/Eco Project is taking first steps to inventory, map and analyze the information infrastructure of the urban-rural, multi-county Sacramento Valley region. Data sharing among many public and private entities, regulatory agencies and research organizations will be required. The means, significance and value of this effort will be in the correlation of telecommunications mapping with the overlay mapping of economic development, educational, and other social indicator-based dynamic data. A partnered approach will help to assure data and analysis integrity and accuracy, as well as safeguarding certain sensitive and competitively advantageous data.

The Info/Eco Project proposes utilizing Geographic Information Systems (GIS) and internetworking tools to inventory and map regional telecommunications infrastructure and usage, and to relate this mapping to specific existing and newly gathered technical, demographic, economic and ecological indicator data. The resulting relational database will provide an increasingly detailed geographic model of the economic and social patterns and dynamics, and the associated impacts and implications of existing and required telecommunications facilities, connectivity, tele-media penetration, business and job creation, educational enhancement, community development and policy. The project is designed to be a replicable model that can serve as the basis for more effective and pragmatic 'next step' tele-social decisionmaking, policy recommendations, investments and actions. This project is particularly timely for at least two reasons:

The link between telecommunications and economic growth is being widely touted, but has little solid evidence upon which to proceed. Federal and state agencies are currently investing in and subsidizing NII based telecommunications demonstration projects with public funds, attempting to promote universal access and equity, lifelong learning and economic development. These efforts are coming under increasing scrutiny and political fire. They can only continue if they prove their economic and political worth.

The Telecommunications Act of 1996 has forced a dramatic restructuring of the telecommunications industry, with complex implications for the future of our society. Its implications and impacts are in question. Without a good understanding based upon fact, it will be difficult to protect and promote the public interests of rural areas and urban neighborhoods. The dangers are real enough; in a reasonably competitive environment, cross-subsidies become unsustainable. Even without subsidies, these areas need to know how much and in what ways they should invest in their own infrastructure needs. Currently, the information base with which to guide such decisions is weak. This project's goal is to generate a substantive information resource for improved telecommunications and economic development based decisionmaking at the local, state and federal levels.

Information Economics and Ecology: What's the Matter; What's the Difference; What's the Use?

Most public decisionmakers and corporate leaders do not yet understand the value of this proposed project or the needs that it plans to address. Many others see competitive, regulatory or security and privacy-based impediments to its undertaking. The potential gains inherent in this undertaking, however, outweigh the many perceived difficulties.

The Info/Eco Project is designed to be a direct complement to the high profile and most urgently worthwhile strategic planning and mapping efforts now in process, in the name of "Smart Growth".   These initiatives are largely reactive attempts to address and mitigate the impacts of ever greater human imposition on an increasingly fragile landscape.

The Info/Eco Project is a pro-active effort to address the cause-and-effect changes being wrought by the tele-mediation of society over the next few years, and beyond. It is based on the belief that the evolution of the Internet and convergent media will have at least as great an impact on our geographic urban-rural communities, economic relationships and social processes, as have transportation, energy systems and the industrial economy over the last one hundred years.

The realization of "Smart Communities" and "Smart Growth" must be actively integrated. It is time to truly demonstrate what we intend to be smart about.

10. Evaluation of Three DCN Project Components

Community Partnerships

Successes:

DCN is an example of how social networking is being constructed to sustain new technological initiatives. The robust partnership among regional government bodies, university and schools, libraries and businesses to date, has set an example upon which to continue building and leveraging support. Next phase regional outreach partnering is expected to set examples for the growth and practically serving work of community networking.

Difficulties:

The greatest problem and concern is the fragility of our non-profit cooperative efforts. Like many other community networks, DCN is prey to the marginalizing effects of the dominant commercial marketplace and narrowly self-interested competitive forces in the new boom and bust information economy.

Many individuals in this community use DCN solely as an ISP,; one among many now serving the region, along with free advertising supported online services such as Juno or HotMail. They seem to care little about the fact that a portion of their account payments support free public training, public access terminals, and a range of other geographically rooted community networking services.   Certain institutional partners are also forgetting the initial goal of shared infrastructure development and resources sharing for the greater public good, as original sources of outside funding come to an end and they feel they must compete locally for limited public and private funds.

One of the most time consuming and sometimes difficult tasks of our partnered approach to building a regional information society, is the regular loss of key individuals (community networking champions), especially in the public sector. The necessary reintroduction and orientation of new personnel, is often slow and sometimes frustratingly fruitless, as they enter positions with a narrow set of objectives, limited time and money, or other priority agendas.

Lessons Learned:

Though problematic, these are not unique situations for any planning and development process in evolving local democratic societies. No matter how 'right', the well intended efforts of a few cannot simply be imposed upon the many. Control is antithetical to the flow of information through society. Whether largely successful or not, the steps being taken in early adopter communities are important to be learned from. The networked sharing of mistakes, failures and successes, is vital to the espoused goal of developing 'communities of learning' in a knowledge-based society.

DCN will evolve. It will not long continue to exist in its current incarnation. It will only succeed in serving this community, if it is regularly re-evaluated and continues to adapt to the rapidly changing technical and social context within which it exists.

Technical Network Services and Approach

Successes:

DCN has operated a practical and reliable technical system since its initiation over five years ago. Though not cutting edge or state of the art, DCN has efficiently maintained Sun Unix servers and NT systems serving GIS and web database applications. Through partnership with a commercial ISP (Omsoft Technologies), latest version high speed modems, hubs and routers support dialup, ISDN and DSL subscriber connections. DCN also shares fiber and multiple T-1 line connections to government, schools, university partners, and Pacific Bell.

Difficulties:

DCN is not an ISP. It derives a portion of its income from accounts managed by its ISP partner. There is an increasingly competitive environment among commercial providers, and the role of community networking is still misunderstood by many. This region should probably not expect cable modem services for at least two years yet, and though DCN has helped to provoke DSL service being offered sooner than was anticipated, it is only available to relatively small areas of Davis and larger cities. Suburban and rural areas, with the majority of regional population, continue to be underserved.

Public access systems strategically located, especially in underserved communities, are needed, especially with high bandwidth connections, for access to web, GIS, healthcare and educational applications. Lack of availability and high cost of such high speed wired or wireless connections is still a limiting factor, other than as occasional testbed demonstrations with outside funding.

Lessons Learned:

As a non-profit, receiving public funds, DCN is limited in its ability to do more than act as a catalyst for other regional providers to better serve end-user markets, while it continues to partner with public institutions and non-profits for their improved access and content delivery. As with the previously stated partnerships, this is an evolving arena. While paying attention to global and national technological developments and service opportunities, federal policy initiatives affecting local competition and cooperation among convergent media companies and municipalities, and some of the leading edge exemplary efforts of national organizations and other communities; DCN will attempt to continue serving this regional community.

Success may possibly also mean that DCN will no longer be needed, as ubiquitous connectivity and high quality, low cost tele-media services are ultimately made available by many entities to all who desire and need them. This is not a very likely scenario, unfortunately.

Civic Participation and Decisionmaking

Successes:

DCN recently premiered its WaterWorks web site <www.dcn.org/waterworks>. In this, its first phase, the WaterWorks project is demonstrating the kind of civic processes and applications that make community networks vitally important parts of new local-global information societies. Along with our Voter Information Project, providing candidate financial information, issue based discussions, and links to multi-lateral position web sites, DCN's civic and environmental decision-support projects are beginning to receive greater local encouragement, participation and support.

Difficulties:

Online public decision-support is an important goal. It is also quite difficult to manifest. Local issues, especially about environmental change, resources allocation, or growth, are increasingly complex. More information, and access to still difficult to use online mapping and database tools, will not help most people. Online resources cannot replace humane interaction, meaningful conversation, or physical experience in the environment. Democracy, civic participation and improved decisionmaking processes require a lifelong willingness to learn and to take responsibility for one's actions. Though most worthwhile, our work in this arena is undeniably problematic and still in its infancy.

Lessons Learned:

Individual responsibility is at the heart of successful democratic societies, and may be what distinguishes geographic communities from virtual communities. Limited user feedback is providing useful understandings for how to continue development and improvement of community networking initiatives and decision-support projects like WaterWorks. Though access to online services is important, a greater social difference will be made as community networks develop site-specific tools for educating and involving their constituents in civic processes that may ultimately improve quality of life. Doing so will leverage their ability to grow and evolve with substantial community support.

11. Conclusion

Davis Community Network is pleased to be working in an early adopter community, and gaining some international attention in doing so. In time, if such efforts proliferate and appropriately meet local needs and desires, they will ideally become less noteworthy. Our social attention will then focus on the places and social organizations that are failing; and on the causes and effects of continuous rapid change and economic incongruities, which are wearing upon our best laid social plans. There is much yet to learn about how the networking of communities and society may ultimately benefit and improve the quality of all people's lives.

Examining Community in the Digital Neighborhood: Early Results from Canada's Wired Suburb[1]

Keith N. Hampton and Barry Wellman

Centre for Urban and Community Studies, University of Toronto
Toronto, Ontario, Canada M5S 2G8
khampton@chass.utoronto.ca
wellman@chass.utorontoo.ca

Abstract. Can supportive, sociable and meaningful relations be maintained online? Will life online replace, complement, or supplant life in the flesh? Netville is a residential development located in suburban Toronto equipped with a high-speed network as part of its design. The clustering of homes within this area allowed us to study the social networks, civic involvement, Internet use, and attitudes of residents. We are interested in how living in a residential community equipped with no cost, very high speed access to the Internet affects the kinds of interpersonal relations people have with coworkers, friends, relatives, and neighbors. This paper explores the research goals and methods used in the Netville project and introduces preliminary results on the effect of living in a new residential development equipped with no-cost, very high-speed access to the Internet on neighborhood social relations.

[1] Portions of this work are reprinted with permission from "Netville On-Line and Off-Line: Observing and Surveying a Wired Suburb," American Behavioral Scientist, Vol. 43 No. 3., (November/December 1999) 475-492, copyright 1999 Sage Publications, Inc. This research was supported by the Social Science and Humanities Research Council of Canada, Bell Canada University Laboratories, and Communication and Information Technologies Ontario. At the University of Toronto, we have received support from the Centre for Urban and Community Studies, the Department of Sociology, and the Knowledge Media Design Institute. We thank a host of people for their comments, assistance, and support. At the University of Toronto: Ronald Baecker, Dean Behrens, Nadia Bello, Bonnie Erickson, Nancy Howell, Todd Irvine, Emmanuel Koku, Alexandra Marin, Antonia Maughn, Dolly Mehra, William Michelson, Nancy Nazer, Christien Perez, Janet Salaff, Anne Shipley, Richard Stren, and Carlton Thorne. Others: Ross Barclay, Donald Berkowitz, Damien DeShane, Jerome Durlak, Herbert Gans, Paul Hoffert, Timothy Hollett, Thomas Jurenka, Robert Kraut, Marc Smith, Liane Sullivan, and Richard Valentine. Our greatest debt is to the many residents of Netville who have given us their time and patience, allowing us into their homes, and answering many, many, questions.

T. Ishida, K. Isbister (Eds.): Digital Cities, LNCS 1765, pp. 194-208, 2000.
© Springer-Verlag Berlin Heidelberg 2000

1   Introduction

A connected society is more than a populace joined through wires and computers. It's a society whose people are connected to each other. For the past two years we have been looking for community online and offline, locally and globally, in the wired suburban neighborhood of "Netville." We want to find out how living in a residential community equipped with no cost, very high speed access to the Internet affects the kinds of interpersonal relations people have with coworkers, friends, relatives, and neighbors.

Advances in personal computer technology, and the rise of computer mediated communication (CMC), have ignited a debate into the nature of community and the effects of cyberspace on social relations. Despite the breathless "presentism" of the current discourse [33], scholarly debate on the nature of community did not originate with the introduction of new computer technologies, but arose out of earlier concerns about the transition from agrarian to urban industrial societies [3] [23]. The discourse surrounding this debate has argued community to be *lost*, *saved*, and even *liberated* in the industrial city [26] [35]. The effect of new communication and information technologies on community and society is the latest chapter in this ongoing debate.

Early urban theorists[2] worried about the effects of urbanization on community just as modern dystopians suggest that the lure of new communication technologies will withdraw people from face-to-face contact and further disconnect them from their families and communities [7] [20]. Yet, several scenarios are possible, indeed each scenario may happen to different people or to the same person at different times. In an "information society" where work, leisure, and social ties are all maintained from within the "smart home," people could completely reject the need for social relationships based on physical location. They might find community online, or not at all, rather than on street corners or while visiting friends and relatives. New communication technologies may advance the home as a center for services that encourage a shift towards greater home-centeredness and privatization. At the same time the location of the technology in the home facilitates access to local relationships, suggesting that domestic relations may flourish, possibly at the expense of ties outside the household.

Whatever happens, new communication technologies are driving out the traditional belief that community can only be found locally. Cyberspace has enabled people to find each other through electronic mail (e-mail), group distribution lists, role-playing games, and Web chat rooms (the list is incomplete and obviously evolving). For more than one hundred years, researchers have confronted fears that community is falling apart by searching for it in localities: rural and urban villages. For the most part, their investigations have adhered to the traditional model of community as little groups of neighbors intensively socializing, supporting and controlling one another [31]. Since the 1970s, some of us have argued that community does not have to be local. It is the sociable, supportive, and identity-giving interactions that define community, and not the local space in which they might take place [22] [25].

We are not members of "little-box" societies who deal only with fellow members of the few groups to which we belong: at home, in our neighborhoods, workplaces, or in cyberspace [34]. Social ties vary in intensity, are multistranded, crosscutting, and

---

[2] For example see Park (1925) and Wirth (1938).

diverse. They extend across our environment to kinship and friendship relations that traverse a variety of social settings and are maintained through a multiplicity of means that include direct physical contact, telephone, postal mail, and more recently fax, email, and online environments.

Our research has been guided by a desire to study community offline as well as online. We are interested in the totality of relationships in community ties and not just in behavior in one communication medium or locale. In this we differ from studies of "virtual community" that only look at relationships online[3] and from traditional sociological studies of in-person, neighborhood-based communities [10] [15] [37]. The former overemphasizes the prevalence of computer-only ties while the latter ignores the importance of transportation and communication in connecting community members over a distance. Unlike many studies of CMC that observe undergraduates in laboratory experiments,[4] we are keenly interested in studying people in real settings. We are taking into account their social characteristics (gender, socioeconomic status and the like), their social positions (prominence, power), and the broad nature of their participation in social networks. We wonder how the tie between A and B is affected by the presence of absence of their tie with C [28], and how their community involvement intersects with their institutional involvements (work, unions, church, bowling leagues, etc.) and their attitudes toward society (social trust, alienation, etc.) [19].

This paper looks at the research goals and methods of the Netville project and explores preliminary results on a subsection of the total social relations maintained by the residents of Netville, those within their local neighborhood.

2   Research Goals

The Netville project addresses the following questions:
1. Can supportive, sociable and meaningful relations be maintained online as they heretofore have in public (such as cafes, street corners) and private (such as homes, clubs).
2. How do online relationships articulate with offline relationships? Will life online replace, complement, or supplant life in the flesh? How do ties with the same persons incorporate online and offline relationships?
3. What will be the fate of community? Will it atrophy as people stay home to work, learn, and entertain themselves online? Will it foster new solidarities as people get drawn into compelling virtual communities? Will it encourage limited involvement in specialized, partial communities as people surf between interest groups?
4. Will the Internet amplify "glocalization": on the one hand, intensely local – indeed, domestic – involvement; on the other hand, wider ranging social ties maintained in part through computer-mediated communication?
5. Will the Internet encourage social integration and civic involvement? Will it foster social networks and transitive relationships ("friends of friends") that cut across group boundaries, build online institutions, and articulate pressing concerns?

---

[3] see some of the chapters in Smith & Kollock, 1999
[4] see the review in Walther, et al., 1994

3   Netville: The Research Setting

Netville is a good place to investigate these questions. It is a newly-built development of approximately 120 homes, most with three or four bedrooms plus a study.[5] These are detached, closely-spaced, single-family homes in the outer suburbs of Toronto.[6] The typical Netville house, 2,000 square feet on a 40 foot lot, costs about CDN$228,000 in 1997 (US$171,000). The price is 7 percent less than the average price in 1997 for a new home in the same area[7], or 13 percent less than the fourth-quarter median for the Metropolitan Toronto new-home market [2]. Netville is similar to other developments in the area and is in an area of rapid population growth and home construction.

Netville looks like many other developments except that as you enter you pass a chuckwagon[8] with the saying "Canada's First Interactive New Home Community, *Welcome Pioneers*" written across it's canvas. It is one of the few developments in North America where all of its homes were equipped from the start with a series of advanced communication technologies supplied across a high-bandwidth local network. For two years the local network provided residents with high speed Internet access (including electronic mail and Web surfing), computer-desktop videophone (but only within Netville), an online jukebox, a number of entertainment applications, online health services, and local discussion forums, all provided free of charge.[9] In return for all of this free, very high-speed access to the information highway, the residents agreed to be studied by the corporate and nonprofit members of the "Magenta" consortium. This agreement was only lightly enforced and often forgotten by the residents. No resident was ever denied service for refusing to participate, and no data were ever collected without the residents' knowledge.

Netville's local network is a dual hybrid fiber coax technology with an ATM (asynchronous transfer mode) backbone. A coaxial cable drop wire from a coax node was brought into the home where it connects to a PCCU (Personal Computer Connection Unit) located in the basement. The PCCU connected a minimum of five computer ports within each home to the local network. Unfortunately the PCCUs installed in homes were limited in that they only allowed one household port to connect to the local network at a time. A substantial number of households installed independent software, or rigged up internal networks, to circumvent this limitation. Users could reliably expect a bit rate of 16.96 Mbps upstream and 13.57 Mbps downstream across the network. The Magenta consortium provided computer and

---

[5] To protect privacy, "Netville" is a pseudonym as is the "Magenta" consortium. The final number of homes is in flux as new ones continue to be built.

[6] Quite "outer": It takes an hour to drive to downtown Toronto without traffic; two hours during rush hour. This may have increased the attractiveness of using computer-mediated communication with friends, relatives and coworkers living in the main centers of Toronto.

[7] Based on unpublished data provided by the Canadian Mortgage and Housing Corporation, 1999.

[8] The chuckwagon was a covered wagon used on long journeys as a frontier kitchen on wheels by early homesteaders of the Canadian and American west.

[9] In addition to the free services, approximately 20 percent of residents purchased additional in-home computer-based technologies, such as: within-household networks, advanced home security systems, and "smart home" technologies.

software support and the major telecommunications member of the consortium staffed 24-hour help lines to support the network.

As technology developed and fashions changed, the telecommunications company responsible for the network decided that the hybrid fiber coax technology used in the development was not the future of residential Internet services. As the telco viewed Netville as a site for technical rather than social research[10] they terminated the field trial early in 1999 to the dismay of the residents who had grown to love the system and assumed it would be there indefinitely [13].

The people living in Netville are largely lower-middle class, English-speaking, and married. About half have completed a university degree [11]. Some are first-time home owners, others were looking for a convenient suburban home, while some were attracted by life in a wired suburb. Those with older children often moved to Netville from a nearby suburb and plan to remain there for the foreseeable future. Those in the early stages of raising a family have less settled plans. More than half of all couples had children living at home when they moved into the community, but as with most newly occupied suburbs a baby boom has since ensued. Most are white, but an appreciable number are racial and ethnic minorities. However, race and ethnicity is less an organizing factor in Netville than lifestyle, stage in the life-cycle, and to a lesser extent socioeconomic status. Residents work at such jobs as technician, teacher, police officer, and small business person. Their median household income in 1997 was CDN$75,000 (US$50,000).

Only a minority of Netville residents were experienced with technology when they moved in. Yet these families are somewhat more involved with home technology than most Canadians. Seventy-eight percent had a personal computer in their homes prior to moving to Netville, as compared to 57 percent of Canadians in 1997 [4]. The great majority of Netville homes have more than one television, own a videocassette recorder, and own a compact disc player: these rates are higher than the Canadian average [11].

Approximately 65 percent of Netville homes participated in the high bandwidth trial and had access to the network for up to two years. To our surprise, the other 35 percent of households were either unable, or unwilling, to participate in the trial despite the no-cost, low-fuss manner in which equipment and service were provided. These households provide a convenient comparison group for studying the effects of computer-mediated communication.

4   Research Design

Our research objectives led us to gather information about the residents' community ties online and offline, globally and locally. We have concentrated on learning about residents' interactions within Netville, personal networks (which extend well beyond Netville), civic involvement, Internet use, and individual attitudes. We have relied on a variety of research methods to increase the validity and reliability of our research

---

[10] To our dismay, and surprise, we could never interest the engineering-driven arm of the telco responsible for this experiment to see this as a window into how people would use technology of the future.

including ethnographic observation, surveys, monitoring an online community forum, and focus groups.

4.1   Ethnographic Observation

Netville's small and compact area made it feasible and desirable to live in the research setting. In April 1997, one of us, Keith Hampton, began participating in local activities (community barbecues, meetings, etc.,). Hampton moved into Netville in October 1997 (living in a resident's basement apartment) for a stay that extended until August 1999. He identified himself to all residents he encountered informally and in groups as a student and researcher interested in Netville. Given the widespread public interest in Netville, residents were not surprised about his activity. They treated him kindly and respected his decision to live in Netville as a full participant.

Hampton worked from home, participated in online activities, attended all possible local meetings (formal and informal), walked the neighborhood chatting, and completed a community ethnography similar to that of Gans (1967) in the New Jersey suburb of Levittown. Observations of the day-to-day experiences of the community provided details about how residents used the available technology, information about local social networks, information about domestic and neighborhood relations, and details of the residents' use of time and local space.

Survey data is useful in tapping information on individual behavior, preferences, and opinions. Yet, the ethnographic observations tell much of Netville's story. The ethnography serves as a record of the group perspective, not in the aggregate reporting of statistics, but in a contextual historical account of the day-to-day events and activities of local residents. The ability to have a participant observer physically present in Netville provided first hand access to information that would have been difficult to collect through surveys, or it would have gone unreported, unobserved and unquestioned during surveys or through the online forums.

For example, residents frequently talked online about burglaries in the community: who was robbed, who witnessed what on the night of the burglary, and future plans for prevention. When a suspicious fire burned down a house one week before its new occupants were scheduled to take possession, nothing related to the fire was ever discussed online. Over the following days, when residents were approached by Hampton on the street, they each recounted a similar story surrounding the house fire, revealing a network of community information that existed externally to the online forum. Residents also wondered why the fire was never discussed online: We believe that it would have crossed an invisible line between the provision of support and aid and community gossip. The online forum was almost exclusively used for the search and provision of various types of support. Since the owners of the burnt-out home were not yet community residents they were not members of the local email list and could not benefit from online offers of support. This suggests that Netville's email list goes a long way in meeting expectations for increasing local support and interaction, but may avoid the sometimes repressive nature of local gossip.

Netville was damaged by a major storm in June 1998 that caused power outages and the shutdown of the local network. Residents mobilized offline, when in the past similar activity had largely been achieved online, to check on the safety of their neighbors and their property, as a series of car prowlings and attempted burglaries were discovered from the same night. Community cliques and organizers were identified. These were based on geography and not on the friendship and interest groups observed online. The observation of, and participation in, mutual support and cooperative strategies in face of what was a relatively small scale disaster revealed the seeds and context to how residents would react to future problems.

The opportunity to conduct a detailed ethnography provided a unique source of information and played a key role in developing rapport with participants. The insights gained through observation and daily interaction were instrumental in developing the kinds of questions asked in our surveys. Moreover, Hampton's visibility and credibility in Netville were vital to convincing many residents to take time from their busy lives to respond to our survey.

Hampton's relationship to community participants became particularly important when the field trial ended. Although most residents were angry at the telco partner and Magenta, because Hampton was a Netville resident – and subject to the same loss of high-speed service – our research was able to continue. Residents continued to be interviewed, and our research goals took on an additional dimension as we studied how residents responded to the threat, and subsequent fact, of the loss of their high-speed service.

4.2   Surveys

Our survey obtained information on geographic perception, personal and neighborhood networks, neighboring, community alienation, social trust, work, experience with technology, time-use, and basic demographics. Learning about the residents' social networks – in Netville and outside of it – is a central concern. It is the nature of these networks that will show if personal communities are abundant, strong, solidary-fragmented, and local-nonlocal. Hence the survey used modified versions of social network protocols used by Wellman in earlier research [27].

To obtain information about network ties within Netville, we presented residents with a list of up to 271 adult residents of Netville, asking them "do you recognize this person?" [5]. In addition to asking whom they recognized we were able to collect more detailed information on each name selected, such as: if they socialized, how often they socialized, and how they kept in touch. Reaction to this question type was very positive, almost all seemed to enjoy the exercise, and many reported how interesting they found the question type [12].

To elicit information about socially close members of the residents' personal networks, wherever they live, residents were presented with thirteen "name-generator questions" [6] [27] [1]. For each question, respondents were asked to provide a list of names, using only first names and last initials to create a sense of anonymity and reduce any fear that we would attempt to contact those people listed. There was no limit on the total number of names that a respondent could provide. Once respondents listed names, the survey software created a master list of all the people listed and asked for more detailed information on each member of the personal network: demographics, where and how they met, how often they communicated, and through what means.[11]

---

[11] For a complete discussion on social network questions and the use of computer assisted interviewing (CAI) in the Netville project see Hampton, 1999.

The survey was launched in April, 1998 with intentions to administer the survey to all household members 18 years of age or older during both a pre-move and post-move interview. The pre-move survey was to be administered approximately three months prior to moving into Netville, and the post-move survey approximately one year after living in the community. An adapted version of the pre-move survey was to be administered to all residents who had moved into Netville before they could be contacted for a pre-move survey. Unfortunately, we were forced to move from a pretest-posttest survey design to a single cross-sectional survey of people already living in Netville. There were a series of construction problems, and the telco partner unexpectedly announced plans to withdraw from the field trial and discontinue supplying Netville with access to the high-speed local network. The discovery that a sizeable minority of homes were not connected to the network made comparative analysis possible and the loss of longitudinal information more palatable. We modified the survey for use with people already living in Netville and continued interviewing.

When the Magenta consortium and the telco partner publicly announced the end of the experiment, Netville residents quickly mobilized and used their networked connectivity in an unsuccessful attempt to obtain the continuation of the field trial. Netville residents did not become complete technological have-nots when the trial ended. They are using 56Kb dial-up service (provided free for six months by the telco partner), waiting and hoping for ADSL service, or they have signed up with the high-speed "@Home" cable modem service. This means that a few interviews undertaken in 1999 are more retrospective than is usual in survey research, reporting about past experiences with the local network as well as their continued experience with high-speed Internet access via the @Home network.

As all of our surveying has been computer assisted, data preparation for statistical analysis largely avoids the data entry phase. *SAS* and *SPSS* are being used for statistical analysis, including special procedures developed by our group for personal network analysis [29] [17].

In an ideal situation it would be appropriate to collect survey data at least twice, pre and post-move. Given the potential complications of doing research in a setting with many factors beyond the immediate control of the research team it may only be possible, and indeed prudent, to complete one wave of surveys over as short period of time as possible. In the end, we were able to interview a cross-section of residents, including a small number of people who "intended" to move into Netville but never did, in addition to those who had lived in the community for up to two years and had access to the high-speed network for none to two years.

4.3   Focus Groups and Monitoring of the Online Community Forum

As ethnographic observation and surveying have taken the bulk of our time and attention, here we briefly review two other data gathering techniques.

Online Community Forum: The community email list has been one of the more detailed and revealing sources of information. All Netville residents participating in the field trial were automatically subscribed to it. The list provided information on community activities, social networks, the provision of local support and aid, and proved to be a forum for community issues. The list was publicly available to Netville residents and messages were easily recorded without interfering with residents' activities. Since the list was publicly available, and participating residents agreed to have their online activities monitored in exchange for access to the local network, there are few privacy issues beyond protecting the identity of participants in publications. The content of these forums has been completely saved and will be analyzed using *Nud.ist* textual analysis software.[12]

Focus Groups: Focus groups were held by Magenta every six months starting in June, 1997. These groups discussed the challenges of living in a wired suburb, experiences with available technologies and services, and expectations for future technologies and services. Although aimed primarily at future planning for members of the Magenta consortium, the focus groups gave us opportunities to meet small numbers of residents, build rapport, and clarify information obtained through surveys and ethnographic observation. In March 1999 we interviewed key members of the Magenta consortium including the developer, the head of the consortium, and various trial managers.

5   Preliminary Results

Despite the availability of local ties, the majority of all active social relations are with those outside of the local area. In North America neighborhood relations typically represent less than one quarter of all active social ties [6] [32]. North Americans typically know about a dozen of their neighbors well enough to speak with them (usually on the street), but few know more than one neighbor well enough to consider them among their closest social ties [26] [30] [32]. The reasons for this lack of social contact at the local level are not directly associated with a loss of civic society or a decrease in community involvement. Rather, propinquity is a limited factor in determining friendship formation. People are much more likely to associate with those that are more like themselves in terms of lifestyle, stage in the lifecycle, beliefs, and participation in common activities, than what can be easily found through physical availability.

The car, telephone, and airplane are indispensable in the maintenance of contemporary social relations and in the provision of most companionship and emotional aid. Yet, despite the extent to which contemporary relationships have overcome the limitations of space, physical proximity still plays some role in the formation of social ties. Physical access promotes the sharing of small and large services, such as household items, aid in dealing with organizations, and help with housework and repairs [36]. Neighborhood relations are particularly important during the early stages of settling into a new housing development [6] [8] [9] [16].

When residents first move into a new residential development, the only thing that they knowingly share is that they have all chosen to settle in the same neighborhood. As a result physical closeness becomes the easiest and most available method for the formation of social contacts. Since all residents share the experience of being both

---

[12] Although technically feasible, because of ethical concerns and because we feared it would upset the residents, we did not monitor private email messages within Netville or from Netville residents to members of their personal communities living outside of the neighborhood.

strangers and new home owners, they are likely to develop social contact with everyone who is easily accessible [9]. It is at this time that the location of front doors, kitchen windows, and porches help determine who is most accessible and with whom people are likely to develop early social contact. As relationships develop, the extent to which neighbors share common characteristics becomes more apparent and people are able to choose the degree of social closeness they wish to maintain in each relationship. As time progresses, children start new schools, people join organizations, and through a variety of different social settings people find others more like themselves to form lasting social relations outside of the local area. Gans (1968) suggests that the process of selecting neighbors for stronger social relations, from those with whom one will eventually only become "neighborly" (i.e., say or wave "hello" on the street), is typically completed within three months of social contact. Regardless, as time progresses, local spatial patterns become less important for friendship formation [16].

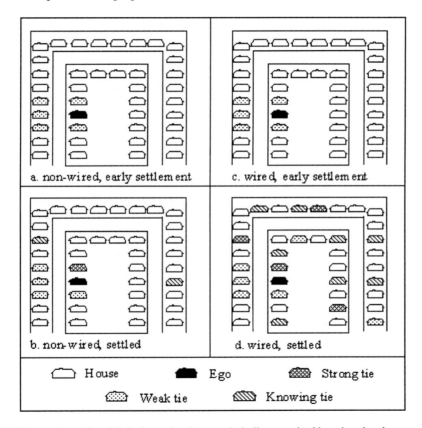

Fig. 1. Comparison of social tie formation in a newly built non-wired housing development to social tie formation in a newly built "wired" development.

Figure 1 is an example of how the formation of social relationships in Netville differs from relationships formed in traditional non-wired housing developments.

Figure 1a depicts a hypothetical example of how early social relations might form in a newly settled non-wired residential development. Social contact is with those who are most easily available and the strength of the social relation is relatively weak, based on the recency of tie formation. Figure 1b depicts social relations in the same non-wired setting at a time period greater than three months from that depicted in Figure 1a. At this time social relations in the immediate area vary in strength, extending to no more than the twelve houses in the immediate proximity to the home, and almost never extend around corners, or to the other side of the block [8] [9] [16]. Figure 1b also introduces a new type of social relationship, the "knowing tie." Knowing ties can be described as those people with whom you have never experienced any direct social contact, but yet you have some specific knowledge of their personal characteristics. Possible examples include knowledge, through information provided by another neighbor or through observation, of a neighbor's occupation or hobbies.

Figure 1c and Figure 1d are examples of the pattern of social relations found in Netville based on ethnographic observation, analysis of the community email list, and preliminary analysis of the network of neighborhood social ties. Figure 1c is identical to the initial stage of social contact found in the non-wired development. However, there are significant differences between what has been observed in Netville (Figure 1d) and what is typically observed in non-wired developments (Figure 1b). There are a greater number of strong ties, weak ties, and knowing ties within Netville. Social contact is no longer limited through accessibility, but extends around corners and to the other side of the block.

Table 1. Number of Netville residents recognised by name and socialized with depending on whether the respondent was connected to the high-speed network.

	Mean	S.D.	Min.	Max.
Number of people residents recognize by name in Netville:				
Wired	26.7	19.1	4	91
Non-wired	9.4	4.9	3	19
Number of Netville residents people talk to on a regular bases:				
Wired	6.8	7.3	0	38
Non-wired	3.7	3.3	0	11
Number of residents who have invited other Netville residents into their home in the past six months:				
Wired	4.1	4.3	0	16
Non-wired	2.9	3.0	0	10
Number of residents who have been invited into the home of another Netville resident in the past six months:				
Wired	4.1	3.7	0	18
Non-wired	2.7	2.9	0	10

Table 1 summarizes the difference between Netville residents who were connected to the high-speed network and those who were not, in terms of the number of Netville residents that they recognize and socialize with.[13] Wired residents recognize almost three times as many neighbors, talk with nearly twice as many, and have been invited, and have invited, one and a half times as many neighbors into their home in comparison to their non-wired counterparts. These results suggest that there is something significantly different about wired Netville residents that makes them more likely to have a greater number of local social contacts, of various strengths, that are more widely spread across the local area. These results are consistent with the following comments from Netville's community email list:

"I have walked around the neighborhood a lot lately and I have noticed a few things. I have noticed neighbors talking to each other like they have been friends for a long time. I have noticed a closeness that you don't see in many communities."

"I would love to see us have a continuation of the closeness that many of us have with each other, even on a very superficial level. Do not lose it, we know each other on a first name basis:"

"If this had been a regular subdivision no doubt I would know my neighbors but I would not know those of you around the corner and down the road"

One possible explanation for the higher levels of social interaction among Netville residents connected to the high-speed network is that they were somehow friendlier, or more community orientated, when they moved into Netville than those who were never connected to the network. However, this seems unlikely as everyone who moved into Netville had the same expectation of being connected to the network. There was no preset method in selecting who would, and would not, be connected to the network. Failure to connect all residents to the network was a result of organizational problems internal to the Magenta consortium. A more likely explanation is that there was something about being connected to the network that contributed to greater social contact. One possibility is the use of the community email list.

The community email list served a number of purposes in the community including early introductions, invitations to social events, the sharing of information on local services and organizations, and providing a forum for mobilization against the developer and eventually the Magenta consortium [13]. Preliminary analysis of the first ten months of email messages sent over the community list revealed that 80 percent of all messages dealt either with local activities or local support, 21 percent were requests for some type of aid or support, 21 percent involved selling items or services from the home, 19 percent were messages believed to contain information of a common local concern, 10 percent were offers of aid or support, and 7 percent were aimed at forming local activities [11].[14] In addition a number of smaller personal distribution lists were created allowing clusters within the community to maintain discussions about specific interests. The email list increased levels of communication, improved knowledge of each other (for example, occupations, hobbies, and individual

---

[13] Note: Numbers reported in Table 1 represent preliminary findings and should be considered approximate until more detailed analysis can be performed.

[14] The discussion list was created in July 1997 and continues to be used as of this paper.

backgrounds), and increased the speed at which residents could mobilize to counter perceived threats.

The success of the community network and the local discussion list in encouraging social contact within Netville does not necessarily mean that the introduction of a similar technology in other neighborhoods will always increase social contact.[15] Netville is a unique situation in that it was a trial of a new high bandwidth technology, it was provided free of charge, and it was part of a new housing development. Existing neighborhoods have existing communication patterns and consist of individuals with established social networks. People have a limited amount of time to spend in social contact with others in a given day. If established social networks and existing means of communication provide much of the companionship, aid, and support individuals need, there is little incentive to divert time and energy towards new and less certain means of maintaining and forming these ties. The same can be said about any "virtual community," that unless it fills some missing need in the lives of the intended user group, it is unlikely that it will meet with expectations for high levels of social interaction.

6 Conclusion

This paper has focused on an introduction to the methodologies used in the Netville project and briefly explores some preliminary results. Key to the methodology behind this project has been the use of multiple data collection methods to increase the reliability and validity of our results. The use of surveys, an ethnography, online records and focus groups enabled us to clarify and refine our data continuously, as well as to collect the best information possible, given the evolving nature of our field site.

In studying community, on or offline, it is imperative to recognize that community does not have to be local, but that it is the sociable and supportive aspect of interaction that defines community and not the local space in which interaction may take place. It must be recognized that relationships extend beyond the neighborhood and include a personal network of friends, relatives, and coworkers that can extend across the city or around the world. Similarly, the study of virtual communities should not be limited to interactions that take place in that setting, but should look at how these interactions fit into the entire set of social ties that make up the multiple communities in which most of us are involved. That said, it is important to realize in assessing our early results that we have yet to analyze the social networks of Netville residents that extend beyond the local setting or into the very local setting of the household. How does the maintenance of a greater number of local social contacts affect relations with other network members? How does the availability of free, very high-speed, Internet access affect how people maintain ties with social network members?

---

[15] Netville received much publicity. The publicity and the intrinsic sense of being involved in an innovative use of technology may have made some residents susceptible to the "Hawthorne effect": people self-consciously modifying their behavior on account of their being studied. Fieldwork suggests that only a small number of residents may have been affected in this way.

Preliminary analysis suggests that the Internet supports a variety of social ties, strong and weak, instrumental, emotional, social and affiliative. Relationships are rarely maintained through computer-mediated communication alone, but are sustained through a combination of online and offline interactions. Despite the ability of the Internet to serve as a global communication technology, much online activity is between people who live (or work) near each other, often in Netville itself. In Netville, the local network brought neighbors together to socialize, helped them to arrange in-person get-togethers – both as couples and as larger groups (barbecues, etc.) – facilitated the provision of aid, and enabled the easy exchange of information about dealing with the developer. The high rate of online activity led to increased local awareness, high rates of in-person activity, and to rapid political mobilization at the end of the field trial. The extent to which the use of no cost, very high-speed access to the Internet influenced the personal networks of Netville residents remains to be explored in more detail.

References

1. Campbell, K., Lee, B.: Name Generators in Surveys of Personal Networks. Social Networks, Vol. 13 (1991) 203-221
2. Canadian Mortgage and Housing Corporation.: Ontario Housing and Market Report: Fourth Quarter. Canadian Mortgage and Housing Corporation, Ottawa (1997)
3. Durkheim, E.: The Division of Labor in Society. Free Press, New York (1964) (Original work published 1893)
4. Ekos Research Associates.: Information Highway and the Canadian Communications Household: Overview of Findings. (1998)
5. Erickson, B., Nosanchuk, T. A.: Applied Network Sampling. Social Networks Vol. 5. (1983) 367-82
6. Fischer, C.: To Dwell Among Friends: Personal Networks in Town and City. University of Chicago Press, Chicago (1982)
7. Fox, R.: Newstrack. Communications of the ACM, Vol. 38 No. 8. (1995) 11-12
8. Gans, H.: The Levittowners. Vintage Books, New York (1967)
9. Gans, H.: People and Plans: Essays on Urban Problems and Solutions. Basic Books, New York (1968)
10. Gans, H.: The Urban Villagers: Group and Class in the Life of Italian-Americans. Free Press, New York (1982)
11. Hampton, K.: The Wired Suburb: Glocalization On and Offline. Paper presented at the annual meeting of the American Sociology Association, San Francisco California (1998)
12. Hampton, K.: Computer Assisted Interviewing: The Design and Application of Survey Software to the Wired Suburb Project. Bulletin de Methode Sociologique. No.62 . (1999)
13. Hampton, K.: Collective Action Online in a Wired Suburb. Mobilization, forthcoming (2000)
14. Hampton, K., Wellman, B.: Netville On-Line and Off-Line: Observing and Surveying a Wired Suburb. American Behavioral Scientist, Vol. 43 No. 3. (1999) 475-492
15. Liebow, E.: Tally's Corner. Little, Brown and Company, Boston and Toronto (1967)
16. Michelson, W.: Man and His Urban Environment: A Sociological Approach (revised). Addison-Wesley Publishing Company, Reading, MA (1976)
17. Müller, C., Wellman, B., Marin, A.: How to Use SPSS to Study Ego-Centric Networks. Bulletin de Methode Sociologique, No. 64 (1999) in press.

18. Park, R.: The Urban Community as a Spatial Pattern and a Moral Order. In Turner, R. H. (ed.) Robert E Park on Social Control and Collective Behavior. University of Chicago Press, Chicago (1925) 55-68
19. Putnam, R.: Bowling Alone: America's Declining Social Capital. Journal of Democracy, Vol. 6 No. 1, (1995) 65-78.
20. Slouka, M.: War of the Worlds: Cyberspace and the High-Tech Assault on Reality. Basic Books, New York (1995)
21. Smith, M., Kollock, P. (eds.): Communities in Cyberspace. Routledge, London (1999).
22. Tilly, C.: Introduction. In Tilly, C. (ed.), An Urban World. Little Brown, Boston (1974) 1-35
23. Tönnies, F.: Community and Organization. Routledge and Kegan Paul, London (1955) (Original work published 1887)
24. Walther, J. B., Anderson, J. F., Park, D. W.: Interpersonal Effects in Computer-Mediated Interaction: A Meta-Analysis of Social and Antisocial Communication. Communication Research, Vol. 21 No.4, (1994) 460-487
25. Wellman, B.: Who Needs Neighbourhoods? In Powell, A. (ed.), The City: Attacking Modern Myths. McClelland and Stewart, Toronto (1972) 94-113
26. Wellman, B.: The Community Question: The Intimate Networks of East Yorkers. American Journal of Sociology, Vol. 84 No.5, (1979) 1201-1231.
27. Wellman, B.: Studying Personal Communities. In Marsden, P., Lin, N. (eds.), Social Structure and Network Analysis. Sage, Beverly Hills, CA (1982) 61-80
28. Wellman, B.: Structural Analysis: From Method and Metaphor to Theory and Substance. In Wellman, B., Berkowitz, S. D. (eds.), Social Structures: A Network Approach. Cambridge University Press, Cambridge (1988) 19-61
29. Wellman, B.: How to Use SAS to Study Egocentric Networks. Cultural Anthropology Methods Bulletin, Vol. 4. (1992) 6-12
30. Wellman, B.: Which Types of Ties and Networks Provide What Kinds of Social Support?. Advances in Group Processes Vol. 9. (1992) 207-235.
31. Wellman, B. (ed.): Networks in the Global Village. Westview, Boulder, CO (1999)
32. Wellman, B., Carrington, P., Hall, A.: Networks as Personal Communities. In Wellman and Berkowitz (eds.), Social Structures: A Network Approach. Cambridge University Press, Cambridge (1988)
33. Wellman, B. Gulia, M.: Net-Surfers Don't Ride Alone: Virtual Communities as Communities. In Wellman, B. (ed.), Networks in the Global Village. Westview Press, Boulder (1999) 331-366
34. Wellman, B., Hampton, K.: Living Networked in a Wired World. Contemporary Sociology, Vol. 28 No. 6, (1999) 648-654
35. Wellman, B. Leighton, B.: Networks, Neighborhoods and Communities. Urban Affairs Quarterly, Vol. 14. (1979) 363-90
36. Wellman, B., Wortley, S.: Different Strokes From Different Folks: Community Ties and Social Support. American Journal of Sociology, Vol. 96. (1990) 558-88.
37. Whyte, W.: Street Corner Society: The Social Structure of an Italian Slum. 3rd edn. University of Chicago Press, Chicago and London (1981)
38. Wirth, L.: Urbanism as a Way of Life. American Journal of Sociology, Vol. 44. (1938) 3-24.

On-line Forums as an Arena for Political Discussions

Agneta Ranerup

Department of informatics, Göteborg university,
PO Box 620, 405 30 Göteborg, Sweden
agneta@informatik.gu.se

Abstract. This text describes experiences of four on-line discussion forums that are used in a Swedish local government context. More precisely, these experiences come from a special kind of Digital Cities that are implemented and run by local government. The main issue that is treated in the following is how aspects such as the implementation of the forums, functional features of the forums, and activities to increase access to Internet affect the on-line debate. Lastly, three strategies for how the amount of debate in the on-line forums might be increased are outlined.

1 Introduction

The main aim of this text is to present experiences of on-line discussion forums in a Swedish local government context. In particular, we will discuss various aspects that are likely to affect the debate in on-line forums, but also strategies that might be used to increase the number of contributions to the debate. There are several reasons why these experiences are of value to the research field of Digital Cities. We will in the following focus on how information technology (IT), like the Internet, is being used for improving democracy, or more particularly, on how it can be used for interactive contacts between politicians and citizens. This issue has not been treated in depth in previous broader descriptions of Digital Cities, civic networks, community networks and the like [5, 31]. As a contrast, other research can be found that treats on-line discussions about political issues, albeit with a focus on Usenet political newsgroups and AOL forums [34]. However, they are much more loosely connected to 'real world' communities and cities than the on-line forums that will be in focus henceforth.

The on-line forums that will be described are situated in two Digital Cities, each with a span of functions that are similar to many other such cities (i.e. functions to provide tourists, private business, and citizens with information). They have booth been initiated by local government, and are being run by local government. This arrangement can be seen as a contrast to other circumstances, such as when a Digital City is run by e.g. organizations with a more commercial interest [5]. Furthermore, according to writers like Buchstein [6] it is more likely that IT will have democratic effects if it is used in connection with existing political institutions. The following

T. Ishida, K. Isbister (Eds.): Digital Cities, LNCS 1765, pp. 209-223, 2000.

experiences will present examples of problems, as well as possibilities, in a context that has close connections with local government. Lastly, we will find experiences of how Swedish cities use the Internet. A recent survey indicates that 98 percent of Swedish cities have a kind of web site that sometimes can be characterized as a Digital City, or alternatively, gives a more limited scope of possibilities to its users [25]. In spite of the high penetration of Internet, only about fifteen percent of the cities provide some kind of on-line forums. The following text will present experiences from two of these cities.

2 Background and Issues of Interest

In this section we will define aspects that are likely to affect the debate in the on-line forums that will be in focus henceforth. The first such aspect is the initiation and implementation of the on-line forums. There are several alternatives that might apply. Sometimes Digital Cities, community networks, civic networks and similar phenomena are initiated by different voluntary organizations as e.g. in Amsterdam [5, 11] Santa Monica [10] and Seattle [28]. Alternatively, they can be initiated by local government as in Bologna [31], or by researchers as in Athens [32]. The first alternative is sometimes described as initiatives 'from below', and the others as initiatives 'from above'. According to experiences as well as research, the chances of getting active citizens and a lively debate are higher in some situations, e.g. where citizen groups are involved when the networks are implemented [9, 14, 28]. However, the extent to which citizens are allowed to participate in the implementation process varies considerably. Against this background we will focus on the initiation and the implementation of the web site as well as of the on-line forums, with a special focus on whether the user participation has been sufficient to result in a lively on-line debate.

According to researchers [33] as well as practitioners [24] high access to IT is one of the most important factors to get democratic effects. One such democratic effect would e.g. be when there is a lively debate in an on-line forum. It has been argued that in a near future, due to market forces, access to IT in general and to the Internet in particular will not be a problem in countries like e.g. the US [26]. Irrespectively of whether we consider this to be a true vision or not, during the time-period that is focused in this research (1997-1998) access to Internet in Sweden was not as high as 50 percent. In other words, access was far from universal. As a consequence, at the time being we might expect activities to increase access for citizens, and also activities to increase access for politicians. Hence, we will in the following be discussing if the activities aiming at increasing access to Internet in connection with the on-line forums have been adequate to result in a lively debate.

In research there is also a discussion about the functional aspects of the on-line forums as such, and how they affect e.g. the size of the discussion. First, there is the question of whether the debate is censured or not. A milder form of regulation is when a moderator reads the contributions before they are published [10].

The technical structure in itself might also affect the debate simply because technological artifacts such as on-line forums create a space of possible actions [30].

This way of reasoning is of course inspired by Actor-Network Theory [1]. For example, one possibility might be to avoid censorship and moderators, and provide an open, unstructured on-line forum where the contributions are published in a long list. Another possibility might be to provide some kind of tree-structure where different issues in the debate can be separated from each other [4, 8]. However, both alternatives enable and restrict the behavior of users. Another functional aspect is that the contributions sometimes are removed from the on-line forums after a certain amount of time. Alternatively, they are placed in some kind of archive for a longer period of time and an interested citizen might easily get an overview of previous discussion [8].

In other words, the main research question in the following is *how aspects such as the implementation process, activities to increase access, and functional features of the forums affect the debate in the on-line forums.* Moreover, with our experiences as well as previous research as a source of inspiration, there is a more open discussion about *how the amount of debate in on-line discussion forums in a local government context might be increased.*

In the following text we will find experiences of on-line discussion forums in three districts in the city of Göteborg, and one forum in the city of Sölvesborg in Sweden. The author has made 23 longer interviews with civil servants and politicians in these two cities. Furthermore, shorter interviews have been made with local politicians (six), and members of the use groups (nine) in one of the cities. Also, the debate in the on-line forums has been investigated regarding its size, contributors, and issues in the debate. The study was conducted between January 1997 and December 1998 in Göteborg, and between January 1998 and December 1998 in Sölvesborg.

3 Experiences of On-line Discussion Forums
3.1 On-line forums in three districts of Göteborg
3.1.1 The initiation and implementation of the forums
One important feature in the background of the on-line forums is the reorganization of the Local Authority of Göteborg in 1990 into 21 districts. These districts have their own councils, with the authority to decide how to spend their budgets within a framework of centrally set economic, political and legal limits. Decentralization has meant that responsibility for a number of elements of government – including schools, child care, libraries and social welfare – has been devolved to a unit with a comparatively small population and geographical spread. The district reform was also intended to increase the democratization of local government, as well as to result in increased participation of citizens in government [24]. Despite these intentions the democratic goals have been attained to a much lower degree than the efficiency goals, according to recent evaluations of actual results [16].

The on-line discussion forums in Göteborg were implemented as part of a bigger project, the DALI-project, aiming at using IT to improve local government services and to enhance democracy in local government. The acronym DALI stands for 'Delivery and Access to Local Information and services'. The project was financed partly by the European Commission, partly by the city of Göteborg. At this point of time (i.e. in the first half of 1996) Göteborg had already started to renew its technical infrastructure by implementing Lotus Notes as well as Internet technology. A prerequisite for the districts in order to take part in the DALI project was that they had embarked on this project of technical renewal. This meant that three districts out of 21 were qualified to participate in the DALI project, and agreed to do so. The names of those districts are Askim (21,000 inhabitants), Kärra-Rödbo (9,000 inhabitants), and Härlanda (19,000 inhabitants). Göteborg as a whole has 460,000 inhabitants.

The project group in Göteborg consisted of a technical consultant, a few civil servants from central and district levels, as well as a few others who worked with IT-issues in the local government administration. According to this group, the project should focus on implementing a web site containing information and an on-line discussion forum in each one of the three districts. The group made a suggestion about how this web site should be designed. Since December 1996, citizens of Askim, Kärra-Rödbo and Härlanda have been able to access the three web sites that are owned by the districts ('the DALI-system').

The European Commission supported the DALI project economically on condition that groups of potential users were to be engaged in the systems development process. As a consequence, various user groups have been involved in the development process from autumn 1996 to spring 1997. In Härlanda and Kärra-Rödbo the participants were recruited from the local political parties that are represented in the district council, whereas in Askim the participants were recruited from other local organizations such as the boards of private schools, child care institutions, and organizations of pensioners. There were several meetings between the systems developers and the groups of potential users, where the former delivered short presentations of the Internet and the DALI-system. Moreover, after a few months, the groups of users were able to express their reactions to the appearance of the system (late 1996).

As a part of the DALI project three public computers were placed in each of the three districts (see next section). This meant that the user groups also discussed what the instructions for the public computers should contain, as well as where they should be placed. Views of a more critical character were also put forward, as e.g. on how to make the DALI project known to the citizens in the districts, which was considered important. However, when subsequently asked if their own organization used the Internet and the DALI, only two out of nine user representatives knew this to be the case. According to these experiences, at the time of the interviews (late 1997) very few of them used the Internet in local government politics apart from the politicians that were involved in the DALI project itself.

3.1.2 Increasing access to the technology

As mentioned above, the district web site and the on-line forums of the three districts could be accessed from computers in private homes, or from nine public computers. Furthermore, as part of the DALI project, computers were distributed to four of the leading local politicians in each one of the three districts that took part in the project. There was also an intention of spreading Internet access to schools in the districts, which are very similar to schools in other cities in Sweden. This process progressed gradually in the three districts.

Parallel to this there was an objective in the city of Göteborg to spread the access to Internet by other measures. Very late in the period that was investigated, in December 1998, an agreement was made with an Internet supplier about providing citizens with Internet access at no cost except for the communication as such. In February 1999 this offer had been accepted by 30,000 inhabitants according to official informants [18].

3.1.3 The functional structure of the on-line forums

As was indicated above, the DALI-system was implemented as a separate web site owned by the districts of Askim, Kärra-Rödbo, and Härlanda in Göteborg, with a connection to the web site of Göteborg. The functional structure of the web sites and the on-line discussion forums can be described as follows: There is an administrative information section that contains information about the opening hours, addresses, and activities of various municipal services, such as child care, schools, social services, libraries, sports facilities etc. There is also some information about how to apply for services. However, there are not facilities to make application for service via the Web. The section for current issues contains the political proposals of the district council, and revised protocols of its decisions. There is also local news of a general character, such as the menus of schools and the restaurants for elderly, information about cultural events, as well as special events in schools etc.

The on-line forums themselves enable moderated, publicly accessible interactive discussions regarding current political issues. They are accessed by a button on the entrance page of the districts. In these discussions, citizens and local politicians can participate. The issues in the debate, as well as the headings under which the contributions are published, can be chosen according to the preferences of those who participate. If the contributions become too many the moderators remove them from the forum after a couple of weeks, but they can easily be fetched from the archive. A citizen who wants to make a contribution must fill in his/her name, but can remain anonymous when their contribution is published. In each one of the three districts there is a civil servant that checks the contributions to the debate Mon-Fri before they are published. However, according to city informants, not many contributions have actually been censored. Unfortunately, two on-line forums, the ones of Härlanda and Askim, have been closed during summer vacations, when the moderator was out of duty. Lastly, the local government web sites contain lists of some of the local politicians and their electronic mail addresses. This way, direct contacts between citizens and politicians are made easier.

3.1.4 The debate in the on-line forums

Table 1 shows the contributions to the debate in the three districts of Göteborg, as well as those who contributed. In one district (Askim) a significant amount of contributions were made, whereas in the two other districts the debate was much smaller. Furthermore, the debate in the districts of Kärra-Rödbo and Härlanda almost came to a complete standstill in 1998. Citizens, as compared to politicians and civil servants, made the vast majority of the contributions. However, Askim had two politicians who made rather many contributions to the debate.

Table 1. Contributions to the debate in Göteborg

	Askim	Kärra-Rödbo	Härlanda
1997			
citizens	107	37	28
politicians	31	7	2
civil servants	2	4	2
1998			
citizens	91	13	8
politicians	20	2	3
civil servants	4	1	0

In Askim, most contributions treated traffic issues (the regulation of specific roads etc.). Another important issue was whether or not the district of Askim should be a part of Göteborg in the future. This issue got its own heading in autumn 1997, but before this point of time contributions could be found under various headings. Furthermore, in 1998 this debate transformed into a discussion about the rules according to which the districts get economic support from the central authority of Göteborg. One could also find other smaller debates on various issues, something that applied to the districts of Kärra-Rödbo and Härlanda too. A few of these were primary school issues, child care issues, and environmental issues. Of special interest is e.g. a debate on primary school issues in Härlanda in 1997 with several contributions. However, the politicians chose to answer through other means than the on-line discussion forum.

3.2 Experiences of an on-line forum in Sölvesborg
3.2.1 The initiation and implementation of the forum
Sölvesborg is a rather small town in the south of Sweden, with 16,500 inhabitants. Two features in the initiation process of the on-line discussion forum in Sölvesborg are of special importance. The first is the fact that the municipality of Sölvesborg during the 90:s has been providing two Information offices for their citizens where a broad spectrum of information about local government services and other kinds of services can be found. These offices have been using IT during their whole existence, but as new kinds of technology developed in the middle of the 90:s they were replaced by modern systems.

Also, in Sölvesborg there have been several attempts to renew the technical infrastructure of the local government administration at large with the help of various sources of funding. As an example, Sölvesborg received financial support from the European Commission for a pilot study about technical renewal in the middle of the 1990:s, but a few years later an application for a further phase of their project was turned down. However, Sölvesborg received economic support from Swedish sources (NUTEK and KK-stiftelsen) for a smaller project aiming at providing citizens with services via Internet. As a consequence, by the end of 1997 the local government web site of Sölvesborg contained an interactive service where parents could apply for child care through the Web, as well as an interactive on-line discussion forum. At that point of time the municipality also got economic support for providing schools with Internet access.

The forum was designed by a small group of civil servants that had previously worked with the Information offices, and by a technical consultant. The leading politician of Sölvesborg also supported the introduction of the on-line forum on the local government web site. However, no other kinds of potential users were asked to participate in the process of design.

3.2.2 Increasing access to the technology

The citizens of Sölvesborg have access to public computers and Internet at the Information offices, as well as at the libraries. No public computers have been installed in connection with the introduction of the on-line forum. Furthermore, no politicians have been given access to computers and the Internet as a part of the process in which the forum was introduced, but four politicians already had access to Internet at their offices. Consequently, the citizens have a means of communication with four of the politicians through Internet, and the local government web site presents their email addresses. Also, as was said above, there is a continuous process of implementing Internet at the schools of Sölvesborg.

Furthermore, as was mentioned previously, an application for a further phase of project of technical renewal in Sölvesborg was turned down by the European Commission. As a consequence, one idea that had to be abandoned was to provide all citizens with Internet access at a reduced cost.

3.2.3 The functional structure of the on-line forum

The web site of Sölvesborg contains information about local government services, links to services that other public agencies provide, as well as information aimed at tourists. The on-line forum is accessed through a button on the entrance page, in a similar way as the forums in Göteborg. As opposed to the forums in Göteborg, the one in Sölvesborg has, between December 1997 and December 1998, been open for discussion about only one issue at a time. In 1998 this issue was chosen by the project group that consisted of civil servants, with the assistance of the leading local politician. There has been one issue suggested for discussion during the spring of 1998, and another in October-November. In December citizens were allowed to discuss issues according to their own choice, as well as a suggested issue.

After the debate on a certain issue has come to a complete standstill, the contributions are removed from the web site. They remain in the system, but can not easily be accessed by citizens. The issues for discussion are shortly introduced with the help of a text, as well as relevant maps etc. Citizens wanting to contribute must provide their name, but it must not necessarily be presented on the screen. The different contributions to the debate are shown on a long list, with the latest on top. The date, the signature/name of the contributor, as well as 20 words from the contribution are also shown on the screen. In Sölvesborg there is no moderator that checks the contributions before they are published, except for an automatic control of whether they contain 'forbidden' words. Unfortunately, the on-line forum of Sölvesborg has been closed between July 1998 and October 1998, partly due to the summer vacations and a lack of interesting issues for discussion.

3.2.4 The debate in the on-line forum
The first suggested issue that citizens were invited to discuss was whether a big natural museum aimed at tourists should be built or not. During a period of six months approximately 50 contributions were made on this issue. Seven were made by politicians, and the rest by citizens. A third of the contributions dealt with pros and cons of building the museum, a third with how it should be financed, and a third treated the debate in itself. For example, the citizens wanted the politicians to be more active in the debate, and they wanted new issues to be brought into the debate. The forum was closed from July to October 1998, but after that a second issue for discussion was introduced. Now the forum welcomed citizens to discuss if some of the streets in Sölvesborg should be for pedestrians only. The result was a discussion with 19 contributions, most of them in favor of that suggestion. However, five of the contributions asked for new issues to discuss. This resulted in a completely open discussion, as well as a debate on where a new big road in the area should be built. In the open debate the citizens discussed environmental issues, as well as issues such as whether a special ceremonial arrangement should be introduced when immigrants received their Swedish citizenship. All in all, citizens made 81 contributions, politicians made 15 contributions, and a civil servant made one contribution to the discussion in the on-line forum.

4 Which Aspects Have Affected the Debate?
4.1 The initiation and implementation of the on-line forums
In both cities the introduction of the on-line forums took place within a larger project with the aim of improving the technological infrastructure and services of local government, as well as improving democracy in local government. But there have been very few activities in the two cities that have allowed various groups of citizens and politicians to participate in the implementation process, and in that way become more deeply involved in the future of the web site and the on-line forums. There was one exception to this. In the implementation of the forums in Göteborg, potential user groups were allowed to participate in the implementation process during a limited period of time. However, these groups were dissolved a few months after the web sites and on-line forums had been introduced to the public. Consequently, the project management did not take full advantage of this potential for creating a stable interest in the on-line forums. In other words, there have been no strategies, with the exception of some very rudimental activities, for how an active interest in the on-line forum could be created. This could be compared to previous research that states continuous user involvement as a necessity in order to create a lively interest in e.g. a community network or a Digital City [9, 14, 28].

4.2 Activities to increase access to the technology

In both cities there has been an intention to provide various groups, as e.g. citizens, children at school, and politicians, with access to Internet. The most ambitious activities to increase access have taken place in Göteborg, but Sölvesborg has not been far behind. All in all: both cities seemed to agree about the fact that increased access to technology is important when Internet is used to improve democracy in local government. However, what is most obvious is the comparatively small interest of the politicians in increasing their own access to technology. It is very likely that the limited access to technology in this group has led to a less vivid debate. In each district council or local government council only a few of the politicians had the most fundamental facilities for being able to participate in the discussions in the on-line forums (a computer, access to Internet etc.). If all politicians got access to Internet they could publish their e-mail addresses on the local government web site, and as a consequence, exchange messages with citizens more in private.

The assumption that the politicians actually are willing to discuss with citizens is very reasonable when considering their role as politicians. As a matter of fact, this is a fundamental assumption in a report in which politicians themselves discussed how to improve democracy in local government [16]. For this reason, their lack of the most basic infrastructure for participating in on-line conversation is of course very harmful to potential democratic effects.

Lastly, according to recent statistics, in May 1999 50.3% of the Swedish population between 12-78 years of age used the Internet actively, and the access-rate is steadily rising [13]. Thus, the problem of limited access in the population at large in Sweden, as well as in the other Nordic countries, Canada and USA might become less important.

4.3 The functional structure of the on-line forums

A comparatively lively debate took place in the district of Askim where the choice of issues in the debate was left to the citizens. At the end of 1998 the on-line forum of Sölvesborg also welcomed a debate about issues according to the choice of citizens. Therefore it seems likely that an open debate is a necessity, albeit not a guarantee, for a debate that attracts citizens. The need for openness might not be without exceptions though. Previous research describes, not very surprisingly, the idea that censorship and moderators limit the freedom of expression in a debate. Yet, all kinds of moderation does not have to be negative if one aims at creating a lively debate in an on-line forum. For example: in the forums in Göteborg as well as in Sölvesborg there were some kind of moderation; in the form of a moderator, and a list of 'forbidden' words. In spite of these arrangements citizens initiated a discussion of issues that local politicians most probably would not have chosen. The most obvious example is the discussion in Sölvesborg about ceremonial arrangements when immigrants receive their Swedish citizenship. Another example is the discussion about whether the district of Askim should be a part of Göteborg in the future or not. On the other hand, a completely open choice of issues can be negative if it results in contributions that by some citizens are considered to be offensive, and they for this reason choose to withdraw from the discussion [10].

A more strictly functional aspect of a forum is if the contributions are published in a long non-structured list, or in some kind of tree-structure. The former was the case in Sölvesborg, and the latter in the forums in Göteborg. Our experiences suggest that citizens should be allowed to make a rather open choice of issues in the debate. However, the open choice must be combined with some kind of structure that gives citizens an overview of the debate. A list that contains 50 contributions or more as in Sölvesborg might be of limited value here. The functional structure of the forums in Göteborg is more likely to meet this demand.

Lastly, in Göteborg as well as in Sölvesborg the on-line forums were closed during summer vacations. This is negative as it interrupts the act of checking up the debate that might have become habitual to some citizens. There are always limitations as to what extent citizens are allowed to participate in a democratic process. But limitations such as these are most likely to be harmful when one wants to create a lively debate in on-line forums. In addition, it ought to be fairly simple to solve this problem.

5 Strategies for Implementing On-line Discussion Forums

5.1 The value of on-line debate

In the previous chapter we discussed the influence of different factors on the on-line debate. In this section there will be some further comments on the differences between the districts in Göteborg, as well as on the value of this kind of on-line debate at large. First, the debate in Askim contained many more contributions as compared to the other two districts. How can this be explained? Askim had two politicians that actively contributed to the debate, which is a different situation from the other districts. Furthermore, the citizens were also more willing to contribute. Thus, the attitude towards using on-line discussion forums *per se* is an issue for further studies. However, there must be some other factors that affect an on-line debate than those we have discussed. One such factor is the local political climate, or in other words, whether it exist any 'hot topics' to discuss or not. This was defined as an important factor by some of the politicians themselves [24]. Due to restrictions of space and time, the author has limited the focus of discussion to the factors that have been defined above. This does not mean, however, that there are no other factors of importance. Against the background of previous research, the factors that we have focused here were judged as very important in relation to on-line discussions, despite the existence of other factors of relevance.

All in all: some citizens seem to be interested in using Internet to participate in a political debate, but the on-line forums have not yet been used to capacity. Even so, their utility has to be emphasized. In our investigation, we have only focused on citizens and politicians who are actively taking part in the debate by posting contributions. However, a complete description of actual usage should also include more passive users such as 'lurkers' who do not post a message themselves [34], a behavior that also can be seen as a way of participating in a democratic process. There are informal evidence that there might be a significant amount of lurkers in this kind of forums [25]. Recent research about what is considered as more successful Digital Cities like the Iperbole in Bologna, and other similar sites, describes that they contain a comparatively small amount of political debate [2]. This being the case despite a target population that can be counted in millions rather than tens of thousands, as regarding the forums that have been studied here. Lastly, as already has been pointed out, the forums that we have discussed are of a special value since they have clear connections with an already existing political institution [6].

5.2 Three potential strategies
What strategies could make the on-line forums more successful in this particular of context?

A first strategy would be to introduce a certain quality of many community networks into this genuinely Swedish context, i.e. that they are implemented with the help of various citizen groups and local organizations [28]. Moreover, in most community networks users are continuously being involved in the implementation process [23], as well as afterwards. Therefore, with the community networks as a source of inspiration, local citizen groups, e.g. the parents of children at school or in child care, or the relatives of elderly that receive service from local government, might get access to Internet at a reduced rate. As a consequence, they could build their own virtual community or network. As a first step, the citizen groups might find it useful to share information among themselves, as well as discuss various issues on-line. They could also be offered an opportunity to participate in the implementation process in association with the local government web site and its on-line forum. In this way, the common group interest of parents or relatives to participate in a virtual community that exists [15] will be used as a ground for activity. This as opposed to a situation where a common place of residence is taken as a sufficient guarantee that the on-line debate will be lively [8].

A strategy like this might be criticized for being a way of colonizing citizen groups, so that they become a part of the political structure of local government [7, 20]. However, many citizen groups and non-governmental organizations are themselves eager to take advantage of modern technology [12], which makes them very suitable as testbeds for how Internet could be used in practice to improve democracy [21]. This might also be a way of including citizen groups that are working with school issues, child care issues etc in a democratic structure that counteracts the risk of fragmentation, which might appear in situations where an organization focus on only one kind of issues at a time [19, 20]. The latter is a risk that is noticed by current research in political science [20].

A second strategy would be to make use of the interest to participate in a debate on other issues than local government politics that many people have, according to other experiences [31]. Or put simply: we could try to sell the discussion forum as a local chat area where the choice of issues is left to those who participate. This is a way of using the pleasure of chatting without any limitations regarding issues that can be discussed etc [17, 34]. The many discussion groups that exist on Internet as a whole might serve as an argument to prove that these kinds of discussions are fruitful. Also, this strategy is interesting as compared to the assertion that the issues to be discussed in an on-line forum must be suitable for the 'target group', or in other words they are supposed to be chosen by others than the discussants [29]. As a contrast, in this second strategy the discussants themselves are in a position to influence the agenda for discussion. However, the ultimate goal of on-line discussions is not necessarily that one arrives at a common point of view. Instead, as is argued by Robins [27], the on-line forum might serve as an arena for a discussion between participators with different standpoints. In other words, the on-line discussion might be of value in itself even if it does not result in the kind of common values and community spirit that are associated with e.g. community networks [27, 28].

Lastly, a third strategy might be to more seriously involve the politicians in the on-line forum as such. The importance of this kind of strategy was emphasized in the discussion in the on-line forums where many of the contributors wanted the politicians to become more active in the debate. Moreover, Benjamin Barber, one of the great theorists of deliberative democracy, argues that citizens not only have the right to speak, but also the right to be heard [3]. As a consequence, this third strategy should also include that all politicians should be given access to Internet, as well as an email address that is published on the net and otherwise whenever there is a chance of doing so. Another part of it would be to emphasize how important it is, for the sake of democracy, that the politicians actually contribute to the debate in the on-line forums. In fact, the very participation by the politicians in itself makes it even more likely that the debate will actually affect the political process [21]. We could also suggest that politicians might use the Internet in general, and the forums in particular, as a tool for collecting the opinions on various 'hot' issues according to their own choice. Hopefully, several politicians will take part in such a process where issues are generated. In Sölvesborg, only one politician took an active part in the discussion about important issues that could be introduced in the on-line forum. Furthermore, according to our experiences the discussions about one single issue at a time can not be characterized as a success. Consequently, a conclusion that could be drawn is that politicians from several political parties should contribute to such a process to create a discussion about the broadest possible range of issues.

As thus, this strategy would be a way of more actively using Internet in an already established political context. As mentioned in the introduction, this has been defined as a critical success factor for Internet to be able to improve democracy [6, 21, 29]. However, as we have shown above, in spite of the seemingly close connection between the forums and local government, this has not been done to a sufficient degree. But, is this not a defensive strategy, in which we only use a fraction of the immense potential of the technology? Mark Poster, a Professor of History, answers that:

> "In response I can assert only that the 'postmodern' position need not be taken as a metaphysical assertion of a new age; that theorists are trapped within existing frameworks as much as they may be critical of them and wish not to be; that, in the absence of a coherent alternative programme, the best one can do is to examine phenomena such as the Internet in relation to new forms of the old democracy, while holding open the possibility that what might emerge might be something other than democracy in any shape that we may conceive it given our embeddedness in the present. Democracy, the rule by all, is surely preferable to its historical alternatives. And the term may yet contain critical potentials since existing forms of democracy surely not fulfil the promise of freedom and equality" [22: 214-215].

And the author is bound to agree.

6 Conclusion

In our four cases there have been no strategies, with the exception of some very rudimental activities, for how an active interest in the on-line forum could be created. Neither have the on-line forums yet been used to capacity. This is in line with previous research that states continuous user involvement to be a necessity in order to create a lively interest in e.g. community networks or a Digital City. Also, according to our experiences a clear focus on how the politicians should be given access to technology seems to be advisable. Lastly, open choice of issues for discussion is to be preferred. However, this kind of policy should be combined with a functional structure of the on-line forum that gives an overview of the debate as well as continuous access to it.

Intuitively, the potential of on-line discussion forums as used for political discussions is immense. However, for being used successfully, more mundane aspects, such as those that have been described here, must be taken care of.

References

1. Akrich, M.: The De-scription of Technical Objects. In: Bijker, W. E. , Law, L. (ed.): Shaping Technology/Building Society. Studies in Sociotechnical Change. MIT Press, Cambridge Massachusetts, (1992) 205-224.
2. Aurigi, A.: Digital City or Urban Simulator. Lecture Notes in Computer Science (in this volume), Springer-Verlag, (2000).
3. Barber, B.: Strong Democracy. Participatory Politics for a New Age. University of California Press, Berkely (1984).
4. Benson, T. W.: Rhetoric, Civility, and Community. Political Debate on Computer Bulletin Boards. Communication Quarterly 44, 3 (1996) 359-378.
5. Besselaar, P., Beckers, D.: Demographics and Sociographics of the Digital City. In: Ishida, T. (eds.): Community Computing and Support Systems. Social Interaction in Networked Communities. Springer, Berlin (1998) 108-124.
6. Buchstein, H.: Bytes that Bite: The Internet and Deliberative Democracy. Constellations 4, 2 (1997) 248-263.
7. Castells, M.: The Information Age, Volume II. The Power of Identity. Blackwell Publishers, Oxford (1997).
8. Croon, A., Ågren, P-O.: Four Forms of Virtual Communities, (Fyra former av virtuella gemenskaper, In Swedish). Human IT 2 (1997) 9-20.
9. De Cindio, F.: Community Networks for Reinventing Citizenship and Democracy. In: Papers for the EACN Workshop on Community Networking and the Information Society: Key issues for the New Millennium. European Association for Community Networks, Paris (1999) http://www.canet.upc.es/fiorella99.html [19990516].
10. Docter, S., Dutton, W. H.: The First Amendment Online: Santa Monica's Public Electronic Network. In: Tsagarousianou, R., Tambini, D., Bryan, C. (eds.): Cyberdemocracy. Technology, Cities and Civic Networks. Routledge, London & New York (1998) 125-151.
11. Francissen, L., Brants, K.: Virtually Going Places: Square-hopping in Amsterdam's Digital City. In: Tsagarousianou, R., Tambini, D., Bryan, C. (eds.): Cyberdemocracy. Technology, Cities and Civic Networks. Routledge, London & New York (1998) 18-40.
12. Hallam, E., Murray, I.R.: World Wide Web Community Networks and the Voluntary Sector. The Electronic Library 16, 3 (1998) 183-190.

13. http://www.sifointeractive.com/index2.html [19990618]
14. Howley, K.: Equity, Access, and Participation in Community Networks. Social Science Computer Review 16, **4** (1998) 402-410.
15. IT-commission.: Digital Democracy. A Seminar on Technology, Democracy, and Participation. Report number 2/97 (Digital demokrati. Ett seminarium om teknik, demokrati och delaktighet. IT-kommissionens rapport 2/97, in Swedish). Sweden (1997).
16. Johansson, L. et al.: The District Reform in Change. (Stadsdelsreform i utveckling, in Swedish). Report to the City Council of Göteborg 20th of August 1998. City of Göteborg (1998).
17. Jones, S.: The Internet and its Social Landscape. In: Jones, S. (ed.): Virtual Culture. Identity and Communication in Cybersociety. SAGE publications, London (1997) 7-35.
18. Jurnell, S. (1999).: Director of the Internet-supplier Utfors, private communication 16th February 1999.
19. Lievrouw, L. A.: Our Own Devices: Heterotopic Communication, Discourse, and Culture in the Information Society. The Information Society 14 (1998) 83-96.
20. Montin, S.: New Forms of Local Democracy (Lokala demokratiexperiment exempel och analyser, In Swedish). Demokratiutredningens skrift nr. 9, SOU 1998: 155. Stockholm (1998).
21. Olsson, A. R.: Electronic Democracy (Elektronisk demokrati, in Swedish). SOU 1999:12. Stockholm (1999).
22. Poster, M.: Cyberdemocracy: The Internet and the Public Sphere. In: Holmes, D. (ed.): Virtual Politics. Identity and Community in Cyberspace. SAGE Publications, London (1997) 212-228.
23. Ranerup, A.: Participatory Design through Representatives (Användarmedverkan med representanter, in Swedish, with Summary in English). Ph.D. Dissertation, Report 9. Department of Informatics, University of Göteborg (1996).
24. Ranerup, A.: Contradictions when Internet is Used in Local Government. In: Heeks, R. (ed.): Reinventing Government in the Information Age. Routledge, London New & York (1999) 177-193.
25. Ranerup, A.: A Comparative Study of On-line Forums in Local Government in Sweden. Department of informatics, Göteborg university (work in progress).
26. Resnick, D.: Unequal Access: A Pressing Moral Problem? In: Proceedings of the 4th ETHICOMP International Conference on the Social and Ethical Impacts of Information and Communication Technologies. Luiss Guido Carli University/ De Montfort University/ SCSU, Rome (1999).
27. Robins, K.: Cyberspace and the World We Live In: Body & Society 12 **3-4** (1995) 135-155.
28. Schuler, D.: New Community Networks: Wired for Change. Addison-Wesley, New York (1996).
29. Smit, E. Y. M., Van Boeschoten, R. M.: Deliverable 3: Forum Workshop. Impressions and results. Forum: A Workshop on Public Debates on the Internet. ISPO 97066. Commission of the European Communities, Rotterdam (1998).
30. Stolterman, E.: Technology Matters in Virtual Communities. Positioning Paper for the Workshop Designing Across Boarders: The Community Design of Community Networks. PDC '98/ CSCW '98, Seattle, Nov. 1998, USA (1998) http://www.scn.org/tech/-thenetwork/Proj/ws98/index.html [19990618].
31. Tambini, D.: Civic Networking and Universal Rights to Connectivity: Bologna. In: Tsagarousianou, R., Tambini, D., Bryan, C. (eds.): Cyberdemocracy. Technology, Cities and Civic Networks. Routledge, London & New York (1998) 84-109.
32. Tsagarousianou, R.: Back to the Future of Democracy? New Technologies, Civic Networks and Direct Democracy in Greece. In: Tsagarousianou, R., Tambini, D., Bryan,

C. (eds.): Cyberdemocracy. Technology, Cities and Civic Networks. Routledge, London & New York (1998) 41-59.

33. Tsagarousianou, R., Tambini, D., Bryan, C. (eds.): Cyberdemocracy. Technology, Cities and Civic Networks. Routledge, London and New York (1998).

34. Wilhelm, A. G.: Virtual Sounding Boards. In: Hague, B. N., Loader, B. D. (eds.): Digital Democracy. Discourse and Decision Making in the Information Age. Routledge, London & New York (1999) 154-178.

Towards the Integration of Physical and Virtual Worlds for Supporting Group Learning

Fusako Kusunoki[1], Masanori Sugimoto[2], and Hiromichi Hashizume[3]

[1] Tama Art University,
2-1723, Yarimizu, Hachioji, Tokyo, 192-0394, Japan
kusunoki@tamabi.ac.jp
[2] University of Tokyo,
7-3-1, Hongo, Bunkyo-ku, Tokyo, 112-0033, Japan
sugi@r.dl.itc.u-tokyo.ac.jp
[3] National Center for Science Information Systems,
3-29-1, Otsuka, Bunkyo-ku, Tokyo, 112-8640, Japan
has@rd.nacsis.ac.jp

Abstract. In this paper, we describe a system that integrates physical worlds (physical cities) and virtual worlds (digital cities), and its applications to supporting group learning. We have so far constructed several systems for supporting collaborative learning. One of the aims of CSCL (Computer-Supported Collaborative Learning) is to promote mutual learning through interactions and discussions among learners. Our previous experiments, however, have shown that these systems may not be so effective for supporting interactions and discussions at times. In order to enhance interactions further, a system should support externalization of each learner in an easily recognizable manner. Through such externalization, learners can actively collaborate or conflict with each other through discussions.

The proposed system integrates a board game and a computer simulation, is used for studying urban planning and environmental problems. Each learner externalizes and represents his/her own ideas on a board game, which allows him/her to actively participate in a learning situation and to share the representations with other learners. The computer simulation calculates and visualizes the status of the city being constructed on the board game, in terms of air pollution, water pollution, etc..

Thirty fifth-grade pupils who had studied environmental problems in school participated in the experiments. The experiments showed that our system is effective for enhancing interactions, activating discussions, and raises learners' engagement.

1 Introduction

In this paper, we describe a system that integrates physical worlds (physical cities) and virtual worlds (digital cities), and its applications to supporting group learning. We have so far constructed several systems for supporting collaborative learning [7][8]. One of the aims of CSCL (Computer-Supported Collaborative

T. Ishida, K. Isbister (Eds.): Digital Cities, LNCS 1765, pp. 224–235, 2000.

Learning) [6] is to promote mutual learning through interactions and discussions among learners. Our previous experiments, however, have shown that these systems may not be so effective for supporting interactions and discussions at times [8]. In order to enhance interactions further, a system should support externalization of each learner in an easily recognizable manner. Through such externalization, learners can actively collaborate or conflict with each other through discussions.

The proposed system integrates a board game (physical world) and a computer simulation (virtual world) [1][14], and is used for studying urban planning and environmental problems. Each learner externalizes and represents his/her own ideas on a board game, which allows him/her to actively participate in a learning situation and to share the representations with other learners. The board game is composed of a checkerboard, game pieces ("houses", "factories", and "trees"), and geographic objects ("mountains", "rivers" and other similar elements of nature). The computer simulation calculates and visualizes the status of the city being constructed on the board game, in terms of air pollution, water pollution, etc.. In order to link between the board game and the computer simulation, Radio Frequency Identification (RFID), which is one of the object identification and data transfer technologies, is used. Tags and readers are embedded in pieces and a board, respectively, and the computer simulation can automatically recognize arrangements of pieces on the board.

When learners use the system, they first set up a board by arranging geographic objects in order to construct a city resembling their own. Each learner puts a piece on the board in turn. When he/she completes his/her move, the computer simulation visualizes the current and future status of the city. After reviewing simulation results, the learner considers what move to play next. For example, if he/she has noticed that air pollution will be a problem in future, he/she may change his/her initial idea and place a "forest" piece. Finally, when the design of the city is complete or time has run out, the computer simulation diagnoses the design of the city and points out planning problems.

Thirty fifth-grade pupils who had studied environmental problems in school participated in the experiments. The experiments showed that physical worlds (physical cities) on the board game are useful for enhancing interactions among learners, and virtual worlds (digital cities) in the computer simulation provide effective stimuli and feedback for learners' further interactions, such as their collaborations and conflicts. Consequently, our system could activate learners' discussions and raise learners' engagement [11]. The integration of the board game and the computer simulation was also successful in that both were used smoothly by the pupils. During post-experiment interviews it was determined that the usage of the system was not difficult, and was enjoyable (most of the pupils stated that they would like to play the game again).

This paper is organized as follows: In Sec. 2, the underlying philosophies and theoretical backgrounds of this work are described. In Sec. 3, the configurations of the proposed system are shown. Section 4 gives the experiments and evaluations with the system. Section 5 concludes the paper.

2   Backgrounds

2.1   Failure of Group Learning

Use of computers in today's school education has come to a transitional phase. While there is a possibility that the potential through using computers may be utilized in education, some are concerned that it may not go beyond mere information exchange [13]. Conventionally, in school education, computers were used by pupils for their individual studies, but now there is a new issue as to how to make full use of computers in a group learning environment. Devoted school teachers respond rather negatively to the importance of "learning from each other" in future education and the idea of collaborative learning supported by a computer. They know full well that the conventional "group" learning method aiming at "learning from each other" did not work and strongly feel that "individual learning" of each pupil should be more emphasized. Group learning failed because children tend to yield to the judgement or "authority" of the group in such an environment and end up "leaving matters to others", "following others blindly", "reinforcing confusion", "causing inefficiency" and "allowing high-handed behavior of a strongman", all of which are harmful effects that are likely to occur in group decision making [5] .

2.2   For Effective Support of Interactions

For Supporting Information within a Group In group learning, individual members may not speak or take action with each other. As a result, they may "leave matters to others" and allow "high-handed behavior of a strongman". It is known that interactions among pupils does not increase as much as expected when computers are simply applied to school education [7] [8]. This is mainly because, among other reasons, uneven knowledge levels of individual learners are not taken into consideration in a typical group learning situation and there are differences in their ability to externalize thinking. In previous studies, we had tried to overcome difficulties caused by learners' uneven knowledge levels through active discussions and interactions induced by using computers with the view to deepening their understanding of problems and enhancing the effect of learning. This time, we developed a mechanism for facilitating externalization of thinking for any knowledge levels or persons with "heterogeneous" knowledge and designed a system that would increase interactions by focusing on the unevenness. At the same time, we incorporated games in the system [4] so that even those who are not good at externalizing their thinking can participate without feeling inept.

To maintain vigorous interactions among learners with different knowledge levels, it is necessary to keep them from focusing on the difference or comparison of each other's knowledge. This can be achieved when learners are directly involved with the authenticity of the subject instead of showing off their knowledge. In other words, it is effective when "the contents for learning are authentic". If the subject is authentic and can be represented in different ways, children feel free to reveal their own perceptions because others would take them as unique views. This allows children to exchange opinions on equal terms. Background knowledge or accumulation of past "studies" barely matters in such a situation.

Using Experience as a Base To make contents authentic, it is necessary that the subject is linked with activities in a specific experience (real experience of the outside world away from a computer). Such an experience must lead learners to an "intellectual quest", which should be deepened through the support of others. To allow this, the experience should be related to something that is practiced publicly in the culture or society and learners should be able to see that. They should be able to realize that it is not just a "fiction" or "something that happens in a book (or computer)". In addition, the contents should be such that allows verification of the validity of learners' views or conclusions and withstands examination from different viewpoints. In other words, the contents should indicate a trajectory of participation in the culture and community from marginal to full participation and allow access to full participation [9].

Diversifying and Activating Externalization of Thinking To facilitate externalization of thinking in spite of different knowledge levels among learners, the contents must be such that can incorporate a context of activities in which learners play the "lead". There should be a story which makes learners feel as if they are doing things as a character. That is why there is a possibility that educational software which incorporates "games" works effectively. The "game" factor provokes moderate competition among learners, but study would not progress if the contents are nothing but fun. It is necessary to help establish a common objective among learners to work together and reach shared understanding while maintaining competition and support the process of their collaboration in spite of confrontation and conflict. Children should be able to understand the frameworks of others' thinking through playing a game and change their own frameworks based on what they learned. It is also important that children learn to collaborate through vigorous interactions and define conflicting points.

The contents should thus be able to reflect learners' thinking, close to their interests, but not just fun. Even though learners start with playing a game and are motivated through the "entertainment factor" in the beginning, they should gradually be motivated by the challenge of "participation" in the activities which are connected to real science or culture. "Non-consensus-forming collaborative learning" is achieved here–children overcome "power scheme" resulting from different knowledge levels, foster camaraderie (in playing a game) and learn in a collaborative manner while they continue to appreciate each other's differences. The most important thing is that the partners with whom children interact in playing a game are real people that exist in reality and that children "can learn from each other because of different views" through such interactions with the "real people" because it does not involve power struggle or emotional conflict.

2.3   Physical and Digital Cities for Supporting Group Learning

Based on the discussions in this section, we claim that the integration of physical and virtual worlds (physical and digital cities in this work) provides a novel way of supporting group learning. Through the collaborative construction of physical cities on the board game, learners can externalize their own ideas, interact with each other, and actively participate in a learning situation. Digital cities in the computer simulation not only provide learners with effective feedback for their further thinking, but also enables learners to try a "what if game", such as "if a factory piece is placed, how this city will be in the future?". Our system deals with authentic contents (urban planning and environment problems), which are critical and open problems in our society, and therefore, necessary to find a solution through collaborations, conflicts and negotiations with others.

The effects of the system described here are due to the integration of physical and virtual worlds, not to either of them. We believe that digital cities linked with physical cities provides learners with a new environment for group learning.

Fig. 1. A board game that supports the learning of urban planning and environmental problems

3   Configurations of the System

In this section, we describe the configurations of the system: its components (Sec. 3.1), the technology for integrating physical and virtual worlds (Sec. 3.2) and usage of the system (Sec. 3.3).

3.1   Components of the System

Figure 1 shows an overview of the system. Components of the system are a board game, scenario cards, and a computer simulation. The board game consists of a checkerboard, game pieces, and geographic objects. The checkerboard has 20×24 squares (its size can be changeable), each of which is three centimeter square. There are three kinds of game pieces: "houses", "factories", and "trees". One game piece is put in one square on the checkerboard. Geographic objects include "mountains", "rivers", and other similar elements of nature. These objects are arranged on the checkerboard by learners in order to construct a city resembling their own.

Fig. 2. An example of scenario cards

Scenario cards give learners a certain direction or contextual message regarding their learning situation. Figure 2 shows an example of these cards with messages such as "You cannot build a house next to a factory", "You should be careful of the increase in air pollution in your city". Before putting a game piece on a board, a learner must draw a card. Based on its written message, a learner confirms the status of the city through the board and a computer simulation, and talks about his/her next action with other learners. The cards, therefore, enhance learners' reflections and promote their paying attention to the board, computer simulation, and other learners.

An example image of a computer simulation is shown in Fig. 3. When a learner completes his/her action, a computer simulation recognizes the arrangements of game pieces on the board and calculates future status of a city. In the simulation model, eight parameters related to a city's environment (amount of carbon/nitrogen/sulfur-dioxide discharged by factories, population of a city etc.) are considered. The status of city's air, water and soil pollution are anthropomorphically visualized in the upper left of Fig. 3, as this makes it easier for learners to relate to the simulation. When a serious environmental problem happens, the simulation not only changes its visualization (i.e., changes the expressions of each object in the figure), but also shows a textual message, such as "the air is heavily polluted" in the center of the image.

3.2   Integration of Physical and Virtual Worlds

In order to integrate a board game and a computer simulation, the radio frequency identification (RFID) system [12] is used. RFID is a non-contact object identification and data transfer technology. The RFID system consists of two components: an antenna (with a transceiver and decoder) and a tag (Fig. 4). An antenna emits radio signals to activate a tag, and reads/writes data to the tag in an electromagnetic field produced by the antenna. An antenna combined with the transceiver and decoder is called a reader. It decodes data encoded in a tag's integrated circuit (IC) and passes the data to an attached personal computer.

Tags and readers are embedded in game pieces and a checkerboard, respectively. In our current implementation, one reader is embedded in each square on the checkerboard, and one CPU is attached to every 4×4 squares as shown in Fig. 5. When a computer simulation starts the detection of the arrangement of game pieces on the checkerboard, it first sends a read-command to all the CPU's. Then, each CPU sequentially activates and controls 16 antennas on 4×4 squares, so that each of them activates a tag and reads its data. Finally, the computer simulation receives data of tags from the CPU's.

Due to the limitation of the current RFID technology, the data transmission speed between a reader and a tag is not so fast. This may cause serious communication delays when the size of a checkerboard becomes large. The configuration of the board described here, however, makes the communication time theoretically independent of the size of the checkerboard[1]. This is an important feature to enable learners to expand the board and construct a large scale city.

3.3   Usage of the System

When learners use the system, they sit around a board, set it up by arranging geographic objects. The first learner draws a card and puts a game piece on

---

[1] It takes within 0.5 second to gain information on arrangements of game pieces.

the board by following the direction of the card. Each learner does the same in turn. Every time a learner completes his/her move, the computer simulation recognizes the arrangement of game pieces on the board, calculates the future status of the city, and visualizes it.

Fig. 3. An example of a computer simulation which visualizes future status of a city being constructed

After reviewing the simulation results, the learner can change his/her move and put a different piece on a different place. For example, a learner, who first has put a "factory" piece, has found that air pollution will be a serious problem in future, he/she may change his/her initial idea and puts a "tree" piece. Finally, when the design of the city is complete or time has run out, the computer simulation diagnoses the design of the city and points out planning problems.

Fig. 4. An antenna (left) and a tag (right)

The integration of physical (a city on the board game) and virtual (a city in a computer simulation) worlds can enhance interactions among learners and their own reflections. All the learners can actively participate in the design of a city through interacting with artifacts, such as putting game pieces. Therefore, each learner can be an active designer, not a passive learner [2][3]. The computer simulation returns effective feedback to a learner's action, which stimulate his/her further thinking and discussions among learners, for example, why his/her action causes air pollution and what he/she should do next. The learning environment provided by the system allows learners to share their action space with each other, and freely come and go between physical and virtual worlds. This raises learners' engagements [11] and promotes learners' active collaborations and conflicts.

4   Experiments and Evaluations

4.1   Overview

The experiments were carried out in a Japanese public elementary school located in Yokohama city in Kanagawa prefecture. Thirty fifth-grade pupils who had studied environmental problems in school were divided into six groups of five. Due to the time limit of one school period, we carried out the experiments over three days. Each experiment lasted twenty minutes.

Before starting the experiments, brief instructions, such as the usage and rules of the system, were given to the children. Two video recorders were used to record the experiments. One was placed in a fixed position to record the motions and interactions of the children around a board, while the other was used to record the expressions and actions of each children making a move, such as placing a piece on the board. A post- experiment interview of each group was also carried out.

CPU   Antenna

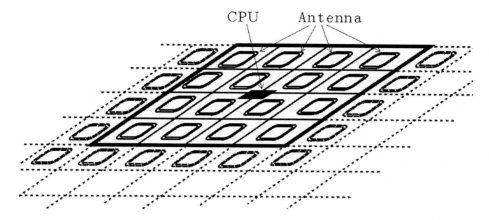

Fig. 5. An arrangement of antennas and CPU's on a game board

4.2 Evaluation

The children did not interact very frequently in the early phase of each experiment. We believe that this is because there were few pieces on a board at these times so pieces could be placed relatively freely. As an experiment went on, however, interactions among the children became remarkable. Every learner read aloud what was written on a scenario card that he/she had drawn (although we did not ask them to do so). In this manner, the message or direction of the card was shared with the other children, who then discussed which piece should be used next. Some children even offered advice of where to place a piece. Collaboration and conflict among the children occurred regularly during these moments.

The children also externalized their ideas at the same time. Every time a piece was placed, all the children paid attention to the computer simulation. The results of the simulation (improvement or deterioration of the city's status) excited the children and led them to further externalize their own ideas.

In our current system, the number of different pieces and rules are not large. However, some groups tried to extend the system by creating new rules, such as "there must be vacant land near houses or factories", or by proposing new pieces, such as "a park".

Throughout the experiments, we were able to confirm that a board game can enhance interactions among learners and is an effective medium for collaboration and conflict. The integration of a board game and a computer simulation was also successful in that both were used smoothly by the children. During post-experiment interviews it was determined that the contents and usage of the system was not difficult, and was enjoyable (most of the children stated that they would like to play the game again).

Several issues, however, were not made clear with these experiments. In one group, there was one leader type pupil who had strong control over the other players. Interactions among the children in this group were not so obvious as that in the other groups. In future research we would like to clarify the influence of individual personalities on a group.

Another important issue is related to distributed cognition [Norman93]. In another group, one child watched the computer simulations and always informed others of the results. In our experiments, the tasks given to the children were not so complex: each child should have been able to understand, judge, and decide what to do by him/herself. The relation between task complexity and distributed cognition will be investigated in the next experiment. Finally, the extensibility or evolutionary design of the system is critical [Fischer98]. It should support learners' addition or modification of artifacts based on their needs in their learning processes. Such systems seem to raise learners' engagement and promote further externalization, interactions and collaboration.

5   Conclusions

Using the experience of our previous system for supporting group learning, a new system that integrates a board game and a computer simulation was proposed in this paper. Several experiments were carried out in a public elementary school in which it was shown that the system could enhance interactions among learners and could promote collaboration and conflict during their learning processes.

Recently many systems that support learning focus on the utilization of multi-media technologies. However, the learners in most of these systems are just passive receivers of information and are not active participants of the learning situation. The system we proposed in this paper enables learners to interact with real objects, represent their own ideas, share them with other learners and confirm these ideas through a computer simulation. This allows learners to be active participants, and raises their engagement in the learning process. We think that the system and its evaluations show one of the critical issues regarding the use of multi-media technology in learning support systems: how to raise learners' motivation, and the importance of interacting with physical and virtual worlds.

References

[1]   Arias, E., Eden, H., and Fischer, G.: Enhancing Communication, Facilitating Shared Understanding, and Creating Better Artifacts by Integrating Physical and Computational Media for Design. In *Proc. of Designing Interactive Systems (DIS'97)*, (1997) 1-12

[2]   Fischer, G.: Beyond 'Couch Potatoes': From Consumers to Designers. In *Proc. of Asia-Pacific Computer and Human Interaction (APCHI'98)*, (1998) 2-9

[3]   Fischer, G.: A Group Has No Head: Conceptual Frameworks and Systems for supporting Social Interaction. *IPSJ Magazine*, No. 40, Vol. 6 (1999) 575-582 (In Japanese)

[4]   Kafai, Y.: *Minds in Play: Computer Game Design as a Context for Children's Learning*, Laurence Erlbaum Associates (1995)

[5]   Kameda, T. : *Gogi no chi wo motomete: group no ishi kettei*, Kyoritsu Shuppan (1997) (in Japanese)

[6]   Koschmann, T. (Ed.): *CSCL : Theory and Practice of an Emerging Paradigm*, Lawrence Erlbaum Associates (1996)

[7]   Kusunoki, F., Hori, K.: How to Make Their Opinions Open: Scaffolding School Pupils in Collaborative Learning. In *Proc. of Artificial Intelligence in Education - Knowledge and Media in Learning Systems (AI-ED'97)* (1997) 618-620

[8]   Kusunoki, F.,: Making an Interactive Environment of the Pupil, by the Pupil, for the Pupil. In *Proc. of World Multiconference on Systems, Cybernetics and Informatics (SCI'98)* (1998) 386-391

[9]   Lave, J. and Wenger E.: *Situated Learning: Legitimate Peripheral Participation*, Cambridge University Press (1991)

[10]   Norman, D.A.: *Things That Make Us Smart*, Addison Wisley (1993)

[11]   Norman, D.A. and Spohrer, J.C.: Learner-Centered Education, *Communications of the ACM*, Vol. 39, No. 4 (1996) 24-27

[12]   RFID (Radio Frequency IDentification): http://www.rfid.org

[13]   Sayeki, Y.: *Shin Computer to Kyoiku*, Iwanami Shoten (1997) (in Japanese)

[14]   Sugimoto, M, et al.: Computer-Supported Collaborative Learning by Utilizing Different Systems, In *Proc. of the 9th Annual Symposium of Japanese Society for Artificial Intelligence* (1998) 125-130 (in Japanese)

Digital City for Disaster Reduction
– Development of Pictogram System
for Disaster Management –

Haruo Hayashi[1], Satoshi Tanaka[2], Kazunori Urabe[3], Haruhide Yoshida[3],
Satoshi Inoue[3], Hideki Shima[3], Nobuhisa Deki[4], Jun Kasagi[5], Takahiro Nishino[5],
and Masasuke Takashima[6]

[1] Disaster Prevention Research Institute, Kyoto University, Uji Kyoto, Japan,
hayashi@drs.dpri.kyoto-u.ac.jp
[2] Disaster Prevention Research Institute, Kyoto University, Uji, Kyoto, Japan,
tanaka@imdr.dpri.kyoto-u.ac.jp
[3] GK Kyoto Inc., Kamigyo-Ku, Kyoto, Japan,
urabe@gk-design.co.jp
[4] Sekisui Jushi Inc., Chuo-Ku, Osaka, Japan,
dekin@sekisuijushi.co.jp
[5] R2 Media solution Inc., Nakagyo-Ku, Kyoto, Japan
junk@r2ms.co.jp
[6] Graduate School of Infomatics, Kyoto University, Sakyo-ku, Kyoto, Japan,
takashim@drs.dpri.kyoto-u.ac.jp

Abstract. The purpose of this study is to apply digital city concept for the development of a pictogram system for natural disaster reduction. Long lasting and tangible achievement of IDNDR is needed which may be used in all over the world for many coming generations. As Neurath said "Words divide, pictures unite", pictograms could be a powerful communication tool as well as an educational tool to improve global disaster awareness. In this project, we formed a multi-disciplinary team to compile "A Database of Pictograms for Natural Disaster Reduction", which we intend to release our copyrights to be used widely and freely as an achievement of IDNDR through internet. We developed the lexicon and grammar of the pictograms for natural disaster reduction. Over 700 pictograms in use were collected for evaluation, and new designs were also added to complete the list of concepts related to natural hazards and their disaster management. Home page will be introduced for worldwide participation in this project as a first step towards the digital city for disaster reduction.

1. Introduction

Digital City has been developed for the real cities existing in the world. It has been popular in various businesses, especially for the tourist business. Through the internet, people could reach the latest information of the city at any time with spectacular visual images. We believe that this digital city concept could apply to other fields such as the introduction of an academic discipline.

In this study, a new possibility for Digital City for the disaster management community is proposed. The disaster management community has various stakeholders such as disaster researchers in multi-disciplinary fields, practitioners of disaster management at various levels of government, and the people in the impacted area. The international organizations, such as Red Cross and Red Crescent, World Bank, OCHA, and other UN agencies, are also recognized as the important stakeholders. These stakeholders play important roles in the disaster management. They need the knowledge of all fields related with disaster management, however, any single person can not be a master of whole disaster management related fields. In addition, it is fairly difficult to predict the exact time and location that a disaster occurs. It means that we could not specify who are involved in the disaster before it happened.

In order to make the disaster management more effective, the Digital City concept would be useful tool for developing a common information basis to integrate the relevant information for anybody who needs that information.

2.   Words Divide, Pictures Unite

With a rapid population growth in the 20th century, many people are now living in a more disaster prone area where nobody used to live. With a rapid development of transportation systems, many people are now travelling a lot both domestically and internationally. As a consequence, people are now becoming a more vulnerable to disasters because they are getting less aware of the hazards and disasters of the area where they are.

Recent statistics on disasters showed a continuous trend towards ever-increasing number of catastrophes with ever-increasing costs (Munich Re, 1997). With this trend, natural disasters will soon become a "budget time bomb" which no government could afford the costs. Thus, it is important to solicit the participation of the people in disaster management. Increasing hazard awareness of the people and improving their disaster reduction capability is the key for maintaining the sustainability of the world from natural disasters,

At the General Assembly of the United Nations, it was unanimously decided to designate the last decade of the 20th century as the "International Decade for Natural Disaster Reduction (IDNDR)". Since 1990, a number of conferences and symposia have been held to substantiate the spirit of IDNDR at various venues all over the world, and their achievements have been published in the form of many proceedings and pamphlets. However, it is always difficult to disseminate information because of different languages.

3.   What Pictograms Can Do

In 1999, IDNDR will end formally. However, it should be a time for new beginning to make a safer and sustainable world by applying what we have learned and achieved during IDNDR. The "Pictogram System for Disaster Management" hopes to be one of such long-lasting and tangible IDNDR achievements by making use of picture language.

As Otto Neurath wrote "Words divide, and pictures unite", a pictogram system, or a picture language system, has been successful since 1930's as an international communication tool. Pictograms are those graphic symbols, which are already familiar with us as icons and signs at various public scenes, such as traffic signs, and information signs at railway stations and airports.

There has been no systematic attempt yet to make use of pictograms for natural disaster reduction. We believe the pictogram system be useful for public education tool to improve their awareness to reduce the number of casualties and refugees from natural disasters

4.   Pictogram System for Disaster Management

There are at least three different ways to use pictogram systems: 1) icons, 2) signs, and 3) educational tools.

4.1.   Icons

With a rapid development of computer technology, it is now common to use GIS (Geographic Information System) technology for disaster management, hazard intensity, Damages due to disasters, as well as the resources for mitigating and preparing for disasters can be displayed on screen so that disaster managers understand them spatially. Many systems based on GIS have been developed by various disaster management organizations. These different systems make use of icons to represent important elements for disaster management. At present, however, there is little agreement among the icons used. Different pictograms are used for representing the same concept, and the same pictogram means different thing.

When we look back the history of pictogram, the U.S. Department of Transportation (USDOT) made great contribution for the development of pictograms. USDOT published "Symbol s and Signs" in which 34 pictogram designs used at ports and harbors. In this book, many pictograms in use were collected and evaluated so that USDOT recommended what they think best. USDOT also released the copyrights of their recommended designs to facilitate their use at various ports and stations all over the world. Just like the USDOT did for the public signs at ports and harbors, we need to have some kind of de facto standard designs related to disaster reduction. By providing a common design, it would be a great help for better disaster management that needs the coordination among many different organizations and jurisdictions. We name these de facto standard pictogram designs as the "lexicon" of pictogram (see Fig. 1).

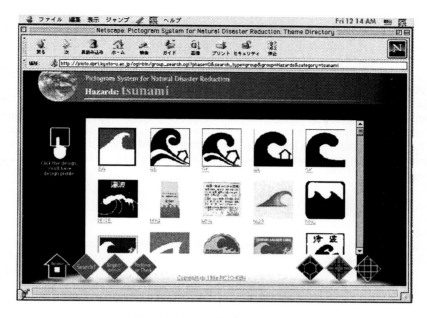

Fig. 1. Tsunami pictograms in use

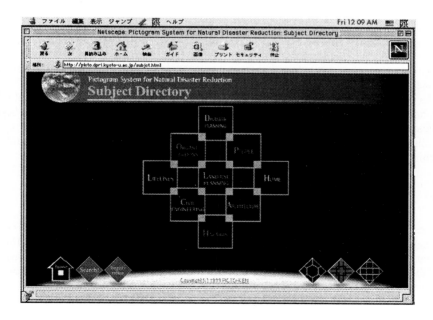

Fig. 2. Different Disciplines Relevant to Disaster Management

As to the design work, it is our goal to have a complete list of pictograms in a coherent manner. In order to realize this goal, we need to design our own when no pictogram in use is available. The following design principles have been adopted for our new designs: 1) Use a distinctive design as much as possible; 2) Use a concrete design as much as possible; 3) Use a simple design as much as possible; and 4) Use the design that can be correctly understood under different condition of visibility.

As shown in Fig.2, disaster management consists of various disciplines from hazards to contingency planning. Since nobody could be the expert of all disciplines, the coordination among the experts in different disciplines are essential element of disaster management. The lexicon for the pictogram system could be a great help for establishing the coordination among various disciplines relevant to disaster management..

4.2. Signs

As you might know, it is possible to create a new "Kanji (Chinese Characters)" by combining other kanji. For example, " 明 " (Brightness) consists of "日" (Sun) and "月" (Moon). Just like kanji formation, we should be able to create new pictograms by some syntactic rules for combining pictograms. Since the world of disaster is not a fixed one, something new would always be added to our knowledge and experiences with every new disaster. Accordingly the pictogram system for disaster reduction should not be fixed. It should be flexible to add new designs into an existing system in a coherent manner. We name the syntactic rules used for the pictograms for disaster reduction as the "grammar" of pictogram.

For the pictogram system for disaster management, we adopted the following principles: Whenever we have the international standard, we respect that. Thus, we respect all the rules and designs used in ISO7001. If we have national standard in some country, we respect that in that country. For example, we respect the designs defined in ANSIZ535 for the United States.

As for the pictogram system for disaster management, we think it should be emphasized the following three aspects: 1) Signs for safety and danger, 2) Signs indicating directions, and 3) Sings indicating degrees and quantity. These three groups of signs may be indispensable elements for making signs, which should be compatible with ISO7001/3864/4196 (see Fig. 3).

4.3. Educational Tools

By establishing the lexicon and grammar, the pictogram systems for disaster management can be a basic communication tool as well as a basic educational tool. When Otto Neurath, an Austrian philosopher and educator, started to use pictograms for the first time, he called them as ".ISOTYPE", which is the abbreviation of "International System of Typographical Picture Education". As the director of the Social and Economic Exhibition Hall in Vienna in 1920's, Neurath designed many

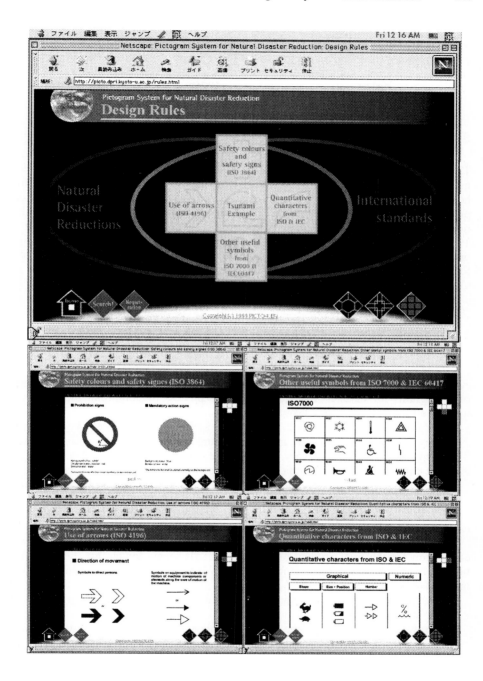

Fig. 3. Grammatical signs taken from ISO7001/3864/4196

statistical charts with simplified pictures, with his intention to use them as a powerful tool for the dissemination of the scientific knowledge. In that sense, scientific education is a prime goal of pictograms. The pictogram system for natural disaster reduction, thus is the tool of scientific education on natural hazards and their disaster reduction.

5. Team Approach

The development of Pictogram System for Disaster Management was started in 1993, using Tsunami warning sign as a prototype (Hayashi, 1993). It was unsuccessful, however, at the beginning. It was a severe lesson learned from this failure that the pictogram system for natural disaster reduction project should be a real multi-disciplinary collaboration. A new multi-disciplinary project team was established in 1997 with disaster researchers, graphic designers, computer system engineers, sign products makers, legal experts, and disaster managers. One other important element for success is financial support, which this project was supported by the "National Council for the Promotion of IDNDR in Japan" for the last two years.

6. WWW Site for Pictogram System for Disaster Management – A New Beginning

As the final product of this project, we initially intended to compile a reference book of pictograms for disaster management. In the process of compiling the reference book, the following step were taken:
1) We identified the concepts to be included in the reference book. For example, they are hazards, damages, mitigation countermeasures, preparedness, disaster response, relief, and recovery. We also keep updating the concept list.
2) We collected a total of 700 pictograms in use from 48 different sources.
3) We formed a database classifying them into sub-groups based on various dimensions of design theme.

With this database, we planned to evaluate them to recommend the best design for each concept. This process was to be documented in the reference book.

Constructing the database over 700 pictograms, we now come to a very different conclusion for the final product of this project. It seems for us that the reference book is not the best way to present the ideas. We think we should take into account the following points:
1) We are now really at the beginning , not the final stage, of the pictogram project for disaster management.
2) We would like to welcome any new input from all over the world: New examples of pictograms in use should be added to broad our understanding. New original designs will also be welcomed to the database. The database should keep growing.
3) It is much more informative to overview all the pictograms in use rather than to look for a one best design. For example, Red Cross and Red Crescent are different in design but same in meaning. It is impossible to select one over the

other. By learning two designs side by side will be the most informative way of presentation.

4)Everybody who wants to participate should participate in design evaluation process.

5)Different people may want to search pictograms with different purposes in mind.

6)If people want to use the pictogram design, they may have it in the digital data form.

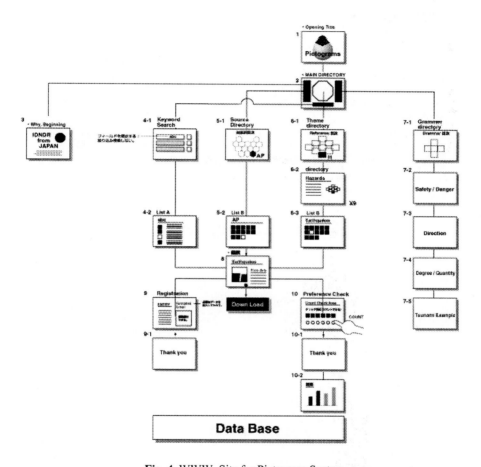

Fig. 4. WWW. Site for Pictogram System

Taking into these points account, we now reach the conclusion that we should open up the WWW site for Pictogram System for Disaster Management as a forum for those who wish to participate in this movement. In this WWW site, people can find all pictograms for a particular concept, they can show their preference in pictograms, they could register their original designs, they could introduce new pictograms in use, and they could download the pictogram they need, as presented in Fig. 4.

244   Haruo Hayashi et al.

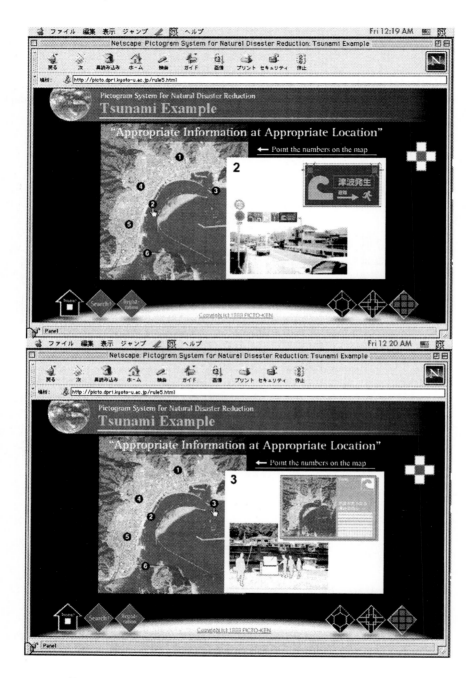

Fig. 5. Tsunami Warning Sign System – A prototype for application

7.   Tsunami Warning Sign System – A Prototype for Application

As an example of real life application, let us present as a prototype of the application of pictogram systems for reducing the tsunami damages in a small town in Shikoku Island, Japan (see Fig. 5). This town is facing the Pacific Ocean, and has been hit by devastating tsunami attack almost every 100 years due to the Nankai earthquakes. This town has a population of 4000 people, and famous for the beach that attracts many visitors. At the railway station, and at the harbor, there are signboards that tell the visitors the potential hazard, and the warning and evacuation systems (1, 2). This board also helps showing all the pictograms used. The electronic sign boards hanged over the road will change its display from road information to show the evacuation directions when the earthquake of over Ms6.6 occurs (3). At the major intersections, the directions for evacuation will be signed up (5). The poles used for emergency public address system are also used to let the people learn how high the past tsunami attacks were, so that people could have a sense of how high they should go (4). The evacuation sites, such as the top stories of the engineered structure more than three stories and the bridge, and is indicated by the green banner as the goal for evacuation (6). This banner can be glowed even in the dark. By combining these elements for the evacuation from tsunami attack, we could have a sign system with pictograms.

8.   Conclusion

In this paper, we showed that Digital City concept can be applicable not only for real cities in the world but also those virtual cities such as representing the systematic knowledge for disaster management, using as an example the of development of pictogram system for disaster management. For more details, please visit our website at "http://picto.dpri.kyoto-u.ac.jp/". .As long as those fields which need decentralized participation from all over the world to represent the diversity and to keep growing by the continuous efforts of the people from all over the world, they can be well realized by using Digital City concept as the basis for their development.

References

1. The American National Standard Institute: Environmental and facility safety signs, ANSI Z535.2. (1991)
2. Hayashi, H.: The development of international ISOTYPE system for the mitigation and prevention of natural disasters, Emergency Planning '93. (1993)
3. International Organization for Standardization: Public information symbols, ISO7001, 2nd ed. (1990)
4. Munich Reinsurance Co., Topics, Munich: Munich Re. (1997)
5. Neurath, O.: International Picture Language, Harper & Row. (1934)

The Digital City's Public Library: Support for Community Building and Knowledge Sharing

Scott Robertson

MediaOne Labs, 10355 Westmoor Dr., Suite 100,
Westminster, Colorado, 80021 USA
srobertson@mediaone.com

Abstract. Libraries are hubs for social and intellectual interactions in communities and organizations. Virtual libraries should serve the same purpose. In this paper an online library is described that places knowledge sharing and community building at the core of its design. The library system supports personal web sites that are visible to the entire community. Personal topic profiles for library research services, information services choices, and collaborative research requests provide people with views of each others' activities and interests. Collaboration and interest-matching tools help people to share knowledge and to form special interest communities. The paper also discusses design features necessary for building community in virtual situations: semantically-rich places, perspective and identity, interaction opportunities, and facilitators.

1 Introduction

The public library is a community resource in most major cities. In addition to providing information in the form of books, videos, CDs and other media, the library serves an important community-building purpose. In this paper, I address a simple question: Should digital cities have digital libraries and, if so, what should digital libraries be like? I will also describe a corporate digital library with community-building features that can serve as a model for digital public libraries.

It is important to start with a significant assumption: libraries are not just places where information is stored and where people go to find things. Although this is an important part of libraries, ethnographic studies of behavior in libraries show that library patrons spend considerable time interacting with staff members and with one another [1], [7], [9], [12], [13], [15]. In fact, libraries serve as informal meeting places for people with common interests and can be instrumental in the formation of special interest groups [3], [8], [12], [13].

Information relevant to the ongoing activities of a community or organization will tend to flow into a heavily used library. For example, if a school district begins a program on environmental education, the library serving the district will begin to receive many questions about environmental issues from students. Staff members will

T. Ishida, K. Isbister (Eds.): Digital Cities, LNCS 1765, pp. 246-260, 2000.

notice relevant library materials being checked out. Similarly, if a corporation begins planning a new product launch or a strategic acquisition, the corporate library will begin to receive requests for specific market information, or for corporate financial information, from a variety of sources involved with the corporate action. Indeed, it is something of a sport of research librarians to figure out what is going on in the community they serve.

Librarians use the information about community activities to help them determine what is most relevant to their clients. For example, a corporate research librarian might provide different information in a company profile if he or she thinks the profile will be used to negotiate a merger instead of to enter a competitor's market. Because one of the research librarian's roles is to filter and focus information, inferences about community activities, as reflected through the goals of the researcher's clients, are very important in guiding the researcher's work.

Because of the immersion of librarians in the activities of their communities, public libraries often serve as "information hubs" and librarians become informal networkers. A library patron may ask the librarian for information about AIDS, for example, and be referred to community groups or even other individuals who have similar interests. The librarian knows about these resources because of his/her history of interactions and role as a broad-spectrum information provider.

In order for this type of informal networking to take place, it is important for the library to be part of a community. A mail order clerk at a book warehouse might find out information about many of the customers' interests, however if the customers are scattered over a wide geographical area and have no other ties to each other, then the knowledge about potential networks is useless. However, if the same person is in a "community," either because of co-location or by being in a virtual situation, then informal networking can be very useful. The digital public library can serve as the appropriate virtual situation.

2 Features Necessary for Community

Community-building in situations like libraries depends on several features:
1. **The Places**: It is important to have an environment where structure and meaning overlap. For example location and topic are related in libraries.
2. **The Perspectives and Identities**: It is important to have the ability to see what other people are doing. For example, in a library it matters what sections of a library other people are in, how often they do certain things, and what reading materials they are selecting.
3. **The Interaction Opportunities**: Meeting places such as conference rooms, chat areas, hallways, etc. make it possible for people who notice each other to interact.
4. **The Facilitators**: Individuals such as library staff members notice what people are doing over time and can become community facilitators.
    In this section we discuss each feature in real and virtual contexts.

2.1 Places

The observed behavior of others in a situation contributes to a sense of the situation's ambiance, or social atmosphere. This sense is often important in determining whether people like a place or situation and whether they will return. Retailers have always been sensitive to the ambiance of their stores and strive to create various feelings. This has generalized easily into e-commerce applications (since, among other things, it is not far from the notion of the "feeling" or "ambiance" of print publications). But this type of ambiance is generally created, both in real and virtual settings, by using the physical features of the environment: hot or cold colors, crowded or empty spaces, graphical elements, and messages.

Another type of ambiance comes from the behavior of people in the environment. The sense of a "quiet" place versus a "busy" place is a determination made on the basis of what people are doing. In places like libraries or bookstores, many content-rich social interactions and observations occur. Because the physical layout of libraries or bookstores is related to the topics in various sections, people tend to notice others in the same sections and can assume that there are common interests [1], [4]. For example, a person standing in a certain area of a library or carrying a stack of books can be quickly identified as a "nature lover" or "poetry fan" based on the area they are in or the type of books they are carrying. A person pulling a book off of a shelf may invite a comment such as "That's a good book," or "There's a better book on that topic." The collection of such observations and interactions provides an "information ambiance" and creates a social value for institutions like libraries.

An interesting example of carrying the information ambiance of a certain type of store into cyberspace is amazon.com, which allows readers to comment on books and shows what other books people have bought in association with any particular book being browsed. These traces of the activities of other people add a richness to the amazon.com experience that moves it closer to the experience of a real bookstore and farther from the experience of a mail-order house.

2.2 Perspectives and Identities

If virtual places such as digital libraries are to support community building and knowledge sharing, then the patrons have to be identified and observable to each other. Being able to see others is taken for granted in the real world, but it is not common in virtual space (collaborative games being an exception). In fact, invisibility and privacy are hallmarks of cyberspace. Even when people must be visible to each other, in chat areas for example, identity fabrication is common. However, invisibility blocks community building and knowledge sharing. It precludes the creation of a social atmosphere based on observed behaviors.

It is important to clarify here that the issue for community is identity of the participants of a space to each other. With the advent of serious e-commerce applications, it is becoming more common on the web for people to be identified to a website and to have their activity recorded by a merchant or site owner. However, a million people could use the same site ("be in the same place") at the same time and never see each other (again, in a strange anti-community way, websites work to eliminate evidence of others such as performance degradation).

Identity, in these cases, does not have to encompass a broad range of personal characteristics. Consider again the case of a person taking books from a shelf in a library: It is enough to initiate a meaningful conversation if their presence and behavior is visible and if the content of the materials they are choosing is visible. It is not necessary to know much more about them.

For a community over time to develop, however, it is important to learn who people are and how to find them, at least in the context of the library. There are many groups that meet in particular places at particular times in which the participants only know each other's names, relevant interests and purposes, and histories that are relevant to the group. This slice of identity and behavior is enough to support special-interest communities.

Thus, the following aspects of identity need to be supported in the design of digital libraries if they are to have social value:

Identity via Purpose. This is the way people know each other in many commercial and informal transactions.   A library staff member may have people identified by their goals when they come into the library, e.g. "the guy who reads all the nature books," "the woman who always looks at telecom stocks on the internet," or "the vice president who is always asking questions about downsizing." These identities are not personas developed and displayed by the library clients, rather they are observed identities that arise from behaviors in the context of the library itself. Thus in cyberspace, they can not be entirely represented by client-crafted homepages, but instead have to be the result of some mechanism that creates a visible record of client activities.

Asynchronous Visibility. If identities are to be derived from behavior, then it follows that the behaviors have to be visible. Unlike real life, where co-presence in time is usually required to observe others, in virtual space it is possible to record behavior and make the traces visible. Buying habits are recorded by amazon.com so that, when a new buyer is looking at a book, they can be informed about what others with similar interests have done in the past by observing the information provided by the virtual environment. It is like seeing someone else in a bookstore who is holding a collection of books that includes one that you are interested in, however it is asynchronous.

2.3 Interaction Opportunities

To support community building and information sharing, an environment must provide "affordances" for interaction, or places where interaction is invited and supported. Everyone has had the experience of being with someone interesting but in a situation where interaction is impossible (e.g. a noisy airport lobby). Quiet places with seating, usually provided in libraries, are physical spaces that provide invitation to and support for interaction.   What would constitute "virtual affordances" for interaction?

Some interaction venues, "chat rooms" and "instant messaging" in particular, have become well established in cyberspace. Turning these into virtual affordances would be possible by pairing them with community-of-interest features. Referring again to the amazon.com feature   in which a customer can view other books bought by customers   with similar interests, imagine instead that a customer was alerted when a customer with similar interests was currently on line. Or imagine that one could view a list of customers with similar interests. A chat could easily be established with such customers, thus taking the book buying application out of the realm of a buying recommendation exercise and into the realm of community-building instead (of course, from the vendor's point of view it would also have to increase the probability of buying more products). Such processes should be part of any virtual environment such as a digital library.

2.4 Facilitators

Most mediated chat environments have realized the importance of moderators or facilitators.   Individuals who facilitate community building are people who can observe the behavior of others in a common environment and make connections among them. This is often a critical role for librarians. Library staff can and do get informal "interest profiles" of their clients by noticing where the clients spend their time and what they request or check out.

Facilitators play two critical roles. One is bridging the time gap that separates people with whom they interact. Thus a librarian may see one client on Monday mornings and another on Wednesday afternoons, but be able to network these people who would otherwise never meet. A more significant role (and one less easily automated) is to determine the goals of clients and proactively make inferences about their needs. This is the most valued service of the research librarians in the two corporate contexts discussed in this paper.

3 A Model Virtual Library for Community Building and Knowledge Sharing

We recently developed and deployed an intranet-based system for handling research requests at two corporations, U S WEST, a telecommunications company in the western United States, and MediaOne, an international broadband and wireless company. The system is designed to address issues of client identity and community, and to leverage the knowledge that is implicit in librarians' interactions with their clients.   Here we discuss highlights of the system.   A more detailed technical description can be found in [16] and [17].

Figure 1 provides an overview of the system architecture. One part of the libraries' websites consists of a set of interconnected web pages with typical library functions, e.g. a library catalog and checkout service, library staff pages, descriptions of services offered, and categorized links to various other internet and intranet sites. We will not discuss these components of the websites since the focus in this paper is on the community-building and knowledge-sharing aspects.

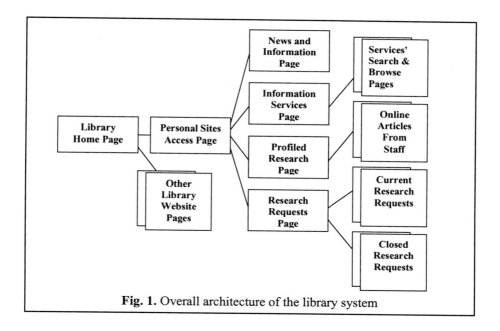

Fig. 1. Overall architecture of the library system

3.1 Library Clients' Personal Sites

Preliminary discussion of requirements with the library staff showed clearly the significance of the social and interpersonal aspects of research interactions. Staff members were very concerned that an intranet-based request handling system would complicate, or even eliminate, the personal relationships between them and their clients. They were justifiably concerned about removing the research activities from their "community context" [12], [13].

To address this issue, each client of the library and each staff member was provided with a "personal website." The personal websites have evolved into a set of customizable web pages from which clients not only view their research requests, but also access online research services, get library news, and receive personalized information that is filtered and "pushed" by the library staff.

The personal web sites are viewable by other employees, so they not only serve to deliver customized information to the client, but also reflect the client to others who may browse the pages. The contents of personal web sites, as they evolve, provide client "identities in cyberspace," at least as far as their interests *vis a vis* the library go. The personal websites are linked to many lists of online library activities and to research requests. The idea is to provide the online equivalent of special interest areas, or ways for people who are in one part of the library website to find others whose interests or activities are related.

Visitors to the corporate library websites enter their user ID to gain access their personal website. Once client's are in their personal website (or other employees are in a personal website), cgi scripts control the display of information as they navigate through their personal web pages. A navigation bar near the top of the personal website pages allows clients to move to "News and Information," a "Profiled Interests" page for profiling their interests and receiving pushed articles, a "Services" page for accessing research services and databases, a "Requests" page for making research requests, and a page for administering their password (see Figure 1).

3.2 News and Information

The top page of a client's personal website provides news and information. When this page is accessed, a cgi script reads contact information about the client from a client database and current news from a news database. The client database is kept up to date by frequent synchronization with the company's human resources database. News and information is authored by library staff through their personal websites. By displaying contact information on a personal website, it makes it easy for another employee who is browsing the site to reach the person.

3.3 Information Services

Most libraries subscribe to several online information services. These services provide primary research and analysis in various areas including marketing, technical information, demographic trends, consumer data, and business intelligence. This information is used primarily by research librarians, however the library system also makes this information available directly to clients. Clients are thereby able to perform simple searches themselves, freeing library staff to answer more detailed research requests.

When a client goes to their "Information Services" page, a cgi script checks their services profile. The profile contains information about the services to which a client subscribes. Icons providing access to only those services are returned on the client's page. When an icon is selected, the browse and search capabilities for that service appear. Clients may subscribe and unsubscribe to services as they please.

In addition to making a considerable amount of information available to all employees, the information services personal web page also serves a community-building function when someone else looks at it. The particular services to which a client subscribes reflect something about that client's interests. Finding that a client subscribes to the same services, market intelligence reports on European wireless for example, is a bit like noticing someone in your favorite section of the library. It serves as an interest-based point of recognition and suggests potential shared concerns.

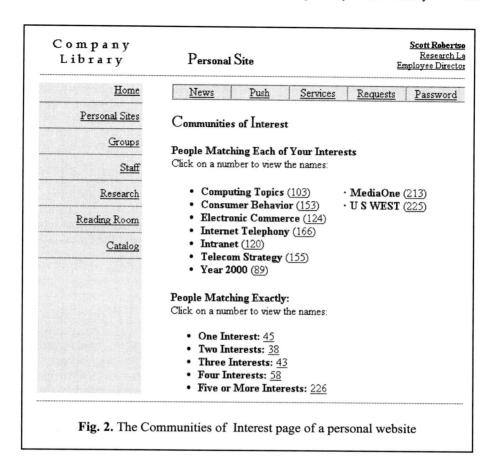

Fig. 2. The Communities of Interest page of a personal website

3.4 Personal Interest Profiles and Push

Librarians have traditionally served as informal keepers of information about the interests of their clients. Proactive librarians look for material relevant to their clients' interests, or find information in the course of their work, that they pass on to clients as a personal service. In fact, clients who find librarians that are particularly attuned to their needs soon regard them as invaluable resources. Automated "push" systems accomplish something similar by combining search agents with personal interest profiles in order to push information, but they lack the knowledge of clients' goals and the contexts of clients' interests that librarians have. In this system we combined the knowledge of the librarians with automation for push.

Research librarians who find interesting material may send it to the system from their personal websites. They do this by copying the material to a special directory on the library web server. Articles in this directory show up on a researcher's personal website where they can be categorized and comments can be attached. In turn, clients may profile themselves by selecting the business categories that they are interested in. When a client accesses their "Profiled Research" page, cgi scripts compare the client's interests with categorized articles and then return links to those articles to the client's page.

Even more than the information services profile of a client, the personal interest profile of a client is an important knowledge source for community-building. In fact, "Profiled Research" pages contain a link called "Communities of Interest" which compare the interest profiles of a client to all other clients. A client's "Communities of Interest" page, shown in Figure 2, returns information about other employees who have various degrees of match in terms of interests. A number follows each of the client's interests, indicating how many others share that interest. When a number next to an interest is clicked on, a list of employees who match the selected interest is provided. The list includes contact information and, more importantly, links to each personal website so that a client can browse the personal websites of other employees who share their interests.

3.5 Research Requests

Library clients may make complex research requests of the library research staff. The staff uses a number of the relevant resources of the library to gather information in response to the request. The client is usually provided with several research articles and interpretations in a highly collaborative research interaction. Collaboration, knowledge sharing using research requests, preservation of client identity, and enabling special interest groups were at the core of the design of the web-based research request system.

Figure 3 shows a mapping of the task analysis of a typical research request scenario onto the system design. Client actions are in the left column while researcher actions are in the right column. Even though only client and researcher actions are shown, note that other clients can browse ongoing research request pages and participate in the question/comment activities.

When a client accesses their "Research Requests" page cgi scripts use databases of current and archived requests to generate a personalized list of requests. From this page, a client may browse or search their own (or all) archived requests. They may also go to any ongoing research request or open a new research request.

The "New Request" link brings up a form on which a client enters the research request and some other details such as the due date. It is not necessary for the client to enter any personal information on the form since the form is retrieved from their personal website and their information has already been bundled with it. When the form is submitted a data file for the specific request is created. This file will hold all information about the request while it is open and is used to generate a unique "Research Request" web page. A researcher is automatically assigned and notified by email of the impending request. The request also shows up in a pending list on the staff member's personal website.

When each research request is made, a new "Research Request" web page is created. The "Research Request" page reflects all of the properties of the request and operates as the focus for all interactions involving the request. These include making comments, attaching articles, recording research, and closing the request.

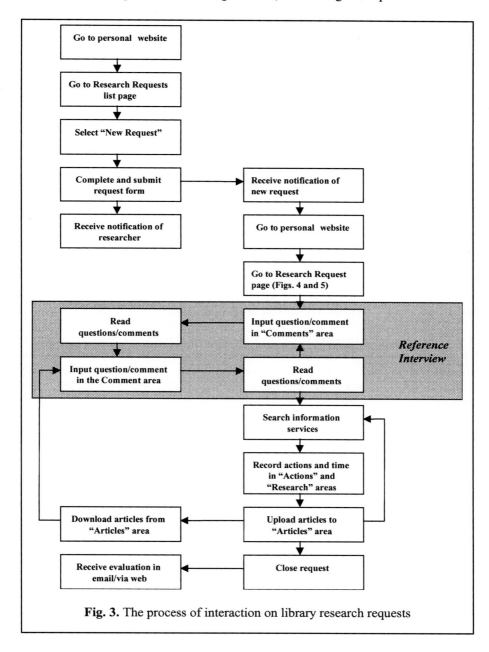

Fig. 3. The process of interaction on library research requests

Figure 4 shows a "Research Request" page just after a request has been submitted. The request is identified by number in the page header. Relevant dates also appear in the page header. The request itself, which consists of a title and description provided by the client, appears in the main portion of the page. At the bottom of the main portion of the "Research Request" page is information about the client and the researcher. This personal information is always kept with the request and reinforces the fact that the request is an interaction between two people. The personal information about the client and researcher is linked to their respective personal websites. Thus people browsing the request can find out what other interests the client may have by going to their personal website and looking at other current and past requests and at other aspects of the client's personal website. A client can also skip to their researcher's personal web page and look at other work being done by that researcher.

At the top of every research request page are links for posting comments, posting actions and research activities, uploading articles, and closing the request. These support the various types of interactions that take place around a research request. When any of these links is followed, a form appears in which the appropriate information is entered. When a comment, attachment, research record, or close request form is submitted, the request data is updated and the "Research Request" page changes. Figure 5 shows, articles, comments, and research activities posted on the request page.

Comments. One of the first things that happens when a research request comes into the library is that the researcher contacts the client for clarification and elaboration (see also [12], [13]). Research librarians describe this as the "reference interview." It is during the reference interview that researchers try to determine the underlying goals of their client in order to better target their research activities and tailor their response. Information revealed during the reference interview is critical for understanding the request. It is also highly transient and ephemeral in that interview information is only maintained in the researchers' memories as they interact with their clients. The comment capability is intended to capture some of the reference interview material.

The comment feature supports asynchronous interaction. Any client or library staff member can contribute to the comments on any current research request. This makes it possible to extend the dialog beyond the dyad of the researcher and his/her client. The contributor's name appears before each comment with a link back to the contributor's personal website. In this way it is possible to learn about who has made a comment, examining what organization they belong to, what research they have requested, what their interest profile looks like, and so on. Thus, the comment feature not only supports the reference interview, but also other interactions that arise while the request is open. When a research request is ultimately closed, the comments become part of the permanent archive and are indexed along with other material in the request.

Company Library | **Research Request 1999-1079** | Open: Sep 27, 199
Comments | Articles | Research | Actions | Close | Due: Oct 1, 199
| Time: 0h, 0

Home

Personal Sites

Groups

Staff

Research

Reading Room

Catalog

What is the future for digital libraries?
What trends are there in information retrieval for libraries? How
many online libraries are planning to include support for
collaboration as part of their design? What companies currently
have extensive online libraries?

Client: Scott Robertson
Research Lab
10355 Westmoor Dr. / Suite 100
Westminster, CO 80021
tel: 303.404.8125
fax: 303.555.6666
email: srobertson@mediaone.com

Researcher: Linda Sole
9785 Maroon Circle / Suite 200
Englewood, CO 80112
tel: 303.555.2976
fax: 303.555.2988
email: lsole@mediaone.com

Switch Researcher

Fig. 4. A Research Request Interaction page just after a request has been
submitted

Research and Actions Performed. Once a researcher is satisfied that they
understand the research request, they begin working with various information services
and internal collections to formulate a response. Usually, the researcher begins
incremental delivery of results to the client and provides feedback about how the
searches are going and what is being found. This allows the client to reformulate the
request as necessary.

Part of the administrative overload for researchers involves keeping track of the
amount of time spent using various research tools and databases and allocating the
time among client organizations. Prior to development of the system, this time was
recorded monthly in a database, usually from recollection. The current system allows
researchers to post research activities as they happen on the "Research Request" page.
This supports both informing the client of ongoing research activity and keeping track
of the time at the moment research activities are posted.

Uploading and Downloading Articles. The primary deliverable of the researchers in
the library is reports pulled from the various information sources that they use.
Researchers post electronic documents on the "Research Request" pages and clients
pick them up by simply clicking on their titles. Researchers may also include
comments with the articles. Article titles and associated comments are posted on the
main part of the "Research Request" page. If the researcher has selected the option
for client email (the default is "yes"), then the client also receives email each time an
article is posted. The email contains hyperlinks to the posted article(s), so a client
may go directly to the article(s) if they use a web-enabled email system. Alternatively,
the client may download an article by clicking on its title on the "Research Request"
page.

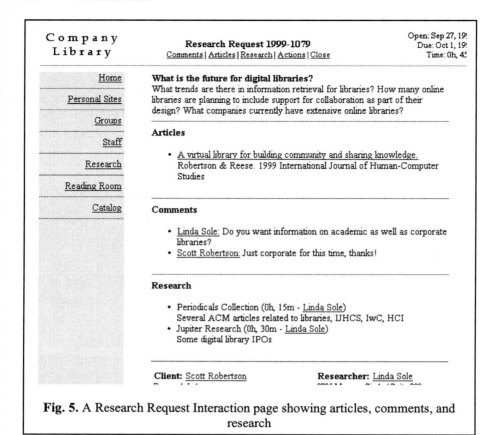

Fig. 5. A Research Request Interaction page showing articles, comments, and research

Articles can be posted incrementally as long as the research request is open. Other people browsing research requests also have access to the articles. Thus, inadvertent discovery of interesting material is enabled by publicly posting the articles in the context of ongoing research requests.

Closing and Archiving the Request. When all relevant research has been conducted and delivered to the client, the request can be closed and the "Research Request" page is archived along with with metadata that the research librarian chooses to include (e.g. keywords). At that point, the "Research Request" page contains all of the information about the progress of the research activity. The saved page is picked up by the library web server's site indexing tool and by the corporate intranet web crawler. It can then be found by searching both within the library website or from the company-wide intranet search page. Client and staff personal web pages, and group pages, have filtered views of the research request archive so that they can retrieve their archived requests. Since personal and group pages are public, it is also possible to browse all of the research done for an individual or a group.

3.6 Overview

A client's library-specific "intranet identity" consists of all the information presented on the personal website. Unlike many customizable, or personalizable websites, the libraries' personal websites are public, visible to anyone on the corporate intranet. In fact, several processes are available which direct clients to other client's sites based on shared interests. These are the connection processes that mimic community-building practices in real libraries [1], [3], [8].

4 Conclusion

The library system developed for these corporate environments was designed to incorporate several "knowledge management" features, specifically:

- Capture of "ephemeral" information that is usually lost (e.g. conversations).
- Explicit relationships and easy navigation among related pieces of information in disparate sources.
- Widespread availability of information.
- Enabling connections between people who would otherwise never find each other.

Knowledge building and information sharing, while currently touted as important for productivity in industry, are also at the center of "community." Features like the ones described here would work equally well for the public libraries of digital cities and could produce extremely exciting knowledge resources for citizens.

Willingness to share knowledge is one of the most basic changes in culture and technology that can lead to effective use of a group's or an organization's information resources [5], [6], [11]. Knowledge sharing involves breaking organizational boundaries and undermining traditional lines of control [14]. One resource for this purpose that is appearing in some organizations is the corporate "knowledge center," a clearing house for diverse sources of information staffed by professionals who keep track of cross-organizational goals and needs [2], [6], [10], [18]. Knowledge centers are natural outgrowths of forward-looking libraries, and tools such as this will be at the center of successful knowledge centers.

These library systems support some of the intangible, relationship-related aspects of a corporate library. They build a structure for information from research interactions and personal interest profiles. They encourage knowledge sharing and seek to enable in cyberspace some of the serendipitous interactions that arise in information-rich landscapes such as real libraries and bookstores [1], [3], [8]. Hopefully, the system described here can serve as a foundation for development of virtual public libraries for digital cities.

References

1. Bishop, A.P., & Star, S.L.:   Social informatics of digital library use and infrastructure. In Williams M.E. (ed.). Annual Review of Information Science and Technology, **31** (1996) 301-401
2. Chase, R.: Knowledge Navigators. Information Outlook, Sept. (1998) 17-26
3. Constant, D., Sproul, L., & Kiesler, S.: The kindness of strangers: The usefulness of electronic weak ties for technical advice. Organizational Science, **7** (1996) 119-135
4. Covi, L., & Kling, R.: Organizational dimensions of effective digital library use: Closed rational and open natural systems models. Journal of the American Society for Information Science, **47** (1996) 672-690
5. Davenport, T.H.: Information ecology. Oxford Univ. Press, New York (1997)
6. Davenport, T.H., & Prusack, L.: Working Knowledge: How organizations manage what they know. Harvard Business School Press, Boston (1997)
7. Ehrlich, K, & Cash, D.: Turning information into knowledge: Information finding as a collaborative activity. Proceedings of Digital Libraries '94, Texas A&M University, College Station, TX, June (1994)
8. Hinds, P., & Kiesler, S.: Communication across boundaries: Work, structure and the use of communication technologies in a large organization. Organizational Science, **6** (1995) 373-393
9. Levy, D., & Marshall, C.: Going digital: A look at assumptions underlying digital libraries. Communications of the ACM, **38** (1995) 77-84
10. Marshall, L.: Facilitating knowledge management and knowledge sharing: New opportunities for information professionals. Online, Vol. 21 (1997) 92-98
11. Miyagawa, S. & Kaneko, I.: Design and development of community oriented tools. Lecture Notes in Computer Science (in this volume), Springer-Verlag, (2000)
12. Nardi, B. & O'Day, V.: Information ecologies: Using technology with a heart. MIT Press , Cambridge, MA (1999)
13. Nardi, B., & O'Day, V.: Intelligent agents: What we learned in the library. Libri, **46** (1996) 59-88
14. Ranerup, A: Online forums as an arena for political discussions. Lecture Notes in Computer Science (in this volume), Springer-Verlag, (2000)
15. Rao, R., Pedersen, J.O., Hearst, M.A., Mackinlay, J.D., Card, S.K., Masinter, L., Halvorsen, P., & Robertson, G.G.: Rich interaction in the digital library. Communications of the ACM, **38** (1995) 29-40
16. Robertson, S., Jitan, S., & Reese, K.: Web-based collaborative library research. Proceedings of the Second ACM International Conference on Digital Libraries. ACM Press, New York (1997) 152-160
17. Robertson, S. & Reese, K. A virtual library for building community and sharing knowledge. Int'l Journal of Human-Computer Studies, **51** (1999) 663-685
18. Williams, R.R., & Bukowitz, W.R.: Knowledge managers guide information seekers. HR Magazine, January (1997) 77-81

Agent Community with Social Interactions for Worker and Job Hunting

Takayoshi Asakura[1], Takahiro Shiroshima[1], Toshiaki Miyashita[2]

[1] Human Media Research Laboratories, NEC Corporation
8916-47 Takayama, Ikoma-city, Nara 630-0101, Japan
{asakura, sirosima}@hml.cl.nec.co.jp

[2] NEC Software Kansai, Ltd.
1-4-24 Shiromi, Chuo-ku, Osaka-city, Osaka 540-8551, Japan
t_miyashita@knes.nec.co.jp

Abstract. We propose an agent community model for investigating workers and jobs on open computer networks. We call it the LOJ/LOT model, and it is a multi-agent model that provides a knowledge-intensive community like a market for human resources. This model also includes social interactions for getting jobs. LOJ and LOT stand for "look for jobs" and "look for talent (worker)", respectively. The LOJ/LOT model has three characteristics as follows. (1) Agents recruit workers or jobs on an open space on the Internet. All users who want workers or jobs can use these agents that have several recruiting tactics and specific requirements for workers or jobs. (2) Agents can ask other agents for information about job contract partners. The information is gathered through social interactions, and is safely kept. (3) If matchmaking fails, agents introduce other candidates using social links created from e-mail, Web page links, chat logs and so on. There are two major problems in providing the service of worker and job hunting with this model. These are legal issue and a privacy issue. If we settle these problems, Digital City will grow with the business and regional community. In the future, Digital City will be able to connect the real world to the virtual world on the Internet.

1 Introduction

In recent years, the working style of office workers has changed. This change might be caused by three factors: social factors, personal factors and business factors. Social factors mean that computers and the Internet have come into worldwide usage and that women have increasingly entered the workforce. Personal factors mean changes in lifestyles. A worker has only to work when he/she needs to. Business factors refer to the spread of "work sharing-styled employment" for retired people, creation of fluid organizations for quick correspondence, and outsourcing. With these factors, new working styles are being created. For example, many job search processes now

T. Ishida, K. Isbister (Eds.): Digital Cities, LNCS 1765, pp. 261-274, 2000.
© Springer-Verlag Berlin Heidelberg 2000

exist on the Internet [CareerSite 99] [iccweb 99]. In addition, job matching service for people with disability starts on the Internet [Miyagawa 00].

On the other hand, multi-agent systems have been developed in universities and companies all over the world. It is difficult, however, to find useful multi-agent systems in the public domain. If multi-agent systems can be applied to the public domain, they can be recognized as an agent community. The problem will then be finding useful applications for daily life and ordinary people. If a multi-agent system is applied to job hunting, we might get one solution to a new work style in the near future.

We propose a model of an agent community for investigating workers and jobs on computer networks. Our model, the LOJ/LOT model, is a multi-agent model for a knowledge-intensive community like a market for human resources, and it includes social interactions for getting jobs.

In chapter 2, we explain the new working style in a business community. These working styles are SOHO, part-time jobs at home and border-less offices. In chapter 3, we explain our definition of Digital City and relations between a business community and Digital City. In chapter 4, we propose a multi-agent model for a part-time job at home, which this is one of the new working styles in a business community. In chapter 5, we discuss potential problems about worker and job hunting in the network.

2   New Working Style in a Business Community

2.1   Present Overview of Working Style

SOHO (Small Office, Home Office)
SOHO is a working style for those who work at home instead of an office. Workers bring their jobs to their homes. When FTTH (Fiber to the home) is constructed and a person's home is always connected to a company by a high-speed network, ordinary software for office applications can be used.

Part-Time Job at Home
People who undertake jobs at their homes for various clients without belonging to any particular company are gradually increasing. Generally speaking, workers in these jobs receive job contents and hand over their work to a client through the Internet. Therefore, it is not necessary to go to a company. The style of such part-time work at present is limited to certain kinds of jobs such as translation, editing and software programming. However, the number of applicable jobs will increase as the Internet spreads since this part-time work at home can reduce the fixed expenses of a company. We can see this now in the increase in the number of contract staff sent out by temporary employment companies.

Border-Less Office

Many companies frequently change their organization according to movement of their markets. Several companies make projects to advance their business plans instead of keeping fixed organizations. Other companies divide one division into many small divisions to manage the skills of their workers.

2.2 Worker and Job Hunting

When companies recruit the part-time employees, they ordinarily use advertisements, magazines, employment agencies, human relationships and the temporary employment companies. The companies, of course, wish to hire people with high abilities (we call this workers or talent). On the other hand, workers want good jobs where they can use their abilities. Providing better solutions for both sides is the central role of forming a business community. We called this "worker and job hunting" and try to realize it by "matchmaking with a multi-agent system", as shown in figure 1.

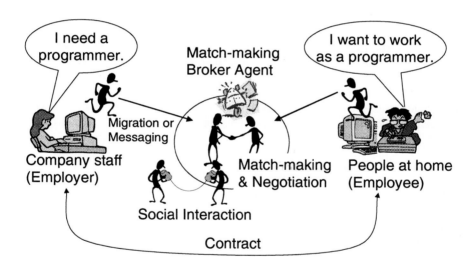

Fig. 1. Matchmaking with a Multi-agent System

The desires of the employer and employee are reflected in the matchmaking process.

A job contract often fails during a job offer or job hunting even if both sides are satisfied with some conditions. This is because it is difficult to fulfill each other's requirements and to objectively evaluate skills, jobs and companies. Therefore, the matchmaking process must play a role in such intervention and sufficiently recognize both sides. Moreover, when the contract fails during the matchmaking process, they must be a system for immediately introducing another job and worker.

The system must support not only matchmaking but also contracting and payments.
These activities take a lot of time and result in troublesome effort for both employer and employee.

People contract with an unknown person or company.
In this case, information about the contract partner is very important, since people must decide the partner by only using information about the contract partner.

2.3   Social Interaction by Exchanging Individual Information

When people make contracts, they try to collect information about a partner. In addition, people who make a contract with a company or a job hunter on a computer network become careful because they do not know a partner's achievements and history. The individual or company will make sure that a partner is reliable. However, more information is necessary in order to make the contract with a better partner. In the public domain, people collect information about a contract partner from the mass media and from other people who have worked with the contract partner in the past. Therefore, the system must be able to mutually exchange an individual and company's information. On the other hand, an evaluation of a potential contract partner requires objective and subjective information. It is desirable that the objective evaluation be automatically done based on a common criterion.

2.4   Toward a Business Community

We described "worker and job hunting" in a previous section on the premise that companies still exist. From the viewpoint of a company, "worker and job hunting" is a assignment of tasks belonging to a project to people not belonging to the company. This is a type of out-sourcing witch means that a company flexibly uses manpower outside of the company. If out-sourcing spreads worldwide, an employee who does not belong to the company may undertake many jobs. Therefore, the company trusts the employee. When an employee is not able to finish many jobs by himself/herself, the employee hunts for other people and dispatches jobs to other people. The employee becomes a manager who contracts with a company. From another viewpoint, the manager is a virtual employment agency, and the manager and the contracted employees construct a network business community.

On the other hand, when a border-less office spreads to many companies, the division of a company has less value. This reduces jobs in the division, and there is an increase in jobs undertaken across divisions. An employee works at his/her discretion, and gets paid. This border-less office means that "a company" is created (exist) in a company. From yet another viewpoint, we can regard a division in a company as "a company". The border-less office makes for an agile organization and promotes the utilization of the human resources in the company. This is a kind of the business community in a company.

Through the evolution of this business community, a virtual company will finally come into existence on the Internet. The virtual company is a virtual organization constructed with each people having the same purpose on a network. The virtual company has many phases. These phases are hunting skills when it is necessary, constructing projects, creating products and selling products for profit. Finally, the virtual company is dispersed when the project has been completed. Perhaps, such a working style in the virtual company is the final working style on the Internet. Of course, companies still exist, and the virtual companies coexist with existing companies. Our final purpose is to support each phases of the virtual company. The first step is "worker and job hunting".

3   Business Community at Digital City

3.1   Digital City: A Virtual World with Reality

We explain our definition of Digital City. Digital City is a virtual world with reality. Since Digital City is based on a real world, virtual objects should exist in Digital City like in the real world. In other words, Digital City is a contact point between the real and virtual world.

We focus on reliability in Digital City. The objects in Digital City correspond to objects in the real world. Therefore, the objects in Digital City are as reliable as those in the real world. For example, when people shop in Digital City, which exists in the real world, they can rely on a shop. If the shop inconveniences them, they can go to the real shop.

Therefore, we can have confidence in Digital City, and applications/services for providing confidence are suitable in Digital City. One such service is worker and job hunting.

3.2   Authentication of Worker and Job Hunting at Digital City

Why do people participate in Digital City? On the Internet, we can communicate by e-mail, and we can search and view a lot of information. For a user to use the Internet and participate in Digital City, Digital City should provide services beyond the Internet. One of these services is based on the regional property of Digital City. For example, it provides regional contents (guidance or information to temples, shrines, etc.), or other information about a regional community. The former is service for people outside of the community, the latter is service for the people in the community. It is necessary to continuously provide services that bring value to users so that they return to Digital City. One such service is "worker and job hunting".

When a regional company searches for regional people in the real world, it is no different from an employment office in the real world. It is more efficient that we do matchmaking for a region but as well as the whole world so that a partner can be found easily. Thus, a virtual town in Digital City might be helpful.

If a company that wants to look for workers and people who want to find jobs have residence in Digital City, they can do matchmaking with each other regardless of whether it is the real or virtual world. To improve reliability, Digital City should include a registration system for matchmaking participants. There are two ways of authentication, "self control" and "administration".

In the "self-control" authentication, participants as volunteers authenticate each other. In this case, a volunteer administrator may not have much authority for researching participants, so a matchmaking service should strictly authenticate the matchmaking participants. In the "administration" authentication, a local government authenticates participants as an administrator of Digital City. In this way, the reliance of a matchmaking target improves simply by having residence in Digital City.

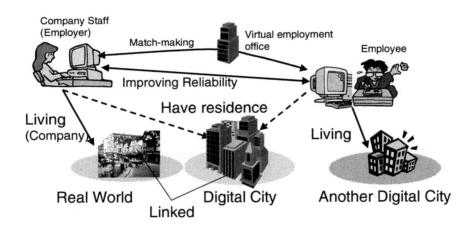

Fig. 2. Reliability of Digital City

3.3   Digital City in the Future

In the future, when Digital City is established, cooperation with other Digital Cities will become important in "worker and job hunting". If an administrator of Digital City guarantees the reliance of participants in Digital City, matchmaking between Digital Cites can become possible. Even in such a condition, matchmaking between a company and people in the same region should occur prior to matchmaking in different regions. Thus, each Digital City will be of great value to the matchmaking candidates. In other words, matchmaking without consideration of region eliminates the concept of region in Digital City.

Companies will have residence in a Digital City to get workers. People will have residence in Digital City to get good jobs. When Digital City becomes more advanced and communication increases among participants of Digital Cites, Digital City or a town in Digital City will become specialized. In addition, Digital City might have a new regional property for matchmaking. For example, in the real world, there are securities firms on Wall Street (Kabuto-Cho in Japan), or companies in the information industry that come to Silicon Valley. The same may occur in Digital City.

A search for workers and jobs supports a continuation of Digital City and a gathering of participants. A content related to the real world and the virtual world is useful for Digital City. In addition, matchmaking based on the regional property of Digital City brings new a regional property, i.e., the specialization of a category of business.

4 LOJ/LOT Agent Model

Our LOJ/LOT agent model provides a service that supports a consistent process from the matchmaking process to the contract execution with the cooperation of various agents. This model is based on a Client-Server model, and it includes migration agents to protect privacy and to reduce the communication cost.

For example, the company sends the agent that has requirements for the workers to the negotiating place. The worker at home sends the agent that has the job requirements to the negotiating place. Then the agents return to the company or home when it is necessary for the agent to interact with the user.

4.1 Overview

Figure 3 shows the LOJ/LOT Agent Model.

First, we explain the model by describing the outline of its operation. Suppose that the staff of a company wants a worker with some skills in order to advance a new business plan and the staff member has a LOT agent (look for talent agent). The staff member inputs requirements to the LOJ/LOT open space with information about job contents and pay, the appointed date of delivery, and so on. Then he/she sends the LOT agent with the requirements to the LOJ/LOT open space. Suppose that a person who wants to get a job has a LOJ agent (look for job agent). He/she inputs his/her requirements with information concerning job contents, his/her career, convenient working days, and so on. The job seeker sends the LOJ agent to the LOJ/LOT open space. Each agent sent to the LOJ/LOT open space is authenticated by the authentication agent, who confirms the following:

Are both the LOJ and the LOT agents the regular program or not?
Are both agent senders registered as regular members of this community or not?

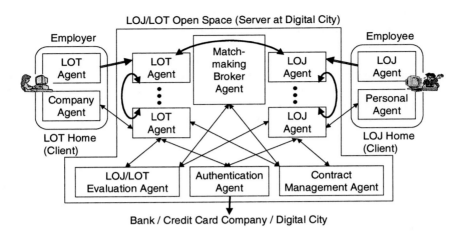

Fig. 3. LOJ/LOT Agent Model

If these confirmations are completed, the system finds appropriate partners who match each other's requirements. At this time, both senders can get the information about the partners from the LOJ/LOT evaluation agent. In the next step, each agent negotiates these requirements among the appropriate partners' agents. Finally, when the best partner is found, the corresponding LOJ/LOT agents make a contract through the contract management agent.

When the work is completed, the LOJ agent sends a result to the contract management agent. After the job content is confirmed, the contract management agent delivers it to the employer through the LOT agent. At the same time, the contract management agent delivers the job pay information to the employee. Each LOJ/LOT agent has some matchmaking and negotiation tactics. Once the LOJ/LOT agent is injected into the open space, it works with pre-contractual requirements based on these tactics. The user, of course, can change these tactics.

LOJ/LOT Open Space
The open space is the place where all services concerning worker/job offers, payment are provided. The agents and the other modules that exist in the LOJ/LOT open space are the matchmaking broker agent, the LOJ/LOT evaluation agent, the authentication agent, the contract management agent, the bank channel, and the credit card channel. Moreover, the agents to be injected from the employer and the employee are the LOT agent and the LOJ agent, respectively. Matchmaking can be done at any time among the injected agents. The open space must support the life cycle of agents.

LOT Agent
This agent looks for agents of workers to mediate between the employer and other agents. The LOT agent is generated in the LOT-home place of the employer and it moves between the open space and the LOT-home place. It moves to the open space

with the employer requirements and it gets the list of available workers, and returns to the LOT-home place. The employer selects some candidates from the list. Then, the LOT agent finds a negotiation partner by working with the matchmaking broker agent. After the matchmaking, the LOT agent negotiates salary requirements and so on with the LOJ agent. Finally, it concludes a contract. During the matchmaking, the LOT agent gets the information about the workers from the LOJ/LOT evaluation agent and other LOT agents. The LOT agent, therefore, has a chance to change the tactics and reset the requirements of the user.

Company Agent
This is a general term for various agents that support the employer. The company agent consists of the LOT management agent for managing information about the employer, the project management agent for managing the progression of the work, and so on. The LOT management agent provides information on the attributes of the company to the LOT agent when requested.

Personal Agent
This is a general term for various agents that support employee. The personal agent consists of the LOJ management agent, schedule management agent, and so on. The LOJ management agent maintains the employee's information and provides information to the LOJ agent when requested. The schedule management agent manages the work schedule.

Matchmaking Broker Agent
This agent performs matchmaking between the LOT agent and the LOJ agent by taking account of the requirements of both agents. Whenever a new LOJ (LOT) agent is injected to the open space, the execution of matchmaking starts. Both the LOJ (LOT) agent and the matchmaking broker agent work according to their respective tactics. For example, suppose that the service of the matchmaking broker agent is a toll service. Also suppose that the result of matchmaking in the open space affects the income of an open space provider. This might work to form more matchmaking according to the tactics.

LOJ/LOT Evaluation Agent
This agent provides the evaluation information of the injected LOJ (LOT) agent, namely, the employer and the employee. The evaluation information is generated by electronic questionnaires, which are sent to the employer and the employee after executing the contract.

Authentication Agent
This agent authenticates the injected LOJ (LOT) agent at the LOJ/LOT open space. The authentication agent verifies if the user and agent are authentic. If this model will be applied to worker and job hunting system on Digital City, authentication agent will link to the authentication mechanism provided by Digital City.

Contract Management Agent
This agent manages the total process until the contract completion. When the contract is agreed upon, the control is switched over from the matchmaking broker agent to the contract manager agent. The contract management agent manages the contract execution and performs the contract task. The contract task is mainly the transfer of money.

4.2   Agent Protocols Used by the LOJ/LOT Model

New agent protocols for worker/job hunting are introduced in this section. These protocols are classified into the recruiting protocol and the partner's information exchanging protocol.

The recruiting protocol is the definition protocol covering the beginning of worker and job hunting to contract completion. The partner's information exchanging protocol is the protocol for collecting the information on a partner in the contract.

Recruiting Protocol
Figure 4 shows an outline of the recruiting protocol and depicts its basic flow. As the LOJ (LOT) agent acts according to its tactics in each phase, the flow is not always the same as the flow shown in figure 4. For example, the Contract Net Protocol [Smith 80] [FIPA 97] or the Multistage Negotiation [Conry 88] can be applied to the negotiation phase.

- The Retrieval Phase
  The employer gives a requirement about the worker to the LOT agent. The employee gives a requirement about the job to the LOJ agent. They inject these agents into the LOJ/LOT open space. Each agent asks the broker agent for those people who agree with the requirement. There are, in fact, various mechanisms in the matchmaking, but we do not describe them in this study. The broker agent ties the employer to the employee to satisfy the requirements of each. The matchmaking broker agent returns the result of the matchmaking to the LOJ (LOT) agent. Each agent receives the list of results. The LOJ (LOT) agent returns to its home, and shows its user the collected candidate list. The user chooses the candidacy of negotiation, and the negotiation phase begins. At this time there is a temporary contract, since there is the possibility that the temporary contract will be canceled depending on the future negotiation. If the result of matchmaking is unacceptable to the LOJ (LOT) agent or the user, the LOJ (LOT) agent changes the candidacy and does the matchmaking request again. The matchmaking broker agent stops the matchmaking by receiving the message sent from the LOJ (LOT) agent.
  If there is no appropriate candidate, the LOT agent can not collect the candidate. In this time, the next phase is the introduction phase.

- The Introduction Phase
  If there is no appropriate candidate, the broker agent looks for candidates of introduction. A candidate of introduction is a user who has requested the broker agent

to do matchmaking in the past. This user may have ability similar to one wanted by a company. If there are such candidates, the broker agent introduces candidates to the LOT agent. If the user of the LOT agent decides the negotiation partner, the next phase is the negotiation phase.

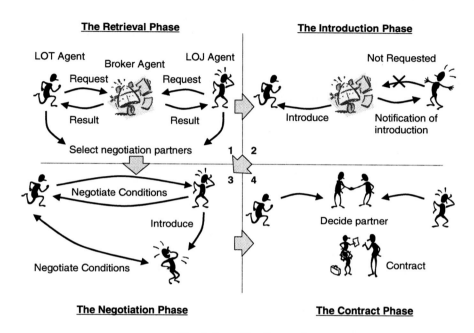

Fig. 4. Recruiting Protocol

- The Negotiation and Contract Phase

In this phase, negotiation is done based on the requirements. If the employer or the employee has already reached an agreement, this phase is unnecessary. The LOJ (LOT) agent delivers a message to the LOT (LOJ) agents and the negotiation begins. The LOT (LOJ) agents ask the LOJ (LOT) agent to make concessions. If the LOT (LOJ) agents can accept the request, the LOT (LOJ) agents send the acknowledgement message to the matchmaking broker agent. If the LOT (LOJ) agents reject the request, the LOT (LOJ) agents send the message of rejection to the broker agent.

This negotiation is based on the negotiation strategy of each agent. This is same as [Maes 99]. If the LOJ (LOT) agent accepts the partner, it sends the message of acceptance to the LOT (LOJ) agents of the negotiation partners. If the LOT (LOJ) agent receiving the message has no problem, it returns the message of acceptance, and the negotiation is completed.

The contract partner's decision and then the contract conclusion are taken over by the contract management agent.

Contract Partner's Information Exchanging Protocol

Figure 5 shows an outline of the Contract Partner's Information Exchanging protocol. This is the communication protocol when the contract partner's information becomes necessary in every phase of the recruiting protocol. The contract partner's information is divided into objective information and subjective information.

We assume that LOJ agent A (of user A) will contract with LOT agent B (of company B).

If LOT agent B has contracted with LOJ agent C in the past, the evaluation agent observes the status of the completed contract, for example, was the appointed date of delivery met, etc. When the LOJ agent requests an evaluation of the candidates, the evaluation agent returns the objective information.

If user A demands more information about company B, the LOJ agent A requests subjective information from the LOJ agent C of user C that contracted with company B in the past.

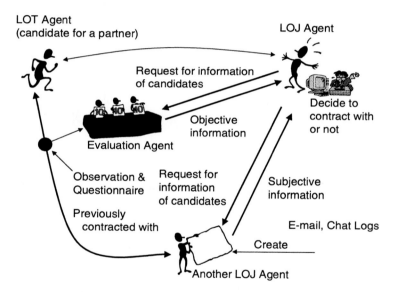

Fig. 5. Contract Partner's Information Exchanging Protocol

At this time, the LOJ agent A checks the user's score of the subjective information. This score represents how many times the user has replied to other users' requests. If the user's score is less than a threshold, the user cannot get the subjective information about the partner. This method realizes a "give and take" situation.

The user who receives objective/subjective information from other agents decides to contract with the candidate or not.

5 Potential Problems

There are two major problems in the worker and job hunting service using a LOJ/LOT model.

The first problem is a legal issue. In Japan, a fee-based private matchmaking service between an employee and an employer is now against the law according to three major labor laws. Therefore, providers of such a service in Japan charge companies to register job offers. However, an ideal method would change the employer and employee for successful matchmaking. Such a method is standard in buying and selling on the Internet. For that purpose, we will have to request that the Ministry of Justice relax the three major labor laws after due consideration of the risk of human selling and buying.

The second problem is related to privacy. A security problem exists in this LOJ/LOT model. Many profiles of matchmaking participants can be distributed over the Internet for deciding the partner, and these profiles can be stored in Digital City too. Perhaps, matchmaking participants will not want this personal information to be made available. For the participants to trust this system, matchmaking service providers (Digital City management or Internet service providers) must be reliable organizations, and privacy protection laws must protect these personal profiles.

6 Conclusion

In this paper, we have proposed an agent community model for the realization of a new work style. The key point of the new work style is the formation of a business community. The LOJ/LOT agent model and protocols are introduced to support worker and job hunting with the goal of forming a business community. However, there are many problems to be solved, for example, protecting against inappropriate access to the open space, settling delivery claims, and authenticating matchmaking. Even if these problems are solved, we think that our agent model and protocols can be applied to the formation of a business community.

A search of worker and job hunting supports a continuation of Digital City and a gathering of participants. In addition, matchmaking based on the regional property of Digital City brings a new regional property, i.e., the specialization of a category of business. Such a service supports the prosperity of Digital City, and Digital City will grow with the business and regional community.

Several tactics and the utility function of the LOJ/LOT agent can be implemented as the service components. Therefore, if the agent's user exchanges the component, the tactics of an agent can be easily changed.

The Internet does not have a mechanism for guaranteeing users reliability. Digital City can provide this mechanism. Digital City will become a portal to the Internet for communicating with reliable users on the Internet. The application of "worker and job hunting" supports to users' actions on the Internet. Some users will work at home through the Internet, and some users will work at a office for a company. Many people will shop in the virtual world on the Internet as in the real world. The activities of real world will affect those of the virtual world, and vice versa.

Acknowledgements

The authors would like to thank Mr. Masao Managaki, Mr. Yosuke Takashima and Mr. Satoru Fujita for their helpful comments and discussions.

References

[careersite 99] http://careersite.com/ (1999.6)
[Conry 88] S.E.Conry, R.A.Meyer, V.R.Lesser : "Multistage Negotiation in Distributed Planning", A.Bond and L.Gasser (eds.) : "Readings in Distributed Artificial Intelligence", pp.367-384, 1988.
[FIPA 97] FIPA : "Agent Communication Language", FIPA97 Specification, Part 2, pp46-50, 1997.
[iccweb 99] http://www.iccweb.com/ (1999.6)
[Smith 80] R.G.Smith. : "The Contract Net Protocol: High-level Communication and Control in a Distributed Problem Solver", IEEE Trans. Comput., Vol.C-29, No.12, pp.1104 - 1113, 1980.
[Community 98] T.Ishida (Ed.): "Community Computing and Support Systems", Lecture Notes in Computer Science, Vol.1519, Springer-Verlag, 1998.
[Maes 99] P.Maes, R.H.Guttman, A.G.Moukas: "Agent that Buy and Sell:Transforming Commerce as we know It", Communications of the ACM, Vol.42, No.3, pp.81-91, 1999.
[Miyagawa 00] S.Miyagawa, I.Kaneko: "Design and Development of Community Oriented Tools", Lecture Notes in Computer Science (in this volume), Springer-Verlag, 2000.

The Motion Generation of Pedestrians as Avatars and Crowds of People

Ken Tsutsuguchi[1,2], Kazuhiro Sugiyama[2], and Noboru Sonehara[2]

[1] NTT Open Lab,
2-4, Seika cho, Soraku-gun, Kyoto 619-0237 Japan
kent@digitalcity.gr.jp
[2] NTT Cyber Space Laboratories,
1-1, Hikari-no-Oka, Yokosuka Kanagawa 239-0847 Japan

Abstract. In the digital city, creating and displaying human animation is a significant problem. This paper describes two applications of human walking animation: pedestrian as avatars and pedestrians as crowds of people. Animating controlled avatars which start, stop, and turn interactively makes it possible to realize the digital city, we describe how to build a walking motion generation module to create plane walking animation. Animating a large number of avatars or virtual bodies is expensive and is a serious barrier to enhancing the digital city. We describe a method that offers cost-effective animation. This method divides the figures in the scene into far and near groups. The movements of the former are updated less often. The proposed methods can produce computer animation scenes rapidly that still offer good animation quality.

Keywords: digital city, computer animation, motion reduction, avatar, pedestrian, human walking.

1 Introduction

Digital cities provide new communication place not only for research and business but for social activities via internet. Various technologies have been developed and applied to the digital city including networking, social interactions, agent communications, and computer graphics.

"Digital City Kyoto Project" tries to establish a "real" city by strongly connecting the digital Kyoto to the physical Kyoto. NTT Open Lab is now constructing a Digital City Kyoto prototype and is conducting various experiments on it [1]. The Digital City Kyoto prototype has a three layer model architecture which includes information, interface and interaction. In the interaction layer, creating and displaying moving human figures is a significant and challenging problem. Realism is enhanced by creating a virtual population that moves around the digital city. Figure 1 shows an image from the Digital City Kyoto prototype. If the user could interact with the digital city or other avatars as a resident of digital city, and, if the digital city were to contain many walking people, the "*virtual*" city would become a "*real*" city.

T. Ishida, K. Isbister (Eds.): Digital Cities, LNCS 1765, pp. 275–287, 2000.

This paper introduces a technology that can generate human walking motion in a three dimensional (3D) digital world, and describes how this technique will be built into the interaction layer of the Digital City Kyoto prototype. In this paper, we discuss the problems and techniques of animating two types of walking human figures, "pedestrian as avatars" and "pedestrians as crowds of people". This technique is based on a human walking animation system, *World Wide Walk* (*WWWalk*) [14]. We extended *WWWalk* and applied it to these 2 forms of human animation.

Fig. 1. Gion, Kyoto; (a) from the "Digital City Kyoto"[1], (b) with pedestrians.

One module for the interaction in the digital city creates 3D walking avatars in the 3D space to bridge users and the digital city environment or residents. By using walking avatars, we can walk around and realize the digital city on a "human scale", and can see 3D scenes from the viewpoint of a walking avatar. We constructed an extended module of *WWWalk* system, which can control avatar from state information including position, direction, velocity, mode and viewpoint. Throughout this paper, we use the word *mode* to refer to the walking state; the modes are "starting", "walking" and "stopping".

The other module creates crowds of people walking. Adding a virtual population makes it possible to activate the digital city, and crowd itself provides information to the user, for example, showing which place is popular. Unfortunately, animating a large number of moving objects is computationally expensive with existing techniques because all objects are regenerated and displayed frame by frame. In this paper, we introduce a method that can generate a large number of pedestrians rapidly. This method divides the figures in the scene into far and near groups. The movements of the former are updated less often. We measured the rendering effect using various combinations of parameters. The results clearly show the benefit of the new method.

Throughout this paper, we concentrate on the plane walking case. The next section introduces the basic technique used to generate the human walking motion. Section 3 describes the avatar making module, and section 4 describes an application that generates a large number of pedestrians. Experimental results and our goal are given and section 5 concludes the paper.

2   Walking Motion Generation

We integrated our 2 modules into a walking animation system based on *WWWalk* [14]. *WWWalk* treats the human body as an articulated rigid body with 40 degrees of freedom as shown in Figure 2 and can generate appropriate human walking motion on arbitrary walking paths in 3D virtual environments. This system permits the prior calculation of motion data.

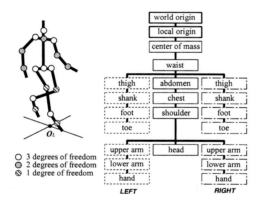

Fig. 2. The human figure model.

As shown in Figure 3, the procedure of *WWWalk* is as follows:
1) load 3D environment.
2) input 3D human figures property including height, weight, default stride and make 3D human figure.
3) set walking path in 3D scene.
4) calculate boundary values for locomotion steps which include step length, step height, the turning angle between 2 steps and the angles of body.

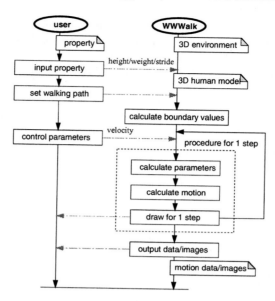

Fig. 3. The procedure of *WWWalk*.

5) for each step, do following:

    5.1) input control parameter (velocity).

    5.2) calculate locomotion parameters which include step duration or the number of frames per step, step number per minute.

    5.3) generate one step motion.

    5.4) draw updated scene per frame.

6) output the resulting motion data or image sequence.

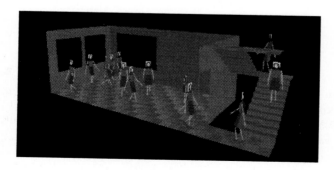

Fig. 4. An example of generated animation using *WWWalk*.

In motion generation, the position of the center of mass and 5 angles are calculated dynamically and the remaining values are calculated kinematically. Figure 4 shows an example. As shown in this figure, *WWWalk* can generate realistic walking motion in a very easy way, there is one problem: all boundary conditions are pre-calculated so walking direction or mode cannot be modified. To make *WWWalk* suitable for the virtual city, the walking mode or walking direction should be changed interactively following user control. The next section describes the extension of *WWWalk* for our module.

3   Pedestrian as Avatars

Generating pedestrian as avatars controlled by the user is a very useful technique. For example, by making a link between avatars and people walking in the corresponding physical city, we can realize communication between digital tourists and physical residents.

The roles of avatars are:
(1) realizing and interacting with digital city environments,
(2) interacting with other avatars.
(3) reflecting real data into the digital city.
In this paper, we concentrate on (1), i.e., controlling the pedestrian. (2) and (3) are not implemented and significant future works. To make it possible control virtual pedestrians, the avatar should start, stop, turn, and so on interactively.

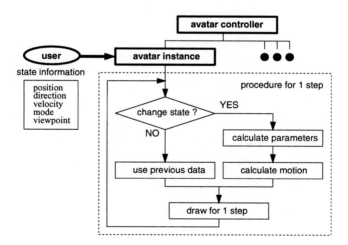

Fig. 5. Avatar module animation.

For such cases, it is useful to apply the motion generation method based on "footprint approach". The foot position or the path of walking is determined first, and the walking motions are then calculated to match the given footprints or walking path. For example, Girard [8], Overveld et al. [16] applied kinematic motion generation, van de Pannee [15] and Torkos [13]applied dynamic translation between foot positions and Ko et al. [10] introduced *VRLOCO*, which estimated next footprint positions from input body center position and facing direction and moved the human body to follow them with many types of planer locomotion.

In the plane walking case, although these approaches were suitable, we applied *WWWalk* system because it can be extended to the non-plane case, such as walking in buildings and on slopes and stairs. As shown in Figure 5, the animation of each avatar instance proceeds is as follows:

1) read the state information for the avatar including position, direction, velocity, mode and viewpoint according to user control.
2) if the state has changed, use the motion data of previous step and go to 4). Otherwise, calculate the boundary conditions and locomotion parameters for next step and go to 3).
3) calculate one step motion and store the motion data in memory.
4) display the one-step motion.
5) go back to 1).

Figure 6 shows a scene from an avatar's viewpoint. Human like avatars are controlled by the "avatar controller" in Figure 5.

Fig. 6. The scene from an avatar's viewpoint.

4   Pedestrians as Crowd

As described in section 1, if the scene of digital city were to contain many walking people, the *"virtual"* city would become a *"real"* city. However, the calculation cost for generating and displaying a large number of pedestrians is excessive.

Various methods have been created to minimize the cost of rendering 3D scenes. Most popular techniques employ simple geometric forms and are effective in reducing the "display" time. The critical problem is hidden surface removal (for example, [12]) which is essential for high quality animation. Nowadays, many works use the LOD (Level Of Detail) approach. This approach aims to reduce the number of polygons or vertices while preserving appearance attributes (for example, [4][5][7][9][11]).

The "calculation" time can be decreased by changing the motion state according to some criteria. Funkhouser et al. predefine states and switch between them according to heuristic criteria including distance of viewpoint, velocity of object and displayed size [6]. Carlson et al. applied the LOD approach to animation; that is, the motion generation method was switched according to some criteria [3]. The generation methods include dynamic simulation, kinematic model, and point mass model.

All of these works assume that the entire scene is updated every frame. Our approach differs because it changes the frame rate or updating period, not the motion status or geometric data. The new approach can be extended by adding these related works. In this section, we offer a method that can generate a large number of pedestrians rapidly. The key to this method is using different scene update periods in different regions. Pedestrians are divided into several groups according to their distance from the viewpoint. Pedestrians close to the viewpoint are rendered and updated more frequently than the others. We will detail our method in following subsections.

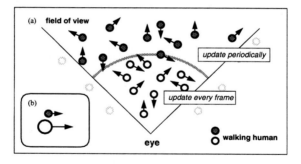

Fig. 7. The concept of our method: (a) field of view, (b) display window.

4.1   Motion Reduction

Objects far from the view point are generally perceived to move slowly in the display window compared to those nearby, see Figure 7. The proposed method updates objects close to the viewpoint in every frame, while objects far from the viewpoint are updated periodically. This greatly reduces the cost of updating the image.

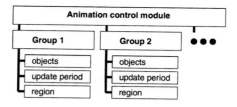

Fig. 8. The concept of the group.

To implement the above approach, the pedestrians are first classified into several groups according to their distance from the viewpoint. As shown in Figure 8, each group has its own updating period P, area and members.

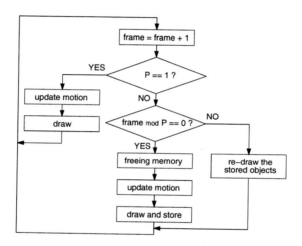

Fig. 9. Flow chart of the proposed method.

Because all graphics objects must be redrawn even if they are not updated, we adopted the memory store algorithm as known as the "display list". The regular drawing mode is often called the "immediate mode"[2]. Figure 9 shows this procedure:

1) *increment frame.*
2) *if $P = 1$ then draw using immediate mode and back to 1), else go to 3).*
3) *if $f mod P = 0$ then do the following, else go to 4).*
   3.1) *free display list.*
   3.2) *update motion using matching P frames from previous update.*
   3.3) *draw updated scene and store in memory as display list.*
4) *render the display list and return to 2).*

Moreover, using the display list can also reduce the drawing cost compared to immediate mode.

4.2   Experiment and Result

To simplify the experiments, a static background image, see Figure 1, was used and the pedestrians moved on the road surface. We added three conditions as follows to acquire useful data:
- **The number of human figures in each group is preserved.**

    A *walker* that leaves the viewing region is immediately replaced by a new walker in the same group.
- **The number of polygons or vertices is the same for each pedestrian.**

    That is, hidden surface removal or polygon reduction is not used.
- **The motion generation method is the same for all pedestrians.**

    We used pre-calculated motion data (straight walking paths).

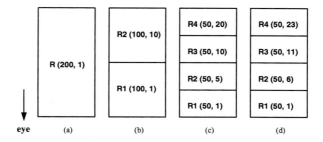

Fig. 10. The groups examined.

We generated 200 people evenly spaced throughout the viewing area, and measured the calculation time for drawing 100 frames while changing the following conditions:

1) **the updating cost.**

   We changed the updating cost from load level 1 up to 1000. This cost includes the calculation of the distances between people and the digits are relative values.

2) **the updating period.**

   We changed the updating period from 1 (immediate mode) up to 20 (one update per 20 frames).

3) **the number of groups.**

   We tried 4 types of grouping. As shown in Figure 10, The human figures were divided into groups. In this figure, a group is indicated as $R_i(N, P)$, where R is the region, N is pedestrian number and P is upgrading period.

   Figure 11 shows the result of experiments described above. All calculations were performed using an SGI OCTANE^{TM} (R10000/195MHz). Figure 11 (a) shows that, for 200 pedestrians in one group, as the updating period increases, the calculation and drawing time strongly decrease if the load level (updating

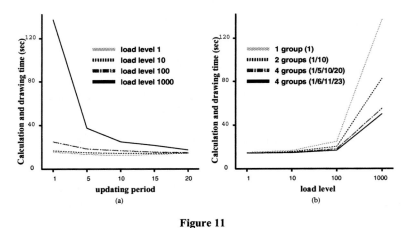

Figure 11

Fig. 11. Calculation time (100 frames) for 200 pedestrians; (a) one group (b) various grouping patterns.

cost) was high. Figure 11 (b) shows that using multiple groups significantly reduces the calculation and drawing time, especially when the load level is high.

In the case of 1 group, of course, discontinuous motion is obvious when the P is large. For example, when the updating period is set to 20, no one moves for 20 frames and then, suddenly, all of them "jump" by a large amount. Increasing the number of groups greatly reduces this motion discontinuity.

Figure 12 shows a scene animated using our method. The grouping pattern shown in Figure 10(d) was used. The benefit of the new method is clearly seen; increasing the number of objects 30 times increases the time taken for calculation and drawing only 20 times. Later tests will examine more closely the quality of animation offered by the new method.

Given that interactive applications such as the digital city must also handle a wide range of other tasks related to the moving objects, the new method is seen to be essential as these other tasks will occupy some part of the processor's capacity thus reducing the power available for calculation and drawing. Extending our method by combining it with other methods, for example, geometric data reduction, would reduce the calculation and drawing cost even further.

5   Discussion

As described in this paper, our technology makes it possible to create highly controllable pedestrians in a very easy way. The possibility of applying our technology to digital cities includes:

- **For the developers or maintainers of digital cities**:

They can design and create dynamic digital city at a small cost. As the amount of control parameters for moving pedestrian is small, our technology

Fig. 12. Animation scene (load level=1000), t means calculation time for 100 frames; (a) no pedestrians, (b) 10 pedestrians, (c)100 pedestrians, (d) 300 pedestrians.

Fig. 13. An example of displaying popular places.

will be suitable for network application like digital city. Moreover, our motion reduction technique can be applied to display other moving objects including cars, buses and animals.

• **For the information contributors**:

They can use walking people as showing some informations which include advertisement, access ranking or congestion. Figure 13 shows an example which indicates the popular place.

• **For the web users**:

They can walking around in the digital city via walking avatar, or humanoid tour guide will take them on a journey to the digital city.

Our goal includes to support those who join the digital city by supplying the technologies which make it possible to create various dynamic digital contents as they like, i. e., *"everyone who joins the digital city can create and feel his own digital city."*

6   Conclusion

This paper has presented method of generating pedestrians in the digital city and two application modules. One module generates pedestrians as avatars. We described how to introduce human walking animation into the 3D scene and creating 3D animation under the control by the user. In our module, the user can change state information interactively and can generate desirable walking sequences efficiently.

The other module generates crowds of pedestrians and we described a new approach to reducing the calculation cost in animating large numbers of pedestrians. The main point of this approach is to update the pedestrians according to their distance from the viewpoint. Experiments involving the animation of large numbers of pedestrians confirmed the efficiency of the proposed method.

We are now trying to port our modules into PC's application. Remaining tasks are to extend our method to cover walking within building or on stairs, and to conduct subjective tests in order to optimize the parameters of the method.

References

1. Ishida, T., Akahani, J., Hiramatsu, K., Isbister, K., Lisowski, S., Nakanishi, H., Okamoto, M., Miyazaki, Y. and Tsutsuguchi, K.: "Digital City Kyoto: Towards A Social Information Infrastructure," *Cooperative Information Agents III, Lecture Notes in Artificial Intelligence*, M. Klusch, O. Shehory, G. Weiss (Eds.), Springer-Verlag, Vol. 1652 (1999) 23-35

2. Woo, M., Neider, J. and Davis T.: *OpenGL Programming Guide Second Edition.* Addison-Wesley (1997)

3. Carlson, D. A. and Hodgins, J. K.: Simulation Levels of Detail for Real-time Animation. *Porc. Graphics Interface '97* (1997) 1-8

4. Cohen, J., Olano, M. and Manocha, D.: Appearance-Preserving Simplification: *Porc. SIGGRAPH '98* (1998) 115-122

5. Eck, M., DeRose, T., Duchamp, T., Hoppe, H., Lounsbery, M. and Stuetzle, W.: Multiresolution Analysis of Arbitrary Meshes. *Proc. SIGGRAPH '95* (1995) 173-182

6. Funkhouser, T. A. and Séquin, C. H.: Adaptive Display Algorithm for Interactive Frame Rates During Visualization on Complex Virtual Environments. *Proc. SIGGRAPH '93* (1993) 247-254

7. Garland, M. and Heckbert, P. S.: Surface Simplification Using Quadric Error Metrics. Proc. SIGGRAPH '97 (1997) 209-216

8. Girard, M.: Interactive Design of 3D Computer-Animated Legged Animal Motion. *IEEE Computer Graphics & Applications* **7**(6) (1987) 39-51

9. Hoppe, H.: Progressive Meshes. *Proc. SIGGRAPH '96* (1996) 99-108

10. Ko, H. and Cremer, J.: VRLOCO: Real-Time Human Locomotion from Positional Input Streams. *Presence* **5**(4) (1996) 367-380

11. Luebke, D. and Erikson, C.: View-Dependent Simplification of Arbitrary Polygonal Environments. *Proc. SIGGRAPH '97* (1997) 199-208

12. Manocha, D., Hudson, T. and Hoff III, K. E.: Visibility Culling using Hierarchical Occlusion Maps. *Proc. SIGGRAPH '97* (1997) 77-88

13. Torkos, N. and van de Panne, M.: Footprint-based Quadruped Motion Synthesis. *Proceedings of Graphics Interface '98* (1998) 151-160

14. Tsutsuguchi, K., Suenaga, Y., Watanabe, Y. and Shimohara, K.: Human Walking Animation System in Three-dimensional Modeled Scene. *Trans. IPS Japan* **38**(4) (1997) 787-796 (In Japanese)

15. van de Panne, M.: From Footprints to Animation. *Computer Graphics Forum* **16**(4) (1997) 211-223

16. van Overveld, C. W. A. M. and Ko, H.: Small Steps for Mankind: Toward a Kinematically Driven Dynamic Simulation of Curved Path Walking. *The journal of visualization and computer animation* **5** (1994) 143-165

Image-Based Pseudo-3D Visualization of Real Space on WWW

Masahiko Tsukamoto

Department of Information Systems Engineering, Graduate School of Engineering,
Osaka University
Yamadaoka 2-1, Suita, Osaka 565-0871, Japan
tuka@ise.eng.osaka-u.ac.jp

Abstract. The conventional approaches for constructing real-space-based 3D space on WWW are costly much in initial modeling and in network access in its operation. The recent trend in such construction, i.e., the image-based rendering (IBR) approach, focuses on more convenient handling of the real space, but the obtained space is usually constrained by the difficulty in image analysis. In this paper, aiming at relaxing the modeling cost of the real space and the accessing cost on WWW, we propose a simple approach where we use scenic images such as those taken by a digital camera or a video camera without distorting them. By enlarging or shrinking an avatar image and pasting it on a background scenic image according to the user's input, we can visualize the depth of the scene as pseudo 3D space. We call the method the *image-based non-rendering (IBNR)*, intended as an antithesis to IBR. In our system, we emphasize on two points: the *scene independency*, i.e., each scene is more independent of other scenes, and the *platform independency*, i.e., usual WWW browsers can be used in the walk-through of the space without extra plug-ins.

1. Introduction

Recently, several types of 3D space have been used in the Internet for a variety of purposes such as games and commercial transactions. This is partly because of the technological evolution in processing and representing such space with reality by using high-performance 3D hardware. Typical 3D space as in 3D games consists of a lot of buildings, rooms, and objects that are each composed of millions of polygons. As a result, a user can feel as if he/she is really in such space and is absorbed in the space.

In general, constructing complex 3D space with high reality is very costly. In fact, existing 3D applications were produced with a lot of money by large companies. However, those who want to construct such 3D space are not only such corporations but also small companies, shops, and personal users. We can assume that some may want to exhibit their paintings in their own 3D museum constructed on WWW, while others may wish to pigeonhole their digital resources, e.g., schedule information, E-mail, and other business materials in a virtual room. However, high cost for construction prevents these users from building elaborated 3D space for their own purposes. Even if a user constructs 3D space with little cost, the resulting space usually becomes poor and unattractive. Moreover, when they employ WWW for such

T. Ishida, K. Isbister (Eds.): Digital Cities, LNCS 1765, pp. 288-302, 2000.
© Springer-Verlag Berlin Heidelberg 2000

space, other technical problems arise, including the slow response, incomprehensive operations, and implicit effects of user's operations, and the incomplete execution caused by the lack of necessary plug-ins.

In this paper, we propose a method for constructing pseudo-3D space with low cost based on pictures taken by digital camera. We call this method the *image-based non-rendering (IBNR)*. In IBNR, pictures taken in the real space are used as the background of a WWW page, and a picture of a person is pasted on the background picture to be served as an avatar. By appropriately enlarging and shrinking the picture of the avatar according to the user's instructions, we can express the depth of a scene. Moreover, by linking such scenes, we can construct a large-scaled pseudo-3D space on WWW.

The rest of this paper is organized as follows: First we introduce the basic concept of IBNR in section 2, and then we show the detail of an IBNR scene in section 3. Next, we explain our design and implementation of the system for realizing IBNR in section 4. We compare the IBNR with other approaches in section 5. In section 6, we summarize the paper and mention our future plan concerning IBNR.

2. The Approach

2.1 Scene

A simple method for constructing complex space with reality is the use of a picture taken in the real space as it is as the background. Based on this idea, we propose an approach called IBNR. We use this phrase as an antithesis to a recent VR trend, i.e., *image-based rendering (IBR)*, where images are, in many cases, deeply analyzed and distorted to construct a 3D model. In contrast, in our IBNR approach, images are used without any analysis and distortion.

In IBNR, first we should prepare a scenic image such as that shown in Figure 1 and eight human images such as those in Figure 2. In these human images, a person should be directed to the front, back, right, left, and their intermediates. Next, as shown in Figure 3, we should give the trapezoid of the scenic image to specify the floor region where a user can move by using an avatar. In what follows, we sometimes use the word 'user' for the avatar.

Fig. 1. A scenic image for a background

Fig. 2. Human images for an avatar

Fig. 3. Floor information

Based on this configuration, the system can construct the scene which a user can immerse himself/herself in and walk through. As shown in Figure 4 (a), the picture in Figure 1 is used as the background and one of the pictures in Figure 2 is composed in an appropriate size. A person's picture is enlarged and shrunk by the user's input to represent the depth of the pseudo-3D space. In this figure, if the user presses a key (e.g., 't') assigned to the 'forward' operation several times, the avatar picture is enlarged gradually as shown in (b), which is as if the avatar steps forward in the space shown in the background picture. If a user wants to change the direction of the avatar, he/she can input another key (e.g., 'f') assigned to the 'rotate to left' operation by which the picture is changed as shown in (c). Then, if the user inputs 't' several times to step forward, he/she obtains the scene shown in (d), which means the direction of the avatar's step is changed. An example of such key configuration is 't' to go forward, 'f' to rotate to the left, 'h' to rotate to the right, and 'b' to go backward.

2.2 Pseudo-3D Space Constructed by Multiple Scenes

We can construct large-scaled pseudo-3D space by linking a lot of scenes constructed in the previous subsection. In this subsection, we describe the way to construct such space.

(a)   (b)

(c)   (d)

Fig. 4. Example scenes of IBNR

In Figure 4 (a), if the user repeats forwarding and the avatar comes out of a predefined floor region, i.e., the bottom side of the trapezoid shown in Figure 3, the scene automatically changes to another one, as shown in Figure 5 (a). This scene is constructed in a similar manner to the scene shown in Figure 4, where the background image, the trapezoid region, and the linkage information are different. Note that, in the situation Figure 5 (a), if a user turns back and moves to the back, the scene again changes back to Figure 4 (a) where the avatar appears with his back-side image in the front of the scene.

If the user turns back in Figure 4 (a) and steps forwarding, the scene changes to Figure 5 (b), where the view point and the direction of the scene are different from those of Figure 4 (a) but the basic mechanism is completely same. If the user repeats forwarding in Figure 5 (a), the scene changes to (c). Moreover, in the situation (c), if the user turns right and steps forward, the scene changes to (d).

In each picture in Figure 4 and 5, there are two, three, or four arrows at the right top area. These arrows represent the directions to which other scenes are linked from the scene. Upward, downward, leftward, and rightward arrows respectively show that there are scene at the back, front, left, and right of the scene.

A scene is described by HTML, JavaScript and Java, and therefore can be displayed by a normal WWW browser. In each scene, at most four URLs are attached to represent the front, back, right, and left neighbors of the scene. Of course, an attached URL is not necessarily an IBNR scene; it can be a normal WWW page.

(a)   (b)

(c)   (d)

Fig. 5. Example scenes of IBNR: when the scene is changed

Figure 6 (a) and (b) are typical WWW pages, which are linked by IBNR scenes. These pages are respectively linked from the left, and the right sides of the Figure 4 scene and if a user presses the 'Exit' button, the Figure 4 scene is again displayed where the avatar appears at the left or the right sides of the scene. Such normal pages are also effectively used in the entrance of a building, an office, and a room to put a separation of a sequence of scenes.

In genral, there are many WWW functions which are used for variety of purposes. These functions can also be utilized in constructing IBNR contents. By using the cookie, we can construct a 3D content where a scene is changed if a user visits the place after visiting another certain place. Several interesting contents with scenario are typically seen in RPG and sound novels. An example of such contents is as follows: A user cannot come into a building if he/she does not visit a place and obtain a key. Another example is that the shutter is closed if a user turns on a switch in another scene.

We can use a page that plays a video. In IBNR contents of a zoo or an aquarium, if a user comes close to a cage or a watertank, the video which shows animals in the cage or fish in the watertank is played. If an avatar goes into a train or a car, the video which shows the avatar going in the vehicle and the vehicle going out is played. Such dynamic contents can enrich the IBNR contents.

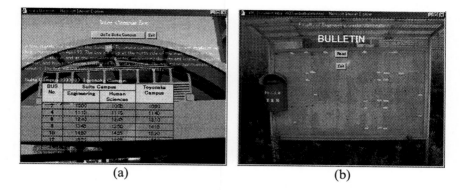

(a)   (b)

Fig. 6. Regular WWW pages linked by an IBNR scene

3. System Design

We designed and implemented the IBNR system. In our system design, we emphasize two points: the *scene independency*, i.e., each scene is more independent of other scenes, and the *platform independency*, i.e., any WWW browsers can be used to visit the space without assuming any special configuration, such as plug-ins. These two points bring content creators the following merits:

- Multiple creators can simultaneously construct contents that are linked to each other.
- Different versions of IBNR can be used in the same content.
- Each floor region may be loosely defined. A creator is not required to care for the global constraint on topology.

In this section, we show the detail of the IBNR system design.

3.1 Scene

A scene is composed by a background image and an avatar image. The composition is based on its floor information and the user's input. The information attached to a scene is divided into four categories; the background information, the floor information, the avatar information, and the object information. They are described in the remaining subsections of this section.

We provide two versions of the system for a scene-change mechanism. One is the *simple version* which does not preserve detailed information on scene change, while the other is the *cookie version* which uses the cookie function of WWW on scene change to preserve avatar information. Each scene can employ either or both of these

Fig. 7. Four initial stages of a scene in the simple version

versions. Furthermore, two scenes employing different versions can be linked to each other.

In the simple version, a scene creator should prepare four HTML files for one scene. These files are identified by the last character of the file name, 'f', 'b', 'l', and 'r', which stand for 'front', 'back', 'left', and 'right', respectively. They represent the entry direction. That is, when the scene name is 'x0', there are four files 'x0f.html', 'x0b.html', 'x0l.html', and 'x0r.html' and they are different in the initial status of an avatar. In Figure 7, (a), (b), (c), and (d) show these four initial stages of a scene.

The simple version has a problem due to its simplicity. We explain it by using an example of the scene change from Figure 5 (c) to Figure 5 (d). In this case, even if the user has almost finished crossing the marked crosswalk and turns to the right, like Figure 8 (a), it appears in the center of the crosswalk after the change, like Figure 5 (d). Moreover, even if the avatar comes out diagonally from Figure 5 (c), like Figure 8 (e), the system shows the same result, i.e., the avatar appears in his back. The approximation of the simple version sometimes prevents user's recognition of the topological connection of the scenes, and possibly causes user's discomfort. Such difference may escape the user's attention when the width of a floor region is narrow, such as in a corridor and a sidewalk, but can be conspicuous when the background image is widely open space such as a plain or a plaza.

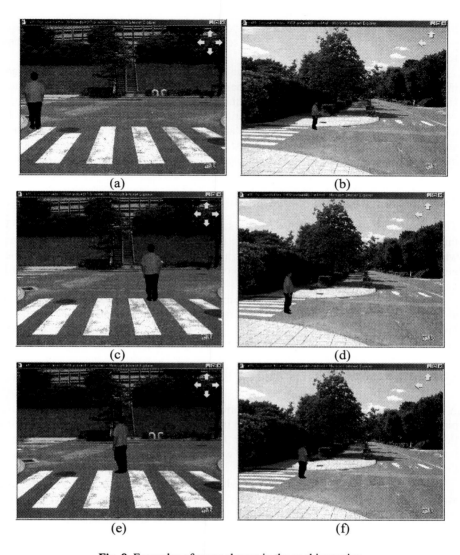

(a)

(b)

(c)

(d)

(e)

(f)

Fig. 8. Examples of scene change in the cookie version

To solve the problem, we provide the cookie version. In this version, we prepare four files 'x0xf.html', 'x0xb.html', 'x0xl.html', and 'x0xr.html' for the scene 'x0'. Consider that the user comes to this scene from another scene. Before the scene changes, the system saves the status of the avatar, i.e., the location and the direction by using the cookie. After the scene changes, the system loads the cookie information to determine the initial location and direction of the avatar.

In Figure 8, we show examples of such scene changes. Remember the back side of (a), (c), and (e) is linked to the left side of (b), (d), and (f). If a user moves out from the scene in a left position like (a), he/she appears in a back position of the new scene, like (b). If he/she goes out in a right position like (c), he/she appears in a front position like (d). If a user exits the old scene diagonally like (e), he enters the new scene diagonally like (f).

Besides the use of the cookie, there are some other ways to share avatar information between two successive scenes. One is embedding this information into a URL. In this method, it is also easy to link the URL-embedded pages with a simple version scene and a cookie version scene. It is also possible to construct a scene by using CGI and ASP. A creator can select an appropriate version in describing a scene according to its property and purpose. Such flexibility is due to the scene independency property of the IBNR approach.

3.2 Background

The background of a scene is typically a scenic picture taken by a digital camera. In this picture, it is required that there is no person and no obstacle in the floor space where the avatar can move, and therefore a creator should remember this point when he/she takes a picture. In the construction of a scene, a creator should specify the file name of this picture.

The background of a scene can be not only a camera picture but also a snapshot of a VRML browser, and a painting or a drawing. It is also possible to use real-time video image taken by a camera fixed at a certain place. In this case, other mechanisms, e.g. a streaming plug-in, are necessary to display the live video.

3.3 Floor

A floor is a region in the real space corresponding to the area in the background picture where the avatar can move around in the scene. We assume that the shape of a floor is a rectangle and the rectangular floor in the real space corresponds to a trapezoid area in the picture. In addition, we assume that the top and bottom sides of the trapezoid are horizontal.

A scene creator should specify the width and the depth of the floor, and they are scaled by a unit that is uniform in the scene, called the *scene unit*. These two parameters only affect the displayed size and the moving step of the avatar. That is, the larger the width is, the smaller the avatar is, and the larger the height is, the more steps the avatar takes to move from the front to the back.

A creator should also specify the four coordinate points of the trapezoid in the picture to indicate the rectangular floor of the real space. The origin of the coordinate system is at the top left corner of the picture. The horizontal direction is served as the X axis (increase rightwards), and the vertical direction is served as the Y axis (increase downwards). The unit is a pixel. This coordinate system is called the *picture coordinate system*. On the other hand, the avatar's location is based on the *floor coordinate system*, whose origin is the point of the rectangular floor which corresponds to the bottom left vertex of the trapezoid of the picture. The X axis is the front side of the trapezoid (increase rightwards), and the Y axis is the left side of the trapezoid (to increase upwards / backwards). Let the bottom left, bottom right, top left, and top right coordinates of the trapezoid in the picture coordinate system (x_{bl}, y_{bl}), (x_{br}, y_{br}), (x_{tl}, y_{tl}), and (x_{tr}, y_{tr}), respectively. Let the location of the avatar in the floor coordinate system (X_a, Y_a). We use the lower case for a variable name in the picture coordinate system or the pixel scale, and the upper case for a variable name in the floor coordinate system or the scene unit scale. Let W_a and H_a be the width and the height in the scene unit scale of the avatar, respectively. Let W_f and D_f be the width and the depth of the floor. Here, $y_{bl}=y_{br}$ and $y_{tl}=y_{tr}$ should be satisfied. Now, we assume that the camera orientation of the background picture is parallel to the floor.

Based on this configuration, we can calculate the coordinates and the displayed width and the height of the avatar image in the following manner. First, we can derive the Y coordinate of the vanishing point of the left and right sides of the trapezoid, y_q, in the picture coordinate system as follows:

$$y_q = y_{tl} - (x_{tr} - x_{tl})(y_{bl} - y_{tl})/((x_{br} - x_{bl})-(x_{tr} - x_{tl}))$$

By using this parameter, the Y coordinate of the avatar, y_a, is expressed as follows:

$$y_a = (y_{bl} - y_q)(y_{tl} - y_q)\, D_f /((y_{tl} - y_q)\, D_f + Y_a\, (y_{bl} - y_{tl})) + y_q$$

Then the X coordinate is as follows:

$$x_a = ((W_f - X_a)((y_a - y_{tl})\, x_{bl} + (y_{bl} - y_a)\, x_{tl}) + X_a\, ((y_a - y_{tl})\, x_{br} + (y_{bl} - y_a)\, x_{tr}))/(W_f (y_{bl} - y_{tl}))$$

The width w_a and the height h_a of the avatar are

$$w_a = ((y_a - y_{tl})(x_{br} - x_{bl}) + (y_{bl} - y_a)(x_{br} - x_{tl}))\; W_a\; / \; (W_f (y_{bl} - y_{tl})),$$
$$h_a = w_a\, H_a\, /\, W_a\, .$$

The last information that a creator should specify for the floor is the link information, which represents the linkage to other pages from the front, the back, the right, and the left sides of the floor. To each side, he/she should specify a linking URL and a segment of the corresponding side in the trapezoid. The segment can be described by its lower bound and upper bound coordinate values in the floor coordinate system. A user goes to the indicated WWW page if he/she goes out from the current scene by crossing a segment.

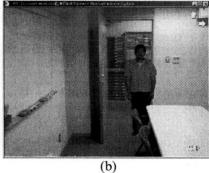

| (a) | (b) |

Fig. 9. Example scenes with objects.

3.4 Avatar

As for the avatar, a scene creator can specify the file header name. Consider the it is 'a0'. Eight files 'a01.gif', 'a02.gif', ..., and 'a08.gif' should be prepared in the same directory. Each picture includes a person's figure; as shown in Figure 2, 'a01.gif', 'a03.gif', 'a05.gif', and 'a07.gif' are respectively for the front, left, back, and right sides of the person, and the rest files are for their intermediates. The background of each picture should be transparent. The length of a step of the avatar should also be described in the scene unit scale. Furthermore, in the simple version, a creator should describe the initial direction of the avatar; front, back, right, left, or their intermediates, and the initial location of it.

3.5 Objects

An object is an optional scene component. A scene creator can specify the file name of a picture and the coordinate (x, y) in the picture coordinate system. The system pastes the picture in front of the scene and the avatar at the specified coordinate. Example uses of objects are Figure 9 (a) and (b), where a picture of shrubbery and a picture of a table are respectively pasted at the lower left and the lower right of the scene.

4. Implementation

We provide two versions for each scene; the JavaScript version for Microsoft Internet Explorer 4.0 or later, and the Java version for other browsers including Netscape Navigator. When a user visits a scene, the first visiting page is its entry page and the JavaScript program included in the page determines the browser type to switch to the appropriate version. An example of the Page description is shown in Figure 10.

```
<html><head><title></title><script language="JavaScript1.2">
<!--
var        Background="scene00/Dscf0039s.jpg", FloorWidth=240, FloorDepth=500,
           AvatarX=90, AvatarY=500, AvatarWidth=60, AvatarHeight=170;
var        BottomLeftX=-15, BottomLeftY=568, BottomRightX=533, BottomRightY=568,
           TopLeftX=348, TopLeftY=345,TopRightX=479,TopRightY=345, AvatarDirection=1;
var        LeftURL="busstop.html", FrontURL="d20b-m.html", RightURL="bulletin.html",
           BackURL="d23r-m.html";
var        LeftSegmentFrom=0, LeftSegmentTo=500, FrontSegmentFrom=0,FrontSegmentTo=240,
           RightSegmentFrom=0, RightSegmentTo=500, BackSegmentFrom=0,
           BackSegmentTo=240;
var        AvatarStep=30,        AvatarStepX=21, AvatarHeader="avatar/u";
var        SceneObject="", SceneObjectLocX=0, SceneObjectLocY=0;
//-->
</script><script language="JavaScript1.2" src="ibnr_simple.js"></script>
</head><body><script language="JavaScript">
<!--
showScene();
//-->
```

Fig.10. Scene source example

To reduce the creator's burden, we prepared a file generation tool written in Perl. In this tool, a user specifies the parameter values according to the system guidance. Then, the system generates three files; the entry page, the page of the JavaScript version, and the page of the Java version.

We have already constructed some contents of IBNR and the total number of the created scenes is more than 500. Some of them are accessible via the Internet [4]. Some pages use the cookie function to memorize the user's visit, and the information is used in other pages to change the scene. These contents are similar to adventure games, which we believe can fascinate the visitors in walking through the constructed space.

5. Discussions

5.1 Related Work

There are some technologies that represent 3D space in the WWW environment, such as Microsoft ChromeEffects [8], MetaStream [9], and Web3D Consortium VRML-streams [15]. They realize transmission of 3D information in the Internet. In representing 3D information, there are several languages including VRML, X3D [7] and OpenGL, and they are currently extended to include a lot of new features. These are typically the geometry-based approach and it has been pointed out that the modeling cost is very high and the resulting space is far from reality. Thus, the approach seems not suitable for the construction of cyber space based on the real space.

Recently, many IBR techniques are exhaustively developed, such as MPI-Video [5], QuickTimeVR [11], and 'Tour into the picture' [2], and there have been a lot of contents with high reality by using pictures taken in the real space. In these systems, a picture of a real scene is analyzed and distorted to invent an imaginary scene from an arbitrary viewpoint. They have been successful in constructing virtual space with reality, but it is also costly to analyze pictures, to transmit 3D data through the Internet, and to construct virtual space. Moreover, special hardware or plug-ins is usually required to display the space. Further, the reality is sometimes lost because of too heavy distortion of pictures. On the other hand, IBNR resolves these problems by fixing the viewpoint and using an avatar. The compensations are mainly caused by the lack of a 3D model. A user cannot touch, move, and destroy any object taken in the background picture without using an ad-hoc contrivance. With the same reason, the user cannot change the viewpoint. It should also be noted that the avatar behavior is strongly restricted by the prepared pictures. That is, if a creator wants to add several actions to the avatar, a lot of files should be prepared for all possible combinations of each action.

There are several approaches that simplify the rendering process in IBR such as LDI [10] and MLI [14]. 3DML[16] is also an IBR approach based on a simplified geometry model. The important points of IBNR are the simplicity brought by the fixed viewpoint and the use of avatar, the use of multiple scenes to build up a large scaled content, and the WWW-based design to achieve scene independency and platform independency.

Here, note that, in IBNR, an avatar plays an important role to represent the 3D topology of each scene. If a user successively visits multiple scenes, he/she can know the topological connection by the avatar's direction on scene change, and the scale of the scene by the avatar's size shown in the scene.

The space representation method used in IBNR has already been used in some games such as Capcon Biohazard (or Residential Evil) [1] and Square Parasite Eve [12]. However, IBNR is different in the following two points; 1) The contents can be shown on WWW via the Internet, and 2) several kinds of multimedia contents such as camera pictures and videos can be used to construct the space.

The relationship to MPEG-4 [6] and SMIL[3] is also important. We can integrate these technologies as a resource format of IBNR to allow a creator to use more flexible multimedia contents in scene description.

5.2 Usage

Main advantages of IBNR are 1) easy construction of cyber space based on the real space, and 2) easy access to the constructed space using WWW, while disadvantages are mainly related to 3D operations. Therefore, it is difficult to use IBNR in the applications which require complex actions, view point change, and 3D object handling. Based on this observation, we can find several applications where IBNR is useful. A user can virtually experience the real space by IBNR, and it can be applied to trip simulation, construction simulation, building guidance, and geographic guidance. The conventional applications of cyber space, such as cyber-mall, museum, and gallery, can also be applied to IBNR. We can consider personal use of such space. The pictures taken in a trip can be use to compose an IBNR content, which are sometimes better for recollection than an album and video because it is interactive. Considering the 'easy access' property of IBNR, it can be applied to education, amusement, and advertisement on WWW.

Here, we mention our related project to show our original motivation in developing IBNR. IBNR was originally developed as a browser of the 'invisible person' system [13]. The 'invisible person' system is aimed at the integration of virtual space and real space for constructing a communication environment for users in real space and users in remote place, i.e., virtual space. In this system, the real space is completely modeled as virtual space and the events occurred in the real space is immediately reflected to the virtual space and vice versa. A remote user visits such virtual space via the Internet to become an invisible person. People in real space can communicate with invisible persons around them by using their handy computers. In our previous system, we employ a normal VRML browser for remote people, and IBNR can replace this browser. It provides an easy way for constructing virtual space based on real space that can be accessible via the Internet. In this way, IBNR is useful in such mixed reality systems.

6. Conclusion

In this paper, we have proposed a method to construct pseudo-3D space easily on WWW. In our design of IBNR, we have emphasized on two kinds of independency, i.e., the scene independency and the platform independency. It is better than the other GBR and IBR approaches in the viewpoint of 'easy to construct' and 'easy to access', and therefore suitable to large-scaled heterogeneous space, such as digital cities.

There are several possible extensions of IBNR some of which we are currently implementing. The scene editor is used to set IBNR information including the floor information. By using this editor, a creator can specify the floor through GUI and more promptly create a piece of content. In order to represent legacy contents written in VRML, X, OpenGL, and so on in IBNR, we need converters to generate IBNR scenes from the VRML and X files. In this case, the problems are how many scenes are suitable for a given piece of content and how to select a viewpoint for each scene. The multi-user version of IBNR will be useful communication space for those who want to use the context in the real space in their communication. We are currently developing this version.

Acknowledgement

The author wishes to thank Prof. S. Nishio, Prof. F. Kishino, Prof. K. Tanaka, Prof. Y. Kitamura, and Prof. M. Arikawa for their valuable comments on IBNR. He is also grateful to Mr. T. Ogawa, Mr. Y. Sakane, and other members of Nishio Laboratory for their helpful comments and suggestions on this research. This work is supported by Research for the Future Program of Japan Society for the Promotion of Science under the Project "Researches on Advanced Multimedia Contents Processing"(JSPS-RFTF97P00501).

Bibliography

[1] Capcon: Biohazard,http://www.capcom.co.jp/gallery/consumer/1996/bio.html (1999).

[2] Horry, Y., Anjyo, K., and Arai, K.: Tour Into the Picture: Using a Spidery Mesh Interface to Make Animation from a Single Image, Computer Graphics Proceedings, Annual Conference Series 1997, Proc. ACM SIGGRAPH, pp.225-232 (1997).

[3] Hoschka, P.(Ed.): Synchronized Multimedia Integration Language (SMIL) 1.0 Specification, http://www.w3.org/TR/1998/REC-smil-19980615 (1998).

[4] IBNR Project, Nishio Laboratory, Osaka University, http://www-nishio.ise.eng. osaka-u.ac.jp/IBNR/ (1999).

[5] Katkere, A., Moezzi, S., Kuramura, D.Y., Kelly, P., and Jain, R.: Towards Video-Based Immersive Environments, ACM Press, Vol.5, No.2, pp.69-85 (1997).

[6] Koenen, R. Ed.: Overview of the MPEG-4 Standard, ISO/IEC JTC1/SC29/WG11 N2725, http://drogo.cselt.stet.it/mpeg/standards/mpeg-4/mpeg-4.htm (1999).

[7] Lee, R.(Ed): X3D Phase 1 Requirements: XML Tagset, http://www.web3d.org/ news/x3d/x3d-reqs.h3h.html (1999).

[8] Microsoft Corp.: Chromeeffects, http://www.microsoft.com/HWDEV/presents/2melt98/melt982n.htm (1999).

[9] Microsoft Corp.: MetaStream Transform, http://www.microsoft.com/DirectX/dxm/help/dxt/reference/effects/metaspec.htm (1999).

[10] Shade, J., Gortler, S.J., He, L., and Szeliski, R.: Layered Depth Images, in Computer Graphics, Proc. ACM SIGGRAPH 98, pp. 231 (1998).

[11] Shencahng, E.C.: QuickTimeVR – An Image-Based Approach to Virtual Environment Navigation, Computer Graphic Proceedings, Annual Conference Series 1995, Proc. ACM SIGGRAPH 97, pp.29-38 (1997).

[12] Square: ParasiteEve, http://www.square.co.jp/pnewfr.html (1999).

[13] Tsukamoto, M.: Integrating Real Space and Virtual Space in the 'Invisible Person' Communication Support System, Nishio, S., and Kishino, F. (Eds.): Advanced Multimedia Content Processing, Lecture Notes in Computer Science 1554, Springer, pp.59-74, Osaka (1998).

[14] Umans, C., Halle, M., and Kikinis, R.: Multilayer Images for Interactive 3D Visualization on the World Wide Web, SPL Technical Report #51, http://splweb.bwh. harvard.edu:8000/pages/papers/mli/paper.html (1997).

[15] Web3D Consortium: VRML Streams, VRML Streaming Working Group, http://www.web3d.org/WorkingGroups/vrml-streams/ (1998).

[16] 3DML Tutorial, http://www.flatland.com/build/tutorial/ (1999).

Dynamic Zone Retrieval and Landmark Computation for Spatial Data

Hiroaki Kawagishi, Kengo Koiso, and Katsumi Tanaka

Graduate School of Science and Technology, Kobe University.
Rokkodai, Nada, Kobe 657-8501 JAPAN,
TEL & FAX: +81-78-845-7643
{kawagisi,koiso,tanaka}@db.cs.kobe-u.ac.jp

Abstract. In this paper, we will introduce a method of dynamically retrieving zones containing clustered objects satisfying the conditions given by the user and computing objects with the most distinct characteristics which we call landmarks. These operations would help the user retrieve and browse the spatial data dynamically in the following ways. Determining the zones would provide one with a general information of the spatial distribution of the objects one wishes to see, thus freeing one from unnecessary browsing. Computing the landmarks would provide one with descriptive information on the zones which were dynamically retrieved. We will discuss algebraic operations for zone retrieval and computational expressions for describing landmarks.

1 Introduction

Digital cities of different nature are emerging on the World Wide Web. AOL's Digital Cities[1] functions as the portal site for the major U.S. cities. De Digitale Stad[2] of Amsterdam is designed to form a virtual community for its citizens and visitors from outside. Virtual Helsinki[3] and Digital City Kyoto[4] have three-dimensional physical model of the cities which serve as media for integrating urban information.

We are interested in the creation of the three-dimensional physical model of the city as media for managing information. The three-dimensional models provide intuitive presentations which are easy to understand even for strangers. In Digital City Kyoto and Virtual Helsinki, they have linked the three-dimnensional model to various information such as homepages available on the World Wide Web.

In the field of GIS, there are research projects for integrating video data, GPS information, and attribute information. Tokyo University has developed the GIS interface for making links between the attribute information of spatial objects to the live video data[5]. "Name-At"[6] is an augmented reality hypermedia system which provides overlaid visualizaiton of attribute data on top of the live video data.

If we are to construct a three-dimensional model of the physical city, we have to construct a continuous three-dimensional space from which we can specify zones where we want to browse in detail.

T. Ishida, K. Isbister (Eds.): Digital Cities, LNCS 1765, pp. 303–313, 2000.
© Springer-Verlag Berlin Heidelberg 2000

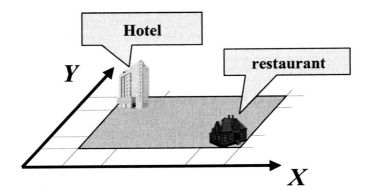

Fig. 1. Zone Retrieval

of all sizes and combinations. Algebraically, a spatial glue may be expressed as below. This is also a two-dimensional extension of the interval glue operation [11] proposed for video data retrieval.

$$\alpha \oplus \beta = r[c_s^{\alpha \oplus \beta}, c_e^{\alpha \oplus \beta}]$$

α and β are objects such as a hotel and a restaurant, and r is the region or the minimum bounding rectangle obtained from the spatial glue operation denoted by $\alpha \oplus \beta$. The values $c_s^{\alpha \oplus \beta}$ and $c_e^{\alpha \oplus \beta}$ are the coordinates which determines the location of the minimum bounding rectangle. In actual computations, there may be more than one hotel or restaurant so we will be dealing with sets of objects $A = \{\alpha_1, \alpha_2, \ldots, \alpha_n\}$ and $B = \{\beta_1, \beta_2, \ldots, \beta_n\}$.

In order to find all possible regions which can be obtained from the objects, we compute two kinds of spatial glue operations. The first one is the pairwise glue in which you select one object from each set.

Pairwise Glue

$$A \bigoplus B = \{a \mid \alpha \in A, \beta \in B, a = \alpha \oplus \beta\}$$

The second one is the powerset glue in which you select at least one object from each set.

Powerset Glue

$$A \bigotimes B = \{a \mid A' \subseteq A, B' \subseteq B, A' \neq \o.B' \neq \o. \ a = \bigoplus(A' \cup B')\}$$
$$where \bigoplus(\{a_1, \ldots, a_n\}) = a_1 \oplus \ldots \oplus a_n$$

In order to retrieve all possible zones, we can compute the powerset glue. The calculation cost of the powerset operation, however, is large but it has been proven that the powerset operation can be transformed into pairwise glue operations. For proofs, please refer to our paper titled "InfoLOD and LandMark: Browsing and Retrieving Spatial Data" [12].

$$A \otimes B = (A \oplus A \oplus A \oplus A) \oplus (B \oplus B \oplus B \oplus B) \tag{1}$$

3.2   Filtering Operation

We explained that we define a zone by specifying a minimum bounding rectangle containing the spatial objects with attribute data satisfying the conditions specified by the user. Within the zones, however, there may be other objects which may not satisfy the conditions you specified. We allow such exceptions because the landuse of a city, especially a large one, is complex and heterogeneous.

As explained in the previous section, there may be a large number of zones of all sizes. Some zones may contain only one object whereas some may contain hundreds of them. Here, we want to discover zones where the objects we want are clustered together in great numbers. In order to extract such zones, we need to filter the answers we get by the spatial glue operation.

We define the spatial noise as the space which are not occupied by objects with the attribute data satisfying the conditions specified by the user. Figure 2 shows the objects which satisfy the criteria specified by the user and the noise contained within the zone retrieved by the spatial glue operation. We define a threshold value for the maximum spatial noise ratio and remove zones with the spatial noise ratios exceeding the value. This can be done by applying the spatial noise filter to the formula 1 as below.

$$F_N (A \otimes B) = F_N ((A \oplus A \oplus A \oplus A) \oplus (B \oplus B \oplus B \oplus B)) \tag{2}$$

For more detailed explanation of the algorithm and proofs, please refer to our paper titled "InfoLOD and LandMark: Browsing and Retrieving Spatial Data" [12].

4   Landmark Algorithm

4.1   Landmark

In visualizing a large number of spatial objects, it is often useful to control the visualization instead of rendering every single object in full detail. We have been engaged in the research in controlling the visualization of attribute data based on the notion of level of detail, namely InfoLOD[7],[8],[9] algorithm which stands for level of detail for information. In this paper, we propose LandMark algorithm to select the object with the most distinct characteristics to represent each region retrieved by the spatial glue operation described in the previous

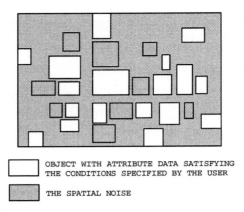

OBJECT WITH ATTRIBUTE DATA SATISFYING
THE CONDITIONS SPECIFIED BY THE USER

THE SPATIAL NOISE

Fig. 2. Spatial Noise in Retrieved Zone

section. By using LandMark algorithm, the user can watch the representative landmark objects before browsing the spatial data of the zones retrieved.

Kevin Lynch stated in his idea of cognitive mapping[10] that one of the elements which constitutes the image of a city was a landmark. It is usually a tower-like structure which serves to be a symbol of a city or a district. The notion of landmark is usually static, but we discuss here the dynamic extraction of a landmark object from a region discovered by the spatial glue operation. We defined the landmark object as the object with the most distinct characteristics and the highest spatial occupancy in a given zone.

4.2   Computing Landmark Factor

For a given region r, and let $O(r)$ denote a set of the object contained in the region r is expressed as follows.

$$O(r) = \{o_1, o_2, \ldots, o_n\} \ , (n \geq 0)$$

We define the landmark object as the object with the most distinct characteristics in a given region. For a given region r, the landmark object o_{LM} is an object such that $o_{LM} \in O(r)$, and $LM(o_{LM}) = max(LM(o_1, \ldots, o_n))$, $((o_1, \ldots, o_n) \in O(r))$.

$LM(o_i)$ is the landmark factor of the object o_i which can be calculated in the equation.3 below.

$$LM(o_i) = \frac{|o_i|}{|r|} * \frac{1}{\sum_{o_j \in same(o_i, r)} \frac{|o_j|}{|r|}}$$

where $o_i (o_i \neq \phi)$ is a object in r, $|o_i|$ the area of the base of o_i itself, $|r|$ the area of given region, $|o_j|$ the area of the objects having the same keyword or feature vector as $|o_i|$. The function $same(o_i, r)$ signifies the object having the same value for attribute A.

$$same(o_i, r) = \{o \mid o \in O(r), and\ o_i.A = o.A\}$$

where $o.A$ denotes the attribute A of o. The first part the equation.3 signifies the "dominance" or the areal occupancy ratio of the object o_i, and the second part signifies the "uniqueness" or the inverse of the areal occupancy ratio of a set of objects o_j having the same characteristics as o_i. Thus, if the areal occupancy ratio of the object o_i is high (then o_i is large-scale structure comparatively), and if the areal occupancy ratio of objects having the same characteristics as o_i is low (then o_i is distinctive structure), the value for the landmark factor $LM(o_i)$ becomes high.

By using spatial glue operation together with filtering operation, one is able to retrieve regions where objects one wishes to search are found in clusters. One is left with a number regions to choose from, but rendering and browsing all the objects contained in the regions might cause excessive task. Landmark algorithm selects a landmark object for each region so one can get a clue about the region before browsing everything inside indetail.

5   Implementation

5.1   System Description

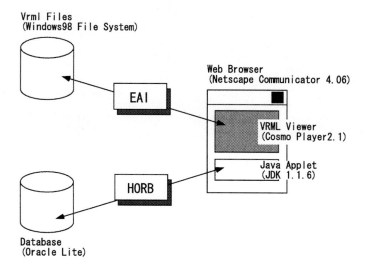

Fig. 3. System Description

Under the assumption that the system would be viewed on the world wide web, we used Netscape Communicator 4.06 as the browser. In order to view the spatial objects stored as VRML[13] files, CosmoPlayer2.1 plug-in was required. And we used Oracle Lite as relational database management system to store georeferenced data.

In order to allow the Java applets to manipulate the VRML data in the browser, the EAI(External Authoring Interface)[14] was used to access the VRML nodes and fields which include the information about the shapes, locations, etc. of the spatial objects viewed in the browser. In addition we use JDBC and HORB[15] needed for Java applets to access the database. The figure 3 shows the configuration of our prototype system.

5.2   Zone Retrieval and Extraction of Landmark Object

We implemented a prototype system based on our concept of dynamic zone retrieval and landmark computation. When the user specifies the conditions for the attribute data of objects, the system computes the zones by accessing the attribute data stored in the databases. After computing the zones, the system filters the answers by removing the zones having excess noise. The system then extracts a landmark object from each zone by computing the landmark factors for all of the objects contained in each zone.

Figure 4 shows a result of zone retrieval. And in figure 5 the same zone is shown.

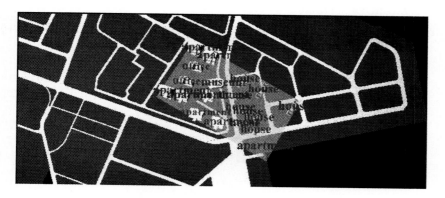

Fig. 4. Presentaion of all objects

In figure 4, all of the objects contained in the zone are visualized with their attribute information. In figure 5, the landmark object and its attribute information is visualized.

You can see that instead of showing every single object, it is effective to limit the number of objects and show the representative object only.

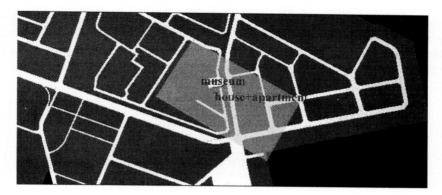

Fig. 5. Selection of a Landmark

6   Discussions

6.1   Possible Application and Extensions of Our Algorithm

Here are some possible applications of our spatial glue operation when considering the actual spatial data.

- continuous spatial data
  Besides the attribute information for architectural objects such as those used in electronic maps, we can also consider continuous spatial data such as environmental data. The temperature, the amount of rainfall, etc., are some of the examples.
- defining a virtual object
  The use of our spatial glue operation is not restricted to the real spatial objects such as buildings. We can also specify a virtual object such as blocks or zones covering a certain area with some common characteristics.
- layered spatial glue
  The spatial data such as those administered by cities are often classified into many different themes and stored in different databases. By specifying different attributes belonging to different themes and executing the spatial glue operation, we can produce various thematic maps. Thus, we will be able to visualize the spatial distribution of various data belonging to different themes and understand their spatial relationships.

6.2   Issues on Coordinate System

One problem regarding the specification of minimum bounding rectangles in order to make approximations for both objects and regions is that the area are subject to change depending on the specification of the coordinate system. For example, by changing the angle of the coordinate system as shown in Figure 6, it is possible to reduce the area of the minimum bounding rectangle the same set of objects. The change in the area would affect the spatial occupancy of the objects within the region, and it would eventually affect the result of the filtering operation. Some principle for determining the coordinate system has to be stated depending on the goal of the operation.

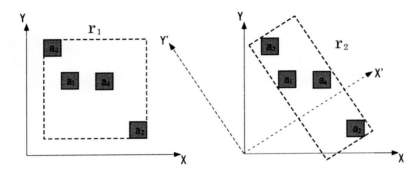

Fig. 6. Noise Reduction by conversion of Coordinate System

7   Conclusions

In this paper, we introduced the dynamic zone retrieval based on user-specified criteria for browsing spatial data, and it is composed of the following two algebraic operations.

- Spatial Glue Operation
  This operation retrieves zones by finding minimum bounding rectangles containing the objects with attribute data satisfying the conditions specified by the user.
- Filtering Operation
  This operation filters the the retrieved zones based on how much space is occupied by the objects with attribute data satisfying the conditions specified by the user.

We also introduced LandMark algorithm for computing the representative object in a given zone based on the uniqueness of the attribute information and its spatial occupancy.

Using our algorithms for dynamic zone retrieval and landmark computation, users can specify the conditions for zone retrieval based on the attribute data of spatial objects and browse the representative objects of the retrieved zones. Users may examine the representative objects in order to decide which zone to browse in detail.

Acknowledgements

This research is partly supported by the Japanese Ministry of Education Grant-in-Aid for Scientific Research on Priority Area (A): "Advanced databases," area no. 275 (08244103). This research is also supported in part by "Research for the Future" Program of Japan Society for the Promotion of Science under the Project "Advanced Multimedia Contents Processing" (Project No. JSPS-RFTF97P00501).

References

1. http://home.digitalcity.com/
2. http://www.dds.nl/dds/info/english/
3. R.Linturi, M.Koivunen,J.Sulkanen ,"Helsinki Arena 2000: Augmenting a Real City to a Virtual One," Lecture Notes in Computer Science (in this volume), Springer-Verlag, 2000.
4. T. Ishida, J. Akahani, K. Hiramatsu, K. Isbister, S. Lisowski, H. Nakanishi, M. Okamoto, Y. Miyazaki, K. Tsutsuguchi, "Digital City Kyoto: Towards A Social Information Infrastructure," M. Klusch, O. Shehory, G. Weiss (Eds.), Cooperative Information Agents III, Lecture Notes in Artificial Intelligence, Vol. 1652, pp. 23-35, Springer-Verlag, 1999.
5. http://shiba.iis.u-tokyo.ac.jp/inte.htm
6. http://www.csis.u-tokyo.ac.jp/ arikawa/Name-at/Name-at.ex1.e.html
7. K.Koiso, T.Matsumoto, K.Tanaka, Spatial Authoring and Orientation-Based Aggregation of Annotated Information, Proceedings of the International Workshop on Urban Multi-Media/3D Mapping, Tokyo, pp.31-38,(1998)
8. K.Koiso, T.Matsumoto, K.Tanaka, Spatial Presentation and Aggregation of Geo-referenced Data, Proceedings of the 6th International Conference of Database Systems for Advanced Application (DASFAA'99). April 1999.
9. Takehisa Mori, Kengo Koiso, Katsumi Tanaka "Spatial Data Presentation by LOD Control Based on Distance, Orientation, and Differentiation" Proceedings of International Workshop on Urban Multi-Media/3D Mapping(UM3'99), September 1999, Tokyo.
10. K.Lynch: The Image of the City, MIT Press, Cambrige, Mssachusetts(1960).
11. S.Pradhan, K.Tajima, K.Tanaka, A Query Model for Retrieving Relevant Intervals within a Video Stream, Proceedings of IEEE ICMCS, Vol.2, pp.788-792, June 1999.
12. K.Koiso, T.Matsumoto, H.Kawagishi, K.Tanaka "InfoLOD and LandMark: Browsing and Retrieving Spatial Data" Proceedings of the 2nd International Symposium on Cooperative Database Systems for Advanced Applications(CODAS'99), pp.39-50, Wollongong, March 1999.
13. J.Hartman, J.Wernecke, Silicon Graphics, Inc. The VRML 2.0 Handbook(Building Moving Worlds on the Web), Addison Wesley Developers Press
14. http://www.cosmosoftware.com/products/ player/developer/eai/eai.html
15. http://ring.etl.go.jp/openlab/horb/

Environment for Spatial Information Sharing

Hiroshi Tsuji[1], Takaaki Yamada[1], Maki Tamano[1],
Tsuneo Sobue[1], and Shuji Kitazawa[2]

[1] Systems Development Laboratory, Hitachi, Ltd.
1099 Ohzenji, Asao, Kawasaki, Japan, 215-0013
{tsuji, t-yamada, tamano, sobue}@sdl.hitachi.co.jp
[2] Systems Engineering Division, Hitachi, Ltd.,
4-6 Kanda Surugadai, Chiyoda, Tokyo
kitaza27@cm.head.sdl.hitachi.co.jp

Abstract. This paper concerns Web-based spatial and local information sharing for digital cities. There are various kinds of spatial information such as geographical maps, illustrated maps, railroad maps and so on around us. Our system provides an environment in which the general users can submit such contents on their favorite map and in which they can view contents submitted from more than two providers on their favorite map. In our system, all spatial information submitted by citizens is linked in special index tables. This paper also shows digital city applications of the presented environments.

1 Introduction

Maps have recently been required to play an important role in the user interfaces providing access to information available from the World Wide Web. We find various kinds of contents and services related to specific areas, and they are apt to be scattered on the Web and inconvenient for viewing at a glance. Spatial information sharing is, therefore, expected to facilitate user access to these contents and services. Integration of such information services based on maps is called map-based information mediation service.

This paper describes the concept, and configuration of our Marche World (MW), which supports map-based information mediation service, and also describes a couple of MW applications. There are three kinds of participants in MW activities for information sharing and exchange:

(1)   spatial information providers,
(2)   spatial information requesters,
(3)   a spatial information mediator.

MW is designed so that general users as well as specific experts can be spatial information providers. One of our target is that everyone join information sharing on digital map.

Marche World has the following function:

(a) it gathers from the providers, a variety of types of contents with spatial keys (electronic maps, illustrated maps, Web pages, etc.)

T. Ishida, K. Isbister (Eds.): Digital Cities, LNCS 1765, pp. 314–325, 2000.

(b) at the mediator, it generates new value-added contents from the original contents,

(c) it delivers these new contents to the requesters.

The basic premise of our MW is that each spatial information provider has a variety of contents - such as geographical maps (including raster data structures and vector data structures), deformed maps, railroad maps and so on - while each spatial information requester would like to browse mixed contents on their favorite map. We should, therefore, focus on the data structure and data flow in the mediator component.

For the mediator component, we present two basic key concepts:

the spatial information header,
the spatial thesaurus.

The spatial information header includes not only index information such as the author and creation date for each spatial information item but also information about the relationship between different spatial information items. The spatial thesaurus is a dictionary that describes the relationships between locations and is used for reference by location name.

It is reported that more than seventy percent of documents includes spatial information. Some documents do not include maps explicitly but instead location addresses, which are a kind of spatial information. Note that a ZIP code is also spatial information because it implies the location. We can regard a specific organization as a kind of spatial information because its buildings are related to its location. In the context of this paper, SDL (Systems Development Laboratory) of Hitachi is located in Kawasaki city, Japan. We present this paper in Kyoto. These facts imply that this paper is also related to spatial information. Our Marche World focus not only precise geographic information but also on this robust and implicit spatial information.

MW is developed for Web-based applications. The systems for the police headquarters and the local government office are used under the Intranet environment. In the police headquarters, the command department for emergencies, the traffic security department for accident management, and other departments share documents including spatial information. Governmental staff shares the information about land, buildings, public life lines, and so on. On the other hand, a restaurant map service system and a medical center search service system are examples of Internet applications.

2   Why Spatial Information Sharing?

First, we would like to review our standpoint for developing Marche World. We have three viewpoints for the system design. These points are also user merits.

1) Legacy geographical information systems [8] and Internet technology.

Traditionally, the geographic information systems (GIS) have been very expensive. Only specific organizations such as police headquarters, gas and electrical energy providers, and telephone companies have used GIS and only for limited purposes. They use GIS every day in order to make their work cost effective. There are no users who use GIS only once a week or once a month for their convenience. Furthermore, only a limited number of persons update the spatial information. They are system maintenance specialists and their own systems require precise maps. They can use neither a deformed map nor an illustrated map. The traditional GIS users cannot tolerate errors nor spatial gaps. The spatial information stored in such systems cannot and need not be shared by the other applications.

Now we have Internet technology, which allows us to share a variety kinds of information including spatial information. So we think there will be some users who use GIS once a week or once a month. Most of them will sometimes accept information less precise than that needed by the traditional users for fun or for just convenience. We have designed MW to make it possible for these new users to share spatial information. The Internet technology will allow a large volume of users to share expensive information.

2) Push and pull technology [7]

Web technology introduces us to push services (delivery) as well as pull service (retrieval). A push service provides new information step by step if requesters specify their interests. Let us consider what a push service for the spatial information is. We would like to propose a new service called a cyber work[10]. In real world, we often select routes according to our interests.

In our cyber work service, an avatar appears in a digital city and takes a walk through a virtual town. The avatar changes his route automatically if he finds his favorite town news: news based on the interests a requester has registered his interest in advance.

The idea can be easily modified. If a requester specifies his current position and destination, the system finds a route for him and presents spot information place by place. To implement such a push service, we designed MW APIs for push service applications.

3) Community computing [1][5][6] and discussion database [4]

Persons often make up communities. Communities facilitates not only information sharing but also discussion. Discussion makes an important role for collaboration. Then, there are systems which support discussion. Discussion databases and net news services are examples. They allow a community to make questions and answers.

We suppose that discussion is similarly useful in the sharing of spatial information. Using digital map, for example, someone might ask "Does anyone knows the fine French restaurant in this area?" or "what is this building?" This is the kind of questions a user does not ask a computer database but instead ask a human database using a computer system. We designed MW as an environment for community computing.

3   System Model for Spatial Information Sharing

We designed Marche World for satisfying the requirements implicit in our three viewpoints. And as mentioned earlier, there are three kinds of participants: Information Providers, A mediator, and Information Requesters. Let us consider the basic MW model as shown in Fig. 1.

To submit spatial information for use by MW, a provider selects an undersheet map and specifies an area or picks a landmark point on the digital map. This is an anchor of the link. Then a variety of different kinds of spatial information such as web pages, and illustration maps are linked. Linkage information is stored as a spatial information header in MW. Then linked information can be the new undersheet for the next linkage. In short, any spatial information can be connected to any another spatial information as undersheet (Fig. 2a). We call this float coordinates management and discuss in detail elsewhere [11].

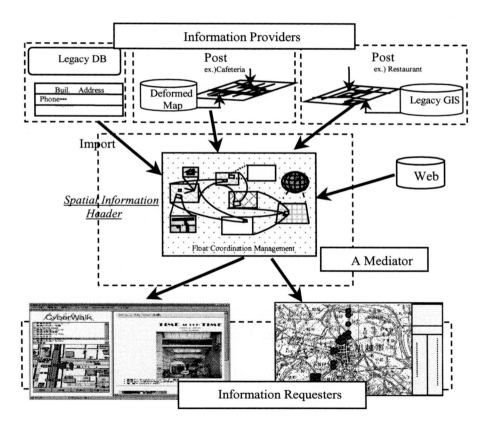

Fig. 1. Basic Model of Marche World

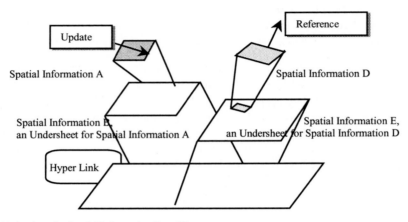

Update

Spatial Information A

Spatial Information B,
an Undersheet for Spatial Information A

Reference

Spatial Information D

Spatial Information E,
an Undersheet for Spatial Information D

Hyper Link

Undersheet for Spatial Information B and E

(a) Float Coordinates Management in Marche World

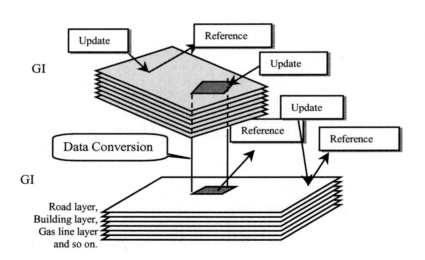

GI

Update   Reference

Update

Data Conversion

Reference

Update

Reference

GI

Road layer,
Building layer,
Gas line layer
and so on.

(b) Traditional Layered Management

Fig. 2. Coordinates Management

Let us compare to the layered method for traditional geographic information management as shown in Fig. 2b. In general there are more than one hundred layers, for example, the road layer, building layer, gas-line layer, and so on. Such management is possible under the premise that the spatial coordinates is severely managed. Then a requester can select any layers from database for their own purpose.

In the case of the strict data conversion for traditional management, however, we had to adjust delicate lags in each area after the coordinate translation. These lags are generated in the accuracy of measurement, input error, projection and so on. Maps inherently contain such errors in themselves. Occasionally, such errors add up to several meters or more. Landmarks located on the map also inherit the errors.

That is, a landmark located at a specific latitude and longitude on GIS-A might be shown incorrectly overlapped on another GIS-B even though at the same latitude and longitude. Especially in Japan, detail maps such as 1/500 scale are often used, therefore, the error adjustment should not be negligible in the distributing and the sharing landmarks on maps.

On the other hand, MW does not use absolute and severe coordinates management; it instead uses a robust and relative coordinates management. Our float coordinates management tolerates errors and spatial gaps. This flexibility allows many new users to participate in the sharing of spatial information.

Consider the simple example shown in Fig. 2. Map-C is used as an undersheet of Map-B and Map-E, and Map-B is also used as an undersheet of Map-A. Hyper structured relationship can be allowed in the relative location definition and can be directly defined in the relationship between two maps if needed. For example, coordinate (20,30)-(40-60) on Map B corresponds to coordinate (30, 40) - (60, 110) on Undersheet and coordinate (5, 10) - (20, 40) on map A corresponds to coordinate (10,15)-(30, 35) on Map B. By following the hyper-linked relationship, MW recognizes a map in the specific location with its base-undersheet coordinates system.

When a requester submits a command for retrieval of spatial information header stored in MW, results are shown on his favorite/ selected undersheet. There are anchors in the output which link to other spatial information. For push services, the application system of MW selects and displays information step by step (in occasion, along the street). Route search algorithms are independent of MW but are easily integrated with MW because MW provides APIs.

The spatial information header includes the category of information, and includes the author's information (copyrights, update date, expiration date, and so on). There is also a flag designating whether or not the information is a question. When a requester finds a question on the undersheet map, the requester becomes a provider and makes a linkage for the question by adding an answer. Note that here is discussion for local communication.

The update and expiration dates play important roles in applications such as advertisement. In general, a bargain sales period lasts only for a specific amount of time, and at the expiration date the bargain information should disappear automatically. Requesters seeing advertisement are interested only in new and valid information. Thus, MW handles live and active information. Fig. 3 shows application of our concept.

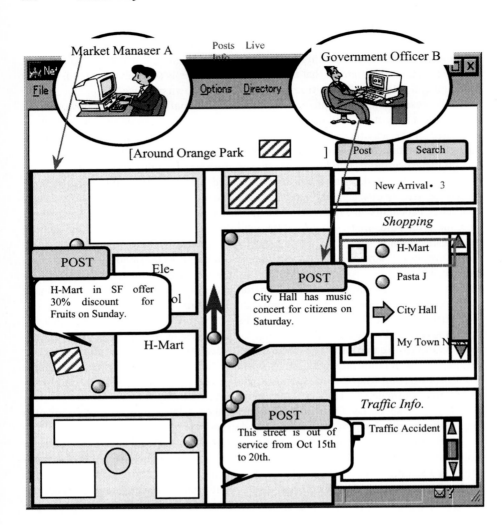

Fig. 3. Live and Active Information in MW

4 Information Flow in Marche World

Let us clarify the information flow from providers to requesters via mediator. As presented before and shown in Fig. 2, all spatial information is linked with undersheet maps. At the first stage, MW provides a basic undersheet map. For user interface matter of information provision, undersheet map may be selected by a human provider or an application software of MW.

For simple case, a provider make a linkage to the point in the undersheet map. For another case, he make it to the rectangle area in the undersheet map. If the spatial information includes an address or a postal code, the provider need not select an undersheet map. MW identifies the location for them by referring to the spatial thesaurus.

A conventional thesaurus includes information about the relationships between words as a dictionary [1]. Typical examples are the relationships between broader (general) terms and narrower (specific) terms. On the other hand, the spatial thesaurus includes the hierarchy of address information. For example,

Kawasaki is a city of Kanagawa prefecture,

Asao is a part of Kawasaki city.

Storing the relationship between the location and coordinates, the spatial thesaurus tells how to transform a location name into coordinates in a digital map.

To prepare enough contents for MW, importing the contents already existing in legacy systems (See Figure 1) is an important task as well as creating new contents. We know many legacy databases include the address fields and/or telephone number fields. By using the spatial thesaurus, these field values can be translated into coordinates. We have experience to extract coordinates immediately from medical center address, where these addresses are stored as values of a large database. Thus the spatial thesaurus allows us to connect MW and legacy databases.

The spatial thesaurus can also be used for automatic spatial Web page collection. Automatic Web page collection technology is described in [3]. An agent, that collects contents and is described in detail elsewhere [11], has the following functions:

(1) find the WWW pages which include the spatial information such as city name and town name by using the spatial thesaurus.

(2) add the extra information to each of the extracted pages to enable its distribution on the MW spatial information header.

Although we know WWW pages include various spatial properties (text, graphics, image, etc.), we implemented an agent that deals with spatial information represented in Japanese text.

To verify the usefulness of the proposed agent, we carried out an experiment with the prototype. Eleven thousand WWW pages are used in the experiment, were collected randomly from WWW sites. The prototype used a Japanese spatial thesaurus, represented as hierarchical structure, so that the target to be extracted was address spatial information.

The agent extracted 23% of the eleven thousand pages as contents including text address information. We verified the correctness of the result manually, and found no noise in this case.

Next, let us use an example in Fig. 4 for considering information flow from the mediator to the requesters. First a user asks system to get shortest path from Namba to Kobe, and the system shows the answer. This output shows a route map. It is a kind of deformed map. Again, MW handles such kinds of illustrated map. The requester asks the system to retrieve restaurants and banks that are located in the area specified on the map. The retrieval condition is transformed into the normal SQL for the spatial information header. It is just an example application.

Note that our spatial thesaurus also stores typical geographic vocabulary used to determine the areas and directions: near, on foot, north, and so on. This allows a requester to specify a retrieval condition such as "a restaurant located within five minutes on foot from Osaka station". MW knows from the spatial thesaurus the coordinates of Osaka station and knows that "five minutes on foot" means 500 meters, and then it can thus find appropriate restaurants by evaluating the data in the spatial information header.

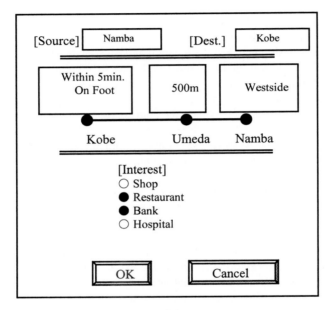

Fig. 4. User Interface Example

5 Applications of Marche World

1) Browsing Local Community "What's New" in Spatial Context [10]

An avatar appears on a displayed map at the left side of the window and then takes a walk in the digital city as shown in Fig. 5. The related information about where the avatar is walking are shown in the right-side frame step by step. The town news consists of basic landmarks, gathered web pages, and posted articles.

A requester expresses his interests to control the avatar's behavior so that he changes his route automatically if his favorite kind of town news is found. Then the user can browse town news in a one-to-one customized spatial context, which involves the user's favorites, popular data and the mediator's suggestion in the specific area. The browsing facility can give a sense of "being there", and requesters can feel a sense similar to that of being in the real city.

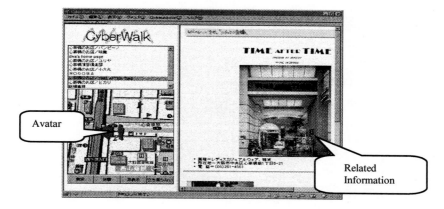

Fig. 5. Cyber Walk for Browsing Local Community

2) Traffic Accident Report Management

Traffic accidents are serious problems in a real city and police therefore try many ways to reduce their frequency. One of these ways is to find out how often they occurred, where they occurred, and why they occurred. Traditionally, police have written volumes of reports day by day, reports including illustrated intersection diagram, pictures, and so on. These reports thus contain a great deal of spatial information.

One MW application was developed to support accident report management. The provider who has a collection of accident reports can, for example, display the related area map and pick out the intersection where the accidents occurred. Then he posts his report by linking to the intersection. In general, he needs the diagram of the intersection as undersheet. If needed for reviewing the cause of accident, he also posts the picture of accident or of the traffic signal. Fig. 6 is a sample output of this application.

Such contents are stored day by day. Then, a requester, who is an analyst of the traffic accident, can make the report from a variety of viewpoint and browse the distribution/ frequency of the accident in a specific area.

6   Conclusion

This paper has described the system concept our Marche World as well as the system configuration and some applications. Typical features are discussed by comparing our system to the conventional geographic information system, push/pull technology, and discussion databases.

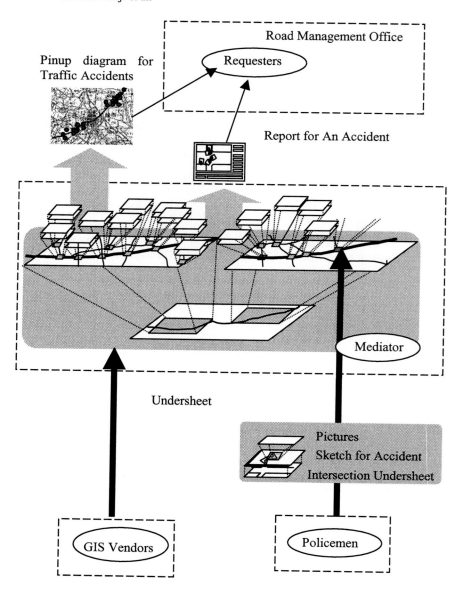

Report for An Accident

Undersheet

Fig. 6. Spatial Information Management In Police Headquarters

Spatial information sharing in MW adopt information mediation as de fact in a service architecture, in where are three roles of contents provider, mediator and requester. The mediator plays a role in matching the demand and supply between the content provider and the requester. As a result, contents can be distributed more widely than they can with the conventional technology.

To link a variety kinds of spatial information, we introduce the spatial information header and the spatial thesaurus. And to provide push/pull service, we designed API of MW for applications. For user discussion on geographic maps, spatial information header and spatial thesaurus is powerful.

We developed a prototype of MW and its applications. Marche World is just a infrastructure for building a new type of spatial information sharing system. Using APIs, we developed a virtual sight-seeing system called "cyber walk" which has push and pull services including discussion. Furthermore, in the police headquarters office system, a variety of documents such as traffic accident reports are linked with undersheet maps.

Acknowledgement

The authors would like to express sincere thanks to all members of Marche World Project in Hitachi, Ltd. Special thanks are also due to Mr. Masanori Kataoka and Dr. Hiroshi Yajima for their useful advice and encouragement.

References

1. Aitchison, J. and A. Gilchrist: Thesaurus Construction. Aslib. (1987)
2. van den Besselaar, P. and D. Beckers: Demographics and Sociographics of the Digital City. In: T. Ishida (eds.): Community Computing and Support Systems. Lecture Notes in Computer Science, Vol. 1519, Springer-Verlag, (1998) 109-125
3. Cheng, F: Internet Agents. New Riders. (1996)
4. Dejean, D. and S. Dejean: Lotus Notes at Work. Lotus Books Pub. (1991)
5. Ishida (Ed.): Community Computing and Support Systems. Lecture Notes in Computer Science, Springer-Verlag, (1998)
6. T. Ishida, J. Akahani, K. Hiramatsu, K. Isbister, S. Lisowski, H. Nakanishi, M. Okamoto, Y. Miyazaki, K. Tsutsuguchi: Digital City Kyoto: Towards A Social Information Infrastructure. In: M. Klusch, O. Shehory, G. Weiss (Eds.): Cooperative Information Agents III, Lecture Notes in Artificial Intelligence, Vol. 1652, Springer-Verlag, (1999) 23-35
7. Petrovsky, M.: Implementing CDF Channels, Computing McGraw-Hill. (1998)
8. Star, J. and J. Estes: Geographic Information Systems, Prentice Hall. (1990)
9. Tokuda, T., K. Tazaki, T. Yamada, H. Mizuno, and S. Kitazawa: On Extraction of WWW Pages with Spatial Information for Mediating their Distribution. Proc. of IEEE/SMC'99 (System, Man, and Cybernetics). (1999) IV-74-79
10. Yamada, T and H. Tsuji: Browsing Local Community "What's New" in Spatial Context. Proc. of First International Workshop on Practical Information Mediation and Brokering and the Commerce of Information on the Internet (I'MEDIAT'98). (1998) 1-8
11. Yamada, T., H. Mizuno, and S. Kitazawa: Map-based information mediation on the Web with float coordinate system. Proc. of IEEE/SMC'99 (System, Man, and Cybernetics). (1999) IV-93-98

Image Maps: Exploring Urban History through Digital Photography

Brian K. Smith, Erik Blankinship, Alfred Ashford III, Michael Baker, and
Timothy Hirzel[1]

MIT Media Lab, 20 Ames Street, Cambridge, MA 02139-4307, USA
{bsmith, erikb, coltrane, mbaker, hirzel}@media.mit.edu

Abstract. This paper describes an integration of geographic information
systems (GIS) and multimedia technologies to create opportunities for people to
explore the history of their cities. We have augmented a digital camera with a
global positioning system (GPS) and a digital compass to record its position and
orientation when ordinary photographs are taken. The metadata are used to
retrieve and present historical images of the photographed locations to
photographers. Another set of tools allows students to annotate and compare
these historical images to develop explanations of how and why their
communities have changed over time. We describe the hardware and software
architectures and learning outcomes that we expect to see in classroom use.

1 Introduction

We think of cities as places where we live, work, and play, but there is also a great
deal that we can learn from them. The city is a "laboratory", a place where we can
reflect on the successes and failures of architectural design and building [6].
Typically, we do not think of cities as learning environments, and we certainly do not
see much emphasis placed on studying cities in most formal, school curricula. In this
paper, we discuss ways for high school students to begin exploring their communities,
to learn about how and why their cities have changed over time.

In the past decade, reform efforts in science education have suggested that students
engage in authentic inquiry around scientific principles [1, 12]. That is, we should be
giving students conceptual and technological tools to help students develop their own
questions and strategies for testing and evaluating hypotheses. The thought is that
learning is best facilitated when students conduct self-directed inquiry. Rather than
giving them "cookbook" laboratory exercises, we should help them understand how to
choose interesting research problems and conduct investigations to verify their
hypotheses about these problems.

These reform ideas are not unique to science learning. We can imagine students
doing similar investigation tasks in the streets of their cities. In most K-12 classrooms,
subjects like history are presented through textbooks and other writings. In general,
students are not given opportunities to explore historical issues in their own
communities. They may take field trips to see local sites of interest, but they rarely

T. Ishida, K. Isbister (Eds.): Digital Cities, LNCS 1765, pp. 326-337, 2000.

use such journeys to investigate how and why their communities have changed over time.

We see opportunities for students to generate their own explanations of historical trends by engaging in "field work" in their cities. This fieldwork is complemented with digitized, archival photographs. Historical photographs provide a glimpse at the architectural, fashion, transport, and cultural trends of a period. By looking at a collection over time, students can reflect on how these trends change over time and their effects on cities. By integrating historical images with geographic information systems (GIS), students can look for spatial patterns and relationships that may vary geographically. For instance, noticing changes in transport throughout the city may give important clues to economic factors affecting city growth.

Rather than just giving students photographs with explanatory captions and narratives, we have developed a software suite, called *Image Maps*, allowing learners to annotate and compare historical images and to detect and explain patterns and relations over time. In this way, we hope to help them become better observers and critics of the real world through the use of imagery as data. To facilitate student inquiry, we have augmented a digital camera with a global positioning system (GPS) and a digital compass to record position and orientation metadata when pictures are taken. When the camera is downloaded, each augmented picture is used to retrieve historical pictures of the photographed location using image and GIS databases. By integrating GIS data with multimedia objects [7, 15], student photographs can be geo-referenced, providing additional data for inquiry. More importantly, students' images of the present are connected to those of the past, providing the basis for inquiries into community change.

2 Learning in the City

The premise of this research is that students can learn critical observation and interpretation skills by investigating changes in their local communities. Many authors describe the changes in urban landscapes [5, 6, 8] while others describe the details of developing organized arrangements for city planning [2, 3, 9]. Such texts provide ways for us to begin thinking about learning from our cities, but they do not actively engage students in conducting the process for themselves. There is much to be learned from becoming an active explorer of one's city [16], and our goal is to assist students in realizing that they can conduct investigations in their neighborhood "laboratories".

Because we do not typically think of cities as places where we can learn, we have to develop supports and strategies to help students proceed in their exploration. In other words, we have to create a methodology for students to use in their daily walks from home to school, a task structure to help them become careful observers and interpreters of the nuances of the city. To do this, we provide students with a set of tools for thinking about city change.

2.1 Learning with Images

Photographs play a large role in this work, providing students with historical evidence to compare against the current city. With photographs, we can see parts of the city fabric that no longer exist, other parts that have been modified or transformed, and still others that are no longer recognizable today. A city like Los Angeles, for instance, once had vast rail services that linked the suburbs to the city center [8]. Today, these rail lines can only be seen in pre-World War II photographs. Within these historical images lies history, a sense of what it was like to live in a city. A bit of introspection can help learners think about why features of the city were transformed or destroyed to make way for new innovations.

Urban planners use historical imagery to study the aesthetics and functionality of city environments [3, 19]. Patterns of urban change can be difficult to explain or justify without using qualitative data such as photographs. Time lapse photography and documenting changes with sequences of photographs are two techniques that allow for analysis of city transformations and communicating hypotheses. We want students to engage on similar strategies. They will use historical photographs to construct temporal chains of evidence to support theories of how and why their cities have changed over time.

We go beyond simply providing images by registering the members of the historical archives to their appropriate geographical locations. By associating the buildings in these photographs with GPS data, students can search on a location to see how features of that location have changed. This may mean that a building has grown or diminished over time. In many cases, students will poll a location only to find buildings that do not exist today. For instance, MIT's famed Building 20 was recently destroyed to make way for a new computer science building; in five years, students going to that location will only be aware of Building 20 through photographs. The images provide evidence for patterns that existed in the past. By geo-referencing these images, they become more connected to specific locations, allowing students to conduct focused inquiry around spatial patterns in their cities.

2.2 Learning by Designing Pattern Languages

In the 1970's, Christopher Alexander and his colleagues introduced the concept of pattern languages to the architectural community [2]. The elements of the pattern language are schemata describing frequently occurring problems in man-made environments and solutions addressing the problem. In the original notation, each pattern begins with photograph displaying a prototypical example of the problem. Accompanying the image is a full description of the problem and evidence for it being a pattern that frequently occurs in architecture. A series of instructions to correct the problem accompanies the pattern, as seen in this description from the "Six-Foot Balcony" pattern:

> Balconies and porches which are less than six feet deep are hardly ever used...Therefore, whenever you build a balcony, a porch, a gallery, or a terrace, make it at least six feet deep. If possible, recess at least part of it

into the building so that it is cantilevered out and separated from the building by a simple line, and enclose it partially [2, pp. 783-784].

These patterns were originally intended for practicing architects and urban planners, but they can be adapted for our purposes of educating K-12 students. One can imagine students using these patterns and instructions to analyze their cities, to develop and understanding for what elements of their communities work and fail with respect to Alexander's pattern language. However, students may gain more by doing the same exercise that Alexander and his colleagues did in formulating the original pattern language. Rather than simply drawing relations between city features and the existing pattern language, we would like students to create their own catalog of design patterns. These student-generated patterns would be created as they travel through their communities and explore historical photographs looking for examples of regularity and variation is architectural features.

To create these patterns, students must annotate images with relevant features that form the basis for describing relationships between parts. The juxtaposition of urban characteristics determine the look and feel of urban space [3], and simple features such as building materials, the heights of traffic lights, and sidewalk layouts can tell us important things about the evolution of a city. By annotating features of the image library with these traits, students can begin to see spatial patterns emerging, patterns that suggest property lines, zoning regulations, and public/private boundaries. When traced over time, these boundaries can provide insights into the complexities of the urban environment's growth.

So we want students to go out into their communities and become explorers and investigators. To help them with their journey, we provide them with an additional source of data to work with, a collection of historical images that can be accessed by their spatial location. These images provide the foundations for developing arguments about how and why a city has changed. In order to organize these arguments, we introduce students to pattern languages as a way to identify regularities and variations in the architectural features of their communities. The design of a pattern library becomes the end goal for the students; their task is to catalog relationships between cities. In a sense, they become urban planners, actively investigating their cities and developing theories about why their construction.

3 Retrieving Images with Images

To get a sense for the types of activities that we hope to see, we provide a hypothetical use scenario, a group of students on a field trip to Harvard Square. These students use our camera to take pictures of buildings and settings in this community that they like and dislike. After doing so, they return to their classroom and download their images into our software (Figure 1). The thumbnails on the right side of the display show students' photographs. When one of these thumbnails is placed into the crosshairs in the upper right, its enlarged image appears at right center, and a set of historical thumbnails matching the location of the selected image are displayed at the top — clicking one of these expands its image at the left center. Figure 1 shows how a photograph of Harvard Square in 1999 retrieves many images of the same location between 1860 and 1980.

Fig. 1. The current retrieval interface. Thumbnails on the right are images taken by students. Choosing one of these displays its larger image and displays an array of historical thumbnails across the top. The left image is the historical photo chosen from the retrieved collection

The students now need to explain why they liked or disliked the objects and regions that they photographed. They do this by creating descriptive ontologies and labeling objects in the images with these features. For instance, Figure 2 shows a list of features that students might develop (*e.g.*, transport types, commercial buildings, road types, architectural features). The historical photos are tagged with these labels, and students can begin comparing images over time to see similarities and differences. As they mark up more photographs, they can begin to retrieve images using their ontological features and describe urban planning patterns [2] that have varied or remained consistent throughout history.

When students are taught to explore their outdoor surroundings, they can become more aware of the intricacies of man-made environments [16]. We assist this process by giving access to historical images that might otherwise go unseen by students. We claim that doing "field work" with our camera, obtaining a record of local history, and working to explain the various changes in the community can lead to new insights about historical, architectural, and social change.

We propose moving students out of the classroom building and into the city itself to study history in its natural setting. Observation and analysis in the field can yield far more authentic results then possible within the classroom [16]. Rather than providing students with textbook explanations of history, we adopt a learner-centered approach [e.g., 14] to engage students in constructing and reflecting on their own explanations of image data. Previous work [11, 13, 18] has discussed the use of video as data in learning and coordinating complex tasks. We build on these projects by allowing students to acquire their own data in the form of photographs, and the annotation tools allow them to construct theories around issues in urban planning and cultural change.

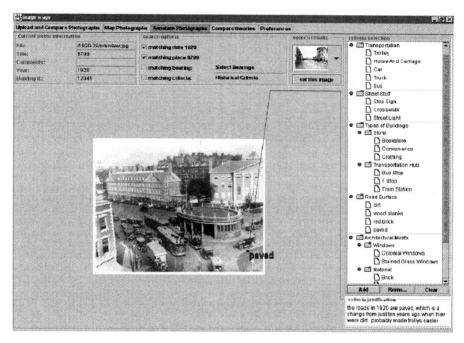

Fig. 2. Annotating images. Students develop ontologies to characterize interesting features of images. Objects in the photographs are labeled with these ontological features and used to develop explanations of community change

4 What Can You Learn From Image Data?

In the above scenario, there are a number of ways that students can learn with historical images provided by the camera. We are currently working to provide students opportunities to learn the following concepts:

1) *Observation and interpretation.* Rather than viewing images as "visual aids" to accompany textual explanations, students are responsible for drawing conclusions from image data. Comparing images across time periods can also provide insights into community change.

2) *Reasoning about urban planning.* We want students to develop hypotheses about the function of architectural structures. For instance, pedestrian crosswalks appeared rather recently in history. Students can pinpoint the time when they appeared and develop theories about why they may have been necessary. For instance, evidence of increased commercial buildings (*i.e.*, more commerce leads to more pedestrians) in the historical images may be correlated with the emergence of crosswalks.

3) *Reasoning about culture.* Images can provide important clues about community culture. For instance, a picture containing a "Buy War Bonds" advertisement is the beginning of a story about America during World War II. We hope to have students explore the meanings behind cultural artifacts found in images, possibly by collaborating with older adults to discover what is was like to live during the 1940's.

4) *Inquiry is an iterative process.* Although students could browse historical images without the camera, we feel that it is important for them to do "field work", to visit locations while constructing explanations of community change. In doing so, we hope they will better understand the iterative nature of inquiry, that returning to the field to make further observations will lead to new insights and questions.

Using GPS data to retrieve relevant historical information from a certain location has been proposed [10, 15], and this is one implementation of such a system. But instead of simply presenting historical synopses, our tools encourage students to build explanatory models using historical data. The "answers" to history are not returned by the system; one uses the primary documents retrieved by the system to build their own interpretations of historical change.

5 Technical Overview

A Kodak DC260 digital camera has been augmented with a Trimble Lassen-SK8 GPS and a Precision Navigation TCM2-80 digital compass. The camera uses Flashpoint Technology's Digita operating environment [4], allowing it to be scripted to send commands to the sensors through its serial port and to embed received data into JPEG images (Figure 3). In this way, the camera's origin and orientation are recorded when pictures are taken.

Our Java application parses the GPS and compass metadata from downloaded images and uses them to access a spatial map of Cambridge, Massachusetts stored in ESRI Inc.'s ArcView GIS. We start at the camera's origin (the point of image acquisition) and trace the orientation vector until we intersect a building or other landmark [17]. This raytracing routine approximates line of sight to return the name of the nearest landmark to the camera lens (Figure 4).

A separate Perl database associates each building name with a set of historical photographs. Each of these images has been hand-indexed with the position and orientation that it was taken from and the year when it was taken. The retrieval engine selects and displays images that closely match the view of the target image. If we cannot find images with similar shot distances and/or orientations, we relax the constraints and return any photographs of the location. We currently test our retrieval algorithms with 1000+ hand-indexed images between Harvard Square and MIT.

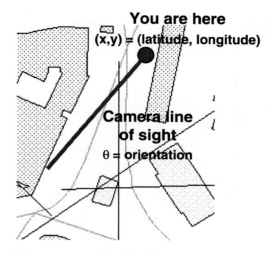

Fig. 3. A segment of the ArcView GIS map for Cambridge, Massachusetts. The red dot shows the current camera position at a GPS coordinate. Orientation is used to trace a vector from the camera origin along its line of sight. The current algorithm simply returns the first building that intersects the line of sight vector

We are expanding our image database to provide students with richer data sources. The algorithm used to retrieve images is still rather simple, and we are developing a more sophisticated engine. For instance, the camera is recording tilt information at present, and we can use that data to disambiguate target buildings (*e.g.*, photographs of tall buildings with smaller ones in the foreground). We will also automatically add student photographs into the image collection to create image records of the present that can be used in future classrooms.

A Kodak DC260 digital camera has been augmented with a Trimble Lassen-SK8 GPS and a Precision Navigation TCM2-80 digital compass (Figure 3). The camera uses Flashpoint Technology's Digita operating environment [4], allowing it to be scripted to send commands to the sensors through its serial port and to embed received data into JPEG images. In this way, the camera's origin and orientation are recorded when pictures are taken.

6 Conclusion

Studying cities is rare in K-12 classrooms, and we are working towards a new class of visualization and modeling applications that use imagery as a primary data source for students to investigate their communities. Rather than simply reading historical accounts, we want to see students arguing and debating about patterns of regularity and variation that can be found by exploring cities and comparing the present to the past. While most scientific visualization tools map quantitative data into visual representations, our students work directly with observational, image data, constructing qualitative models that can be used to predict future outcomes and events. The work described here is a first step towards fusing GIS and multimedia systems to produce new learning experiences through imagery.

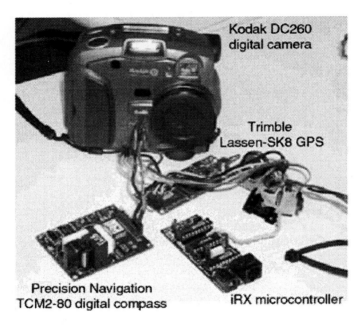

Fig. 4. An "out of the box" view of the camera hardware. A Kodak DC260 digital camera is attached to a Trimble Lassen SK-8 GPS and a Precision Navigation TCM-80 digital compass. This hardware configuration allows recording of position and orientation information into a JPEG image

One of our current concerns is the scalability of the project. Hand-indexing and registering historical images geographically consumes large amounts of effort. The best way to bring photographs into the system may be to allow our students to assist us in the indexing task. To do this, we created a web-based indexing tool (Figure 5) to allow users to contribute photographs to our database. Contributors select regions of the city that they want to add to and position a camera on screen to represent where the picture was taken and the approximate angle of view seen in the photograph. Our applet uses this information to create geographical metadata that can be used to retrieve the image in future searches, and the photo itself is added to our database.

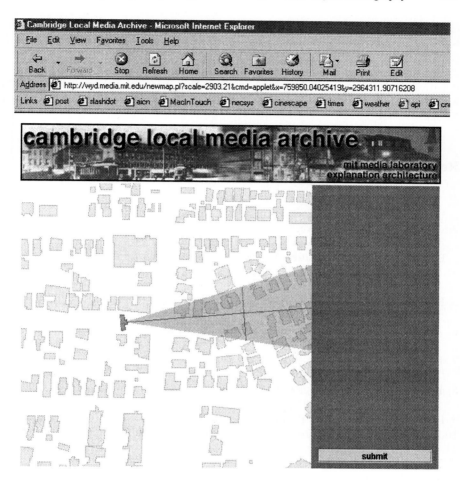

Fig 5. Auto-indexing images into the Image Maps database. Contributors align the graphical camera on the ArcView map at the position where a photograph was taken and adjust the "aperture" setting to show the area covered in the image. The applet uses this information to generate the geo-referenced metadata that accompanies the submitted image so future users of the system can retrieve it

We are hoping that this tool allows us to extend our database without the necessity for hand-indexing each photograph to a location. Also, by allowing people in the community to add to our databases, we hope to gain a much richer perspective on history. It is quite possible that the best historical, image archives are hidden in the photo albums of ordinary citizens, and the availability of this tool might help these images becomes available to a larger community.

Although we have tested the camera ourselves, our first deployment with children (14-16 years old) begins in late 1999. This initial deployment will inform the iterative design of the camera and software tools for constructing explanations about community change. We will also attempt to understand the types of supports that teachers need to provide for this activity to successfully engage students in new ways of thinking about inquiry and their communities.

We would like to thank the Cambridge Historical Commission for their gracious donation of 100+ years of historical images. This work is supported by the MIT Media Laboratory's News in the Future consortium and kind donations from Eastman Kodak.

References

1. American Association for the Advancement of Science: Science For All Americans: Project 2061. Oxford University Press, New York (1990)
2. Alexander, C., Ishikawa, S., Silverstein, M.: A Pattern Language: Towns, Buildings, Construction. Oxford University Press, Oxford (1977)
3. Bacon, E.N.: Design of Cities. Viking Press, New York (1967)
4. Flashpoint Technology: Digita Operating System: Script Reference. Flashpoint Technology, San Jose, CA (1998)
5. Hoskins, W.G.: The Making of the English Landscape. Penguin Books, Middlesex, England (1970)
6. Jacobs, J.: The Death and Life of Great American Cities. Vintage Books, New York (1992)
7. Kraak, M.-J.: Integrating multimedia in geographical information systems. IEEE Multimedia 3 (1996) 59-65
8. Kunstler, J.H.: The Geography of Nowhere: The Rise and Decline of America's Man-Made Landscapes. Touchstone, New York (1993)
9. Lynch, K. Hack, G.: Site Planning. The MIT Press, Cambridge, MA (1996)
10. Mitchell, W.J.: City of Bits. The MIT Press, Cambridge, MA (1996)
11. Nardi, B.A., Kuchinsky, A., Whittaker, S., Leichner, R., Schwarz, H.: Video-as-data: Technical and social aspects of a collaborative multimedia application. Computer Supported Collaborative Work 4 (1996) 73-100
12. National Research Council: National Science Education Standards. National Center for Education Statistics, Washington, DC (1996)
13. Smith, B.K. Reiser, B.J.: What should a wildebeest say? Interactive nature films for high school classrooms. In: ACM Multimedia 97 Proceedings, ACM Press, New York (1997) 193-201.
14. Soloway, E., Guzdial, M., Hay, K.E.: Learner-centered design: The challenge for HCI in the 21st century. interactions 1 (1994) 36-48
15. Spohrer, J.: Worldboard: What comes after the WWW? Available at http://www.worldboard.org/pub/spohrer/wbconcept/default.html (1998)
16. Stilgoe, J.R.: Outside Lies Magic: Regaining History and Awareness in Everyday Places. Walker and Company, New York (1998)
17. Tsui, C.: Multimedia Data Integration and Retrieval in Planning Support Systems. M.S. thesis, Department of Urban Studies and Planning, Massachusetts Institute of Technology, Cambridge, MA (1998)

18. Whittaker, S. O'Conaill, B.: The role of vision in face-to-face and mediated communication. In: Finn, K.E., Sellen, A.J., Wilbur, S.B., (Eds): Video-Mediated Communication. Lawrence Erlbaum Associates, Hillsdale, NJ (1997) 23-49
19. Whyte, W.: The Social Life of Small Urban Spaces. 16mm film. Municipal Art Society of New York, New York (1984)

Navigation Support in a Real City Using City Metaphors

Kensaku Fujii[1], Shigeru Nagai[1], Yasuhiko Miyazaki[2] and Kazuhiro Sugiyama[1]

1 NTT Cyber Space Laboratories, 1-1 Hikarinooka Yokosuka-Shi
Kanagawa 239-0847, Japan
{fujii, nagai, sugiyama}@marsh.hil.ntt.co.jp
2 NTT Cyber Solutions Laboratories, 2-4 Hikaridai Seika-Cho Sohraku-Gun
Kyoto 619-0237, Japan
miyazaki@soy.kecl.ntt.co.jp

Abstract. Digital cities make a wide variety of city metaphors possible. City metaphors can be used as information resources for real city users. To use resources easily, it is essential that digital cities have simple and intuitive interfaces. We are working towards a new interface focused on supporting navigation services in a real city. This paper proposes an approach to improve the interface of digital cities. Proposed approach is realized by dynamically generating intelligible representation of route guide information using city metaphors. Our developed system can generate the pictorial and linguistic representation by selecting truly required information and re-arranging it for easy understanding. Using our system, route guides are available for very small display of a cellular phone. In experiments we verified the effectiveness of proposed interface for navigation support in a real city. Using proposed interface, we can easy browse route information in digital city even with mobile terminals.

1   Introduction

This paper outlines results of experiments with a new interface for digital cities. Digital cities make a wide variety of city metaphors possible [1][2]. City metaphors can be used as information resources for real city users. To use information easily, it is essential that digital cities have simple and intuitive interfaces. Many technologies can be used to support user interfaces in digital city systems. We focused on supporting route navigation – a fundamental activity of real city users. We investigated design and implementation interfaces to support navigation services in a real city.

City metaphors are usually designed as maps. These maps provide geographical information, for example, locations of a destination and routes to a destination. Another role of these maps is to handle information about various activities in a real city. To browse geographical information easily, a 3D interface is proposed [3]. This interface allows easy access to geographically delimited information. Using this interface, people can get information related to various activities in a real city. The information can be listed visually or presented linguistically with 3D maps.

However, a 3D interface is hard to browse route information. Maps are developed to closely correspond to real cities. The accuracy can assist to handle various infor-

T. Ishida, K. Isbister (Eds.): Digital Cities, LNCS 1765, pp. 338-349, 2000.

mation. On the other, this disturbs an easy route browsing and demands high-performance presentation devices. For example, a 3D map fails to clearly show all routes to the destination at the same time because of occlusion of buildings. Additionally, a 3D map fails to clearly show on small or low-resolution displays. When real city users want to get route information, they are usually in mobile environments. We consider an interface to get geographical information easily even with mobile terminals.

We are working towards a new interface to support route navigation in a real city. We propose an approach to dynamically generate an intelligible representation using city metaphors. An intelligible representation is realized by selecting truly necessary information and re-arranging for easy understanding. In this paper we first introduce in Section 2 the useful representation which is examined from a viewpoint of spatial recognition. Then we present proposed method to dynamically generate both pictorial and linguistic representations using same 2D maps. In experiments we evaluate proposed interface to support route navigation in a real city.

2   Analysis of Route Guide Representation

A variety of recognition processes are triggered when people move toward a destination. Such a movement can be achieved using inner recognition resources and external resources. The former include cognitive map, sense of direction and so on. The latter include various clues (guide maps and signboards, etc) or others (ask a passer-by for directions). People usually recognize spatial information by combining external resources with inner resources. If external resources correspond to user's inner recognition resources closely, a movement toward a destination is achieved easily.

Therefore we examined an effective representation of external resources. We paid attention to two kinds of route guide representation - pictorial representation ("see") and linguistic representation ("hear").

2.1 Outline

The route guides consist of semantic information and spatial information. The former provides the meaning of spatial objects such as roads, buildings, and so on. The latter indicates the position or relation of spatial objects. As this consideration, we investigated their characteristics from semantic and spatial viewpoints.

We collected three kinds of route guide maps as pictorial representation. They were displayed on signboards, published in magazines, and hand-written. We sampled 100 maps of each type at random. Samples are shown in Figure 1 - a) signboard, b) magazine, c) hand-written.

We also collected 1,300 route guide sentences as linguistic representation. They were provided in the WWW and personal computer communications. An example is "You are at Gotanda station. Leave east exit, and walk straight along Sony Corporation Street. The destination is next to NTT building."

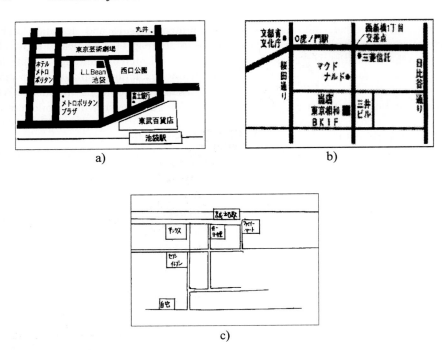

Fig. 1. Samples of pictorial representation a) signboard, b) magazine, c) hand-written

2.2 Analysis from Semantic Viewpoint

We semantically examined spatial objects extracted from collected guides. Symbols of these objects were classified by component type of cognitive map. The components included path, node, landmark, edge and district as given by Lynch [4]. Examined maps displayed on signboards, published in magazines and hand-written contained 702, 676 and 941 symbols, respectively. Examined sentences also contained 3,700 symbols. Results of classification of these symbols are shown in Table 1. As shown in Table 1, the landmark category is used most frequently. On the other hand, the path or node categories are used sparingly. For example, such symbols mean street names, street numbers and so on. These results are probably due to the fact that symbols to describe roads or intersections are rare in Japan [5]. We also classified symbols in the landmark category by attribute type, which is an important factor for easy recognition. Specific types are often used as shown in Table 2.

Based on these results, symbols of spatial objects are selected on the basis of component type or attribute type to enhance easy recognition.

Table 1. Classification by component type of cognitive map

component	frequency a) signboard	b) magazine	c) hand-written	d) sentence
path	0.088	0.080	0.086	0.220
node	0.001	0.008	0.007	0.070
landmark	0.740	0.681	0.750	0.530
edge	0.093	0.097	0.056	0.010
district	0.085	0.127	0.101	0.100

Table 2. Classification by attribute type

attribute	frequency a) signboard	b) magazine	c) hand-written	d) sentence
station	0.078	0.117	0.057	0.426
department	0.003	0.003	0.016	0.096
store	0.142	0.130	0.166	0.094
restaurant	0.051	0.081	0.130	0.088
public facilities	0.078	0.118	0.089	0.087
building	0.148	0.111	0.031	0.051
temple	0.001	0.003	0.016	0.026
school	0.016	0.022	0.058	0.025
hotel	0.019	0.028	0.018	0.022
traffic facilities	0.019	0.020	0.018	0.022
amusement facilities	0.066	0.052	0.053	0.020
bank	0.145	0.124	0.060	0.018
convenience store	0.016	0.049	0.097	0.013
hospital	0.024	0.018	0.015	0.009

2.3 Analysis from Spatial Viewpoint

We examined spatial representation of collected guides. Representations of examined maps could be classified into two types based on route representation. These types correspond to the route map type and survey map type in classification of cognitive map, respectively [6]. Samples are shown in Figure 2 - a) route map type, b) survey map type. The former shows symbols that describe spatial relationship of objects limited on route. The latter shows symbols that describe spatial relationship of objects selected around route. These types reflect a form of spatial knowledge that has been acquired or studied. Results of classification of examined maps are shown in Table 3. It shows that the route map type is more favored, because a departure point is easy specified.

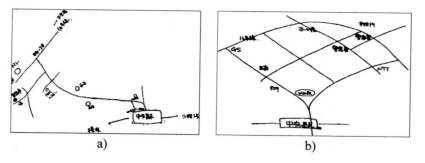

a)   b)

Fig. 2. Samples of a) route map type, b) survey map type representation

Table 3. Classification of exmanied maps by representation type of cognitive map

representation	frequency a) signboard	b) magazine	c) hand-written
route map type	0.71	0.56	0.86
survey map type	0.29	0.44	0.14

We also examined shapes of collected maps. These shapes are often deformed. The angle of intersecting roads tends to be quantized in steps of 45 or 90 degrees. Large step size implies greater simplicity. The deformation by quantization is maybe caused by orthogonalization phenomenon of intersections - a well-known characteristic in recognition psychology [7]. It could assist in recognizing spatial arrangement of roads or landmarks.

Next, we examined spatial representation of collected sentences. These sentences arranged spatial information in a time series. It means to be equivalent to the route map type in classification of cognitive map. Route representations could be classified into two types. One is the direction of movement. An example is "Turn right at police box." The other is the position relative to described objects. An example is "It is in front of police box." Results of classification are shown in Figure 3, which indicated that relative position is frequently used. The tendency corresponds to "people tend to recognize the position of objects using relative position to other objects." The word that shows spatial relationship between objects is defined as "spatial word." Table 4 shows results of classifying 1,500 spatial words in examined sentences.

As these results, representations of the route map type and survey map type in cognitive map are used to generate route guide maps. In addition, it is important from a viewpoint of spatial recognition that the position of roads or landmarks is re-arranged to match the quantization effect. To generate route guide sentences, it is the right way to use the direction of movement and spatial word giving relative position between objects.

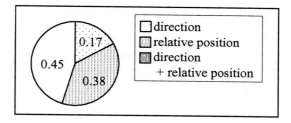

Fig. 3. Classification of examined sentences by spatial representation

Table 4. Classification by spatial word

spatial word	frequency	spatial word	frequency
front	0.012	left	0.112
right	0.107	near	0.102
along	0.088	next	0.057
back	0.049	beside	0.045
foreground	0.032	between	0.027
diagonal	0.021	side	0.019
north	0.018	front on	0.017
n blocks away	0.016	corner	0.015

3   Development of Route Guide System

Based on results of analysis stated above, we developed the route guide system, which automatically generate intelligible route guides using city metaphors.

3.1 Object Selection

So as to select objects used for route guides, we proposed calculation of recognition parameter, which reflect to characteristics of the attribute type and 2D shape[8]. The parameter for the attribute type is set on the basis of appearance frequency in Section 2. In addition, the parameter for the 2D shape is also set using the size and circumference of each object.

The number of selected objects is decided in proportion to the amount of information, which can be displayed on requested terminals at a time. Objects are selected in order of recognition parameter calculated for each object of the area around route.

3.2 Generating Pictorial Representation

To generate the route map type representation, route is calculated using a dijkstra method and other objects for route specification are selected using recognition parameter. For the survey map type representation, in addition to the procedure, objects around route are selected using recognition parameter and connections between these selected objects and route are calculated.

When we generate the deformed map type representation, an angle of two intersecting roads is set at multiples of 45 degrees. However, it is difficult to re-arrange the position of landmarks using simple coordinate conversion, because it is necessary to keep spatial relationship between objects after re-arrangement. We proposed to use the spatial object network, which describes knowledge of their spatial relationship. Refer to [9] in detail. Using this knowledge, the position of landmarks is calculated to retain spatial relationship after re-arrangement.

3.3 Generating Linguistic Representation

To generate route guide sentences, route is represented using a series of phrases giving the direction of movement and spatial word. Objects are selected using recognition parameter stated above. Representations of the direction are generated based on corresponding to an angle formed by intersecting roads. Spatial words are generated based on corresponding to a path between objects using the spatial object network. Path patterns are associated with spatial words in advance. Two objects are selected, a path from one object to another is calculated. According to a pattern of calculated path, spatial word is selected. Refer to [10] in detail.

4   Experimental Results and Discussions

We developed the route guide system that generated the pictorial and linguistic representation by applying proposed method. Route guides are generated from our developed city metaphors designed as 2D maps. Figure 4 shows a sample of 2D maps (scale : 1/2500). Samples of route guide maps are dynamically generated using these maps as shown in Figure 5. Figure 5(a) and (b) correspond to the route map type and survey map type, respectively. Figure 5(c) shows an example of the deformed map type.

Samples of route guide sentences are also dynamically generated using same maps. Figure 6 shows a sample of route guide sentences with corresponding route map type using WWW Browser. This sentence uses the spatial word "diagonally front" to indicate relative position between "Komachido Bldg." and "Sangosho".

We browse these guides using a cellular phone. As shown in Figure 7, our generated guides are available for small display in mobile environment.

Fig. 4. Example of 2D maps (scale: 1/2500)

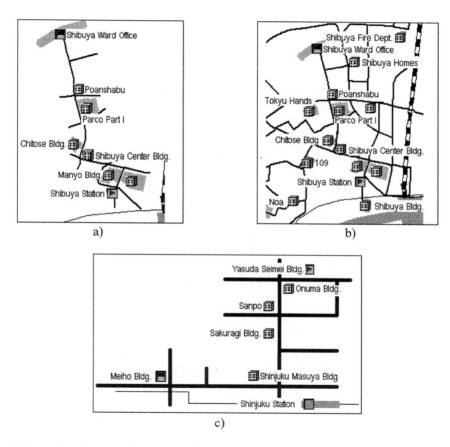

Fig. 5. Examples of route guide maps a) route map type, b) survey map type, c) deformed map type

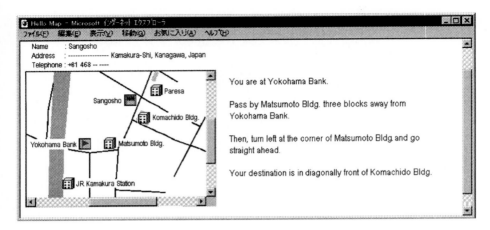

Fig. 6. Example of route guide sentences with corresponding route map type using WWW Browser

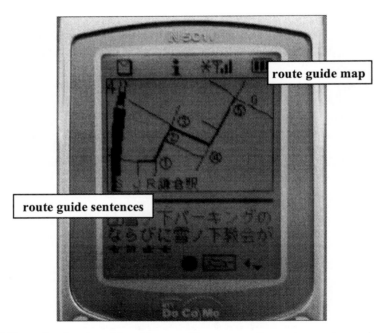

Fig. 7. Example of route guide sentences with corresponding route map type using a cellular phone.

We tested our system by assuming a real activity - a tourist wants to find a restaurant in a real city. A tourist accesses our system and inputs some requirements, for example, a Chinese restaurant near Kamakura police office. As shown in Figure 8, our system provided search results using simple 2D maps and lists. After a tourist selected a specific restaurant, our system provided route guides using the pictorial and linguistic representation as shown in Figure 9.

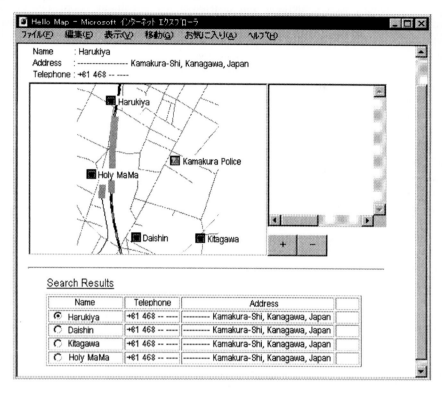

Fig. 8. Example of search results using simple 2D maps and lists

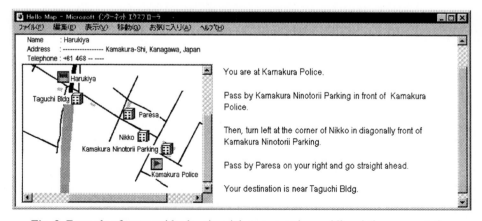

Fig. 9. Example of route guides by pictorial representation and linguistic representation

Using the route guide system in a real city, we examined an effectiveness of our proposed approach. For simplicity only linguistic representation was used. Route guide sentences were generated and distributed by a cellular phone (synthesized speech) and a pager (text). Ten destinations around Kamakura Komachi town were selected from tour guide magazines. Subjects were 5 men and women in their twenties and thirties; all were new to test locations. They moved from one destination to another; their movements and utterances were recorded by a video camera. In this case, 100 sessions were recorded by assigning to each of 10 subjects.

After experiments, we investigated recorded movements, utterances, and subjects' opinions. Deviations from route described by generated sentences and causes of mistakes were identified. We defined the movement failure rate to examine an effectiveness of our proposed linguistic representation. The rate is Out / N, where Out means a number of times subject was unable to return to route and N means a number of cases. In experiments, N was 100 and Out was 9, so the movement failure rate was calculated to be 0.09. As these results, our proposed linguistic representation is effective for navigation support. It well assists people in making it easier to get and understand route guides.

One frequent cause of mistakes was bad data; stored data may not necessarily be correct. For instance, "Matsumoto Bldg." in Figure 6 had a different name at the time of experiments. We must use the latest information as a city metaphor to decrease mistakes. It was additionally found by investigated their opinions that 3D information such as 3D shapes, signboards and texture images are effective for navigation support. Therefore it is necessary to develop city metaphors using these types of visual information.

5   Conclusion

This paper outlines results of experiments with a new interface for digital cities. We are working towards a new interface to support navigation services in a real city. We propose an approach to dynamically generate intelligible representation of route guide information using city metaphors.

With the goal of navigation support, intelligible representation consists of the pictorial representation and/or linguistic representation. The former is generated using representations of the route map type and survey map type in cognitive map. In addition, it is necessary from a viewpoint of spatial recognition that the position of roads or landmarks is re-arranged to match the quantization effect. The latter is generated using representations of the direction of movement and spatial word giving relative position between objects. On the other hand, spatial objects are selected according to specific attributes to assist route recognition.

We developed the route guide system, which automatically generate these representations using city metaphors. Using our system, route guides are available for very small display of a cellular phone. In experiments we verified the effectiveness of proposed interface for navigation support in a real city. Using proposed interface, we can easy browse route information in digital city even with mobile terminals. It was also found in experiments that 3D information such as 3D shapes, signboards and texture images are effective for navigation support and development of city metaphors.

Acknowledgements

Thanks are due to Noboru Sonehara of NTT Cyber Space Laboratories for their extensive assistance throughout this study.

References

1. P. van den Besselaar and D. Beckers.: Demographics and Sociographics of the Digital City. T. Ishida (Ed.). Community Computing and Support Systems, Lecture Notes in Computer Science, Vol. 1519, pp. 109-125, Springer-Verlag (1998)
2. T. Ishida, J. Akahani, K. Hiramatsu, K. Isbister, S. Lisowski, H. Nakanishi, M. Okamoto, Y. Miyazaki, K. Tsutsuguchi.: Digital City Kyoto: Towards A Social Information Infrastructure. M. Klusch, O. Shehory, G. Weiss (Eds.). Cooperative Information Agents III, Lecture Notes in Artificial Intelligence, Vol. 1652, pp. 23-35, Springer-Verlag (1999)
3. Stefan Lisowski et al.: Laying 3DML Interface Groundwork for a Distributed Digital City Kyoto. Interaction '99 (1999)
4. J. Hori.: Adequate Condition for maps. Gengo. Vol.23. No.7 (1994)
5. K. Mori.: Cognitive Map. publicated by science co (1991)
6. Lynch K.: The Image of the City. Cambridge, Mass. MIT Press (1996)
7. K. Kajita et al.: Development of an Automatic Generation System of Deformed Maps. Transactions of Information Processing Society of Japan. Vol.37. No.9 (1996)
8. K. Fujii and K. Sugiyama.: A Method of Generating a Spot-Guidance for Human Navigation. Transactions of the Institute of Electronics, Information and Communication Engineers D-II. Vol.J82. No.11 (1999)
9. K. Fujii and K. Wakabayashi.: A model for Map Recognition based on Spatial Relation. Theory and Applications of GIS. Vol.5. No.1 (1997)
10. K. Fujii and K. Sugiyama.: Route Guidance for Human Navigation Assist. Proceedings of International Conference on Cognitive Science. (1999)

Public Applications of SpaceTag and Their Impacts

Hiroyuki Tarumi, Ken Morishita, and Yahiko Kambayashi

Department of Social Informatics
Graduate School of Informatics, Kyoto University
Kyoto, 606-8501 JAPAN
TEL: (+81) 75-753-5385, FAX (+81) 75-753-4970
{tarumi,ken,yahiko}@i.kyoto-u.ac.jp

Abstract. SpaceTag is an object that can be accessed only from limited locations and time period. SpaceTags are served and distributed from a central server which should be managed by a service provider. Users of the SpaceTag system can access SpaceTags with portable terminals equipped with location sensors and wireless communication device such as mobile phones. Users walk around in a city and find SpaceTags that can be only found at the location. SpaceTag is thus an inconvenient media, but suitable for gaming, advertising, city guide information, etc. A user can also put a SpaceTag at the location where (s)he is, which can be found by other people nearby. This feature also enables local public communication applications. In this paper, we will argue why this inconvenient but simple virtual platform can support various applications for a digital city. We will also argue social impacts of these applications.

1 Introduction

One of the authors visited Florence to present our paper on SpaceTag[6] in June. In the city, I found that many tourists were visiting the Uffizi Museum. Visitors should wait for one or two hours before entering the museum. They were mainly aiming at seeing Botticelli's famous paintings.

However, how many of the visitors are able to admire the real Botticelli's paintings? The paintings are printed on many art books published all over the world. They do not have to come to Florence if their aim is to see the paintings. Maybe most of them come to the museum to satisfy themselves by the fact that they see the real ones, or to tell their friends to say, "I saw the real ones," after returning from Florence.

The Internet and multimedia technologies are improving year by year, or month by month. In near future, a digital museum will probably become able to exhibit Botticelli's paintings with a very detailed image data. Nevertheless, people would still visit Florence to see the real ones. Florence's economy is everlasting.

Then, how is the case of digital art? Simply imagine that Botticelli had had a Macintosh and an Illustrator! Now his digital works would be copied

T. Ishida, K. Isbister (Eds.): Digital Cities, LNCS 1765, pp. 350–363, 2000.

to everywhere through the Internet, because the copyright would have been expired hundreds years ago. Even if the works were still copyright-protected, the download fee would be lower than travel costs. Everyone in the world could saw the *real* ones at home, and Florence's economy would be poorer.

This is one of the problems of digital technologies that very few people point out. They make *only* computer and communication industries rich. One of my friends who is a member of a railway company complained me of digital museum's possible negative effects on the number of passengers.

People are interested in rare things, or things that are hard to get. WWW has made all digital data popular and easy to get. We don't want to deny the value of WWW, but we think that rare and hard-to-get information should also be digitally supported. Imagine a digital city where people can watch plenty of digital arts that can be enjoyed *only* in the city. The city would be rich!

Actually, location-restricted digital art exhibition is one of the possible applications of SpaceTag. The SpaceTag system is a platform to support digital data that can be accessed only from limited locations and in limited time period. Games, sightseeing information, local community communication, etc. are also SpaceTag's applications, as well.

In this paper we will describe the architecture, applications, advantages, and our prototype of SpaceTag system. Possible social problems will be discussed and solutions will be proposed.

2   The SpaceTag System

2.1   Concept

A SpaceTag is a virtual object that can be accessed *only* within limited area and limited time period. Restriction and inconvenience is the essential idea of SpaceTag. Of course, in some applications, it will be more convenient if SpaceTags can be accessed remotely. However, our policy is to give convenience by other media such as WWW, as SpaceTag can be interfaced with other media.

2.2   Architecture

Figure 1 shows the basic design of the SpaceTag system. It basically consists of a server and clients. A user has a handy client terminal.

Server SpaceTags are stored in a database on a server machine, and they are broadcasted from the server to terminals (clients). A server is composed of a database subsystem and a communication subsystem. The server and the database are supposed to be managed by a service provider.

The database is required to manage SpaceTag objects. A SpaceTag is a digital object that has at least the following attributes: *ID, data type, effective zone, effective time period, access rights, channel,* etc.

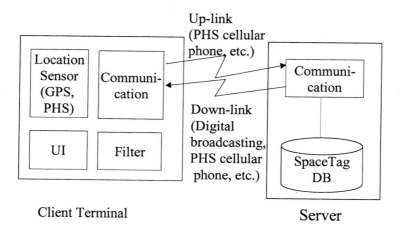

Fig. 1. Configuration of the SpaceTag System

- ID is a serial number given by a server, which is not shown to users. Data types may be text, image, audio, program, VRML, URL, etc.
- Effective zone means the area within which a user can open the SpaceTag. It is defined by a pair of center location and radius. [1]
- Channel is like that of TV broadcasting. For example, tourist channel, communication channel, or gaming channel can be given. If a user selects a channel on the terminal, only SpaceTags that have the same channel attribute are shown.

Since the objects have uniform structure except the multimedia contents, the database can be implemented with standard relational or object-relational database products. Almost all queries are retrievals of SpaceTags that can be accessed from a particular position and time. This fact gives possibilities to tune the database performance for queries.

There are two cases in creating and modifying SpaceTags.

By a service provider: In cases of tourist information and advertisements, etc., information provider (city government or advertising agents) commissions the service provider to manage the SpaceTags. These SpaceTags can be modified or removed only by the service provider.

By end-users: A SpaceTag created by an end-user is transmitted to the server by the up-link communication and stored in the database as a SpaceTag with location attributes of the place where it was created. In this case the SpaceTag

---

[1] Correctly speaking, we have two kinds of zones. Another is the zone within which users can detect the existence of the SpaceTag but cannot open it.

can be removed by the creator or some specified people. Appropriate access right management should be applied.

It must be inhibited for users to access SpaceTags remotely. If it were allowed, remote access would become a popular behavior of end-users because remote access is simply convenient; the basic concept of SpaceTag might be crashed and some applications would become nonsense. If remote access is required, the service provider can select remotely accessible SpaceTags and copy them to WWW, or the company can create SpaceTags whose contents are URLs indicating the open data. The SpaceTag system and WWW can be linked and cooperate in this way.

It should also be inhibited for users to create SpaceTags remotely, in order to avoid SPAM-like SpaceTags. Only the service provider should be allowed to create them remotely.

Communication The SpaceTag system uses two way communication: up-link (client to server) and down-link (server to client).

For the up-link communication, we have adopted a popular digital cellular phone system. Required bandwidth is not so wide, because what are transmitted from clients to the server are some control commands, position data, and SpaceTags created at the client terminal.

For the down-link communication we currently have two options: public digital broadcasting and micro-cell type cellular phone (Japanese PHS (Personal Handyphone System)).

In case of adopting digital broadcasting, surface broadcasting is more appropriate than satellite broadcasting, because broadcasting area is smaller. For example, if a 10 Mbps bandwidth channel is reserved, about 60,000 SpaceTags of 1 KB short text can be broadcasted per minute. If large data like image is contained within a SpaceTag, it is possible to broadcast only indexing information to get the real contents from other network in an on-demand manner, e.g., from the Internet through http or other protocols.

If a micro-cell type cellular phone is adopted, the bandwidth is narrower. In case of Japanese PHS, 64 kbps can be reserved. However, each service area is small enough to reduce the number of SpaceTags to transmit in one area.

Client Terminals As shown in Figure 1, a client terminal has the following functions.

Location sensor: It senses the position of the terminal itself. We have currently two options for the sensor, GPS and PHS.

Communication: It implements the up-link and down-link communication functions. The manner of connection depends on its implementation. If digital broadcasting is adopted, it receives SpaceTags every time. If PHS is adopted, it should be connected continuously or periodically.

Filter: This function selects SpaceTags that should be shown to the user from all received SpaceTags and stores them. The filtering is based on location, time, channel, keyword, or other attribute values. Location, time, and channel-based filtering functions are mandatory; others are optional. If a wide-area broadcasting is adopted as the down-link communication, many SpaceTags might be filtered out by this function, because most of them are not within the neighborhood. Selected SpaceTags are cached on the terminal as long as it can be accessed.

Some optional functions can be appended. Content-based filtering is one of them. Another example is notification service, which is to notify the user when a particular specified SpaceTag is detected.

It should be noted that the filtering function could be modified to show SpaceTags that may not be accessed. Currently we are supposing that this type of cheating does not occur. However, we should design more secure implementation against cheating. Developing one-chip SpaceTag terminal is an example of secure design.

User Interface (UI): It provides the following functions:

 - List up all the SpaceTags that can be accessed.
 - Creation of new SpaceTags. Stylus pen interface, audio microphone, and digital camera (still, motion) are possible future interfaces to create SpaceTags. Currently any Windows files can be stuck as a SpaceTag, on our prototype system.
 - Sticking newly created SpaceTags in the real space, and removing or copying SpaceTags from the space. If a SpaceTag is moved from the space to the terminal (cut operation), a control command is sent to the server and the server removes the SpaceTag from the database.
 - Channel selection.

2.3   Prototype

We have prototyped the first version of the SpaceTag system. For the communication, we adopt PHS for both up-link and down-link. The server is located in our laboratory; Oracle 8 is adopted for the database. Terminals are implemented on usual notebook PCs running Windows, with a client software shown in Figure 2 and Figure 3.

In Figure 3, a user is shown as an icon at the center of the map image. SpaceTags are shown with icons around the user. The user can open a SpaceTag by double-clicking the icon, or a SpaceTag name shown in the list of SpaceTag in the upper-right sub-window. Some SpaceTags, which are not so close to the user, are shown with "?" icon. These SpaceTags are detected by the user, but cannot be opened. Other SpaceTags, which are far from the user, are not shown.

In the lower right sub-window, a list of channels is shown. The use can select a channel in this window to restrict categories of SpaceTags to be shown. In this example, "Hotel," "Sightseeing," "Restaurant," "Advertisement," and some other channels are used.

Fig. 2. A Client Prototype

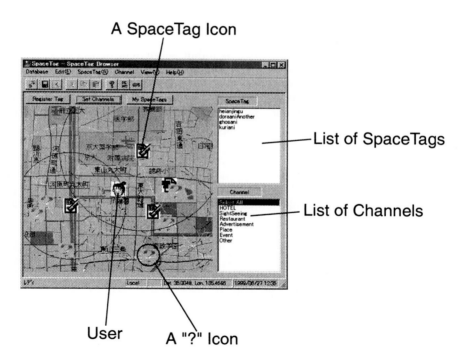

Fig. 3. User Interface of Our Prototype

If the user walks, the map and SpaceTag icons are shifted. SpaceTags getting closer will appear, or the icon will be changed from "?" to usual icons. SpaceTags getting farther will be changed to "?" icon, or disappear.

For the user to stick a SpaceTag, what the user should do is only select a Windows file and drag-and-drop it into the map area. It will be stuck at the place where the user is.

2.4 Future Perspective

In June, 1999, Epson Corporation started to sell "Locatio." It is an integrated handy terminal that has GPS, LCD (3.9 inch), digital camera, and PHS. Its weight is 260 – 290 grams. Its market price is under 100,000 yen (without PHS). For location sensors, it can use GPS and PHS complementarily.

Since its memory and disk space is not enough, currently it cannot be used for a SpaceTag client. However, this product suggests that we will be able to start SpaceTag service in very near future, with very handy terminals.

3 Expected Service of SpaceTag System

The SpaceTag system is intrinsically inefficient because accessibility is limited. Its application is mainly in the entertainment field, rather than the business field. In this section we give some applications we are expecting. Especially, the first three applications can be provided as public services of digital cities.

Public Information Service: Location-dependent public information can be presented by SpaceTags. Examples are sightseeing information that describes and illustrates famous sightseeing points, public announcement to warn people against pickpockets, to show (temporal) traffic regulation, to show the place of an events, etc.

City residents and visitors who have SpaceTag-aware terminals can find such SpaceTags. If channels are separated, visitors find only those they need, like sightseeing information and traffic regulation announcements, while city residents find other SpaceTags (like a SpaceTag that navigates people to a local tax office) as well.

Multimedia Attraction: With SpaceTags, we can implement attractions and entertainment scenes at festivals or events, like fireworks. Digital art exhibition, mentioned in section 1 belongs to this category. If a city offers many multimedia attractions by SpaceTags, many people will visit there to enjoy them.

Local Area Communication: A SpaceTag-powered city gives people opportunities to have communication between them. A SpaceTag put by a person is shown to unspecified people nearby. This means that a SpaceTag can be used for instant communication with people around the user. For example, SpaceTags like bills to ask for help to search a lost child, to offer a ticket exchange at event sites, to look for partners to enjoy themselves, and to exchange information about police speed-traps between car drivers are examples of such requirements.

Real World Adventure Game: SpaceTags can be used for items in adventure games like secret keys, hints for puzzles, instructions, etc. Players carrying terminals walk around a town, getting and putting SpaceTags according to a game scenario. This type of game is better for our health than existing game machines, and realizes multi-player games naturally.

Advertising Event: People must move to access attractive SpaceTags. It causes some economic impacts. For example, suppose that a supermarket chain store announces that some SpaceTags will appear at some of the chain stores on a particular day and people who get the SpaceTag will win a prize. This campaign will gather many customers at all chain stores.

Moving Advertisement: A SpaceTag can be shown as a moving object, by periodically changing its location parameter. Using a moving SpaceTag for advertisement, we can provide a moving advertisement. It is only displayed to small number of people, but sometimes more effective than common advertisement like banners on Web pages. It is because it gives strong impression and sometimes causes rumors about the time and place to watch it. Moving advertisement is very easily implemented by periodically changing the location attribute.

4   Advantages of SpaceTag System

4.1   Overlaid Virtual System

In Figure 4, we categorize location-aware information systems.

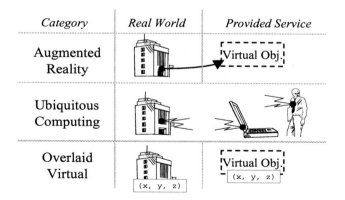

Fig. 4. Location-aware Information Systems

The first category is *augmented reality*. This concept was originally invented in contrast to *virtual reality*. While virtual reality systems just create realistic 3D computer graphics and give interactive interfaces to the graphical objects, augmented reality is intended to give strong relationship between virtual objects and real objects. Virtual objects are used to give information about real objects. Examples of typical augmented reality systems are NaviCam[4], UbiquitousLinks[2], and Augment-able Reality[5]. In their cases, special tags are attached to real objects. The systems detect these tags and retrieve related information.

The second category is *ubiquitous computing* [2]. In this category, small electronic devices are attached to real objects. The device is enabled to communicate with other devices in a wireless manner like radio waves or infrared. This type of device is also attached to portable computers or human users. They detect each other, sense surrounding situations, and give appropriate services according to the situation. Examples of this category include Cyberguide[1] and Active Badge[7].

The third category, *overlaid virtual* include the SpaceTag system and Touring Machine[3] [3]. In this architecture virtual objects have location attributes and shown at the location.

Overlaid virtual systems may be regarded as a subcategory of augmented reality, because virtual objects can give information of real objects. However, overlaid virtual systems can also be used without real objects, and its implementation is quite different from augmented reality systems. Hence we have given a new category.

An overlaid virtual model can also be illustrated as Figure 5. We assume multiple virtual worlds, which have same geometry with the real world. Objects in virtual worlds are mapped on the real world according to their positions. People in the real world can see these virtual objects with a SpaceTag-aware device.

The most important benefit of this architecture is that it is free from real object management. In case of the first two categories, small tags or devices must be attached to real objects. This fact causes the following four harmful costs proportional to the number of objects. Hence we do not think they are realistic implementation for public and open use.

1. Hardware costs of devices or tags.
2. Labor costs to attach them to real objects.
3. Management costs of real objects. Without management, devices or tags might be removed or exchanged by people who are not familiar with the system. Object ID management and maintenance are also included as the management cost.
4. Negotiation costs. Before attaching devices or tags, the system administrator should negotiate with the owner of the object.

---

[2] It may not be the correct definition of ubiquitous computing, but here we use this name to refer to this type of architecture since many ubiquitous computing systems take this architecture.

[3] In [3], they categorize Touring Machine as an augmented reality system, but we re-categorize it because it can be used without real objects.

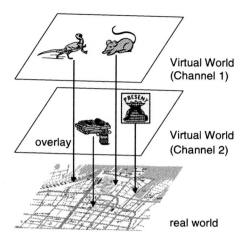

Fig. 5. Overlaid Virtual Model

There is another implementation of augmented reality systems. It recognizes real objects by pattern recognition techniques instead of detecting tags. In this case, real world object management is still necessary. System administrators should collect information about shape, color, and material of real objects.

One of the drawbacks of overlaid virtual system is that it cannot give augmented information to moving objects. However, our standpoint is that lower cost is more important than this drawback.

The difference between the overlaid virtual systems and virtual reality systems is that overlaid virtual systems are not intended to represent 3D virtual graphics realistically, for now. This fact strongly affects the system cost and portability.

Then, what is the difference between the SpaceTag system and Touring Machine? Touring Machine can be regarded as a research prototype to investigate the possibilities of user interfaces for overlaid virtual worlds. Its user interface is a heavy kind of thing including HMD, neglecting high cost and heavy weight. SpaceTag gives a basic architecture and application possibilities of overlaid virtual systems, supposing light-weight and low-cost devices. In future, Touring Machine's ideas of user interfaces will be able to be applied to the SpaceTag System, if device technologies improve them.

4.2   WWW's Complementary Media

As described in section 1, SpaceTag is the opposite of WWW in the sense that SpaceTag supports locally accessible information while WWW supports globally accessible information. However, these two can be connected and used as complementary media to each other.

If a SpaceTag's data is a URL, a person who discovered it can access to the indicated WWW page, which is also a globally accessible data for people who have already known the URL. On the other hand, we can give a WWW page that announces what kind of SpaceTag can be seen when and where, to attract more and more people.

4.3   Economical Effect

As described in section 1, SpaceTag has a potential power to lead people to go out and move. This has a positive economical effect on transportation companies, shops, restaurants, etc.

The supermarket chain store's campaign and the moving advertisement mentioned in section 3 are examples of SpaceTags used as a marketing tool.

4.4   Easy to Popularize

Imagine a city office selling portable terminals to visitors and residents to distribute city information. Few people would purchase them because application is limited. With the SpaceTag system, there are various applications. Games and other attractions are included. It is a very important point to make the system attractive and to sell SpaceTag-aware portable terminals as many people as possible.

Moreover, as stated above, SpaceTag will have positive economical effect to many kinds of industries. This means we can expect that various industries will help the popularization activities.

With all reasons described in this section, we believe that SpaceTag is the only solution as a popular, low-cost location-aware information system.

5   Social Impact

The SpaceTag system would impact on people's life and social systems. In this section, we will describe such problems and propose their solutions.

5.1   Abuse

A possible problem of SpaceTag is its abuse. Users can put slanders and slurs as SpaceTags. SPAM-like advertisements can also be placed as SpaceTags.

To avoid them, a membership system can be considered. Below is an example of membership system.

An institutional member can put SpaceTags everywhere. Examples are national and local governments, advertisement companies.

An individual member can put SpaceTags only where the member exists, but can delete SpaceTags that (s)he has put wherever (s)he is.

A non-member cannot put any SpaceTag. (S)he can read them if the SpaceTag is on a free channel.

It should be inhibited for individual members to create SpaceTags remotely, in order to avoid SPAM-like SpaceTags. Only institutional members should be allowed to create and distribute them remotely.

The SpaceTag service provider can suspend the membership of an individual member if (s)he has put slurs or other troublesome SpaceTags.

Even if a slur SpaceTag is placed, it can be seen only limited number of people. To put more SpaceTags, the malicious user must move about. Nevertheless, the SpaceTags can be easily removed by the service provider. This means that SpaceTag is a less attractive media than the Internet or physical posters, for malicious users who want to SPAM.

There is some subtle usage of SpaceTags. The communication about speed-traps mentioned in section 3 is an example. Such communication between unspecified car drivers interferes with police's business, but free communication between people should be protected. As well as communication on the Internet, communication with SpaceTag should be discussed further from various viewpoints.

The membership system is also beneficial from the viewpoint of the service provider's business. For example, the service provider can propose membership ranks. Highly ranked members who pay high membership fee would be able to access and put more SpaceTags than usual members.

5.2   Right to Attach Tags

As described in 4.1, one of the advantages of SpaceTag is that augmented information can be attached on a physical object without negotiation with the owner of the object. However, this may cause another kind of troubles. Can the owner request for the SpaceTag service provider to remove the SpaceTag?

For example, assume a case that a SpaceTag advertising a steak restaurant is placed at a building whose owner is a vegetarian. This case will happen if the building is at the center of the area where the restaurant's owner wants to advertise. The building's owner does not suffer any damage, but (s)he just want to remove the SpaceTag from his/her place, because (s)he simply do not like it. However, the SpaceTag is not physically attached to the building. To solve this kind of problems, a new law system to deal with SpaceTag is expected in future.

5.3   Communication or Broadcast?

Does the SpaceTag system belong to the category of communication or broadcast? If it belongs to communication, the privacy of communication should be protected by law. If it belongs to broadcast, the broadcasting company, the service provider in this case, should guarantee the quality of contents.

It seems that the SpaceTag system is a kind of broadcast since unspecified people can view the contents. On the other hand, it seems to be a kind of communication, because it is similar to ham radio.

As well known, Web pages have a same kind of problem. A Web page is authored by individuals, distributed by a service provider through the Internet. However, the provider does not guarantee the quality of the contents, at least prior to distribution.

A SpaceTag is very similar to a poster on a bulletin board, but posters are neither communication nor broadcast, from the viewpoint of law. It seems very strange. Hence we expect a new law system, again.

5.4   Location Sensor Infrastructure

Our prototype uses GPS as the location sensor. PHS can also be a candidate of location sensor. However, both have disadvantages. GPS cannot be used underground or in buildings. PHS provides only rough data. Both are weak in providing the Z-axis location data. It is difficult to know on which floor in a building a user is.

We propose that a digital city should provide a universal location identifying system for SpaceTag and other location-aware information systems. It is low cost. It can be implemented only by installing cheap beacons at places where above problems occur. What a beacon should do is only to radiate a constant location data around it.

6   Conclusion and Future Work

In this paper, we have described the function and architecture of the SpaceTag system, presented its possible application services, and discussed its impacts on our life and social systems.

We are now developing a next version of the SpaceTag system. A SpaceTag will be more object-oriented, in the sense that it will have methods to process events and that it will be able to send messages to other SpaceTags and users. Examples of events are receiving messages from other SpaceTags or users, timer events, and location events.

Adopting these features, we will be able to provide new kinds of applications. For example, a SpaceTag can be made look like a pet. We call it "SpacePet." A SpacePet moves about a city, communicate with other pets and other users, and returns to the owner and reports what it has experienced. Different from other virtual worlds, SpacePet may meet other users who do not know much about the SpacePet system. A SpacePet also may find other SpaceTags that are related to the real society. Hence SpacePets and SpaceTags will be bridges between virtual and real world.

We believe that SpaceTag's overlaid virtual architecture is a promising candidate of digital city's location-aware information service, due to its low cost and easiness of popularization. We welcome proposals from companies or city governments to implement the SpaceTag system in a large scale.

Acknowledgments

The authors are grateful to Mr. Megumi Nakano, for his contribution in developing the SpaceTag prototype.

References

1. Abowd, G.D., et al.: Cyberguide: A mobile context-aware tour guide. Wireless Networks, **3** (1997) 421–433
2. Ayatsuka, Y., et al.: UbiquitousLinks: Hypermedia Links Embedded in the Real World. IPSJ SIGHI Notes, Information Processing Society of Japan, (1996) 96-HI-67 (in Japanese)
3. Feiner, S. et al.: A Touring Machine: Prototyping 3D Mobile Augmented Reality Systems for Exploring the Urban Environment. Proceedings of IEEE International Symposium on Wearable Computing '97 (1997), 74–81
4. Rekimoto, J. and Nagao, K.: The World through the Computer. Computer Augmented Interaction with Real World Environments. Proceedings of the ACM Symposium on User Interface Software and Technology (UIST'95), (1995) 29–36
5. Rekimoto J., et al.: Augment-able Reality: Situated Communication through Physical and Digital Spaces. Proceedings IEEE International Symposium on Wearable Computing '98, (1998) 68–75
6. Tarumi, H., Morishita, K., Nakao, M., and Kambayashi, Y.: SpaceTag: An Overlaid Virtual System and its Application. Proceedings of International Conference on Multimedia Computing and Systems (ICMCS'99) **1** (1999) 207–212
7. Weiser, M.: The Computer for the 21st Century. Scientific American (Sep. 1991), 66–75

Location Oriented Integration of Internet Information - Mobile Info Search -

Katsumi Takahashi[1], Seiji Yokoji[1], and Nobuyuki Miura[2]

[1] NTT Information Sharing Platform Laboratories,
Nippon Telegraph and Telephone Corporation
3-9-11, Midori-cho, Musashino-Shi, Tokyo, 180-8585 Japan
takahashi.katsumi@lab.ntt.co.jp, yokoji.seiji@lab.ntt.co.jp
[2] NTT DoCoMo Multimedia Laboratories,
3-5, Hikarinooka, Yokosuka, Kanagawa, 239-8536, Japan
miura@mml.yrp.nttdocomo.co.jp

Abstract. Information on the Internet is becoming more attractive and useful for our daily life. It provides things on the town, happenings on the city, and learning of the real world. If we can utilize such information for the interaction between the human and the city, it can enhance the value and the function of the city. In this paper we introduce the research project *"Mobile Info Search"* in which we study the method of integrating heterogeneous information in a location-oriented way for providing it in a handy form with mobile computing. We have a prototype of *Mobile Info Search* at *http://www.kokono.net/*, a location-based "search engine". Local information such as yellow pages, maps, and relevant Web pages at any location of Japan are provided with a simple interface. From the analysis of test services, we will discuss the user issues and information source issues; What kind of local information is welcomed? What can we learn from collected documents? Through the experience of handling various contents related to the real-world, we describe the potential of the Internet information for the digital city efforts.

1   Introduction

Not only for researches and businesses, information on the Internet is becoming useful for our daily life today. There is much attractive information available. It includes restaurant guides, local maps, public transportation, and weather reports. Moreover, due to the progress of the mobile computing, we can access to the Internet even when we are not in offices or home. We can use Internet just at the city. We think the function of the city is to provide the information and the marketplace for any activities. Though we can get rich information directly from the city, the Internet information from the each constituents of the city has a potential to enhance the value and the function of the city. That what we think about the digital city. A methodology and a service for utilizing such information from the Internet is required for our coming digital city.

This research is to study the computing methodology of overlapping the real world and the information from the network. If we can apply these ideas to the

T. Ishida, K. Isbister (Eds.): Digital Cities, LNCS 1765, pp. 364–377, 2000.

interaction between the real world and us, we can know more about the world and the city. If we use information on the Internet before we go to the city, we will be able to have more chance to find the city deeply. If we use it just on the city using mobile computing, we can know more about the things on the city. For these targets, one goal is to compile the "personalized digital guidebook" automatically from the Internet resources. Commercially there can be a portal site (the server which provides the index to enter the Internet) services for mobile users. And furthermore, not only using but also supplying and sending local information from each user to others relevant to the location, the open space for sharing the local information can be created.

Mobile Info Search is the name of our research project and an Internet based application[1]. The goal of *Mobile Info Search* is to study the location-oriented computing. We now concentrate to integrate local information existing on the Internet into a handy form especially for mobile-computing users. *Mobile Info Search* is characterized by the usage of "location information". Location information represents the geographical position or the area of the information in the form of address strings, longitude-latitude, landmarks,... etc. *Mobile Info Search* uses the location information of Internet resources for information integration. So the location of the mobile user and the location handling such as extraction and transformation of the information source play important role. We call this integration "location-oriented information integration".

Mobile Info Search was implemented experimentally on the Internet in 1997 and has been open to the public since then. Our prototype *Mobile Info Search* service is at *http://www.kokono.net/*[1]. It provides local information ("kokono" information in Japanese) about shops, maps, the weather, transportation, etc.

In this paper we first describe an outline of *Mobile Info Search* in section 2, and two features; *Location-Oriented Meta Search* and *Location-Oriented Robot-Based Search* in section 3 and 4. In section 5 and 6 we discuss the results from the experiment. After a look at related work, we conclude with a summary.

2   Mobile Info Search

2.1   Local Information on the Internet

On the Internet, we can find information related to a certain location. It describes about shops, towns, and sights on the location or about the region itself. We call it "local information" in this article. *Mobile Info Search* uses such resources existing on the Internet.

Most local information today is divided into two types by their stored forms. Database type and static file type. Examples of database-type resources provided on the Internet are shown in Table. 1. They are provided through the CGI program of the WWW server. The access method and the use of location information is vary for each services. A mediation service for these resources is described in the section 3 of *Location-Oriented Meta Search*.

---

[1] see *http://www.kokono.net/english/* for English

Table 1. Database-type resources on the Internet

Services	Location information used for the search
Maps	longitude-latitude
Yellow Pages	address (and categories,... etc)
Train Time Tables	station
Weather Reports	address or region
Hotel Guides	nearest station

Another type of local information is the static file. A manual analysis of static files is show in Table.2. We investigated the existence of Japanese address string for 100 files obtained randomly from the Internet. About 25% of files contains address strings. An automatic method of collecting and structuring these files are described in the section 4 of *Location-Oriented Robot-based Search*.

Table 2. Ratio of the files which contain address strings

Prefecture	City	Town	Chome[2]	Total (any address)
10.7%	13.7%	8.0%	4.0%	24.7%

2.2 Mobile Info Search

A goal of *Mobile Info Search* is to provide local information from the Internet by collecting, structuring, organizing, and filtering in a practicable form. To utilize such local information, *Mobile Info Search* employs a mediator architecture; a software agent between users and the information sources. The architecture of *Mobile Info Search* is shown in Fig. 1. Between users and information sources, *Mobile Info Search* mediates Database-type resources using *Location-Oriented Meta Search* and static files using *Location-Oriented Robot-based Search*. To use *Mobile Info Search*, only Internet connectable PDSs or PCs with Web browsers are required for users. Additionally if the user have a PHS or GPS unit, the user location is automatically obtained [2].

3   Location-Oriented Meta Search

Location-Oriented Meta Search provides a mediation service for database-type resources. It provides a simple interface for local information services which have various search interfaces. Only to select the service such as the maps or the

---

[2] "Chome" is a block number of the town. Japanese addressing method is Prefecture, City, Town, "Chome", "Banchi" (smaller block no.), "Go" (house no.)

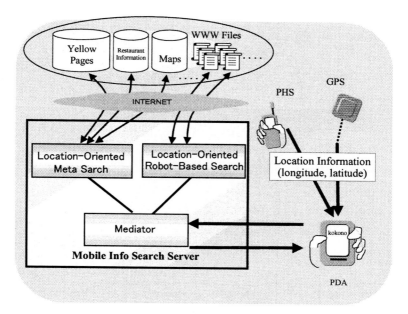

Fig. 1. An architecture of *Mobile Info Search*

yellow pages, users can get information of the location easily from each server. The architecture of *Location-Oriented Meta Search* is shown in Fig. 2.

Search Controller converts the location information and picks the suitable *Wrapper* for the requested service. Both location information from the user and for the information sources are in various form. It can be address strings, longitude-latitude, postal-codes, or landmarks. The *Controller* converts the user location into the location information suitable for the target using the *Location Information Repository*. The repository we constructed on *Mobile Info Search* is the set of location information that can convert each format to others. The *Wrapper* is a software prepared manually for each services. The access method, the request form, and the usage of local information of the target is defined.

Location-Oriented Meta Search performs in following way;

1. to receive user location (longitude latitude) and the name of the target service

   ex. $(x = 139.36.27, y = 35.25.24, target = AYellowPages)$
2. to converts the user location into the location suitable form for the target using *Location Information Repository*

   ex. $(x = 139.36.27, y = 35.25.24) \rightarrow address = "Tokyo, Chuo - ku, Ginza 4"$
3. to determine the search scope of the location for the target

   ex. $"Tokyo", or "Tokyo, Chuo - ku", or "Tokyo, Chuo - ku, Ginza", ...?$
4. to create a query

   ex. $http://www.AYellowPages....co.jp/seach.cgi?address = "Tokyo, Chuo - ku, Ginza 4"$
5. to search

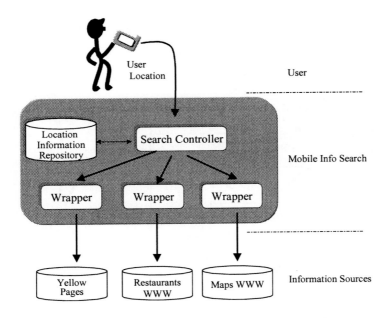

User
Location

User

Location
Information
Repository

Search Controller

Mobile Info Search

Wrapper   Wrapper   Wrapper

Yellow
Pages

Restaurants
WWW

Maps WWW

Information Sources

Fig. 2. An architecture of *Location-Oriented Meta Search*

4   Location-Oriented Robot-Based Search "kokono Search"

4.1   What Is kokono Search

In this section, we introduce the *Location-Oriented Robot-Based Search* called *kokono Search.* "kokono" is a Japanese word means here. *kokono Search* provides the spatial search that searches the document close to a location. Just like other search engines, *kokono Search* employs a software called "robot" that collects documents from the Internet and creates local database for collected documents. While other search engines provide a keyword-based search, *kokono Search* do a location-based spatial search. It displays documents in the order of the distance between the location of the document and the user's location. Fig. 3 illustrates the architecture of *kokono Search.* A brief flow of *kokono Search* described below.

1. to create a location oriented database
   - *Location-Oriented Information Collecting Robot* collects documents from the Internet
   - *Location-Oriented Structuring Parser* parses the obtained document to look up the location information (address strings) and store the documents with the spatial information (longitude-latitude) by consulting the *Location Information repository*

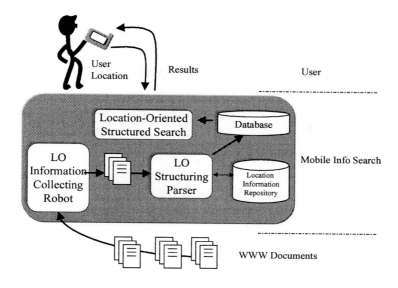

Fig. 3. An architecture *kokono Search*

2. to perform a search
   - to search documents within the distance from the requested location
   - to display the documents in order of the distance

4.2 How to Collect Local Information

Our robot is a special one to collect local information selectively. The ability of *Location-Oriented Information Collecting Robot* is shown in Fig. 4. *Location-Oriented Robot* employs the heuristics to calculate the collection priority. The priority for the uncollected document is determined by estimating the resource is the local information or not. It is estimated local information, if the link letters contain the address strings . For the starting period of collection, this robot works more effective than the normal breadth-first collection robot.

4.3 How to Structure the Local Information

To put the spatial information such as longitude-latitude to the document for the spatial search, we parse the documents to look for the location information. Location information can be address strings, station names, landmarks (ex. "Tokyo Tower"), or postal-codes. In this subsection we describe the extraction of address strings.

We extracted the address strings by following way. There are two major difficulties for address strings extraction; the writing variation and the ambiguity to the other nouns (person's name). We used several heuristics of the address strings.

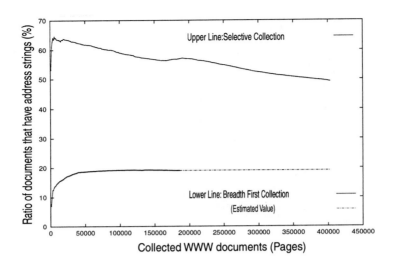

Fig. 4. Comparison between the selective information collection by *Location-Oriented robot* and the breadth first collection

1. to divide document into morphemes by the Japanese text parser
2. to compare noun phrase to the address dictionary (part of *Location Information Repository*) and regard it as an address if it satisfies the following conditions
   - any address strings without omitting the upper address, or
   - cities with address suffix (ex. Yokohama "Shi" (=City)), or
   - towns or block numbers with the city name
   - block numbers with the upper town and city name and meets the street numbers patterns (pattern ex. "1-Chome 2", "1-2", "1 2", ...)

5 Mobile Info Search: An Experimental Service

Mobile Info Search is open to the public on the Internet since 1997. From the address *http://www.kokono.net/* , anyone can enjoy the *Location-Oriented Meta Search* and *kokono Search*. When user access to the *Mobile Info Search*, the index page of the location is displayed (Fig. 5). About 20 WWW services, provided by the courtesy of 8 companies are available. They include following; *kokono Search*, Yellow Pages and Restaurants guide under the Shops information, several maps, train tables, hotel guides and reservations, weather reports, and TV listings. From January to July 1999 about 500 searches a day to some services are done. Fig. 6 shows the *kokono Search* results displayed on the map.

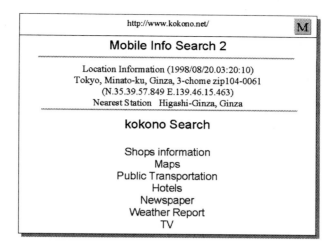

Fig. 5. Index page of *Mobile Info Search*. This page is automatically displayed by accessing *Mobile Info Search*. User's current location is displayed as the address, the longitude-latitude, and the nearest station on the top of the page. *kokono Search* and other seven categories follow. Services for the external sites are requested by selecting the services categorized into the seven menus.

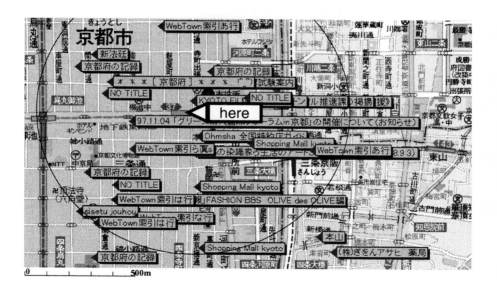

Fig. 6. *kokono Search* results at the Kyoto City Hall. Web pages are automatically located and can be retrieved geographically. All results can be displayed on the map. This is the search result of the Web pages within about 700m of Kyoto City Hall. This map is by ProAtlas (c).

6   Experimental Results

6.1   How They Used the Local Information? -Search Analysis-

We analyzed the user's searches from the log files recorded on the server. We used 39,718 complete searches for analysis from the log files from January to July of 1999.

6.2   Search Trends in General

Classification of all searches requested to *Mobile Info Search* is illustrates on the in Fig. 7. Map is the most requested category of *Mobile Info Search*. Note that the frequency of the request can depend on the user interface. As the map button is located at the third position of the menu and not in highlighted position, map is the basic service for the local information services. Transportation category represents the information about the rail-way station including the time table of the train. This demand reflects the Japanese living style.

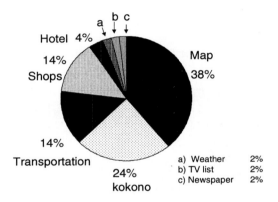

Fig. 7. Search trend of *Mobile Info Search*

6.3   Search Session Analysis

We divided searches into "sessions". We defined a session that a session is a set of searches from one person for one location in succession. If the interval of two searches was less than 3 minutes, they were regarded in succession. 39,718 searches were divided into 20,080 sessions. In about 40% of sessions, plural searches such as map and *kokono Search* are requested together and the average search of plural session is 3.44 times per session (Table. 3). Though this is a open WWW service and user may be a first-time, it is not easy to make users request plural services continuously. A sophisticated and concise way of integrating information from plural source into one screen is required.

Table 3. Session trend of *Mobile Info Search*

	sessions	searches/session
single search	12,047	1.00
plural searches	8,033	3.44
total	20,080	1.98

6.4   Is Digital City Created? -Data Analysis-

We analyzed about half million (479,669) documents collected for *kokono Search* by our robot and found about 40 % (210,369) of documents contained address strings (Table 4). As some documents contains more than one addresses, we collected 1,122,380 total addresses.

The collection rate for addresses is shown in Table. 5. We collected almost every cities, 30.3% of towns, and 6.8% of Chome level addresses of Japan.

Collecting some deeper addresses from the Web pages is not a easy matter. Because some Chome or deeper level addresses are used only for describing the location for personal houses, they may not appear on the Internet.

Table 4. Numbers of collected documents

		Prefecture	City	Town	Chome (Block #)	Total
Documents that have addresses	(A)	210,369	151,272	68,381	32,755	[3]210,369
Addresses collected total	(B)	418,488	501,992	117,066	88,926	1,122,380
Addresses per documents	(B/A)	2.0	3.2	1.6	2.6	5.3

Table 5. Collection rate of documents for Japanese addresses

		Prefecture	City	Town	Chome
All addresses in Japan[4]	(A)	47	3,883	121,172	343,269
Addresses collected unique	(B)	47	3,876	36,799	23,326
Collection rate	(B/A)	100 %	99.8%	30.3%	6.8%

Fig. 8 illustrates the distribution of the local information we collected. This map is drawn only by plotting the longitude-latitude we put to the each docu-

---

[3] As some document contains different level addresses together (ex. City and Town), total value is less than the sum of City, Town, and Chome

[4] from the Address Code Table published under the Ministry of Home Affairs

ments (210,369 documents). This map shows that the location described on the WWW reflects the population distribution.

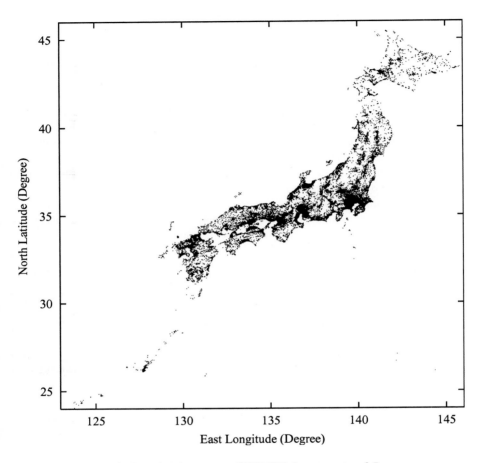

Fig. 8. A distribution map of WWW documents of Japan

Fig. 9 shows the relationship between the populations and the number of Web pages of the prefecture. The dots represent all the 47 prefectures in Japan. We divided Web pages that have addresses (City, Town, Chome) into 47 prefectures they belong to. From the figure, there is a correlation between them. It is interesting that Hokkaido and Kyoto have many famous tourist cities. Nagano is famous for Olympic game. On the other hand, Saitama and Chiba are "bed-towns" of Tokyo and it is said most cities are common ones.

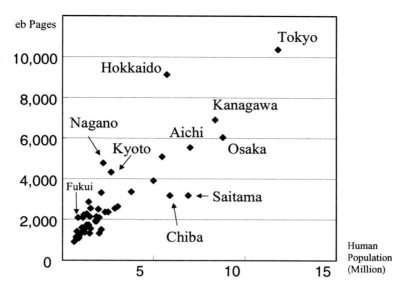

Fig. 9. Relation between human populations and Web pages

7   Related Work

We will mention our related work from the point of information search services and information mediators.

For years, the role of supplement tools for finding something in the city has been left to books or newspapers. Internet has become a useful tool for the city since around the mid '90s. At first, it started as a searching tools / sources. Digital maps including car navigation systems and Yellow Pages services are ones of the pioneers. Our series of real-world related studies started as development of a Yellow Pages server (Internet TOWNPAGE *itp.ne.jp*) since 1995. Succeeding the growth of the real-world related contents, we have been studying information retrieval for mobile users. Intelligent Page [3] was our first effort. We intended software agents to retrieve information from the diverse resources on behalf of the user. Our next effort, Action Navigator [4] used a "recommender architecture" [5] based on the choices made by other users.

Today the activity in this area is distinguished as a "local portal sites" commercially. They collect and organize local information and provide local advertisements. Sidewalk (*sidewalk.com*), Yahoo Get Local (*local.yahoo.com*), and DigitalCity (*digitalcity.com*) are examples.

Our work is based on the work of others.

The idea of overlapping the real world and the information from the network is studied in the field of mobile computing and augmented reality[6][7].

Mediator [8] is a middle-ware service between end users and data resources. It integrates diverse data from multiple sources, reduces it to the appropriate level, and restructures the results. TSIMMIS [9][10] and I3[11] are the major mediation research projects.

There are several Internet-based research applications similar to *Mobile Info Search*. MetaCrawler [12] is a parallel WWW search service. It provides a single interface to the user, collects the results from various search engines, and organizes the results. Bargain Finder [13] and Shopbot [14] both find products by using servers and compare the prices and specification. These research efforts are close to *Mobile Info Search* in their motivations and goals; *Mobile Info Search* differs in its Location-Oriented information structuring and organizing.

In the research field of the digital city, several similar efforts are found. "Helsinki Arena 2000"[15] is the project that augments a real city to a three-dimensional virtual one. "Digital City Kyoto"[16] also tries to reproduce the real city and to create the a social information infrastructure on it. Both projects take the real and virtual world to be tightly linked and the virtual one to be a infrastructure of the city. We believe *Mobile Info Search* and these projects work together to realize the digital city.

8   Conclusion

We introduced Mobile Info Search. Location-Oriented Information Integration is the key word of our project. To support the interaction between the human and the city, the real-world, we are studying the method that integrates useful local information existing much on the Internet in a Location-Oriented way. We described out current two methods, *Location-Oriented Meta Search* and *Location-Oriented Robot-Based Search*. And also described about the experimental results from the test service on the *http://www.kokono.net/*.

Our approach for the Digital City effort is from the side of information retrieval and search. We can feel the city by searching local information on the net. Such information will be growing and may change their forms and roles. We will follow it by studying the technique for processing local-information sources and learn the city by looking the real-world and information together.

References

1. Takahashi, K., Miura, N., Sakamoto, H., Shima, K.: Location Oriented Information Integration. In Proc. Japan World Wide Web Conference '97, http://www.iaj.or.jp/w3conf-japan/97/ (1997)
2. Takahashi, K., Miura, N., Yokoji, S., Shima, K.: Mobile Info Search: Information Integration for Location-Aware Computing. In Proc. IPSJ SIGMBL http://www.kokono.net/~ takahasi/articles.html (1998)
3. Takahashi,K., Nishibe,Y., Morihara,I., Hattori,F.: Intelligent Pages: Collecting Shop and Service Information with Software Agents. Applied Artificial Intelligence Intl. J., Vol. 11, No. 6, Taylor & Francis (1997) 489-499
4. Ohtsubo, R., Nishibe, Y., Takahashi,K.,Morihara,I.: Action Navigator: an Information Service Based on Agent-Communication for Supporting Decision-Making. In Proc. PAAM98 (1998) 629-630

5. Resnick,P., Varian,H.R.: Recommender Systems. CACM, Vol.40, No.3 (1997) 56-58
6. Wellner. P., Mackay, W.E., Gold, R.: Computer-Augmented Environments: Back to the Real World. CACM Vol.36, No.7 (1993) 24-26
7. Nagao, K., Rekimoto, J.: Agent Augmented Reality: A Software Agent Meets the Real World. In Proc. the Second Intl. Conf. on Multi-Agent Systems (ICMAS-96) (1996) 228-235
8. Wiederhold, G.: Interoperation, Mediation, and Ontologies. FGCS '94 Workshop on Heterogeneous Cooperative Knowledge-Base, (1994) 33-48
9. Hammer, J., et al.: Information Translation, Mediation, and Mosaic-Based Browsing in the TSIMMIS System. ACM SIGMOD Intl. Conf. Management of Data (1995)
10. TSIMMIS: The Stanford-IBM Manager of Multiple Information Sources (TSIMMIS). http://www-db.stanford.edu/tsimmis/ (1998)
11. Gunning,D.: Intelligent Integration of Information Technology (I3). http://maco.dc.isx.com/iso/battle/i3.html (1997)
12. Selberg,E., Etzioni,O.: The MetaCrawler Architecture for Resource Aggregation on the Web. IEEE Expert, Volume 12 No. 1 (1997) 8-14
13. Krulwich, B.: Bargain finder agent prototype. Technical report. Anderson Consulting. http://bf.cstar.ac.com/bf/ (1995)
14. Doorenbos, R., Etzioni, O., and Weld: A Scalable Comparison-Shopping Agent for the World-Wide Web. Autonomous Agents '97 (1997)
15. Linturi, R., Koivunen, M. R., Sulkanen, J.: Helsinki Arena 2000: Augmenting a Real City to a Virtual One. Lecture Notes in Computer Science (in this volume), Springer-Verlag (2000)
16. Ishida, T., et al.: Digital City Kyoto: Towards A Social Information Infrastructure. Cooperative Information Agents III, Lecture Notes in Artificial Intelligence, Vol. 1652, Springer-Verlag (1999) 23-35

Fairy in a Smart IC Card: Interfacing People, Town, and Digital City

Takao Terano[1], Toshikazu Nishimura[2], Yoko Ishino[3], and Eiji Murakami[1]

[1] University of Tsukuba,
3-29-1, Otsuka, Bunkyo-ku, Tokyo   112-0012, Japan
Tel:+81-3-3942-6855   Fax:+81-3-3942-6829
{terano, murakami}@gssm.otsuka.tsukuba.ac.jp

[2] Ritsumeikan University,
1-1-1, Nojihigashi, Kusatsu, Shiga 525-8577, Japan
Tel:+81-77-561-4971   Fax:+81-77-561-2669
nisimura@cs.ritsumei.ac.jp

[3] RCAST, University of Tokyo.,
4-6-1 Komaba, Meguro-ku, Tokyo   153-8904, Japan
Tel:+81-3-3481-4486   Fax:+81-3-3481-4585
ishino@ai.rcast.u-tokyo.ac.jp

Abstract. The performance of recent smart IC cards is equal to the one of mi-cro-computers about twenty years ago. Using the functions of smart IC cards, this paper proposes Fairy-Wing: yet another mobile computing system for community computing in a digital city. The system aims at supporting personal information management, information services, and dynamic collaborative fil-tering in order to interface the people, towns, and digital cities. The main fea-tures of the system are that (1) the agents or fairies are small, cheap, and easy-to-use; (2) they are fully distributed among ubiquitous computing environ-ments with and/or without computer networks; and (3) holder-centered infor-mation controlling mechanisms. The application candidates in digital cities in-clude travel navigation, collaborative education, and electronic commerce. This paper discusses the system architecture, feasibility of applications, Group Trip Advisor: a prototype of Fairy-Wing, and future issues.

1   Introduction

Current digital cities [10] on the web usually have only one-way communication routes from virtual worlds to visitors and/or citizens, although people in a digital city should both communicate each other and affect their behaviors and desires to daily life activities. To make such activities easier, we must have new systems to interface people, physical towns, and digital cities. Flexible and reasonable personal data as-sistant systems must be developed. The systems require ubiquitous information serv-

T. Ishida, K. Isbister (Eds.): Digital Cities, LNCS 1765, pp. 378-390, 2000.
© Springer-Verlag Berlin Heidelberg 2000

ices, ease of use with friendly user interfaces, and privacy control mechanisms. Our proposal in this paper aims at satisfying these requirements.

Recent cellular phone systems with web access functions (e.g., I-mode service in Japan) or personal data assistant (PDA) systems with communication capabilities seem to meet the requirements. However, to deploy the systems, we usually assume the following conditions: (1) Every individual in a digital city must have *expensive* personal equipments such as PDAs; (2) The digital city must have large scale *central* servers in order to maintain end user information management systems; and (3) They also must maintain central servers to provide information via *communication networks*.

In this paper, we would like to reexamine the assumptions and propose Fairy-Wing: yet-another mobile information system. The basic idea is that we should utilize smart IC cards [6]. The performance of recent smart IC cards has become powerful enough to be used as simple PDAs with small programs. We call these small programs or agents as Fairies. We use the word Fairy, because the programs in the card are small agent-based ones and the card itself is portable, and cute for users

Fairies are small, cheap, and easy-to-use for naïve users. Fairies are always accompanied with the card-holders or citizens in a digital city and support their communication activities among personal PCs at home and information terminals in towns. They will support the tasks of personal information management, information services, and dynamic collaborative filtering with other citizens. Fairy-Wing is a fully distributed system among ubiquitous computing environments with and/or without computer networks.

This paper is organized as follows: In Section 2, we describe the background, motivation, and objectives of the system. In Section 3, we show the architecture and application candidates of the proposed system. In Section 4, we demonstrate the function of our small prototype: Group Trip Advisor. In Section 5, we give some discussion on the applicability and future issues, and In section 6, concluding remarks are given.

2   Background and Objectives

In this section, we will describe the background, motivation, and objectives of Fairy-Wing from the viewpoint of social requirements [10], [13], [17], hardware and software technology and IC card systems [6], [12], [18], and software technology on agent-based systems[3], [11], [15], [17], [19].

2.1 Requirements for Digital Cities

Systems in a digital city must have the functions of live information providing, electronic commerce, and community formation. However, in the current digital cities, they do not work well. The information on the web is biased and the search engines are not smart. The numbers of customers in digital malls is, at least in Japan, not large and there few charming consumer goods there. Good relationship among the citizens hardly emerges. To cope with these problems, we must examine the following three issues intrinsic in the state-of-the-art digital cities.

Issue 1: The first issue is the skills and the cost of computer equipments. About even recent small personal data assistants, they are too difficult and too expensive for those who are not familiar with PCs. Although the unlimited logical boundaries of virtual spaces in a digital city, there exist physical and mental restrictions among people in digital city. The barriers are much higher than the ones in physical towns, because they cannot directly touch, speak, nor hear with the other persons without computers and networks. They are required to have the skills to retrieve computers and bare costs to have them.

Issue 2: The second issue is the management of a lot of information about the towns and people. In order to make the life smooth, they must maintain large databases in a digital city. First category of the databases is about resources of the digital city. The resource databases must be frequently updated when new stuff is introduced. Of course, catalog and logistic information about commercial goods must be maintained. Second category of the databases is about personal information. They must collect, manage, and provide their personal information. The cost to maintain the information will become too high, even if the local government will control them.

Issue 3: The third issue is security and privacy problems. It is repeatedly reported that companies participated in electronic commerce pay much cost to maintain customer databases, however, there still remain security halls among them. As is stated in [12], there are a delicate balance between protecting privacy of citizens and facilitating the sharing information. Therefore, if a good community will emerge in a digital city, user-centered information control mechanism would be essential.

In summary, information systems in a digital city must cope with the problems: (1) cost and ease-to-use, (2) information management, and (3) security and privacy. To meet the requirements, It is desirable to develop distributed cooperative systems to support personal information management, information service, and dynamic collaborative filtering.

2.2 Smart IC Card System

The smart IC card is a plastic card with an embedded microprocessor silicon chip. To date, it is reported that over one billion smart card have been issued [6]. The main purposes of the IC cards have been limited to e-cashes including advanced credit card or davit card systems, storaging personal information such as health care, and e-tickets for traveling in everyday life. However, the research and development works is too concentrated into security issues and has not attempted to utilize the ability of the smart IC cards as computers, which corresponds to the ones of micro computers twenty years, ago.

Figure 1 illustrates a typical smart IC card, which is used our prototype system described below. The IC card is a thin- non-contact type one recently provided by HITACHI. The IC card is equipped with an 8 bit microprocessor unit, 512 byte RAM, 16 k-byte ROM, and 8 k-byte EEPROM. The information in the card is transported to/from PCs with a reader/writer equipment.

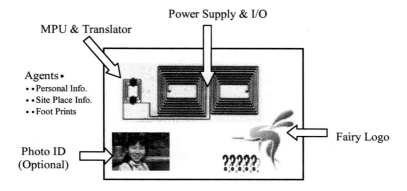

Figure 1.   Illustration of Smart IC Used in Group Trip Advisor

The card is also energized by the electromagnetic induction principle via the reader/writer equipment. The reader/writer is connected with conventional PCs via the RS-232C port. The IC card is processed via interfacing modules in a PC, and thus, handled by conventional programming systems including C++.

The current costs of the IC card and the reader/writer are respectively about 10-20 US$ and 100-200 US$. Thus, from both computation and cost viewpoints, the performance of smart IC card systems is between conventional magnetic cards and conventional personal data assistants. It is reasonable to deploy these IC cards to the citizens and PCs with the reader/writers.

2.3   Coping with the Issues of Information Systems via Smart IC Card

Using the functions of the smart IC card, we think we can overcome the issues discussed above on the information systems in a digital city. The system consists of personal information in the IC card, information services in PCs with and/or without networks, and pointers to the resources of digital cities. We also assume that there exist ubiquitous information terminals in the physical towns and that sufficient information for daily life is available in the digital city. These assumptions are natural to interface people and towns in a digital city.

About **Issue 1**, our approach is that (1) we provide the digital city with holders' personal information within the IC card, and (2) fully distributed systems are developed to compensate the defects of current PDAs and information terminals by integrating both personal and public information. Current PDAs are more flexible than the PCs, because they are fully personalized for the holders. On the other hand, information terminals in a digital city can have much more powerful user interfaces than the ones of current PDAs with a small display and narrow communication channels. Using the personal information in the IC card, according to the context, situation and desire of the users, we can control the functions of a digital city.

About **Issue 2**, we think that our systems will work without central personal information databases and any specific information control mechanisms in the center. End users are responsible with their personal information and usages of the digital city. Fairies contain sufficient personal information to access the services of the digital cities. Thus, users or card-holders can actively control the availability or privacy of the personal information. For example, users can mask any personal information depending on the features of target applications. Fairies will also contain footprints or recent access records to the applications. These footprint information can be used as bookmarks to get services provided by the digital city. The information can be used as the key to directly access the desired information on stand-alone type information terminal. This reduces the development cost on information services among digital cities. For example, users can access the appropriate information of digital cities while moving around the corresponding physical towns.

About **Issue 3**, our policy is that holder centered control mechanisms are essential. Fairies containing personal information are fully distributed. Thus, comparing with the centralized personal database systems, they can avoid complex management tasks for personal information. Users must be responsible with their own information. It will be a desirable feature of the activities of a digital city, if the activities are governed via bottom up manner. As the personal information is contained in Fairies, under the holders' control, they can be dynamically integrated in the information terminals. This enables citizens to support community formation tasks via collaborative filtering. Conventional filtering algorithms usually assume that very large amount of data is available in the analysis and, therefore, the algorithm must be kept simple in order to handle the large data in time. As fairy-based systems will dynamically analyze small amount of the data on user access information, we can implement sophisticated algorithms.

3   Architecture of Fairy Wing

This section describes the architecture of Fairy Wing and the feasibility of the systems.

3.1 System Components and How They Work

The proposed system consists of (1) Smart Cards with fairies for storing and managing personal information, (2) Ubiquitous information terminals with an IC card reader/writer, and (3) Distributed information space of digital cities, which do not necessarily assume the existence of centralized data warehouses nor communication networks. Figure 2 shows the conceptual architecture of Fairy Wing. In the subsequent sections, we will describe the features of each component.

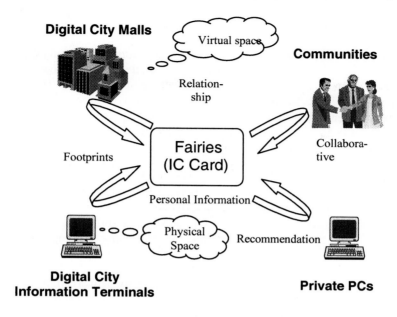

Figure 2. Architecture of the Proposed System

3.2 Smart IC Cards

Fairy Wing cards are flexible, easy-to-use, and cheap mobile terminals corresponding to conventional PDAs. The cards contain (1) the security information, or the ping number of card-holders, (2) personal information, which can be masked per data item by users in order to conceal or reveal the individual information, (3) footprints of the user, which maintain past records of activities in a digital city, and (4) local information, which must be transferred among information terminals. If necessary, each fairy can be transferred into conventional personal data assistant systems or their own PCs. Furthermore, the shape of the equipments with fairies can be designed in any shapes and forms, for example, they can be like a notebook page, leaflet, button, and/or any wearable style. However, we consider the IC card is a good form, because of the portability and the cost requirements.

All information in the cards is under control of the card-holder, thus, he or she must be responsible for managing and maintaining it. For users' convenience and avoidance of loosing damages, the contents of the IC cards can be freely copied only by the card-holder. When the card-holder loose his or her cards, immediately he or she can distribute the information that the card is no more valid among the digital city. This is easily attained by accessing ubiquitous information terminals. Only the user can do is to inform the specific card ID to the digital city. Then the information will be immediately distributed to the whole city.

3.3 Information Terminals

The users interact with a digital city via ubiquitous information terminals, which should be equipped with easy-to-use and look-and-feel interfaces for naïve users (for example, touch screens and voice information guidance are desirable). They have a reader/writer for IC cards. The users start the session by inserting their IC cards to the reader/writer. When Fairy-Wings are inserted into the terminals, the terminal will show the most appropriate information to the user based on the stored information in the terminal and the footprints on the Fairy Wing.

To deploy the terminals, the following functions must be implemented: (1) User identification and privacy control to manage whether which information will be concealed or revealed; (2) Utilities to let the users retrieve, modify, and copy the contents of the Fairy Wing; (3) Communication and storing of user information, (4) Collaborative filtering for user community formation; (5) Information recommendations based on users' profiles, the context, and the information contents of a digital city.

The information terminals are basically client systems connected with information servers in the digital city. However, they are not necessarily networked, if the terminals have enough information for the current users. This is because the fairies contain footprint information, so that the information providing task can be performed in standalone type terminals. This capability will reduce the cost of the system deployment.

3.4 Information Space

The users of Fairy Wing connect the digital city based on the information of fairies and information terminals. In the information space, dynamic filtering [11] and data mining mechanisms [7] will generate appropriate recommendation to the users. These mechanisms will be of use for relationship marketing in e-commerce and community formation among citizens.

Fairy-Wings are used both in virtual and physical information spaces. For example, in the virtual space shown in a private PC, users can explore digital city malls based on the personal information and buy favorite stuff based on the concepts of relationship marketing. They also gather together to the user community based on the filtering mechanisms. On the other hand, in the physical space, user will have appropriate information or recommendation from digital city via information terminals and/or private PCs, based on the footprint information.

The information space can be developed independently with Fairy Wing, because Fairy Wing only bridges the digital city and their citizens via IC cards and ubiquitous information terminals.

3.5 Discussion on the Applicability of Fairy Wing

The most unique characteristics of Fairy Wing are attained by the fact that all the private information is only contained in users' own fairies and no central control and maintenance mechanisms. In summary, the development of Fairy Wing in a digital city will benefit to the citizens in the following points:

(1) Users are responsible for their privacy, thus, they van be active in concealing and revealing private information.
(2) The digital city can provide citizens with appropriate information based on the contents and contexts. As the information controls depend on the information of fairies, the recommendation information can be available even if the information terminals do not have connection with computer networks.
(3) The application systems at each information terminal can be developed separately, because fairies can maintain both static and dynamic personal information.
(4) Complex user management systems are not necessary in the central server systems, thus, system development and maintenance will become easier.
(5) Collaborating filtering systems can be equipped in each information terminal, therefore, interfacing with a specific terminal, users can form communities with the same interests or subjects.

4   Group Trip Advisor: A Prototype

To assess the feasibility of Fairy Wing, we are developing the first prototype system: Group Trip Advisor for Digital City Kyoto. The system aims at advising group trips around sightseeing places in Kyoto of both physical and virtual environments.   As described above, the system intend to realize (1) cost-effective and ease-to-use environments,, (2) distributed information management, and (3) holder-centered security and privacy controls.

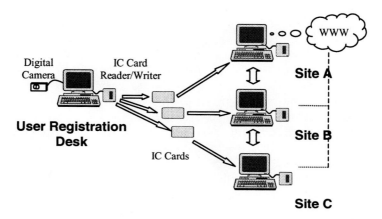

Figure 3. System Configuration of Group Trip Advisor

The system configuration is shown is Figure 3. The current version of Group Trip Advisor consists of (1) one PC for user registration, which is used to issue IC cards with personal information, is equipped with an IC card reader/writer and a digital camera to take photos of users, and (2) Three PCs for information terminals at Site A, B, and C, which are assumed to set at sight seeing places, with an IC card reader/writer. Figure 4 shows the sample IC card used by the prototype and Figure 5 shows the snapshot of the demonstration at Kyoto Digital City Workshop, 1999.

End user interfaces are implemented as the additional functions of a current web browser, therefore, if the users are familiar with web surfing, they can easily enjoy the prototype system. The information terminals provide the users or group visitors to Kyoto City with the explanation of the sites and the recommendation based on the users preferences.

Figure 4. Sample IC Cards Used by Group Trip Advisor.

Figure 5. Snapshot of Group Trip Advisor at Kyoto Digital City Workshop

4.1 Functions of Group Trip Advisor

In the prototype system, users visit some sightseeing places based on the recommendation of the advisor via web browsers. If the users belong to the same group, based on the foot print information, they can get messages of colleagues about sightseeing information at different time and places. Information terminals contain web-browser based interfaces and Fairies are implemented on a thin- and non-contact type IC card, thus can be hold in even a small purse of the users.

We would like to support the following scenario:

(1) Information services for Kyoto sightseeing are provided by Kyoto Digital City itself.

(2) IC cards contain users' profiles (Name, Age, Sex, Hobby, Objective of the Trip, and Place where they like to visit), Footprints (where the user visit and what they zapped at the browsing), and Users' comments on the sites (short chats).

(3) The users' privacy is protected the ping number, users photo shown in front of the card (optional), and concealing items.

(4) At each information terminal, the explanation and recommendation panels are generated based on the users' characteristics, common experience and feelings.

4.2 Implementation of Group Trip Advisor

At each information terminal, Group Trip Advisor consists of the three independent software components: MFCIE, In-Agent, and PGN-Agent. In the current version, they are implemented in C++, JAVA, and Visual Basic.

(1) MFCIE: Browser for Group Trip Advisor

MFCIE has the three functions: (a) providing end users with web-based browsing interface, (b) managing input and output controls of IC cards, and (c) communicating the other programs and systems. It provides users with the registration windows, the favorite lists, their corresponding web pages with voice guidance, and user recommendation pages.

(2) Int-Agent: Collaborative Filtering for Recommendation Generation

Int-Agent generates the recommendations adequate for the users based on both the user information and footprints in the IC cards and the local information on the other users stored at the terminal. The basic mechanism is taken from standard dynamic collaborative filtering algorithm, which is summarized as follows:

(a) Users profiles are gathered via a questionnaire at the registration terminal. The web pages at each terminal have the information on the places and the appropriate activities at the place, beforehand.

(b) The user model is represented by the place-behavior matrix, whose elements describe the strength of users interests on the place-behavior contexts.

(c) When browsing begins, the system records the web pages the user access and their corresponding browsing time. Then, based on the information, the place-behavior matrix is updated using a simple reinforcement algorithm.

(d) Generate recommendation based on the similarity of the user's interests and the records stored at the terminal. The similarity is calculated based on the inner product of user interest vectors.

(3) PGN-Agent: Messenger for Transferring Visitors' Comments

PGN-Agent transforms information stored at a terminal into the other terminal via IC cards. In the current version, the message exchange is performed between given two terminals. The system is used to move the information on Group Trip Advisor among information terminals without using computer networks. The basic mechanism is summarized as follows:

(a) Unique ID is given to each terminal. The information transferred between two terminals is stored in any IC cards with from/to terminal IDs.

(b) If the site a user will visit next is coincide with the to-terminal ID in stored information at a given terminal, the information is moved into the IC card as a fairy.

(c) When the IC card reaches at the corresponding terminal to which the information specifies, the information moves from the IC card into the terminal.

(d) The information is used at the terminal.

4.3 Preliminary Evaluation of Group Trip Advisor

Group Trip Advisor is still under development, thus, the evaluation must be qualitative and somewhat intuitive. However, preliminary experiments and the system demonstration at Kyoto Digital City Meeting reveal the following characteristics of Fairy Wing.

First of all, we have recognized the cost effective ness of the proposed architecture. The cost of IC cards is one-fifth or one-tenth of the ones of conventional PDAs. Also, the additional cost for each information terminal is only for a reader/writer. If there are so many cellar phones or PDAs available in a digital city as is in Japan, the poor capability of the current IC cards would not be welcome. However, the areas where such infrastructure has not been matured, the distribution of IC cards among citizens will be highly promising.

Second, from the developers' viewpoints, Group Trip Advisor is very easy to implement and shows the effectiveness of recommendation functions. This is because: (1) the system is a fully distributed one and the IC cards have only one unique role of interfacing each software component, and (2) each decision by the software components is only made at the corresponding terminal. These conditions have reduced the complexity of the target system. Third, the size of memories available in the IC card is not enough, however, fancy old techniques in micro-code programming in old days will be applicable to enhance the capability of fairies used in the system. Especially, knowledge compiling techniques will work in such small size applications.

On the other hand, from users view points, forth, the system has demonstrated the feasibility to the realistic situations: (3) Users have enjoyed the demo scenario and get interesting information from the corresponding terminal site, although the demo was the virtual one. (4) The processing time is so long that the user must be patient to finish the sessions. These are caused by the fact that the system is apparently transparent between users and browsers, that is, this means that users may feel as if they only use a conventional advisory system. This is both good and bad points of the current implementation. The good point is that users are able to be familiar with such intelligent, agent-based, distributed systems. The bad point is that we must improve the performance of the system so that users do not aware of the fairies in a digital city.

5   Discussion on Further Applications and Future Issues

The proposed architecture Fairy Wing is applicable to various task domains, which have the characteristics of user-centered participants, user-centered information management, user-centered information navigation, advanced information services, distributed easy-to-maintenance [3], [11]. The application candidates include relationship marketing support inter-communities/companies, visitor information assistance at exhibition places, healthcare information service, and collaborative education supports.

The implementation techniques are at the moderate level and can be easily realized. The assumptions we have made in order to implement the applications are not severe; They are summarized as follows: (1) the existence of ubiquitous information terminals, (2) users' succeeding interests in the information services, (3) the small amount of personal information required to run the system, and (4) adequate number of participants entered the system at the same time.

Future issues include that (1) The improvement on the implementation of Fairies in the IC card [1], [6], (2) The development of the information providing functions based on the integration of multi-user information [3],[4], and (3) The development of dynamic and distributed collaborative filtering algorithms, which will be some extensions of data mining techniques [7]. From the theoretical viewpoint, the following issues should be uncovered: (4) Analysis of emergent group behaviors in digital cities [2], [4], [14] and (5) Investigation of design principles for such fully distributed collaborative agent-systems [1], [16].

6   Concluding Remarks

This paper has proposed Fairy Wing: yet another mobile computing system for community computing in a digital city. The system is characterized by the concepts of smart IC cards and aims at supporting personal information management, information service, and dynamic collaborative filtering. We have discussed the advantages of the system and architectural issues. We believe the proposed system architecture is effective in various applications, which will cover physically, virtually, and temporally wide areas. We also think the idea of Fairies will become a good gear to develop advanced agent systems.

The research is supported in part by a Grant-in-Aid of Scientific Research (Number: 10680373 and Digital City Development as the Bases of Social Information Systems) of the Ministry of Education, Science, Sports, and Culture of Japan.

References

1. Aiba, H., Terano, T.: A Computational Model for Distributed Knowledge Systems with Learning Mechanisms. Expert Systems with Applications Vol. 10 (1996) 417-427
2. Axelrod, R.: The Complexity of Cooperation: Agent-Based Models of Competition and Collaboration.Princeton University Press (1997)
3. Bradshaw, J. M., (ed.): Software Agents. AAAI/MIT Press (1997)
4. Brown, R.: Group Processes - Dynamics within and between Groups. Basil Blackwell, (1988)
5. Carley, K. M. , Prietula, M. J. (eds.): Computational Organization Theory. Hillsdale, N.J: Lawlence-Erlbaum Assoc (1994)
6. Dreifus, H., Monk, J. T. : Smart Cards -- A Guide to Building and Managing Smart Card Applications. John-Wiley & Sons (1998)
7. Fayyad, U. M., Piatetsky-Shapiro, G., Smyth, P., and Uthurusamy, R. (eds.): Advances in Knowledge Discovery and Data Mining. AAAI/MIT Press (1996).
8. Ishida, T. (ed.): Community Computing - Collaboration over Global Information Networks.John-Wiley & Sons (1998)
9. Ishida, T. (ed.): Community Computing and Support Systems - Social Interaction in Networked Communities. Springer-Verlag Lecture Notes in Computer Science, Vol. 1519 (1998)
10. Ishida, T., Akahani, J., Hiramatsu, K., Isbister, K., Lisowski, S., Nakanishi, H., Okamoto, M., Miyazaki, Y., Tsutsuguchi, K.: Digital City Kyoto: Towards A Social Information Infrastructure. M. Klusch, O. Shehory, G. Weiss (eds.): Cooperative Information Agents III. Lecture Notes in Artificial Intelligence, Vol. 1652, Springer-Verlag, (1999) 23-35.
11. Jennings, N. R., Wooldridge, M. J. : Agent Technology - Foundations, Applications, and Markets. Springer-Verlag, (1998)
12. Lau, T., Etzioni, O., Weld, D. S.: Privacy Interfaces for Information Management. Communications of ACM, Vol.42, No. 10, (1999) 89-94.
13. Mitchell, W. J.: Designing the Digital City. Lecture Notes in Computer Science (in this volume), Springer-Verlag, 2000.
14. Prietula, M. J., Carley, K. M. and Gasser, L. (eds.): Simulating Organizations: Computational Models of Institutions and Groups. CA: Morgan Kaufman (1998)
15. Russel, S., Norvig, P.: Artificial Intelligence A Modern Approach. Prentice Hall (1995)
16. Terano, T., Kurahashi, S., Minami, U.: TRURL: Artificial World for Social Interaction Studies. Proc. 6th Int. Conf. on Artificial Life (ALIFE VI), (1998) 326-335
17. Van den Besselaar, P. and Beckers, D.: Demographics and Sociographics of the Digital City, In Ishida, T. (ed.): Community Computing and Support Systems, Lecture Notes in Computer Science, Vol. 1519, Springer-Verlag, (1998) 109-125.
18. Vigna, G. (ed.): Mobile Agents and Security. Lecture Notes in Computer Science, Vol. 1419, Springer-Verlag (1998)
19. Weiss, G. (ed.): Multiagent Systems – A Modern Approach to Distributed Artificial Intelligence. MIT Press (1999).

A Warm Cyber-Welcome: Using an Agent-Led Group Tour to Introduce Visitors to Kyoto

Katherine Isbister
Open Laboratory
NTT Communication Science Laboratories
2-4, Hikaridai, Seika-cho, Soraku-gun, Kyoto 619-0237
JAPAN
katherine@digitalcity.gr.jp

Abstract. Like thriving physical cities, successful digital cities will provide many opportunities and approach points for building local social connections and context. This project focuses on bringing cultural outsiders into the Kyoto Digital City community, using a tactic that is well understood in the physical world of travel: the guided group tour. We are creating an interface agent to perform the tour guide role. With careful design of this agent's narration strategies, we can accomplish two goals: providing preliminary cultural and historical context for foreigners who want to learn more about Kyoto, and providing a shared experience, so that they can form relationships that build upon their common interest in Kyoto.

1 Introduction

This project is part of a 3-year initiative at the NTT Open Lab, to build a Digital City Kyoto resource. One key goal of the Digital City Kyoto Project is to create a digital city that has real value and connections for people to the physical world, rather than a stand-alone fantasy or simulation space. The Digital City Kyoto is meant to build upon and complement what is available in the physical city; to work as a digital resource for accessing a geographically and historically real place.

There are many components to building a digital complement to a real city, and there are many tensions involved in forging community around the digital version. Community formation on the net thus far has often been quite free of geographical constraints. Some have hailed this as a powerful advantage of internet communities, allowing people to connect around common interests that are not inherently geographical (Rheingold, 1993). However, the lack of pre-constrained social context and commitment that normally come along with physical community can create problems for digital communities--these can include more frequent trouble-making behavior, difficulty setting and sustaining a workable agenda for the community, and difficulty creating a sense of social continuity (Dibbell, 1999; Kim, forthcoming). One digital city noted that their city is heavily populated by physical outsiders who

T. Ishida, K. Isbister (Eds.): Digital Cities, LNCS 1765, pp. 391-400, 2000.

may not have the same needs and interests as local residents (DDS in Amsterdam reported that 75% of their visitors were from outside Amsterdam, in 1997). How can we encourage visits from outsiders, and also maintain the local flavor of the community that our digital city is tied to? And from another perspective: what is valuable for outside visitors about a geographically-tied resource like the one we are creating?

We believe one large benefit of the digital Kyoto to outsiders will be the ability to learn about and experience some of Kyoto and Japanese culture before, or in lieu of, travelling to the physical location. They may also find it fun to talk with others who are likewise interested in Kyoto and in Japan, and may use the digital Kyoto to help plan a visit to the physical Kyoto. So the digital Kyoto can act as a bridge to the real city and to other people who share an interest in it.

We are creating an agent-guided tour of one location within the digital Kyoto, to provide an opportunity for outside visitors to get a little exposure to the culture of Kyoto and Japan, and to find one another and begin a dialogue. We believe the use of an agent tour guide will allow us to deliver socially meaningful and engaging information to visitors, in a comfortable and familiar format. Most people know what a group tour is, and what one should do while on such a tour. This allows us to provide a familiar and understandable social setting in which visitors can get to know each other, as well as the place itself.

We also hope this agent-guided tour will act as an acculturating influence on newcomers. Social psychologists have demonstrated that people look for cues from others to help them decide how to behave in a new setting and what to expect (Fiske and Taylor, 1991). The author of this paper demonstrated in previous work that an interface agent can provide such cues, and help guide visitors into appropriate behaviors (Isbister and Hayes-Roth, 1998). We hope that our agent tour guide can set a positive tone for experiencing the digital Kyoto, for outsiders. And, by learning a little about the social and cultural background of Japan, outsiders may become more prepared to communicate with people in the physical Kyoto, as well.

We are now constructing a prototype of the guide-led tour. This paper will describe the research that led to the design plan, outline the design plan itself, and describe current progress and next steps.

2 Researching Guided Tours

In preparation for creating the digital Kyoto guided tour, the author went on several guided tours of the real Kyoto, making notes about how various tour guides did their work, and on how tours themselves were operated. She also consulted a manual for training professional tour guides (Pond, 1993). This section will summarize the results of these investigations.

2.1 The Tour Guide Personality and Skill Set

Guided group tours are usually led by an narrator who is knowledgeable about the setting of the tour, and who can deliver this information in an entertaining and comfortable way.

Pond (1993) notes that successful tour guides tend to have the following qualities:
♦ Enthusiasm for the place and for giving the tour.
♦ An outgoing and affable nature.
♦ Sensitivity to cues from others and the surroundings.
♦ Flexibility in dealing with whatever situation may arise.
♦ Knowledge about the location that is wide-ranging and relatively deep.
♦ A sense of humor.
♦ Charisma in directing a group.

She also notes that, since much of tour-guiding is making the place seem to "come alive" for the visitors, story-telling and story-delivery skill are essential for a good tour guide.

Finally, a tour guide has to deal with the mechanics of the group experience. A good tour guide needs to:
♦ Let people know what to expect, generally how long the tour will last, and what will happen.
♦ Set and adjust the pace to adapt to the visitors as well as general time constraints and expectations.

2.2 Tour Contents--What to Talk About and When to Talk About It

Pond (1993) notes that there are particular kinds of contents that most tour takers find interesting:
♦ Interpretation instead of information and facts. People like to hear stories about a place and the people who used it. They like to have their emotions and imaginations engaged, rather than just their intellect.
♦ People like to have information related back to the whole, to key points being made about the place. They like to have a few key messages to remember about the place, to give shape to their impressions and memories.
♦ A wide range of information. Different visitors have different interests, so for a group it's good to hit upon a lot of angles about the place. This will ensure that everyone hears a few things that particularly interest them.
♦ Not too much content--people need time to breathe, to take in what's been said. Silences and time to reflect are important.

In addition, the author of this paper noted during her observations, that tour guides frequently tell stories about how things were constructed or about how they are maintained, if these processes are unique or different from the visitors' daily lives.

The timing of the telling is as important as the contents. Good tour guides are sensitive to how their telling synchronizes with what the visitors are doing. Pond notes that a guide should begin a story about a particular location only once all have arrived there, and should be sensitive to cues from the group that they want to hear more or less about a particular location. She also stresses the need to know when to stop, and allow visitors to simply take in what is in front of them.

3   Design Plans for the Guided Tour

3.1 Design Goals for the Tour Experience and for the Tour Guide

We created a set of design goals for the digital Kyoto tour, after researching group tours and tour guide ideals:
- Visitors should learn a few interesting and useful things about Kyoto and about Japanese culture that they can enjoy recounting to others.
- Visitors should have a chance to interact with other tour group members during the tour, and the tour contents should encourage visitors to do this.
- The tour guide agent should be outgoing, enthusiastic, and charismatic in personality.
- The tour guide agent should make the agenda of the tour very clear, and should adjust length of stories to the pace of the conversation and to visitor interest level in tour narration, as much as possible.
- The tour guide agent's narrative should primarily be stories that have strong human interest and that can evoke conversation among the visitors, covering a wide range of topics.
- The tour guide agent's stories should be selected in part for their value in promoting better understanding and perspective in visitors.

3.2 Overview of the Tour and Tour Guide Agent Features and Structure

For the initial prototype of the digital Kyoto tour, we chose to focus on a single famous and historically rich landmark in Kyoto: Nijo Castle. A tour of Nijo Castle allows our agent to discuss the Edo period in Japan, and the reign of the Tokugawa shogunate, which were crucial in shaping the aspects of Japanese culture that many outsiders recognize as distinctly Japanese. Nijo Castle is a physical reminder of the power struggles and shifts that helped shape modern Japan.

The tour is implemented so that it can be experienced through a web browser. Part of the Kyoto Digital City Project's plan is to create a variety of user interfaces to the digital city resource, all of which are available through the internet. One of these interfaces is particularly suited to crafting a tour--a 3-D navigable model of sections of Kyoto. Using a new technology that allows us to create photo-based navigable 3-D worlds (called 3DML), we have constructed sections of the interior and exterior of

Nijo Castle for our tour (see Figure 1). 3DML models can be embedded in web pages, and can be viewed with the aid of a browser plug-in.

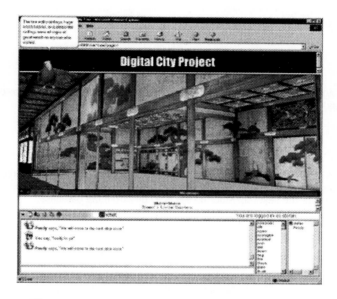

Figure 1. Prototype of the Kyoto Digital City Tour

Visitors join the tour by entering a chat room that is embedded in an html frame set which includes the tour site 3DML model. We are using a commercial chat server called I-Chat to host the tour. I-Chat allows us to synchronize what all of our tour-takers see in their browsers. Using a built-in command, we can display the same url to everyone in the chat room, thus taking all of our tour group members to a new tour stop location.

The tour guide agent's interface to tour takers is the Microsoft Agent character "Peedy". Microsoft Agent is a technology that allows us to script speech and animation coming from a character that rests atop all other windows on the computer's desktop. The character delivers both text and audio (text-to-speech) messages that can be scripted directly into html pages. The character includes a wide range of animated gestures that can be used to liven up story-telling and create an engaging performance from the guide. These gestures include the kinds of expressive and referential gestures that people normally make when referring to their environment (such as gazes and pointing at locations). Using these gestures ties the agent and the environment more closely together, in the way that a human tour guide would be closely referring to the tour site.

The tour is driven by a software agent written in perl, that is actually logged into the tour chat room as an invisible guest. This agent is able to monitor the conversation that occurs in the chat room, and makes decisions about which stories to deliver for each tour stop, based upon the contents of visitor conversations. This agent can then assign new contents (drawing from a database of tour stories) to the html frameset that it will show to all tour members (see Figure 2). The upper frame contains the 3DML location; the lower frame contains the commands that drive the Microsoft Agent's narration.

Tour Guide Agent Process

1. Agent monitors chat contents for key words that indicate level of interest, 'ready to go on' statements, and volume of interaction.

2. When agent gets 'ready to go on' response from majority of tour takers, it uses the cues gathered in step 1 to make a decision about which story to use for the next tour stop. It selects a story from the database.

3. Agent tells I-Chat to display the new story html and tour 3DML to all tour members.

Figure 2. Tour Guide Agent Process

Current methods for tracking visitor interest include noting the amount of conversation among visitors within the chat environment, and searching for positive and negative key words in conversation while at each tour stop. The tour guide agent decides whether to deliver a long, medium, or short version of the next tour stop story, based on tracking these cues. If the agent gets positive key words, and and/or low conversation volume, it will decide to deliver a longer story. If the agent gets negative key words and/or high talk volume, it will decide to deliver a shorter story (see Figure 3). This follows from recommendations for tour guides (Pond, 1993) to adjust one's speeches to the audience. The idea is that, if visitors are happy and receptive, longer stories are okay. But if they are unhappy with the amount of tour guide talk, or busy talking among themselves, tour content should be shortened to adjust to this situation. Later, we hope to build in other gradations and classifications of story and of visitors cues to interpret, as we learn from user logs about which categories are meaningful within this context, and interpretable by the agent.

Volume of Talk	Valence of Conversation Contents	
	Negative	*Positive*
Low	medium length	long length
High	short length	medium length

Figure 3. Story Length Choice Criteria for Agent

The tour guide agent relies on tour takers to help set an appropriate pace for the tour. By asking for explicit "ready to go on" signals from all group members, the agent is able to decide to move on to the next tour stop at the socially appropriate time, when most tour takers are done with the current location.

We also provide an opportunity for visitors to continue chatting in an I-Chat chat room devoted to outside visitors to digital Kyoto. Visitors are instructed in where to find this room so that they can go there at any time to continue discussion with others they may have met on the tour.

3.3 Tour Content Selection and Development

The preliminary tour contents were created to highlight both Nijo Castle itself, and to give some general information about the events and lifestyle of the period in Japanese history in which it was built. To prepare the contents, we collected materials from the Web, educational material from Nijo Castle itself, as well as books about the Edo period, and stories from that time period.

Nijo Castle was the Kyoto residence for the Tokugawa Shoguns. Shogun was the title for the military ruler of Japan. During certain periods of Japan's history, there were Shoguns in addition to the Emperor. The Shoguns had the real economic and military power, but their reign was sanctioned by the Emperor. During the period in which Nijo Castle was built, Kyoto was where the Emperor lived, and so it was necessary for the Shogun to have a base in Kyoto. Thus, Nijo was a military base rather than a primary home--a place where the Shogun would meet with others when in Kyoto. The castle was built directly after the first Tokugawa Shogun rose to power (circa 1603), and was built in a style calculated to impress.

We have focused our 3D development for the tour on four key rooms in the castle: the Shogun's private living quarters, the grand meeting rooms, a reception room, and the weapons room.

The tour currently includes visits to each of these locations. Tour takers progress from the weapons room, to the reception room, to the grand chambers, and finally take a look at the Shogun's private quarters. Along the way, the guide offers information about the purpose of each room and information about historical significance, as well as information about the architecture and decoration. Also, the guide describes aspects of the lifestyle of the people who lived and worked in the castle, and how they relate to the castle itself. Some examples include: castle defenses such as nightingale floors and bodyguard rooms, the sparing use of furniture during this time period in Japan, and the fact that only women could be present in the private quarters of the Shogun.

We have chosen stories that we thought would spark discussion and interest among foreign visitors to the site, and encourage them to learn more about Japan and its culture. We created short, medium, and long versions of each story, to allow the agent to modulate its speeches given the user-interest indicators mentioned in section 3.2.

3.4 Expected Tour Audience

Currently, the Kyoto Digital City project gets about 15% of its traffic from domains that are outside Japan. This includes domains in the U.S., many countries in Europe, as well as a smaller portion from various countries in Asia. Thus, we anticipate that the tour will have visitors from many different countries and backgrounds. Judging from present patterns of general web use, visitors are likely to be fairly highly educated, middle-to-high income, and mostly males who are young-to-middle-aged. We plan to confirm these assumptions by encouraging tour-takers to fill out a brief survey about the experience after they take our tour, which will include a few questions about their demographic.

The current tour is more targeted at American and European visitors, who have had even less exposure to Japanese culture and history than their Asian counterparts. We expect that most tour takers will have never been to Japan, with a few that have made a brief trip to Japan. We expect that tour takers will have very limited exposure to Japan and Japanese culture, consisting mostly of popular media coverage and school history courses (which, in the U.S., give almost no coverage to Japan). Again, we plan to try to confirm these early intuitions about the primary audience through our post-tour survey. There are also plans to create a Japanese language tour, with contents adapted to Japanese visitors who might be curious about Nijo Castle.

3.5 Issues and Plans for Continuing Development

The database structure of the tour contents makes it very easy to add additional stops. However, the hand-created nature of the visual and story contents mean that it is time-consuming to add quality materials. We are exploring the possibility of designing a mechanism for outside content providers to add their own tour stop information. For example, shop keepers on Shijo-Kawaramachi may wish to add information about their own shop sites to our story database, and there may be a way for us to automate a guided tour of this shopping street for visitors.

As far as tour group size, I-chat has preset limits on the number of people who can be in any tour room. I-chat allows 100 people to be active chatters, and 400 to be in a room in total, with the additional 300 as lurkers who cannot speak. However, if we are getting more than about 15-20 people in a tour during our web observation period, we will look at developing a way to shunt extra interested visitors into new tours. A group larger than 20 people is likely to be too large for effective conversation and social experience. If we get large groups during our testing period, we will compare their logged interactions to smaller groups to look for an empirically verified dividing line between what's too large a group, and what is a good size.

We'd of course like to continue to increase the adaptability of the agent's tour to include content modification based on user input, instead of just social cues of talk volume and valence. This way we could more effectively tailor the contents to reflect different tour takers' demographic qualities and particular interests. In future versions of the agent, we'd like to begin to look for and adapt to particular content keywords about the tour sights and topics themselves, words like "ninja" or "architecture" or "tatami". We'd also like to begin grouping content items in demographically meaningful tour categories, so we can offer tours that adapt to certain demographics of visitors.

It would be ideal to test the prototype, recruiting as many foreigners as possible to join in the tour and try it out, then fill out a web-based survey about the tour experience. Logs from the tours could help us assess the value and performance of the agent-led tour for visitors. The log file that was implemented for the tour keeps a record of the decisions about story length that the agent makes, as well as a record of all that was said by tour participants. This allows us to evaluate and adjust the agent's decision-making criteria, as well as its reception by tour-takers. We can also monitor usage of the follow-up chat room, to see if we are getting repeat visitors to the digital Kyoto chat space.

4   Conclusion

To be useful community resources, digital cities must provide social context and orientation for visitors. An agent-led group tour that introduces newcomers to the digital (and physical) city is one approach to setting the right tone and helping to seed community. We hope to learn some lessons from this project that will be of value to the digital city research community, in its efforts to create sustainable and thriving online city communities and resources.

Acknowledgements
Thanks to Stefan Lisowski of Omron Software, and Kenji Kobayashi of the NTT Open Lab for their extensive contributions to this project. I would also like to thank students from the Stanford Japan Center for making contributions during the early design stages. Thanks also to Kaoru Hiramatsu of the NTT Open Lab for creating and maintaining the story database. Finally, I would like to thank Professor Toru Ishida at the Kyoto University Department of Social Informatics and the NTT Open Lab for supporting this research.

References

De Digitale Stad, (1997). *Brochure on DDS 3.0,*
   http://www.dds.nl/dds/info/english/engelsfolder.html.
Dibbell, Julian. (1999). *My Tiny Life: Crime and Passion in a Virtual World*. Owl Books.
Fiske, Susan T., and Taylor, Shelley E. (1991). *Social Cognition*. New York: McGraw-Hill,
   Inc.
Isbister, Katherine, and Hayes-Roth, Barbara, *Social Implications of Using Synthetic
   Characters: An Examination of a Role-Specific Intelligent Agent*. Stanford Knowledge
   Systems Laboratory Report KSL-98-01, 1998. (Presented during IJCAI '97 (International
   Joint Conference on Artificial Intelligence) workshop entitled "Animated Interface Agents:
   Making Them Intelligent," Nagoya, Japan, 1997.)
Kim, Amy Jo (forthcoming). *Community Building on the Web: Secret Strategies for Successful
   Online Communities*. Reading, MA: Addison-Wesley Publishing Company.
Pond, Kathleen Lingle (1993). *The Professional Guide: Dynamics of Tour Guiding*. New York:
   Van Nostrand Reinhold.
Rheingold, Howard (1993). *The Virtual Community: Homesteading on the Electronic Frontier*.
   Reading, MA: Addison-Wesley Publishing Company.

Extending the Services and the Accessibility of Community Networks

Antonietta Grasso*, Dave Snowdon*, and Michael Koch^

*Xerox Research Centre Europe, Grenoble Laboratory, France
^Technische Universität München, Munich, Germany

Abstract. Community networks are community-oriented information and communication systems that are generally patterned after the public library's model of free, inclusive service and commitment to universal access. To serve the community network objectives it is therefore important to have easy and widespread information access. In this paper we present the Campiello system that proposes both enhanced information services and complementary user interfaces to better serve the community network objectives. Enhancement of the services is obtained by introducing collaborative filtering functions to support easier navigation in the information space of the community. To extend access to the community network, a paper-based interface is used, that supports exchange of information with the network, from physical locations spread in town. A large screen based interface is also used, which provides collective easy entry points to the most recent and relevant community information.

1   Introduction

In the last few years there has been much work on virtual communities and how they can be supported with technology ranging from text-based MUDs [8] to 3D collaborative virtual environments (CVEs) [7]. However, there has also been work on community networks in which the aim is to provide support for existing communities situated in specific physical locales such as towns and cities (e.g. [6]). In this second case, since the community already exists, the aim of technology is not to support the existence of the community itself but to provide tools which can augment the existing communication channels in the community, provide awareness of current activities and support a collective memory. The work presented shares the same social motivations driving the community networks, and is based on the assumption that technology advancements can help in better serving the above objectives. In the last two years we have been working on a project that has the goal to explore how technology can be used and enhanced to support both the communities living in cultural towns and the encounter between them and the visitors. The principal project guideline has been to focus not in providing a better virtual environment, but in better connecting activities happening in the real world with the digital representation of the community.

In this paper we first introduce in Section 2 the community networks and where technology can be improved. Then we present the Campiello project and its main

T. Ishida, K. Isbister (Eds.): Digital Cities, LNCS 1765, pp. 401-415, 2000.

technology advancements both on the information services and on the user interfaces. In Section 6 we discuss future research.

2 Community Networks

Community networks are community-oriented information and communication systems that are generally patterned after the public library's model of free, inclusive service and commitment to universal access. Community networks, some with user populations in the tens of thousands, are intended to advance social goals such as building community awareness, encouraging involvement in local decision making, or developing economic opportunities in disadvantaged communities [15]; they are inherently addressing co-located communities. An example of community network is the Rete Civica Milanese (RCM) [6]. RCM is a community network created five years ago to promote a stronger community sense of belonging in the city of Milan (Italy). To achieve this purpose it offers a free registration service to a network where both private and public communication can occur. The basic information unit of the system is the email message, which can be posted either in public or semi-public discussion areas or exchanged among participants; synchronous communication can occur too, through chatting facilities. This basic set of functionality is used to provide an encounter place to virtually all the actors active in town (municipality, associations, commercial entities, etc.). The core of the project is to offer a new kind of *piazza* inhabited by the members of the local community, people sharing history, experiences, and problems connected with Milan.

On the same line, even if sometimes with less explicit emphasis on the civic aspects, are the efforts related to several digital cities. Experiences of this kind are the digital cities of Amsterdam [4] and Bristol [5].

In general these networks, to fulfill their objectives of increasing the sense of belonging to the community, put a high priority in having a system that is easy to use and widely available. The availability and modality of access can be considered a major issue, because only a broad participation in a community network can sustain its growth and wealth. This is true for any kind of community, not only local communities of town inhabitants: the more the network is the image of the real community, the more it encourages community newcomers to participate in it and the risk of drying out diminishes.

2.1   Advanced Information Services and User Interfaces for Community Networks

Community networks are usually based on easy to use software. However we have observed, in our experience of users of such community networks, that technology can improve along two main directions:

- information navigation;
- information access.

From the point of view of information access, we have experienced that when successful, the number of discussion topics can become very large and locating information matching the users' interests can be a complex task. In the same way the location of people sharing the same interests can become very difficult when users are in the order of thousands like in the RCM case. To an extent a user of a community network can suffer from the same information overload problems that a Web user experience. However in the case of the community network it is even more crucial to its growth the possibility to easily benefit from the community generated information. On the side of accessibility, the provision of common access points is part of the agenda of almost every community network. However, up to now all user interfaces to community networks are based on desktop computers. The problem with this approach is that firstly it is not possible to reach all possible users, and secondly, it forces the users to access the network in isolation (alone sitting in front of the personal computer). In the work presented here we argue that it would be an improvement if the community information could be accessed without using a computer and while being with other members from the community.

In the rest of the paper we describe the approach that the Campiello[1] [1, 2, 9] system has adopted to enhance the information services and the user interfaces to community networks.

3 Overview of the Functionality of Campiello

On the basic level, the Campiello system acts as a repository of information that is related to places and events in the city. This information mainly consists of descriptions and comments. Every user of the system can contribute to the information space, but there will be some main actors that provide an initial set of descriptions and continue to feed the system with descriptive information.

For structuring the information space and designing the access to it, we were faced with the well-known tradeoff between structured information system and unstructured 'communication area'. If the system is designed in a structured way it is easy for users to find information. On the other hand if you give users a lot of freedom in creating new information they are more likely to contribute, but this usually leads to a loss in structure and so can frustrate people when they try to find something in the network. For this reason we have decided to model the information services primarily around the recommendation function, while leaving the search and browsing capabilities still available if desired.

The information space consists of a set of items. The major types of items are physical places (e.g. (cultural) buildings, restaurants, and museums), events (e.g. concerts, festivals), and more abstract topics of interest like 'food' or 'parenting'. For search and recommendation issues the items can be related to one or more categories. Additionally, the descriptions or comments of the items can contain links to other items. The system collects explicit and implicit feedback of the user and combines this with a given profile of interests to select information items that might be interesting for the user. This works in a proactive way (i.e. without action by the user) and in a reactive way (i.e. the user tells the system to give him items that match some attributes). More information about collaborative filtering can be found in [15];

---

[1] Campiello is a project funded by the European Union's (ESPRIT LTR #25572, i[3] framework) which is aimed at providing intelligent information interfaces for connected communities.

Knowledge Pump, an existing collaborative filtering system from Xerox used as recommender engine in Campiello, is described in [11, 12].

On top of the information services devoted to improve the flow of information inside and among the different communities, Campiello offers a layer of functionality to support improved communication and contact facilitation. This layer includes services for finding people with similar attributes (e.g. interests) that one could contact for preparing a visit to the town or for whatever.

3.1 Improved Information Services

The goal of Campiello is to provide more than just an asynchronous messages service (although we may well integrate synchronous communications support) – we aim to provide a dynamic community memory and actively push information to people who might be interested in it. To this end we have been developing two novel interfaces and also working on supporting services for managing the information contained in the community memory.

This section will describe the internal services of the Campiello system and subsequent sections will describe the user interfaces that use these services.

3.2 Contexts, Items, People Traces

There are four important types of information stored by Campiello, these are:

1. *Contexts* – A hierarchical classification scheme that can be used to group related *items*. Each context has a title in one or more languages and one or more description in one or more languages. Contexts can also have context specific information associated with any items related to them allowing the knowledge base to be extended. A fragment of contexts hierarchy is presented in Figure 1.

2. *Items* – An item represents a concrete or abstract entity about which information can be collected. Items can be buildings, museum exhibits, cultural events, associations or any "thing" about which people might wish to collect information. Items have a title on one or more languages and one or more descriptions in one or more languages. Items are classified into any number of contexts – for example an Italian restaurant might be classified under:

- restaurants/italian – it's a restaurant!
- architecture – the building containing the restaurant might be of architectural significance
- cuisine/italian/venice – the restaurant might service particular examples of local cuisine.

3. *People* – The users of the system. Campiello stores some basic demographic information about people and a user profile which is composed of 1) a static part indicating a user's preferences such as which contexts they are interested in and 2) a dynamic part composed of the *traces* the user has generated in the course of their interaction with Campiello.

4. *Traces* – As people interact with the system they leave traces of these interactions, which are then used to find correlations between users, and as implicit indications of a user's preferences and interests. Traces can be both implicit and explicit. Implicit traces are generated by actions such as requesting information on an item, sending a message to another user, or a record of a visit to a particular place. Explicit traces are generated when a person explicitly wants to communicate information to the system and other people. Examples of explicit traces include a rating of an item (a score awarded on a linear numeric scale indicating like-dislike) and comments (a text or hand-written comment indicating the users opinion and intended to be communicated to other users, e.g. the hand-written comment in Figure 2).

These four types of information allow Campiello to provide a flexible knowledge base and to allow users to share their opinions of items with others by the medium of comments and ratings.

Rather than relying on users performing searches of the knowledge base or browsing it looking for items of interest, Campiello actively tries to push information to users. The next section will present the architecture of the system and explain how this "information push" is achieved.

Conosci Castello?

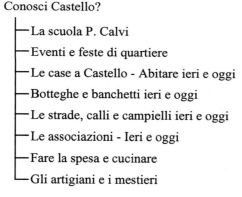

—La scuola P. Calvi

—Eventi e feste di quartiere

—Le case a Castello - Abitare ieri e oggi

—Botteghe e banchetti ieri e oggi

—Le strade, calli e campielli ieri e oggi

—Le associazioni - Ieri e oggi

—Fare la spesa e cucinare

—Gli artigiani e i mestieri

Fig. 1. A fragment of the context hierarchy related to the Castello quarter of Venice

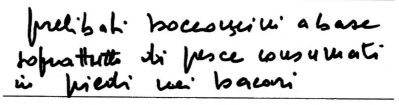

Fig. 2. An example of a hand-written comment.

3.3   The Campiello Architecture

The Campiello system contains a number of components (see Figure 3):
- storage agents – these provide access to and specialised functions on the information stored in the Campiello knowledge base. Internally the information is stored in an SQL database but these modules provide a more convenient API hiding this fact.
- service providing agents – these agents use the knowledge base to provide services to the user interfaces. Currently the most important of these modules is the recommender agent.
- user interfaces – Campiello provides a number of user interfaces which use the storage and service providing modules.

These modules are implemented as Java-based agents and can either run on the same machine or several different machines allowing for some flexibility of deployment and the ability to provide multiple instances of each user interface geographically dispersed throughout a city.

The recommender agent has two main functions:
1.   Finding users with similar profiles (matchmaking)
2.   Recommending items to users which they should be interested in, based on their profiles

These two functions are interrelated. The recommender uses a technique called *community centred collaborative filtering* [10, 14] in which correlations are found between people in each context (community) and then these correlations are used to predict a given person's interest in a given item based on the ratings of the users with which a person is correlated. These correlations are done on a context by context basis since while two people might agree in one subject area (e.g. films) they might violently disagree in another (e.g. restaurants). By restricting correlations to individual contexts we can provide better correlations of interest than by attempting to find overall similarities between users.

For example, suppose a number of users have eaten at several restaurants in Venice. These users have then rated the restaurants and left comments on them that can be seen by other users. The recommender then compares the ratings of the users for each restaurant and derives a value for the correlation between users using the Pearson algorithm [14]. Given the correlations between users the recommender can now predict the users' interests in items that they have not yet seen. If two users tend to agree on their ratings of restaurants and one has rated a restaurant that the other has not then the recommender can use the rating and the correlation factor to predict the other user's interest in this restaurant. If the result of this computation is a score above a given threshold the system might recommend the restaurant to the user when they next interact with the system or it might directly send them information, perhaps by fax or email.

As stated earlier, one of the goals of community networks is to offer widespread access in order to encourage the maximum possible participation and to ensure that sections of the community are not excluded due to lack of access. For this reason Campiello has chosen to focus on novel user interfaces in addition to using a PC based user interface. The sections below describe these new user interfaces: paper and large screen displays.

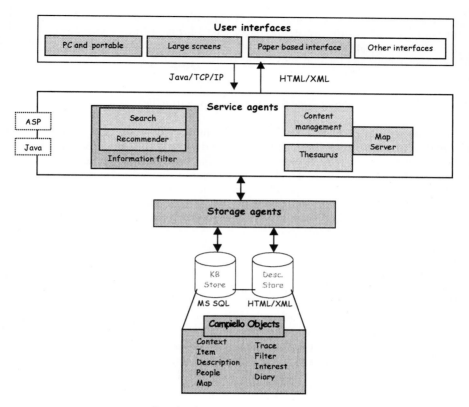

Fig. 3. The system architecture

4   Using Paper to Interact with the Community Network

The paper interface was chosen as an interaction tool for the various advantages it presents (e.g. it is cheap, paper artefacts are easily shareable, and it can be easily annotated) and especially the fact that it is mobile and doesn't require acquiring new skills to interact with computers.

However, a simple means of interaction was needed for the paper interface. The users should be able to navigate through the data and be able to comment and rate on items and be identified. We used a very generic interaction scheme similar to dialog boxes in current computer interfaces. It is based on checkboxes and comment boxes as the basic means of interaction and it is described in the Section 3.4.4. Using this simple interface we aimed to achieve two objectives [10]:

- close the gap between the moment where an experience happen and the moment where an evaluation or comment about it can be given;
- take advantage of existing information collection and feedback generation activities.

Regarding the implementation, in Campiello we make use of some Xerox technology [13, 18] for processing paper-based forms. In this paper however we do not focus on the implementation architecture of this interface, but rather on the user functions addressing the two above objectives.

4.1   Applying the Paper Based Interfaces in Campiello

With the possibility to link the real world and the electronic space through paper, dynamic information can become a real support to local communities, both enhancing the effectiveness of current paper based media, from newspapers and magazines to wall postings and restaurant tickets, and opening the way to a new set of paper artefacts that can exploit completely the potential of this link.

In our work on the project Campiello we are currently dealing with support for connected communities in towns which have a rich culture and hence large numbers of tourists. The major objective of the project is to better connect the local inhabitants of the towns, to make them active participants in the construction of the cultural information and also to support new and improved connections with cultural managers and tourists.

The goals are achieved by creating a bi-directional exchange of information about the town, its places and events.

As described before, the Campiello system acts as a repository of information that is related to places and events in the city. Every user of the system can contribute to the information space but there will be some main actors that provide an initial set of descriptions and continue to feed the system with descriptive information.

Access to the information space is provided through collaborative filtering. Therefore, the system collects explicit and implicit feedback from the users and combines this with a given profile of interests.

Looking at what paper artefacts were already available in the field we identified postcards announcing events which are distributed in a lot of places, and local, topic specific newspaper like information brochures as examples. We planned to enhance these artefacts in a way that they could easily be used for collecting feedback.

4.1.1   Take Advantage of Existing Information and Feedback Generation Tasks

People already collect a lot of information on paper and use paper quite naturally for marking feedback on items for themselves or for friends. If we make this information gathered in paper form and written on paper artefacts available to electronic information systems, the users do no longer have to make an extra effort and much more material and feedback will be available to the recommender system.

There are two ways to tackle the topic of using already established activities:
1)   Firstly one could use the forms which are produced by the recommender system but design them in a way that makes them useful for different tasks. For example these forms can be nice information carriers with room for giving feedback that are worth collecting for a personal diary. One problem here is that it cannot be used to collect new information.
2)   Secondly one could provide means for extracting information from existing paper artefacts which have not been produced by the system. Possibilities are to extract

text from the given paper artefacts and try to relate them to existing items or define new items based on the information.

The general set-up for recommender systems with paper based interfaces is the following: A computer based recommendation systems prints its recommendations on paper and then receives feedback and new items from the user through traditional desktop interfaces *and* scanned paper forms.

Central issues when implementing this setup are where and when the data leaves the information system and how the data comes back to the system.

For processing forms we support two complementary approaches: delayed processing (the user drops the form in a box and it is collected later) and immediate processing (the user does the processing himself – and perhaps gets immediate response).

4.1.2 Active NewsCards

One outcome of our work was what we call an Active NewsCard.

Active NewsCards are flyers (DIN A4) or small (DIN A5 or DIN A6) postcards that show information on one or more items from the information space, enhanced with visible checkboxes and active blank areas. Ticking any of the checkboxes distributed in the content allows the user to:

- express interest in more detailed or related pieces of information or
- give feedback (rating) for an item.

Checkboxes can have different shapes or can be attributed with attached icons to express the different functionality. Blank areas are used to give the possibility to add free comments, which are scanned and saved. Additionally, we are considering using highlighting of text on the NewsCards for input purposes

4.1.2.1 Different Types of Active NewsCards

According to the basic ideas mentioned in the section on paper-based interfaces for collaborative filtering, there are two basic types of Active NewsCards:

- Static NewsCards: These are Active NewsCards edited explicitly by cultural managers and distributed in large numbers in the town. These resemble the information cards already found in several towns. According to the main usage of the feedback elements we distinguish two main subclasses:
  - Information NewsCards: Main goal of the NewsCard is to give information on one of the several items. Therefore, the NewsCard contains a lot of text and images. Feedback elements are mainly used for expressing interest in more information or for giving feedback (ratings and free text). An example is visible in Figure 4.
  - Comment NewsCards: Main goal of this kind of NewsCard is to collect comments and ratings on a specific event/place. It is assumed that the user already knows about the item, so there is little extra information but large areas for writing comments or for giving ratings. Examples for such NewsCards can be feedback NewsCards in restaurants.
- Dynamically created NewsCards: While static NewsCards are created in large numbers for generic users, there is also the possibility to get a personalised

printout of information (e.g. in response to submitting a filled out static NewsCard). These NewsCards usually contain more information and are larger in size. That is why we also use the term Active Newspaper for them.

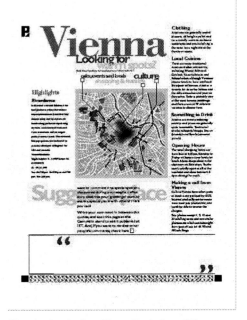

Fig. 4. An Active NewsCard about Vienna

4.1.2.2 Processing of Active NewsCards and New Information

Two possibilities for processing paper input have been implemented in Campiello:

For synchronous processing scan/print stations are available at semi-public places where people can process their NewsCards and immediately receive the results, which can be a personalised NewsCard with requested information. Such places are tourist offices, libraries, hotels and schools. Additionally, synchronous access is available through a fax server.

Alternatively, the users can drop the NewsCard in collection boxes that are mounted at several places (e.g. in restaurants and hotels or at public events) or send them by mail.

Both for comments on existing items and for new items we make use of the fact, that the information we collect is mainly to be presented to users again. Therefore, we do not have to fully transfer it into digital information (e.g. do recognition of handwriting etc) but mainly store the image and relate it to some basic contexts and/or users.

Each Active NewsCard can be associated with another paper "tool" called PID Stickers (see Figure 5), which work as personal identifications. Such a sticker contains a machine-readable id of the user. Attaching a PID sticker to an Active NewsCard makes the system associate content and actions with the user, creating conditions to produce useful information for the recommending and the collaborative systems, which are essential to give valuable services back to the user.

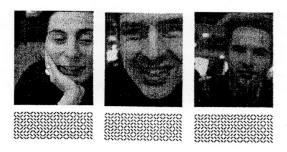

Fig. 5. Example of Personal Identifier (PID) Stickers

5   Using Large Screens to Interact with the Community Network

As described above, the paper user interface allows us to provide information on specific topics and allows users to request more information and provide feedback. What is lacking in this interface is a general overview of the contents of the community memory and information about the topics that are currently interesting to members of the community. This information could be distributed via the paper user interface by providing forms which users can scan to receive updates or by automatically mailing or faxing information to registered users – indeed this is something that we may try at a later date. However, our current approach is to use large screen displays to display broad coverage of topical information in a way that complements the focussed presentation of the paper user interface.

The purpose of our large screen display, the CommunityWall, is to create an environment that fosters social encounters (conversation) using topical information and/or news as a trigger. It provides a focus for social activity in a similar way to existing notice-boards which display notices (ranging from formal printed notices to hand written scraps of paper) concerning current community activities. Using the CommunityWall, we aim to provide information on what are the interesting activities or topics of conversation, who is actively interested and what they are saying. If a topic displayed on the CommunityWall catches attracts someone's attention they can then request that more information be displayed on that item by touching the screen (or using some other means if a touch-sensitive display is not available) or that a NewsCard be printed on that topic on a printer/scanner situated near the display. Once the NewsCard is printed it can be used to comment on the topic. In this way the CommunityWall supports information discovery and an asynchronous communication among members of the community. Furthermore, we hope that if multiple people simultaneously use the display it will help trigger conversations and allow people to meet others with similar interests (since it will be obvious what topics people are looking at).

Given the contexts, items, and traces present in the knowledge base, the task of the CommunityWall is to select the topics that are most representative of the community at the current time and to display information about these topics in such a way that onlookers can see which are the items of current interest to the community. Topics are selected for one of two reasons. Firstly, privileged users, referred to as cultural managers (editors), can mark some items as being of particular interest. Secondly, the CommunityWall monitors additions to the database in order to see which contexts and items are receiving most comments and ratings – these are assumed to be the items that are of current interest and therefore generating lots of "traffic". A set of customisable rules is invoked to prioritise items and decide which are the most interesting at the current moment. Items can be viewed as competing for screen real-estate and those that win are the ones that are generating the most interest, belong to contexts of other items of high interest, or have been marked by a cultural manager as being of particular interest.

Once selected, items displayed are grouped by contexts so that the display has some coherence. Items are represented by a title, a brief description, and comments on the items and pictures of the users who have commented on that item. Onlookers can therefore see what is interesting, who is interested in it and what these people are saying about the item. In order to maximise screen usage while preserving context, older comments (and the associated images of the commenter) are gradually shrunk and thereby progress from being full-size, to being small but legible, to being illegible but still visible, to finally vanishing altogether. The motivation for this is to provide some indication of the volume of comments even if people cannot actually read them all. Optionally, ratings can be displayed alongside particular items to give another form of feedback.

We deliberately chose to display images of people who make comments, which were captured as part of the registration process. Although this might seem to raise privacy concerns we believe that there are good reasons for identifying people in this way. Firstly, people are aware that the comments they are entering are intended to be seen by others. Secondly, we believe that some form of identification may help to encourage responsible comments and avoid obscenity. Thirdly, we hope that people standing in front of the CommunityWall will be able to recognise people who have commented on a topic that is of interest to them and perhaps identify these people if they are also nearby. In this way the CommunityWall can help to facilitate contact between members of a community.

We are currently experimenting with a number of different display and layout styles for the CommunityWall and also working to provide an interface that can be adapted for a number of different settings. Figure 6 shows the current CommunityWall display and Figure 7 shows an earlier prototype of the CommunityWall used for a demonstration at a conference of European projects (IST'98).

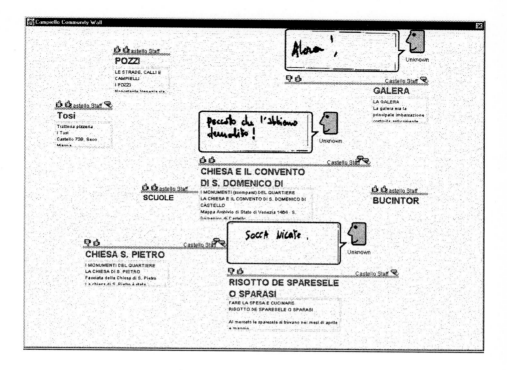

Fig. 6. The CommunityWall on real content from a Venice neighbourhood

6 Conclusion

Campiello is a project based on a multidisciplinary approach supported by different partners with different skills: computer engineers, industrial designers and social observers [1]. Input from these three converging perspectives continuously gets compared and influences the work of the others. In this paper we have focused on the technology as it has been designed on the basis of the industrial designers vision and of the first insights from the social observation in the two towns of Venice (Italy) and Chania (Greece). The next steps of this work will be the refinement and testing of the ideas in real communities with the support of the social observers participating in the project.

Acknowledgements

The work described in this paper is partly supported by the European Community via the Campiello project (ESPRIT LTR #25572). The design of the CommunityWall and of the Active NewsCards originated from the Domus Academy Research Centre, XRCE, and the University of Milan, in conjunction with the project consortium.

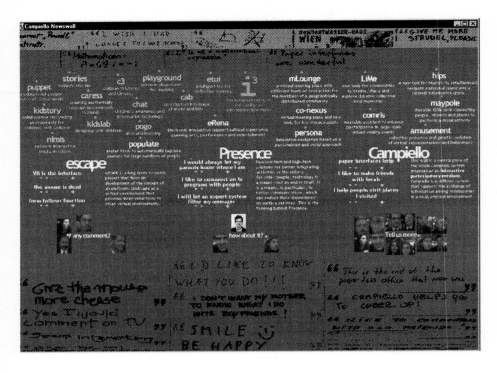

Fig. 7. The first CommunityWall produced for a conference dedicated to i3 projects.

References

[1]   A. Agostini, G. De Michelis, M. Susani. A methodology for the design of innovative user oriented systems. In *i³ Magazine*, 2, March 1998.

[2]   A. Agostini, V. Giannella, A. Grasso, and R. Tinini. Memories and Local Communities: An Experience in Venice. In *Proc. Designing Collective Memories, 7th Le Travail Humain Workshop*, Paris, Sept. 1998.

[3]   S. Benford, D. Snowdon, C. Brown, G. Reynard, and R. Ingram. Visualising and Populating the Web: Collaborative virtual environments for browsing, searching and inhabiting Webspace. *Computer Networks and ISDN Systems* 29, pages 1751-1761, 1997.

[4]   P. van de Besselaar, I. Melis, D. Beckers. Digital cities: design, organization, and use. Lecture Notes in Computer Science (in this volume), Springer-Verlag, 2000.

[5]   A. de Bruine. Digital City Bristol: A Case Study. Lecture Notes in Computer Science (in this volume), Springer-Verlag, 2000.

[6]   G. Casapulla, F. De Cindio, and O. Gentile. The Milan Civic Network Experience and its Roots in the Town. In *Proc. 2ⁿᵈ International Workshop on Community Networking*, IEEE Comm. Soc., ACM SIGCOMM, Princeton (NJ), 1995.

[7]   E. Churchill, and D. Snowdon. Collaborative Virtual Environments: an introductory review of issues and systems. *Virtual Reality: Research, Development and Application*, Springer-Verlag, 1998.

[8]   P. Curtis, and D.A. Nichols. MUDs grow up: Social virtual reality in the real world. In *Proc. IEEE Computer Conference*, IEEE Press, 1994.

[9]   N. Glance, D. Arregui, M. Dardenne. Knowledge Pump: Supporting the Flow and Use of Knowledge in Networked Organizations. In U. Borghoff, R. Pareschi (eds), *Information Technology for Knowledge Management*, Springer Verlag, Berlin, 1998.

[10] N. Glance, D. Arregui, M. Dardenne. Making Recommender Systems Work for Organizations. In *Proceedings of PAAM'99*, 1999.

[11] A. Grasso, A., M. Koch, and D. Snowdon. Campiello – New user interface approaches for community networks. In *Proceedings of Workshop on Designing Across Borders: The Community Design of Community Networks*, Seattle, WA, Nov. 1998.

[12] Grasso, A., M. Koch, and A. Rancati. Augmenting Recommender Systems by Embedding Interfaces into Practices. To appear in *Proc. GROUP '99*, Phoenix, Arizona, ACM Press, 1999.

[13] W. Johnson, W., S.K. Card, S.K., H. Jellinek, H., L. Klotz, and R. Rao. Bridging the paper and electronic worlds: The paper user interface. In *Proc. INTERCHI*, ACM Press, 1993.

[14] P. Resnick, N. Iacovou, M. Suchak, P. Bergstrom, and J. Riedl. GroupLens: An Open Architecture for Collaborative Filtering of Netnews. In *Proc. of CSCW'94*, October 22-26, Chapel Hill, NC, ACM Press, 1994.

[15] D. Schuler. Community Networks: Building a New Participatory Medium. *Communications of the ACM*, **37**(1), 1994.

[16] A. Sellen, and R. Harper. Paper as an Analytic Resource for the Design of New Technologies. In *Proc. CHI'97*, Atlanta, GA, 1997.

[17] U. Shardanand, P. Maes. Social information filtering: Algorithms for automating word of mouth". In *Proc. CHI'95*, Denver CO, May 1995, ACM Press, pp. 210-217, 1995.

[18] Xerox (1998): Information on PaperWare and multifunctional devices from http://www.xerox.com/paperware

Creative Contents Community

A Multimedia Contents Authoring Environment for a New Digital Community

Toshiyuki Asahi[1], Hisashi Noda[1], Daigo Taguchi[1], Kazuhiro Ishihara[2]

[1] Human Media Laboratories, NEC Corporation
8916-47, Takayama-Cho, Ikoma, Nara 630-0101, Japan
{asahi, noda, tagu}@hml.cl.nec.co.jp
[2] Seta Elementary School
4-2-1, Ooe-Cho, Otsu, Shiga 502-2141, Japan
kazu.ishihara@nifty.ne.jp

Abstract. A new paradigm is proposed for a network-based community called the "creative contents community". Typical examples of network based communities are bulletin boards and mailing lists, which have a "free talk" communications style but are not always productive. In the creative contents community, open and flexible human groups are formed with members having different skills, knowledge, viewpoints, etc, enabling them to create multimedia contents with a certain value. One of the models of such a community has many creators providing small pieces of a final output and a producer who gathers and edits these pieces into one artifact. A feasibility study was conducted at an elementary school where groups with creators and a producer were easily formed (i.e. students and a teacher). From the study, a newly developed authoring environment consisting of a Kids editor and a Producer tool was implemented in an experiment to create multi-media contents. The concept of the community model, the authoring environment and the results of the experiment are discussed in detail.

1 Introduction

Although great and rapid advances having been made in the hardware and software that support multimedia in the home, office, school or anywhere for that matter in daily life, opportunities are still limited for large populations of users to utilize the multimedia infrastructure fully. For users to receive a great deal of advantages from the coming information-oriented society, they should be able not only to consume information but also to enhance their creativity by producing and distributing information or software contents by themselves. A shortage of high quality content that can encourage people to participate and stimulate their creativity is widely expected.

On the other hand, networking technologies as represented by the Internet have been producing various types of new communities. Many of these communities

T. Ishida, K. Isbister (Eds.): Digital Cities, LNCS 1765, pp. 416-426, 2000.

presently seem to have common features such as wide open participation, i.e. anybody can join any community freely because of this intrinsic characteristic of the Internet. Undoubtedly, this has been contributing quite a bit to an increasing number of end users and an increasing awareness of the need for popularizing computer literacy. These communities have much potential to produce new values that could not arise before the recent network infrastructures were introduced. This is because people who have very different backgrounds, skills, knowledge and cultures can gather so flexibly. As seen with mailing lists and chat corners, however, there have been many cases of a community being formed just for "information exchange" among "people holding some knowledge in common", not for producing new information or values. As a result, opportunities for deeply enjoying multimedia content or enhancing creativity have rarely been provided even to Internet users who are capable of operating computer tools.

Taking the above two viewpoints into consideration, the authors have come to believe that development of communities is a social necessity. Such communities should be open to a wide range of users and be able to stimulate or enhance creativity through the activities of making multimedia content, which would allow participants to produce yet unknown innovative value as the output of the communities. The authors call such communities "creative contents communities". To form such communities, "self-propagating contents" have been assumed to be essential, and a platform has been developed to promote such contents. To evaluate the effectiveness and usability of the platform in the real world, the platform was implemented in an experiment at an elementary school. The following part of this paper describes the platform which consists of a Kids editor and a Producer tool in detail, and briefly introduces how they can be used in an elementary school lesson.

2 Previous Projects

Groupware or CSCW might have a similar concept to what the authors are aiming at, in the sense that each group has a common objective of producing some artifact. The difference between them is that one side has closed groups while the other has groups open to the public. In other words, while members of communities do not necessarily know each other [1], members of groupware or CSCW know each other, and producing artifacts is somewhat beyond their expectations.

In artistic fields, several cooperative projects have been introduced. One example is the Renga project which introduces an idea from the traditional way of making poems in Japan [2] into modern network systems. Suppose some member presents an artificial work such as a design sketch on the Internet, and then some other member inspired by the work, provides his/her own work on the WWW in relation to the original one. The repetition of this cycle can be expected to yield a growth of the work or other innovative concepts. In this case, the participants are actually closed to certain individuals because they are expected to handle some drawing tools and to have artificial skills of a high level (even though this might not be intended obviously).

Widely known open community projects include digital communities such as Amsterdam Digital City [3], which conveys some real-world regional constraints into its community and supports social events for the everyday lives of its residents. The city offers many public services such as the distribution of information, and encourages communications among residents. This approach may not be productive but is effective at least in constructing a digital community widely open to a large population because the participants share mutual regional interests which in turn brings a feeling of solidarity. Residents can easily get useful (sometimes profitable) information from the community.

3 Basic Concept

As mentioned above, the objective of our research is to develop a platform to promote and control a widely open digital community meaning even computer novices can participate easily in particular and to support creative cooperative work. Ishida has already classified digital community functions into five categories [4]:
 · Knowing each other;
 · Sharing preference and knowledge;
 · Generating consensus;
 · Supporting everyday life;
 · Assisting social events.

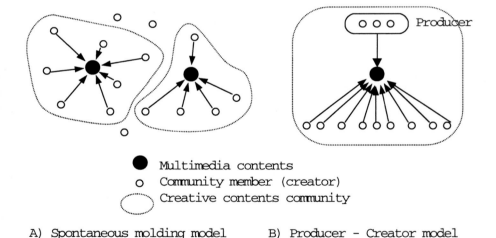

● Multimedia contents
○ Community member (creator)
⬭ Creative contents community

A) Spontaneous molding model   B) Producer - Creator model

Fig. 1. Two models of creative contents communities

If our proposition were to be considered a variation of the community, a 6th function could be added: Creating (multimedia) artifacts. Otherwise, this might be thought of as a new concept situated between groupware and community computing.

Two conceptual models have been considered for our creative contents community, in advance of the design of the project activities (visual images are given in Fig. 1):

A) Spontaneous molding (bottom up) model
On the premise that a weak combined community already exists, members gather quite freely or spontaneously to create certain artifacts together. Guidance or leadership is minimum. Actual examples of this model are few, but the groupwise activities being done to develop Linux might be one example [5].
B) Producer - Creator (top down) model
To create artifacts, an individual or a group called the producer provides the theme and leads members. The producer can control what is to be created by selecting participants or their outputs, and by editing the outputs to some extent. In this case, the community is often formed after the project starts.

The authors developed the platform based on (B) the producer - creator model, because this model is believed to fit in with a wide variety of creation-related activities in the real world, and with computerization of the activity flow. In addition, the authors have also proposed "self-glowing multimedia contents", e.g., templates or examples presented to the participants first, followed by the participants contributing their own contents to add to the core or the list of examples. Metaphorically, the contents seem to grow in number up as the contributions of the participants increase. The addition of contents is assumed to be less bothersome than the creation from zero, even for non-expert computer users or non-artists (the majority of people on the Net).

Lessons at an elementary school were selected as the choice of our feasibility study because the relationship between a producer (= a teacher) and creators (= students) naturally exists, and the needs are generally strong for tools supporting creative activities. The second reason is that by raising the usability level of the system so that even lower class students are able to use it with ease, should help extend the number of application areas, e.g., to the home or public, in the future.

4 Platform for Self-Propagating Contents

4.1 Outline

To achieve the producer - creator type community, the basic system configuration was assumed to include the following sub-systems (Fig. 2).
• Producer supporting environment
Arranges, selects, or edits unit contents contributed from participants so that the output will meet the producer's intent.
• Participants supporting environment
Encourages participation by providing editing tools and viewers for browsing or appreciating contents edited with the contents engine.

- Contents engine

  Stores contents sent from participants, and also occasionally controls the extent of participant participation according to indications from the contents engine (i.e. the producer can control access). An important feature the server should have is flexible distribution control which will guarantee individual privacy, prevent distributed contents from being illegally copied, impose fees on visitors and so on.

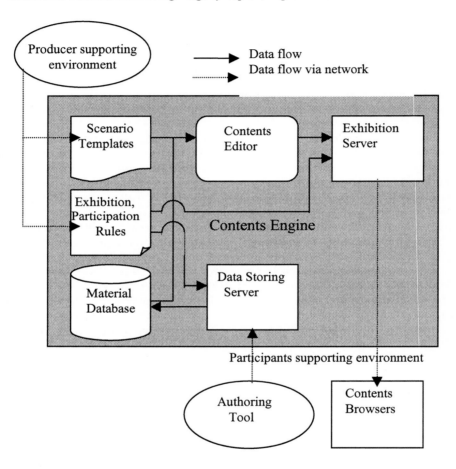

Fig. 2. System configuration of the self-propagating contents platform

As the minimum set for the platform prototype, a "Producer tool" and a "Kids editor" were developed for the experiment at a school. The exhibition server had been developed as a multimedia data container named "MediaShell," but was not installed because the planning for the distribution experiment did not go beyond a local area network this time.

The Kids editor enables users (creators) to make one Web page at a time with bitmaps and text data. The gathering and simple editing of these Web pages can be done with the Producer tool.

Even with the minimum set prototype, multimedia contents of a new type on the WWW can be produced as follows. First, a producer gives members of his/her community what is to be formed on the Net. In the elementary school case, this is usually a theme for activities, such as "make a multimedia map of our town by having each of you gather photos taken around your own home" or "make a graduation album consisting of each of your best memories of your school days". Here, the students make their own pages perhaps with photo data and messages about scenes. These pages are then assembled into a homepage the homepage is opened to the class, the school, or a broader audience, and some of the people in the community who are interested in the homepage can participate and add their own pages. Then, the homepage and the community can grow under the producer's control.

Fig. 3. The screen dump of the Kids Editor

4.2 Kids Editor

A screen dump of the Kids editor is shown in Fig. 3. Because "ease and fun to learn and use" was first considered in designing the editor, the functions were created as follows.

- No notion exists for pages, windows, or scrolling. What users are able to see on the single screen is only the whole canvas on which they can put pictures or text information.
- Users (students) can put bitmap data such as photos taken with a digital camera on the canvas.
- Users can write messages with a single font and several sizes (able to be selected visually), and not the input of point numbers.
- Users can draw freehand style with two kinds of erasers (for small and medium areas).
- A few effects such as shadowing, coloring the texts, changing of occlusive relations, sound attachment to the canvas.
- Users can send the finished canvas (by email) to the producer or save it to a file.
- Users can input text with the keyboard and save data to a "file," this concept was adopted intentionally because it became clear through interviews with teachers that computer literacy training was necessary.

All of the functions are given as icons that are always visible on the screen. No menus, no key commands, no other "tricky" interaction techniques are provided to avoid any increase in the operational complexity.

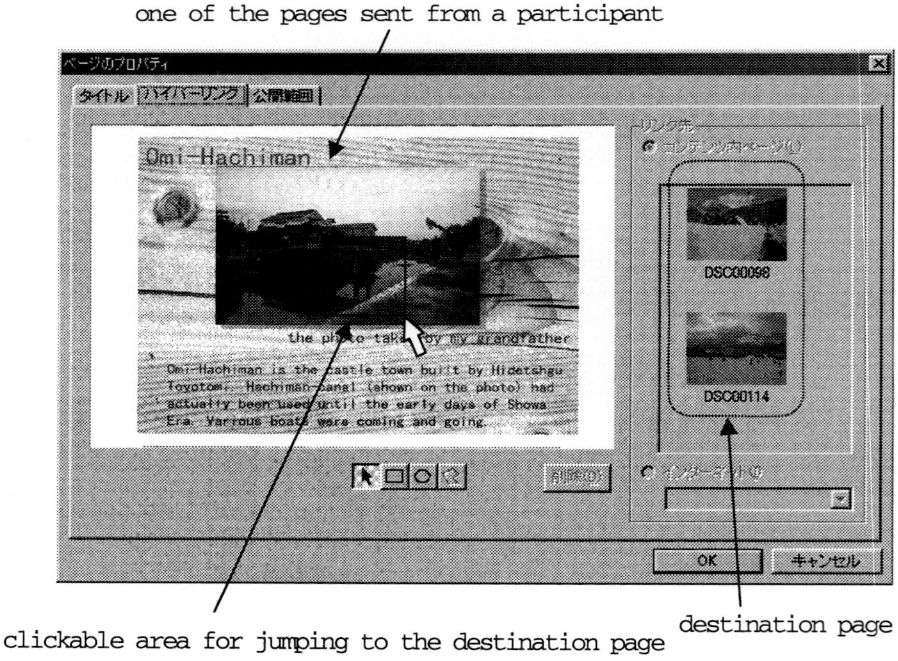

one of the pages sent from a participant

clickable area for jumping to the destination page   destination page

Fig. 4. Hypermedia linkage design with the Producer tool

4.3 Producer Tool

A teacher in a lesson is supposed to use the producer tool. All of the pages sent by students can be browsed as icons on a screen and rearranged quite easily just by dragging the icons to desired positions. The cover and the contents pages are given as templates so that even non-experts of Web page design can readily open the contents to the WWW. The links between the previous and the next pages are given automatically. The additional hypermedia links among the pages can be edited by the teacher, just by indicating the link button areas on one page and then pointing to the destination page icons (Fig. 4). The function that controls where the contents should be issued is planned to implement in the producer tool. This will prevent the contents from too much exposure to the public.

4.4 Browser

For enjoyment of the contents, it is indispensable to have easy-to-use and attractive browsers with which producers, creators, and others can look over whole contents or retrieve certain pages for selective appreciation. Accordingly, a few information visualization techniques have been proposed for the platform. They focus on how to visualize regional and time attributes simultaneously and facilitate understanding at a glance, this is because gathered contents are expected to vary in time and location in many cases. Figure 5 shows the browsers.

- Annual ring browser [7]
  Annual rings are characteristic images recording the passage of time. In this browser, accordingly, the time axis is assigned in the radius direction and the space axis is assigned in the perimeter direction. Therefore, both the time axis and the space axis can be expressed in one screen image. Each page is represented as a word and put on the annual ring browser according to its time and spatial attributes.
- Stratum browser
  Time attributes are simply assigned to layers of the map, i.e., each icons (representing a page) having the same time attributes are put on the same layer. A "Peeping" interaction technique is newly proposed to look into the occluded icons as shown in Fig. 5 (B).
- Chrono-tunnel
  The depth direction of the tunnel is assigned as the time axis. While time travel takes place by walking forward or backward in the tunnel, the user can retrieve a certain page and look at it on a full screen just by clicking an icon put on the side panel. The user can "feel" time elapsing among events simply by walking-through the tunnel.

A producer can select an effective browser from among these according to the contents. The important feature given to these browsers is a reversal linkage function. In a typical homepage design, creators often put textual or graphical buttons in their pages in order to jump to other pages (i.e., other sites). With self-propagating contents, many cases can be foreseen in which a new participant wants someone else using a browser to jump to his/her page. In such cases, the creator can directly stick a button or an icon linked to his/her page on the browser. In other words, participants

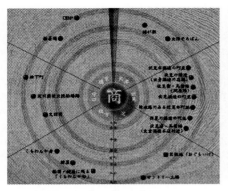

A) Annual ring browser

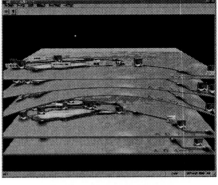

B) Stratum browser

C) Chrono-tunnel

Fig. 5. Screen dumps of browsers

can add their pages indicating how they are presented in the whole contents. Of course, a kind of filtering function is needed if the reversal linkage is open to the public because people will possibly link unsuitable pages (e.g., malicious or commercial ones) to the contents.

5 Experiment at an Elementary School

A feasibility study was conducted in a lesson at an elementary school. The objective of the experiment was to observe how well students (assumed as computer novices) would understand the concept of self-propagating contents, and use the tools. The task was set by a teacher (one of the authors) to the students: "find any kind of welfare facility or device in your town, take photos of it with a digital camera, and then make a page with the photo data along with explanations or comments". The teacher was supposed to collect and edit these pages, and then make a homepage called "a welfare map of XYZ town".

Fig. 6. Photo shots of an open class at an elementary school using the self-propagating content tools

About 150 students in the fourth grade participated in the experiment assumed as an ordinal lesson and 100 pages of contents were put together into one homepage. The homepage could be accomplished and published within three weeks from the start of activities with 45-min classes once a week (which included not only the editing task but also the task of gathering information in the town). The instructions for using the Kids editor was given in 20 minutes. Considering the students had to learn from the concept of "contents" to the operation methods of the Kids editor, we can conclude that this community forming platform seems to be useful and easy to use even for computer novices.

6 Conclusion and Future Research

This paper proposed a new concept for digital communities that are open and creative. "Self-propagating" multimedia contents were also proposed as a centripetal force in the community. A platform consisting of three sub-systems was considered as supporting in promoting community formation. The minimum set for the platform was implemented on PCs for a feasibility study at an elementary school. The study showed easy understanding of the self-propagating contents concept and learning of the Kids editor by the elementary school students.

As mentioned in the Introduction, we believe communities open to a wide range of users and able to stimulate or enhance creativity through the activities of making multimedia content are the key technology for the coming information oriented society. A possible application is like this; people living in the real community are supposed not only as users but reporters in the digital city (in this case, the digital city itself is regarded as the MM contents produced in the community). They can make use of information served in the community and can also have the opportunity to distribute their personal information. Some might use it as advertisement of their own business such as announcement of special sales, and some might use it as report of local events.   All residents can receive and enjoy the merit from that regional information.

Future research plans will be proposed in two directions as follows:
· Contents distribution experiments
As mentioned briefly, one of the essential factors of a contents based community is the distribution control of the multimedia contents.   Security, copyright, and payment issues are the representative hurdles to be cleared through tool development and experiments.   The authors have a plan to spread the experimental field to five or more elementary schools and even to a few public domains.   The "Media Shell" system will be implemented to control to what degree contents are disclosed.
· Innovative multimedia contents
The authors hope to demonstrate that "self-propagating contents" will produce ever-unknown values which will stimulate people's creativity, bring people together, and prompt some to form communities.   The objective of the experiment described in this paper focused the evaluation of the system, not the contents themselves.   One of the challenges is being planned as a "self-propagating map," which will be put on the Net. People will be able to add the highly regional data (just around their residences such as scenes of narrow lanes which would never be printed in published maps), each piece of data will be connected to other pieces according to the spatial relationships in the real world.   If a community spreads wide enough, even a worldwide map is possible that will enable people to make virtual trips and enjoy local scenes and information.

References

[1] Schlichter J., Koch, M., Xu, C.: Awareness - The Common Link Between Groupware and Community Support Systems, in Community Computing and Support Systems, Ishida, T. (Ed.), Springer-Verlag (1991).
[2] Nakamura, R., Anzai, T.: Renga Com, http://www.renga.com/.
[3] Besselaar, P., Beckers, D.: Demographics and Sociographics of the Digital City, CCSS, Springer Verlag, pp. 109-125 (1998).
[4] Ishida, T.: Towards Computation over Communities, in Community Computing and Support Systems, Ishida, T. (Ed.), Springer-Verlag, pp. 1-10 (1991).
[5] Raymond, E. S.: The Cathedral and the Bazaar, http://www.tuxedo.org/~esr/writings/cathedral-bazaar/cathedral-bazaar.html (1998).
[6] Hosomi, I., Nakae, M., Ichiyama, S.: Digital Information Logistics   Architecture "MediaShell" - Its Billing and Utilizing Management, IPSJ reports, Vol. 98, No. 85, 98-EIP-2, pp. 49-56 (1998). (in Japanese).
[7] Noda, H., Asahi, T.: Space-Time Visualization: Annual Ring Metaphor, Proceedings of Advanced Multimedia Content Processing '98 (AMCP98) (1998).

Public Opinion Channel:
A Challenge for
Interactive Community Broadcasting

Shintaro Azechi[1], Nobuhiko Fujihara[1], Kaoru Sumi[1], Takashi Hirata[2],
Hiroyuki Yano[3], and Toyoaki Nishida[4]

[1] Synsophy Project, Kansai Advanced Research Center,
Communications Research Laboratory, MPT,
588-2 Iwaoka, Iwaoka-cho, Nishi-ku, Kobe, Hyogo 651-2492, JAPAN
{azechi, fujihara, kaoru}@crl.go.jp
http://www-karc.crl.go.jp/synsophy/index.html
[2] Artificial Intelligence Laboratory, Graduate School of Information Science,
Nara Institute of Science and Technology,
8916-5, Takayama, Nara, 630-0101, JAPAN
takash-h@is.aist-nara.ac.jp
[3] Knowledge Systems Section, Kansai Advanced Research Center,
Communications Research Laboratory, MPT,
588-2 Iwaoka, Iwaoka-cho, Nishi-ku, Kobe, Hyogo 651-2492, JAPAN
yano@crl.go.jp
[4] Department and Courses of Electrical Engineering, Information and
Communication Engineering, and Electronic Engineering,
School of Engineering, The University of Tokyo,
7-3-1 Hongo, Bunkyo-ku, Tokyo, 113-8656, JAPAN
nishida@kc.t.u-tokyo.ac.jp

Abstract. A novel communication medium is described for sharing and exchanging information and opinions in a community, the "Public Opinion Channel (POC)." The POC collects information and opinions from members of a community and broadcasts them as edited stories. Rather than simply building a passive medium, we are developing an active medium that can provide a means for forming public opinion based on mutual understanding through the information circulation. The POC will enable community members to easily obtain information about the other members of the community and to learn how they can contribute to the community. People using POC will be able to easily get information about the community and thus join into it more smoothly. Building the POC is thus a worthwhile challenge in information and communication technology and it will contribute to the study of digital cities as a city community communication medium.

1 Introduction

In this paper we propose what we call a "Public Opinion Channel (POC)," which is a new communication media [13]. The POC is a kind of interactive broadcast system consisting of three stages.

T. Ishida, K. Isbister (Eds.): Digital Cities, LNCS 1765, pp. 427–441, 2000.

Collection Stage (Collect opinions and information from the community)

Opinions and information are collected using electronic character based media. For example, a community member can send his or her opinion to the POC system by e-mail or through an on-line bulletin board system (BBS). The system can also automatically search for information on the World Wide Web (WWW). In the future, handwritten character information sent by letter or facsimile and voice information sent by telephone will also be recognized.

Summarizing Stage (Summarize opinions or information)

The collected opinions or information are summarized with the focus on clarifying the majority opinion while respecting the minority opinions or on presenting the information concisely. The summary is edited to tell a story.

Broadcast Stage (Broadcast collected opinions or information back to community)

A story based on the collected opinions or information is broadcast to the community by using a script that makes the summary sound natural. The creation of this script is done in this stage.

The POC has two advantages over conventional media: it enables community members to form a mutual opinion by sharing meta-knowledge, and it has artificial intelligence capabilities, enabling it to operate automatically and at low cost.

In Sec. 2, we explain the structure of the POC, describe how people can use it, and describe how its use promotes the circulation of information in a community. In Sec. 3, we assert that the POC is an effective new media and support our contention by comparing it with other media from a social psychological viewpoint. In Sec. 4, we discuss the implementation of a POC. While doing so is technically challenging, we have assembled the equipment for implementing a prototype by using existing technology. Finally, in Sec. 5, we discuss the application of the POC to digital cities.

2   Structure of POC

In this section, we explain the structure of the public opinion channel. As an example, we consider how a POC might be used in relation to a certain event, in particular, the various attractions related to a festival at a shrine (Fig. 1).

2.1   Learning about What Is Going on

Imagine one afternoon, while driving in your car, you are listening to one of the public opinion channels on the radio. An artificial-intelligence announcer with a synthetic voice says "Hello, people. Do you know about the festival to be held at the Akashi shrine this weekend? Along with the festival, various attractions will be held. Let's talk about this festival."

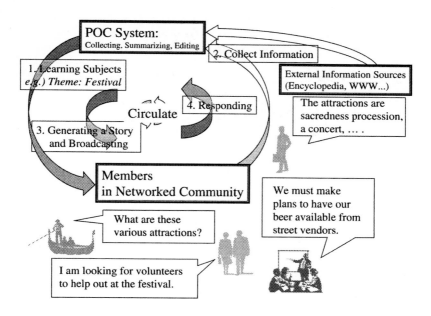

Fig. 1. The concept of the Public Opinion Channel (POC)

In this way, a community member can learn about what is going on in the community. The topic may have been one chosen by the POC itself at random, or it may be one suggested by community members. It may result from the completion of a POC interaction cycle. Because there are various POC channels, a listener can switch between channels to find a topic of interest.

2.2 Opinion/Information Collection

After hearing this broadcast, you have some questions. "What are these various attractions?" "Where will they be held?" "What time does the festival start?" "Where is the shrine located?" You speak these questions to the computer installed in your car. The computer transmits these questions to the POC system immediately.

Another community member may hear the same broadcast at home. She works as a volunteer at the shrine. She is worrying about not having enough volunteers to help out with the festival. She sends a facsimile to the POC stating "I am looking for volunteers to help out at the festival."

In the future, once voice-recognition and handwritten-character-recognition technologies are perfected, it will be possible to collect information via telephone and handwritten facsimile input. At the present, however, an operator would have to convert voice and handwritten input before it can be entered into the

POC system. Therefore, while it will be possible to communicate with the POC by using various means, here we consider only electronic media input. Moreover, the POC system will search for additional information relevant to the subject on the WWW and in electronic encyclopedias. For the shrine festival example, such information as "what attractions are there?" can be collected automatically from the shrine's web site.

2.3   Information Summarization

The information collected will likely be abundant and wide ranging. It therefore needs to be summarized. In our example, the question "where will the attractions be held" will likely generate input from many community members. If each of their responses were broadcast, little time would be left for other information. Therefore, the information should be summarized by the POC system. This leaves more time for other things, such as the request for volunteers. Moreover, the collected information is likely to contain *garbage*, such as meaningless words, slander, and discriminatory terms. The POC system filters out this garbage.

2.4   Story Creation and Broadcasting

The announcer says "Akashi Shrine will hold its annual festival this week, on Friday, Saturday, and Sunday. Additional volunteers are needed. Would you like to help out? If so, please contact Akashi Shrine office at (telephone number). Three attractions will be held along with the festival. They are a sacredness procession, a concert, and a beer garden. The procession will begin at 2:00 p.m. on Friday. It will start at the shrine and end at the beach park. The concert will be held in the city hall. It will start at 3:00 p.m. on Saturday. The beer garden will be on the roof of the Hitomaru Building, across from the main entrance. It will be open all three days, from 11:00 a.m. to 11:00 p.m.. . . . "

If the information collected and summarized was broadcast as is, a POC televiewer or listener would surely be perplexed. It would be like raindrops of unrelated bits of information falling from the cloud of a certain subject. For the information to be coherent, it needs to be broadcast within one context. The POC system thus creates a story that semantically unifies the information.

Advances in artificial intelligence technology will one day make it possible to create this story automatically. Until then, people will still need to perform much of this work. In the future, an agent announcer with a synthetic voice will broadcast the story automatically. For the present, a human announcer is needed. As the first step to full automation, we can develop artificial intelligence system that supports the human announcer, thereby reducing the cost. One day, we should reach the point where an agent announcer and a human announcer can have a dialog. The agent announcer would then truly support the human announcer.

2.5   Community Reaction

Again you are listening to a POC channel and hear a spot about the shrine festival. You may decide to volunteer your services. You may decide to take your children to see the sacredness procession. Or you may know that an internationally famous cellist will participate in the concert, so you submit this information. If you work for the company providing the beer garden, you might submit more information about it, such as the menu. Or if you work for a rival company, you might make plans to have your beer available from street vendors.

A community member can thus learn about what is going on in his or her community by listening to the POC channels. He or she can get information about topics of interest. Moreover, he or she can learn about the problems of other community members. Therefore, community members can share information and help each other by listening to the POC channels.

2.6   Information Circulation

Once a story has been broadcast, people will likely send another opinion or more information to the POC system. The system will collect these opinions and information and use them to modify the story. The reactions to this modified story will be collected, and the story will be modified once again. In this way, information will be circulated and opinions will be developed in the community.

How does this information circulation and opinion development differ from that created by other media? What meaning does the POC have in social psychological contexts? We will address these questions in the following section.

3   The POC: An Effective New Media

In this section, we discuss the uniqueness and validity of the POC. We will do this by comparing it with other media. We will assert the usefulness of the POC from the social psychological viewpoint.

3.1   Comparison with Other Media

The media can be categorized as personal communications (telephone, regular mail, e-mail), article-based communications (net news, BBS), and the mass media (newspapers, magazines, television, radio). The public opinion channel is a new media located between personal communications and mass media (Fig. 2).

The POC has two main features: interactivity and extensive transfer power. Interactivity is also found in personal communications media and article-based communications (ABC). The POC is digital media as ABC. And it is similar to the mass media in that information can be transmitted in large quantities. We next compare the POC with the other three kinds of media in more detail.

We will look at what point other 3 kinds of media and POCs differ from each other.

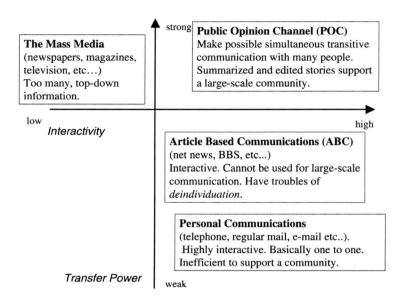

Fig. 2. The classification of media

Comparison with Personal Communications In personal communications, communication is basically one to one. A sender generally sends a message to only one person, though it is possible to have multiple receivers. The roles of sender and receiver normally alternate, so communication is highly interactive. Using personal communications to support a community is inefficient because information is usually sent to only one person at a time, so it can take quite a while to pass the information on to many people.

On the other hand, if a POC is used, information can be sent to many people simultaneously. Moreover, a receiver can receive messages from many senders. The POC thus enables a person to interact with many people simultaneously.

Comparison with POC and ABC The POC is similar to ABC in two ways. Both are interactive media; they make possible simultaneous transitive communication with many people. Both use computer networks.

However, there is a big difference. It is the difference in scale of the community that they can support. For example, in a community with more than 1000 members, using ABC to share opinions would be very inefficient. Each member would surely be drowned in a flood of opinions. This means that ABC cannot be used for large-scale communication. If ABC were used to support such a large volume of opinion sharing, community members, for example the academic society members, would have trouble communicating.

In contrast, the POC has broadcast characteristics. Opinions are summarized and edited before they are distributed. Therefore, a receiving person is not overwhelmed by a flood of opinions. This means a POC can support a large-scale community.

Furthermore, ABC is subject to a social psychological problem, *deindividuation* [16]. It arises from the anonymity found in ABC. It can result in what is called "flaming" [9], or the expression of opinions that would normally be suppressed in regular communication. Its cause is attributed to the loss of social cues due to the anonymity (or general CMC) [6]. When a sender's identity is unknown to the receivers, he or she may act in ways that deviate from the norm. This can lead to harassing those whose opinions differ from one's own by sending antagonistic messages, sometimes over and over again.

Flaming is avoided in POC communication because the POC system edits the information, and in doing so removes the identity of the sender. With this perfect anonymity, it is impossible to flame someone whose opinion you disagree with. Furthermore, if someone were to try and say something slanderous, the POC system would edit it out.

Comparison with Mass Media In conventional mass media, information is transmitted from the top, down to many unspecified receivers. While people in the community can use the mass media to share opinions, the process is inefficient. It requires, for example, getting a letter published in a newspaper or getting a telephone call accepted by a radio call-in show. It is not always clear when one's opinion will be published, or when reactions to it will appear. In addition, it can be cumbersome to dispatch information to a number of people. Claiming that the mass media supports a community would be a difficult position to prove.

In POC communication, various opinions from community members are summarized; they are integrated in a qualitative manner. Minority opinions that do not fit into someone else's frameworks are not disregarded. Only garbage, such as redundancies, meaningless expressions, and discriminatory terms, is thrown away. In this was, a POC televiewer or listener can grasp opinions from all corners of the community. He or she can take into consideration opinions of minority groups and thus form a more balanced opinion. Moreover, he or she can estimate what reception his or her opinion will receive from the community and thus consider how to express it most appropriately. This is the big difference between mass media and POC communication.

Therefore, POC communication is very attractive for large-scale communities. In the following section we will discuss the technologies needed to implement it.

4   Prototypic Implementation

We have explained the concept of the public opinion channel. Implementing one requires producing some actual tools. Along with our colleagues, we have already

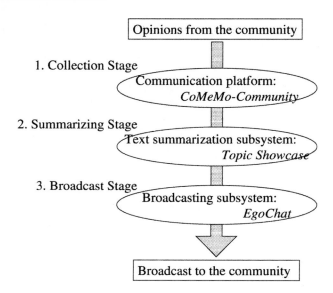

Fig. 3. Prototyipically implemented subsystems of the POC

prototypically implemented some important functions of the POC system (Fig. 3).

Furthermore, we are developing and researching subsystems for each stage. The "CoMeMo-Community" will serve as a communication platform in the collection stage. "Topic Showcase" will serve as a text summarization subsystem in the summarizing stage. "EgoChat" will serve as a broadcasting subsystem in the broadcast stage.

4.1 CoMeMo-Community

The CoMeMo-Community [12] communication platform is based on a talking virtualized ego metaphor. Within this community, each person has a virtualized ego that talks to other virtualized egos on behalf of the real people. Each virtualized ego is represented by a different icon. When given a key phrase, a virtualized ego says phrases associated with the key phrase.

In the example shown in Fig. 4, a virtualized ego might respond to the key phrase "an air conditioner," with such words as "fan," "cool," or "necessity." Furthermore, a virtualized ego respond to the words spoken by other egos. Even with a simple conversation-management facility, such as a key-word or key-phrase chaining, observing the conversations among virtualized egos enables us to gain an awareness of the knowledge and interests possessed by a community. It gives an idea of who knows what and who is interested in what. The talking virtualized ego metaphor brings about a new asynchronous communication channel for a community, a channel in which there is a casual and conversational fla-

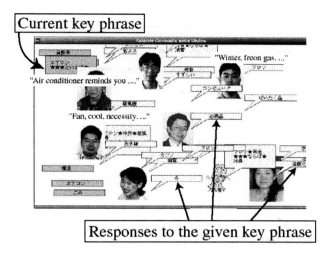

Fig. 4. "CoMeMo-Community" : A communication platform with virtualized egos

vor. Of course, the community members have to share their knowledge with the virtualized egos in advance.

Our first prototype of POC is developed based on using the data style of CoMeMo-Community, associative representations. Those formal data are processed by information summarizing system and broadcast system and stored by the virtualized egos. They will be used repeatedly as shared community knowledge in the future. This function of storing information and providing compatible data style for all subsystems is needed for the collection subsystem of POC. And people who input their opinion to this system are benefited by dispatching their opinions corresponding to appropriate key phrases automatically by the virtualized egos.

Another reason of using CoMeMo-Community as the collection subsystem of the prototype of POC is that this system provide positive reciprocity by virtualized egos for opinion presenters. The virtualized egos immediately respond to the information presenter by showing relevant phrases when he or she inputs their opinions. As mentioned by the researches of the client-centerd therapy [14], positive reciprocity should raise expression motivation and make information expression one after another. We consider those functions of CoMeMo-Community support the community member's information expression and we implement this system as the collection subsystem of POC. In the future work, when the virtualized egos are given the ability to automatically gather data from the Web or other electronic data-bases, the CoMeMo-Community will become a more effective collection subsystem.

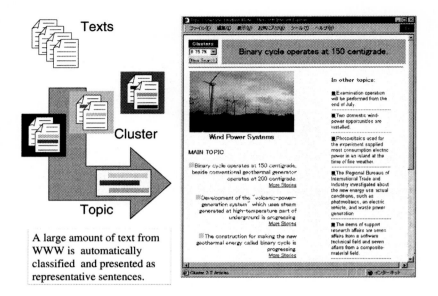

Fig. 5. "Topic Showcase" : Multi-text summarization system

4.2   Topic Showcase

The Topic Showcase [7] summarization subsystem of our prototype POC is illustrated in Fig. 5. It automatically summarizes a large amount of text. It collects text from, for example, the WWW, classifies it automatically according to its statistical features, and automatically presents a representative sentence for each cluster. The diagram on the left shows the interface for selecting a topic word. The one on the right shows the result of a text summarization. The first sentence is a representative sentence, and the others are details about the topic.

The main point using the Topic Showcase as the summarizing subsystem of POC is that this system is designed to summarize wide ranging and a large amount of information. This system can treat only the text (for example the Web pages) now, but it will soon be able to apply to summarizing other written information like protocols of group interviews or dialogues on BBS. Of course, our aim is to develop the Topic Showcase for summarizing opinions from the community tied by the POC. It would be interesting to research the application of the Topic Showcase for POC from a psychological viewpoint as well as from an engineering viewpoint. How can we develop the method of summarizing natural opinions generated from real community member's interaction? This research should be supported by cognitive psychological findings. And in the future, for using as the summarizing system of POC, Topic Showcase should be developed as the system which processes not only written information but also oral information.

Fig. 6. "EgoChat" : Broadcasting subsystem

4.3   EgoChat

The interface of the EgoChat [8] output subsystem is illustrated in Fig. 6. The figures represent virtualized egos, which talk to each other about a key phrase. The system is similar to the CoMeMo-Community, but there are some differences. While the CoMeMo-Community shows the communication processes visually, EgoChat shows them as a voice presentation. EgoChat can use both recorded human voices and artificial, synthetic voices. In addition, EgoChat has conversation schema, and the egos use them to converse. For example, EgoChat has the conversation schema "What does the word...remind you of?" and "Let's talk about...." Consequently, while the CoMeMo-Community shows only a chain of words and phrases, EgoChat generates more story-like presentations. The continuous generation and expression of a story are very important for the POC broadcast system.

4.4   Prototype Demonstration

We developed a POC prototype by combining these three subsystems. It was first demonstrated at our laboratory open house. Information provided by some of the visitors was stored in the CoMeMo-Community and was expressed by EgoChat. Doing this required a lot of human effort. We plan to automate and improve the quality of the processing system.

Although each subsystem was operated by a person, this demonstration showed that even with our POC prototype, the concept of informational circulation is valid. Visitors were interested in the prototype of POC and inputted their opinions and information about that day's topics to collection subsystem. After viewing the broadcasting which contains his or her edited opinions, they were attracted to input information to the POC again. It seemes to prove our concept of information circulation, although we did not have psychological experimentally surveyed data.

5   Application of POC to Digital Cities

POC communication is designed to support a community. One concept of the digital city is to provide infrastructure for networking local communities and to promote social interaction among people who visit or reside in a city [4]. The POC communication also supports this concept. Consequently, it makes sense to include a POC in a digital city as a resident communication media. Doing so will increase the circulation of information in the digital city. Moreover, it should help build resident solidarity and activate the community.

Three potential applications of POC communications to a digital city are searching for information on the Web, sharing opinions among city residents, and providing advertising opportunities.

5.1   Searching for Information on the Web

Information about a city can be found on any number of web pages. The effective use of these pages is desirable for constructing a digital city [5]. The POC system includes a subsystem for searching for information about a certain subject. Moreover, the subsystem summarizes and edits the information found.

There are various approaches to identifying and displaying city information, including using icons [2], [3], animation [15], 2-D mapping or 3-D modeling [5], [10]. They are aimed at developing a user-machine interface that everyone can use. This is a perfect location for a POC as well. The user-machine interface of POC communication is broadcasting, and this is an interface that almost everyone can use. With a POC, it would be possible to broadcast intelligible information about a city.

5.2   Sharing Opinions among City Residents

Sending information about one's neighborhood to the POC should promote social interaction among city residents. This aim at supporting regional community would be consistent with a purpose of digital city [2]. Residents can share information about problems in their neighborhood. Furthermore, they can learn about what people in other neighborhoods have done about the same problem.

A city in which 10,000 or more people live is too large to consider a community. It is difficult for an individual to grasp the situation of so many people. He or she cannot use such large community as the reference group, so that cannot derive social identity [11] from a whole city. More likely, his or her actions will be centered on the area in which he or she lives and works rather than on the whole city. Rather than information about the whole city, people want information about the smaller domestic areas which is directly related with their daily life. However, by sharing information over the POC, people can come to grasp the situation of the whole city. This will enable residents to consider the whole city as the community to which they belong.

Such information sharing will also be useful people just visiting the city. A big problem for visitors is not knowing what is currently happening in the city. A traveler does not have the cues needed to grasp this information beforehand, whereas a resident has such meta-knowledge as "The information being obtained if I go there," and "It being known if I see that." A traveler can obtain knowledge about the city by viewing or listening to the POC. Through it they can obtain the detailed information commonly known by the locals, such as the best places to eat. This acquisition of detailed information is also important to people who have just moved to the city. Since people are continuously visiting or moving to the city, the POC must broadcast the same information on a regular basis.

5.3   Providing Advertising Opportunities

The POC can provide a realtime advertising medium. For example, a store owner could advertise his or her time limited bargain sale on realtime, which is impossible with conventional media. A gallery owner might advertise that a famous artist has unexpectedly dropped in and will be staying until such and such a time. The owner of a restaurant might advertise the specials for the lunch time. Such realtime advertising supports another concept of the digital city, that is, reflect the present situation of the city reflect on a network [5].

Conversely, marketing will made easier because sellers will be better able to understand market demand. Normally, it takes a lot of effort, such as filling out a detailed questionnaire to quantitatively determine what consumers want. And the results do not exceed the boundaries established by the market researcher beforehand. To obtain qualitative data through interviews or free descriptions, it is serious to process the repetition information on an opinion. It depends on the manpower of high cost for processing of qualitative data. Therefore, it is usually not carried out very often [1]. In contrast, the POC can be used to collect and summarize the needs of city residents automatically. The opinions and information sent by residents is qualitative data based on free utterances, so this data very likely matches their actual needs. Obtaining this low cost and highly edited qualitative data should enhance a seller's product development strategy. This process supports another concept of the digital city, that is, stimulating social interaction among the city's residents [3].

6   Conclusion

In this paper we have described the Public Opinion Channel, a new interactive community media that supports the concepts of the digital city. While implementing the POC is technically challenging, a prototype implementation proved its validity. Even though it will take some time for the required technologies to be perfected, interim imperfect systems will still be beneficial. The POC is a system whose implementation can be started now. To achieve a more perfect design, discussions from the engineering and social-scientific standpoints are also required.

Implementing the POC as part of a digital city will enable the dynamic sharing of information among city residents, a key objective of the digital city. Moreover, broadcast may show the form of the man-machine interface which deserves consideration by digital city researches.

The final goal of our research is to investigate by using social-scientific techniques the effect that the POC will have on the structure and activities of a community. How can the POC contribute to a real and/or virtual community? Does the POC make informational circulation and facilitate community communications really? And do those informational supports by POC enhance community activity? Social psychological research on the community which is tied by POC would resolve those questions. And we consider that those research methods and findings would be also useful to research on the social interaction in a digital city.

References

1. Aaker, D.A., and Day, G.S.: Marketing Research: Private and Public Sector Decisions. John Wiley and Sons. (1980)
2. van den Besselaar, P., Beckers, D.: Demographics and Sociographics of the Digital City. In: Ishida, T. (ed.): Community Computing and Support Systems, Lecture Notes in Computer Science, Vol. 1519. Springer-Verlag. (1998) 109-125
3. de Bruine, A.: Digital City Bristol: A Case Study. Lecture Notes in Computer Science (in this volume). Springer-Verlag. (2000)
4. Ishida, T.: Understanding Digital Cities. Lecture Notes in Computer Science (in this volume). Springer-Verlag. (2000)
5. Ishida, T., Akahani, J., Hramatsu, K., Isbister, K., Lisowski, S., Nakanishi, H., Okamoto, M., Miyazaki, Y., and Tsutsuguchi, K.: Digital City Kyoto: Towards A Social Information Infrastructure. In: Klusch, M., Shehory, O., and Weiss G. (eds.): Cooperative Information Agents III. Lecture Notes in Artificial Intelligence, Vol. 1652. Springer-Verlag. (1999) 23-35
6. Kiesler, S., Siegel, J. and McGuire, T.: Social Psychological Aspects of Computer-Mediated Communications. American Psychologist, 39. (1984) 1123-1134
7. Fukuhara, T., Takeda, H., and Nishida, T.: Multiple-text Summarization Method based on Topic Identification and Context Restructuring. Proceedings of the 13th Annual Conference of JSAI. (1999) 555-558
8. Kubota, H., and Nishida, T.: Externalization of Individual Memory by Talking with Quasi-ego Agents. Proceedings of the 13th Annual Conference of JSAI. (1999) 346-349
9. Lea, M., O'Shea, T., Fung, P., and Spears, R.: Flaming' in Computer-mediated Communication: Observations, Explanations, Implications. In: Lea, M. (ed.): Contexts of Computer-mediated Communication. Harvester Wheatsheaf. (1994) 89-112

10. Linturi, R., Koivunen, M. and Sulkanen, J.: Helsinki Arena 2000: Augmenting a Real City to a Virtual One. Lecture Notes in Computer Science (in this volume). Springer-Verlag. (2000)
11. McGarty, C.: Categorization in Social Psychology. Sage. (1999)
12. Nishida, T., Hirata, T., and Maeda, H: CoMeMo-Community: A System for Supporting Community Knowledge Evolution. In: Ishida, T. (ed.): Community Computing and Support Systems, Lecture Notes in Computer Science, Vol. 1519. Springer-Verlag. (1998) 183-200
13. Nishida, T., Fujihara, N., Azechi, S., Sumi, K., and Hirata, T.: Public Opinion Channel for Communities in the Information Age. New Generation Computing, Vol.17, No.4. (1999) 417-427
14. Rogers, C. R.: On Becoming a Person: A Client's View of Psychotherapy. Houghton-Mifflin. (1961)
15. Tsutsuguchi, K., Sugiyama, K., and Sonehara, N.: The Motion Generation of Pedestrians as Avatar and Crowds of People . Lecture Notes in Computer Science (in this volume). Springer-Verlag. (2000)
16. Zimbardo, P.G.: The Human Choice: Individuation, Reason, and Order versus Deindividuation, Impulse and Chaos. In: Arnold ,W.J. and Levine, D. (eds.): Nebraska Symposium on Motivation., Vol.7. (1970) 237-307

Author Index

Lecture Notes in Computer Science

For information about Vols. 1–1706
please contact your bookseller or Springer-Verlag

Vol. 1739: A. Braffort, R. Gherbi, S. Gibet, J. Richardson, D. Teil (Eds.), Gesture-Based Communication in Human-Computer Interaction. Proceedings, 1999. XI, 333 pages. 1999. (Subseries LNAI).

Vol. 1740: R. Baumgart (Ed.): Secure Networking – CQRE [Secure] '99. Proceedings, 1999. IX, 261 pages. 1999.

Vol. 1741: A. Aggarwal, C. Pandu Rangan (Eds.), Algorithms and Computation. Proceedings, 1999. XIII, 448 pages. 1999.

Vol. 1742: P.S. Thiagarajan, R. Yap (Eds.), Advances in Computing Science – ASIAN'99. Proceedings, 1999. XI, 397 pages. 1999.

Vol. 1743: A. Moreira, S. Demeyer (Eds.), Object-Oriented Technology. Proceedings, 1999. XVII, 389 pages. 1999.

Vol. 1744: S. Staab, Extracting Degree Information from Texts. X; 187 pages. 1999. (Subseries LNAI).

Vol. 1745: P. Banerjee, V.K. Prasanna, B.P. Sinha (Eds.), High Performance Computing – HiPC'99. Proceedings, 1999. XXII, 412 pages. 1999.

Vol. 1746: M. Walker (Ed.), Cryptography and Coding. Proceedings, 1999. IX, 313 pages. 1999.

Vol. 1747: N. Foo (Ed.), Adavanced Topics in Artificial Intelligence. Proceedings, 1999. XV, 500 pages. 1999. (Subseries LNAI).

Vol. 1748: H.V. Leong, W.-C. Lee, B. Li, L. Yin (Eds.), Mobile Data Access. Proceedings, 1999. X, 245 pages. 1999.

Vol. 1749: L. C.-K. Hui, D.L. Lee (Eds.), Internet Applications. Proceedings, 1999. XX, 518 pages. 1999.

Vol. 1750: D.E. Knuth, MMIXware. VIII, 550 pages. 1999.

Vol. 1751: H. Imai, Y. Zheng (Eds.), Public Key Cryptography. Proceedings, 2000. XI, 485 pages. 2000.

Vol. 1752: S. Krakowiak, S. Shrivastava (Eds.), Advances in Distributed Systems. VIII, 509 pages. 2000.

Vol. 1753: E. Pontelli, V. Santos Costa (Eds.), Practical Aspects of Declarative Languages. Proceedings, 2000. X, 327 pages. 2000.

Vol. 1754: J. Väänänen (Ed.), Generalized Quantifiers and Computation. Proceedings, 1997. VII, 139 pages. 1999.

Vol. 1755: D. Bjørner, M. Broy, A.V. Zamulin (Eds.), Perspectives of System Informatics. Proceedings, 1999. XII, 540 pages. 2000.

Vol. 1757: N.R. Jennings, Y. Lespérance (Eds.), Intelligent Agents VI. Proceedings, 1999. XII, 380 pages. 2000. (Subseries LNAI).

Vol. 1758: H. Heys, C. Adams (Eds.), Selected Areas in Cryptography. Proceedings, 1999. VIII, 243 pages. 2000.

Vol. 1759: M.J. Zaki, C.-T. Ho (Eds.), Large-Scale Parallel Data Mining. VIII, 261 pages. 2000. (Subseries LNAI).

Vol. 1760: J.-J. Ch. Meyer, P.-Y. Schobbens (Eds.), Formal Models of Agents. Poceedings. VIII, 253 pages. 1999. (Subseries LNAI).

Vol. 1761: R. Caferra, G. Salzer (Eds.), Automated Deduction in Classical and Non-Classical Logics. Proceedings. VIII, 299 pages. 2000. (Subseries LNAI).

Vol. 1762: K.-D. Schewe, B. Thalheim (Eds.), Foundations of Information and Knowledge Systems. Proceedings, 2000. X, 305 pages. 2000.

Vol. 1763: J. Akiyama, M. Kano, M. Urabe (Eds.), Discrete and Computational Geometry. Proceedings, 1998. VIII, 333 pages. 2000.

Vol. 1764: H. Ehrig, G. Engels, H.-J. Kreowski, G. Rozenberg (Eds.), Theory and Application of Graph Transformations. Proceedings, 1998. IX, 490 pages. 2000.

Vol. 1765: T. Ishida, K. Isbister (Eds.), Digital Cities. IX, 444 pages. 2000.

Vol. 1767: G. Bongiovanni, G. Gambosi, R. Petreschi (Eds.), Algorithms and Complexity. Proceedings, 2000. VIII, 317 pages. 2000.

Vol. 1768: A. Pfitzmann (Ed.), Information Hiding. Proceedings, 1999. IX, 492 pages. 2000.

Vol. 1769: G. Haring, C. Lindemann, M. Reiser (Eds.), Performance Evaluation: Origins and Directions. X, 529 pages. 2000.

Vol. 1770: H. Reichel, S. Tison (Eds.), STACS 2000. Proceedings, 2000. XIV, 662 pages. 2000.

Vol. 1771: P. Lambrix, Part-Whole Reasoning in an Object-Centered Framework. XII, 195 pages. 2000. (Subseries LNAI).

Vol. 1772: M. Beetz, Concurrent Ractive Plans. XVI, 213 pages. 2000. (Subseries LNAI).

Vol. 1773: G. Saake, K. Schwarz, C. Türker (Eds.), Transactions and Database Dynamics. Proceedings, 1999. VIII, 247 pages. 2000.

Vol. 1774: J. Delgado, G.D. Stamoulis, A. Mullery, D. Prevedourou, K. Start (Eds.), Telecommunications and IT Convergence Towards Service E-volution. Proceedings, 2000. XIII, 350 pages. 2000.

Vol. 1777: C. Zaniolo, P.C. Lockemann, M.H. Scholl, T. Grust (Eds.), Advances in Database Technology – EDBT 2000. Proceedings, 2000. XII, 540 pages. 2000.

Vol. 1780: R. Conradi (Ed.), Software Process Technology. Proceedings, 2000. IX, 249 pages. 2000.

Vol. 1781: D.A. Watt (Ed.), Compiler Construction. Proceedings, 2000. X, 295 pages. 2000.

Vol. 1782: G. Smolka (Ed.), Programming Languages and Systems. Proceedings, 2000. XIII, 429 pages. 2000.

Vol. 1783: T. Maibaum (Ed.), Fundamental Approaches to Software Engineering. Proceedings, 2000. XIII, 375 pages. 2000.

Vol. 1785: S. Graf, M. Schwartzbach (Eds.), Tools and Algorithms for the Construction and Analysis of Systems. Proceedings, 2000. XIV, 552 pages. 2000.

Vol. 1786: B.H. Haverkort, H.C. Bohnenkamp, C.U. Smith (Eds.), Computer Performance Evaluation. Proceedings, 2000. XIV, 383 pages. 2000.

Vol. 1790: N. Lynch, B.H. Krogh (Eds.), Hybrid Systems: Computation and Control. Proceedings, 2000. XII, 465 pages. 2000.

Vol. 1794: H. Kirchner, C. Ringeisen (Eds.), Frontiers of Combining Systems. Proceedings, 2000. X, 291 pages. 2000. (Subseries LNAI).